REPOSSESSING THE ROMANTIC PAST

New work on British Romanticism is often characterized as much by its conscious difference from preceding positions as it is by its approach to or choice of material. As a result, writing neglected or marginalized in one account will be restored to prominence in another, as we reconstruct the past as a history of the present. This collection of new essays takes as its starting point the wide-ranging work of Marilyn Butler on Romantic literature, and includes contributions by some of the most prominent scholars of Romanticism working today. The essays offer new perspectives on Maria Edgeworth, Coleridge, Austen, Scott, and others, showing that the openness of modern critical perceptions matches and reflects the diversity of the literature and culture of the Romantic period itself.

HEATHER GLEN is Reader in Nineteenth-Century Literature at the University of Cambridge and a Fellow of New Hall.

PAUL HAMILTON is Professor of English at Queen Mary, University of London.

REPOSSESSING THE ROMANTIC PAST

EDITED BY

HEATHER GLEN AND PAUL HAMILTON

CAMBRIDGE
UNIVERSITY PRESS

CAMBRIDGE UNIVERSITY PRESS
Cambridge, New York, Melbourne, Madrid, Cape Town, Singapore, São Paulo

Cambridge University Press
The Edinburgh Building, Cambridge CB2 2RU, UK

Published in the United States of America by Cambridge University Press, New York

www.cambridge.org
Information on this title: www.cambridge.org/9780521858663

First published 2006

Printed in the United Kingdom at the University Press, Cambridge

A catalogue record for this publication is available from the British Library

ISBN-13 978-0-521-85866-3 hardback
ISBN-10 0-521-85866-6 hardback

Contents

Notes on contributors   *page* vii

    Introduction   1
    Paul Hamilton

PART I   DISSENT AND OPPOSITION

1 'Severe contentions of friendship': Barbauld, conversation,
   and dispute   21
   Jon Mee

2 Hazlitt's visionary London   40
   Kevin Gilmartin

3 Shelley's republics   63
   Michael Rossington

4 Memoirs of a dutiful niece: Lucy Aikin and literary
   reputation   80
   Anne Janowitz

5 Holding Proteus: William Godwin in his letters   98
   Pamela Clemit

PART II   REOPENING THE CASE OF EDGEWORTH

6 Edgeworth and Scott: the literature of reterritorialization   119
   James Chandler

7 Maria Edgeworth and 'the light of nature': artifice,
   autonomy, and anti-sectarianism in *Practical
   Education* (1798)   140
   Susan Manly

PART III   DIFFERENT DIRECTIONS

8   Coleridge's stamina   163
     Paul Hamilton

9   Elizabeth Hamilton's *Translation of the Letters of a Hindoo
     Rajah* and Romantic orientalism   183
     Nigel Leask

10   Jane Austen and the professional wife   203
     Janet Todd

11   High instincts and real presences: two Romantic responses
     to the death of Beauty   226
     Jerome McGann

Marilyn Butler: a bibliography   244
     Heather Glen

Index   250

Notes on contributors

JAMES CHANDLER teaches English and Cinema Studies at the University of Chicago, where he is also director of the Franke Institute for the Humanities. He is the author of *Wordsworth's Second Nature* (1984) and *England in 1819* (1998). More recently he co-edited *Romantic Metropolis* (2005) with Kevin Gilmartin. He is currently putting together the *Cambridge History of British Romantic Literature* and, with Maureen McLane, the *Cambridge Companion to Romantic Poetry*.

PAMELA CLEMIT is Professor of English Studies at the University of Durham. She is the author of *The Godwinian Novel* (1993). She has published numerous scholarly and critical editions of William Godwin's writings, two volumes in *Novels and Selected Works of Mary Shelley*, and, most recently, 'Life of William Godwin' in *Mary Shelley's Literary Lives and Other Writings*. She is completing an intellectual biography of Godwin and editing a scholarly edition of his letters.

KEVIN GILMARTIN is Associate Professor of English at the California Institute of Technology. He is the author of *Print Politics: The Press and Radical Opposition in Early Nineteenth Century England* (1996), and co-editor with James Chandler of *Romantic Metropolis: The Urban Scene of British Culture, 1780–1840* (2005), a collection of essays on the urban world of British Romantic writing. His book on conservative culture in the Romantic period, *Writing against Revolution*, will be published by Cambridge University Press in early 2006.

HEATHER GLEN is a fellow of New Hall and Reader in Nineteenth-Century Literature at the University of Cambridge. She is the author of *Vision and Disenchantment: Blake's Songs and Wordsworth's Lyrical Ballads* (Cambridge, 1983) and of *Charlotte Brontë: The Imagination in History* (2002), and editor of *The Cambridge Companion to the Brontës*

(2002). Her edition of Charlotte Brontë's final Angrian tales will appear in summer 2006.

PAUL HAMILTON has taught at the Universities of Nottingham, Oxford, and Southampton and is now Professor of English at Queen Mary, University of London. He has written widely on Romanticism and critical theory. His most recent book, *Metaromanticism*, was published in 2003. Currently he is working on a comparative study of European Romanticism.

ANNE JANOWITZ is Professor of Romantic Poetry at Queen Mary, University of London. She is the author of *England's Ruins: Poetic Purpose and the National Landscape* (1990), *Lyric and Labour in the Romantic Tradition* (1998), and *Women Romantic Poets: Anna Barbauld and Mary Robinson* (2004). She is completing a study of the night sky in the poetry of the late eighteenth and early nineteenth centuries.

NIGEL LEASK is Regius Professor of English Language and Literature at the University of Glasgow. He has published widely in the areas of Romanticism, Orientalism, and travel writing and is the author of *British Romantic Writers and the East: Anxieties of Empire* (Cambridge, 1992) and *Curiosity and the Aesthetics of Travel Writing 1770–1840: From an Antique Land* (2002). He is currently researching a book on Robert Burns and British Romanticism.

JEROME MCGANN is the John Stewart Bryan University Professor, University of Virginia. His most recent book is *The Scholar's Art: Literary Studies in a Managed World* (2006). He writes broadly on literary and cultural issues and is the editor of the standard edition of Byron's Poetical Works as well as the editor of the online *Complete Writings and Pictures of Dante Gabriel Rossetti*.

SUSAN MANLY is a Lecturer at the University of St Andrews. She is the editor of Maria Edgeworth's *Harrington* and *Practical Education*, and the co-editor of *Helen* and *Leonora*, all in the twelve-volume *Novels and Selected Works of Maria Edgeworth* (1999/2003). She is also the editor of a paperback edition of *Harrington* (2004), and the author of several articles and book chapters on Edgeworth, Burke, Coleridge, and Wollstonecraft.

JON MEE is Margaret Candfield Fellow in English at University College, Oxford. His *Dangerous Enthusiasm: William Blake and the Culture of Radicalism in the 1790s* (1992) was based on a thesis supervised by Marilyn Butler. His most recent work is *Romanticism, Enthusiasm, and Regulation:*

Poetics and the Policing of Culture in the Romantic Period (2003). He is currently working on a book on controversy and conversation in the Romantic period that will deal at more length with some of the issues raised in the chapter in this volume. A selected edition of state trials from 1792–4 with John Barrell is to be published in 2006.

MICHAEL ROSSINGTON is Senior Lecturer in the School of English Literature, Language and Linguistics at the University of Newcastle upon Tyne. He has edited Mary Shelley's *Valperga* (2000) and Percy Shelley's *The Cenci* in *The Poems of Shelley*, vol. II, ed. Kelvin Everest and Geoffrey Matthews (2000). With Jack Donovan and Cian Duffy, he is editing *The Poems of Shelley*, vol. III, due to be published in 2007.

JANET TODD is Herbert J. C. Grierson Professor of English at the University of Aberdeen and an Honorary Fellow of Lucy Cavendish College, Cambridge. Her most recent monographs are biographies of Aphra Behn (1996) and Mary Wollstonecraft (2000), and *Rebel Daughters: Ireland in Conflict* (2004), and her most recent editions the letters of Mary Wollstonecraft and Behn's *Oroonoko*. Her *Introduction to Jane Austen* will appear in 2006, along with the final volumes of the Cambridge edition of Jane Austen, of which she is the General Editor.

Introduction

Paul Hamilton

How should we repossess the past? Applied to academic writing now about Romantic-period writing, this is a disingenuous question. It presupposes a scholarly field in which antagonistic critical positions are already drawn up in unignorable fashion. New work on British Romanticism is often characterized as much by its conscious difference from preceding positions as it is by its take on or choice of material. As a result, writing neglected or marginalized in one account will be restored to prominence in another. In fact, for some, such difference has become the point of the critical exercise itself. The past as we construct it becomes nothing more than a history of the present.

The quality of possession, though, is as important as its novelty. Quality of historical recovery, the chapters in this volume suggest, comes both from the critic's ability to respond to the particularity of a piece of Romantic writing and from her awareness of not one but several overarching contexts to which it could have belonged. The historical prism through which these essays view Barbauld, Edgeworth, Scott, Hazlitt, Coleridge, Godwin, and others is consciously chosen, certainly, but in a spirit of dialogue which allows the reader to judge if another angle of approach might have revealed more. Thus the critical conversation continues.

Marilyn Butler possesses this dialogic ability in full, and her work makes sense of the quality of historical sympathy required to repossess the Romantic past in a more than critically opportunistic sense. Butler's work takes the question of historical recovery to be ever-present and never conclusively decided. That is why a book written in honour of Marilyn Butler ought not to be in any way retrospective. That has never been her style. She has always been suspicious of traditional academic expectations and uncomfortable with pure, philosophically unmixed explanations. Her work has always been original, critical, and self-critical, testing disciplinary boundaries, commenting on and revising current historical verdicts by attending to neglected literary possibility – Malthus rather than Burke; Southey rather than Coleridge; the expatriate, liberal Edgeworth rather than Scott; Jane Austen, but in her underestimated role as a contributor to the contemporary 'war of ideas'. But her generosity of interest and her creative eclecticism should not be confused with an undiscriminating latitude. Her historical critique of Romanticism is a sharply intelligent and highly sophisticated one.

The essays in this volume show how her work is being continued. Each is characteristic of its author. Each in different ways addresses itself to issues that have often taken centre stage in Butler's work. They examine the ways in which Enlightenment and Romantic writing could be critical of its own times; they place non-canonical alongside canonical writing in order to illuminate each; they challenge the certainties of established literary history. There is a strenuous tradition of historiography behind a focus like this, and it needs to be acknowledged that Butler's work has been a precursor and stimulator of initiatives in the history of the period too. If I dwell for a while on historical writing in these introductory remarks, it is in order to emphasize a breadth and grounding in Butler's work – the degree to which its historical positioning is thought out – that often goes unnoticed.

Marilyn Butler's work has characteristically avoided the extremes of immanent critique, in which to evaluate a great piece of writing's complex, internal difference from its own project provides sufficient judgement, and sociological reduction, in which literature's complicity with power (or 'the police', as Hazlitt would have said) sanctions a wholesale scepticism concerning its aesthetic value. Instead, it has sought to explore the immediate literary context within which a given work was shaped, and the relation of that context to a number of other larger contexts. It has kept 'major' and 'minor' works simultaneously in focus, troubling their canonical status in interesting and enhancing ways, and enabling them to appear in brighter historical relief by showing how their literary struggle (as Butler put it in her Cambridge inaugural lecture) 'models an intricate, diverse, stressful community, not a bland monolith'.

Butler's sympathetic intimacy with Romantic writing has enabled her sharply to identify its literary ambitions. Her work displays an unusual historical sensitivity to the specific literary choices open to writers at a particular moment. Although it does not take the Romantics entirely at their own evaluation, it is nonetheless inspired by a historically learned realization of their creative departure from other contemporary possibilities, other, equally legitimate ways of writing at the time. It co-opts and re-orchestrates the methods Butler inherited and experienced in her own career: impressionism, formalism, Oxford bibliography, Leavisite moralism, feminism, new historicism of the European and American varieties, post-colonialism. In Marjorie Levinson's best diagnosis, a unifying theory is replaced in her work by the act of showing 'one historical fact . . . *produced* by another'.[1] The canon shines in contradistinction to the archive from which it has emerged, but in that archive must reside the alternatives that made the canon a choice, a risk, an election, a political act, ascriptions that at once acknowledge orthodox achievement while refusing it an absolute authority. Official literary history is shadowed, in Butler's work, by other possible literary choices and histories.

Marilyn Butler's writing is deceptively un-theoretical and accessible. As a result, the force, the subtlety, and the seriousness of her interventions in intellectual debate about Enlightenment and Romantic-period history can sometimes go unobserved. In recent years the more obviously grand narratives of Jonathan Israel, Linda Colley, and Roy Porter have been influential in gripping and shaping non-specialized attention to the British cultural heritage. Butler's work assimilates and already qualifies and questions the large ambitions of such narratives. Like them, it conjures up a British self-image that won't stay still, that is knowing about its difference from Europe, that is interestingly in transition, and that changes with the subtle re-alignments of class and social expression produced by mutating historical circumstance. But in its attention to local, writerly detail it subsumes and refines upon grand narrative, and foregrounds the power of individual agency within history.

The historical presuppositions that Butler's work shares with the major historians from whom she differs can perhaps be summarized as follows. Dissent in the long eighteenth century is both oppositional and conservative: it resists an establishment that it believes has excluded it, and is eager to achieve the establishment of its own tradition that it was disappointed in expecting from the settlement of 1688–9. The new, more tolerant consensus following from the Glorious Revolution was primarily religious but was forged at a time when religious and political sentiments and language were still fairly interchangeable. Nevertheless, they were not the same, and subsequent exclusions of Dissenters from dominant educational institutions, Parliament, the judiciary, hegemonic culture generally, had probably two main effects. The first was recognition of a pressing need for secularization if religious toleration was to be turned into a political franchise: Dissent had to become dissent. The second was the desire to keep up anyway with the dominant state apparatuses by shadowing them with an equally supportive Dissenting establishment. The Dissenting academies at Warrington, Northampton, Tewkesbury, and elsewhere are the obvious formal example of success here, but the informal support for Dissent hosted by clubs, associations, meetings of lobby groups, reviews, correspondence societies, and other groupings has a long tail that, as was shown by gagging acts from the mid 1790s until 1819, was difficult to monitor, never mind police.[2]

Add to this unmanageability the secularizing imperative first mentioned, and the picture of creative dissidence towards orthodoxy in all its inherited forms becomes one of energies working across a very broad front. And the breadth of this front can bring out unusual versatility in the critical writing attempting to understand and record it now. Secularism, in fact, is only a name for the variety of modes of justification replacing that of monolithic religious authority. Secularism belongs with that continuing crisis of the European mind of which Jonathan Israel has provided the most exhaustive account. At its best, interdisciplinary history like Butler's puts aside the limited binary axes of explanation articulating single subject areas, as if itself opposing academically a theological model of doctrinal uniformity with a secular latitudinarianism. It challenges the completeness of sweeping separations into ancients and moderns or traditionalists and radicals because it shows that the same people belong to different sides in different contexts. Israel, for example, argues that 'what was ultimately at stake was what kind of belief-system should prevail in Europe's politics, social order, and institutions, as well as in high culture and, no less, in popular attitudes'.[3] Butler shows that the grand narrative of secularization is actually made up of contested local stories and different time-scales, which can be allowed centre stage without sacrificing an overall idea of progressiveness.

Butler's replacement of the 'bland monolith' with a more difficult 'diverse and stressful community' positions her interestingly in relation to the historiography of her period. The prevailing nostrum of the moment on the long eighteenth century is in all likelihood one deriving from Linda Colley's *Britons*, according to which the egregious event for historians to explain from the early modern period onwards becomes the forging of the nation, not the variety or consistency of competing views suppressed by the national story, the non-conformism of which major historians (Hill, Thomas, Thompson) preceding Colley established so influential a school of study.[4] Whereas J. C. D. Clark had excavated an often cryptic persistence of an authentic ecclesiastical communion in unlikely places in order to ground national continuity, Colley stressed the diversification of establishment positions required to make people sufficiently patriotic about public order to believe in the value of exporting it and to enlist in that colonial enterprise.[5] The moral case for Empire, far from merely euphemizing its commercial gains, actually justified them; they set the standard for good use and equitable practice in an expandable British society. Warren Hastings, for example, was arraigned for allegedly compromising these standards, and Burke's moral victory in his failed prosecution of Hastings was still measured commercially in its impoverishment of the eventually acquitted Nabob. The moral obligation to extrapolate domestic standards to the colonies, after all, is the same argument we still find, carried to extremes, in Wordsworth's *Excursion*. Butler's resistance to literary parochialism lets her criticism alert us to these wider historical debates that texts like *The Excursion* were, in their own way, settling.

Colley's overwhelming case for concentrating on explaining how the national self-consciousness driving the extraordinary British Imperial successes of the Victorian age was produced understandably tends to leave languishing any radical, enlightened dissent. Butler's work, however, encourages us to highlight the importance of accounting for another equally obvious phenomenon, that of progress. It is equally arguable, a story as compelling as the national story of the long eighteenth century, that people typically sensed that things could get better for the species as a whole (another Wordsworthian theme, as he too changes sides),[6] and that advances in medicine, technology, and agriculture applied indifferently to everyone and therefore helped establish ideas of political equality. If we are the same as each other in such formative matters, then why should barriers of birth and class prevail socially? The sentimental impulse in literary culture fed off this scientific indifference; its sympathies were licensed further by ever more comprehensive scientific analyses of our common condition; encouraged to neglect social distinctions, the sentimentalist's range of appropriate sympathetic objects increased correspondingly. (Later attempts to redescribe the burgeoning life-sciences so as to recover the modes of discrimination they had undermined fascinated Butler in her editing of *Frankenstein*.) The discovery of still more material for empathy, and more reliable material at that, powered writings as varied as those of Shaftesbury and Hutcheson, Richardson and Sterne. More than this, as Roy Porter's tableaux of the Enlightenment cumulatively ascertain, sentimentalism softened the commercial impulse, but it did so significantly by lending it an emotional surround capable of replacing religious prescriptions of how to behave with an affectivity just as morally reliable. Porter's interest in 'men devoted to the promotion of a new material well-being and leisure; aspiring provincials, Dissenters, sceptics and political realists resentful at the traditional authority imbued in Church and State' sits happily with his depiction of the effects of a symptomatic transition from good sense to sensibility, when 'the personal became the political', or, less anachronistically, 'what Hazlitt meant by the "cant of religion" yielding to "the cant of sentimentality" . . . spelt a new and crucial phase in the dynamic enlightened quest for truth and freedom'. Commerce and sensibility share the same headlines, and Porter's breadth of example, significantly, outflanks the mediating adjective 'polite' required by Paul Langford's contrasting account of English commercialism.[7] This broadly progressive front held people together by holding up the possibility of change for the better and by implying the entitlement of any member of the species to represent the rest. All manner of possible enfranchisements, including the abolition of slavery, now heave into sight. Again, Porter's work represents a changing body of historical speculation with which Butler's criticism constantly interacts. But her early interest in the progressive core of eighteenth-century social diversity and her grasp of the variety of its transformations within Romanticism were quite distinctive.

Butler's own work pioneered, and the canonical series *Cambridge Studies in Romanticism* she has edited with James Chandler has helped foster, this richer view of things. We have come to see that 'the production of social order', to quote a recent sub-title from the series, was far more complex in this period than the production of legitimacy. Founded on conflicted notions, the social order that survived the challenge of the French Revolution poses the question of how it was that a certain kind of conformity, a sense of national belonging, was what actually changed things most effectively for the better. Our book therefore begins with this question at its most general, with one of the most casual ways of belonging to a company, that of 'conversation'. Conversation is not synonymous with argument, although a relatively uninhibited public sphere, as Habermas famously showed, can prefigure and so make a case for political possibility. But conversation clearly manages potential conflict or dispute between people towards productive ends. Jon Mee deepens our understanding of Dissenting opposition by emphasizing divisions within its counter public sphere.

One pole of Dissenting conversation looked towards the rehabilitation of existing constitutionalism. For women, the bluestocking group led by the wealthy and resourceful Elizabeth Montagu and friends offered such a forum. Anna Barbauld, despite invitations to align herself with the bluestockings and participating to a degree in their activities, tended towards a second pole, which gathered those loyal to the principle of opposition as the heuristic principle of all human exchanges. This trust in 'much arguing, much writing, many opinions' belongs to a severer non-conformist tradition linking Milton's 'good old cause' to Godwin's privileging, in his *Enquiry*, of communicative action as the guiding light of philosophical explanation. Barbauld, in Mee's description, is located at a particularly expressive moment in the development of this dialogic arena, when the Dissenting ideal of 'conversation' as a transforming dialectic is being countered by notions that a culturally effective politeness has to be separated from enthusiasm or Dissent's Puritan past. Instabilities in Dissenting allegiances and a largely secular progression beyond these oppositions are talked through. Ideas of progress and education change when increasingly they are written about by women. Critics have treated these subjects separately and in depth. Mee's depiction of Barbauld's historical situation captures the tensions and uneasy alliances (in the Joseph Johnson circle, for example) produced in action by these competing or, better, 'conversing' interests.

William Hazlitt, nothing if not critical, is an essential figure in any investigation of the revisions of Dissent and the varieties of secular developments open to it. Are his writings to be valued as one literary future open to Dissent? Can Dissent find a manifesto in his secular, omnivorous, cultural day-to-day critical commentary, journalism in the best sense? Would this description do justice to the 'contrarian' but defining character of Hazlitt's political stance, one so distinctive in its opposition that it can look anachronistic, idiosyncratic, and wilfully nostalgic for a future promised but not delivered by the French Revolution? Kevin Gilmartin raises and answers these questions in a fashion that acknowledges the range of stamped and unstamped radical literature with which Hazlitt's writings negotiated. A political front as broad as this must risk contradiction and paradox; but in the process it may express most effectively the inconsistencies of the un-institutionalized life of radical London. Hazlitt was no communitarian, but Gilmartin shows that his writings are charged with the dialogic energies that a successful political opposition would have to orchestrate. Gilmartin argues that Hazlitt's unflinching catalogues of the good and bad of London life replace conventional Romantic utopianism (the Lakeland republic of Wordsworth's vision) with a vigorous, materialist, inclusive acceptance that a consistently admirable life is unavailable: 'vanity and luxury are the civilizers of the world, and the sweeteners of human life'.

Hazlitt's phrase offers no Mandevillean solution but advocates a knowledge that must get its hands dirty in proportion to its claims to be authoritative and comprehensive. Gilmartin suggests that Hazlitt's vivid immersions in London life, its politics, its pugilism, sports, theatres, topographies, voice a collective fantasy, the 'liberating' abstraction of a 'popular Leviathan', shared by more apocalyptic writers at the Blakean end of contemporary

radicalism. He is fascinated by the fixation of the popular imagination on
unworthy (monarchical) individuals, by the diminishing of the idea of the
People by abstract schemes for their betterment such as those of Godwin
or of Bentham. But his fundamental refusal to distinguish between supporting the People and celebrating individual aspiration finally locates him
as a figure uniquely expressive of those unresolved rhetorical negotiations
with which the heirs of Dissenting radicalism had to deal.

Shelley, on the other hand, wrote a defence of poetry in which the possibility of reactivating past writing in the service of new causes appears lim-
itless. Michael Rossington's discussion of Shelley's republicanism is therefore a discussion of his 'republics'. The historical adaptability of Shelley's
radicalism unrealized it in Hazlitt's eyes; to him, Shelley, symptomatic
of his generation, substituted for 'representations of things, rhapsodies of
words'.[8] Rossington fits Shelley's republican 'latitude' to Butler's insistence
on Shelley's internationalism, itself an historicizing updating of the French
Revolutionary rhetoric for post-Napoleonic times. Romantic oppositional
thought, one sees, has as many shapes as its uses of history. Rossington's
discussion of one period in Mary and Percy Shelley's continuous attempt
to keep alive the idea of an English republic explores the historicist tactics
they enlisted in furthering this project. Two relevant geographies become
the unusual bearers of this political investment and desire: Marlow, near
Windsor, where the Shelleys stayed in 1817, and a European context more
specifically evoked by stays in Switzerland and then Italy. Rossington's main
point is that these different venues enhance each other's presence: remem-
brances of one locale from the other consolidate and then colour in the
republican tradition of each. An English republican tradition that never
enjoyed establishment status after the Interregnum obviously has little celebrating its existence in the way of public monuments. It must therefore be
materialized inwardly, memorialized informally by the geography of its
protagonists, or through the adjacent, supportive traditions of mainland
Europe with its much more varied history of actual republican government.
Rossington shows that these strands are woven together in the Shelley circle's writing and behaviour so as to furnish a republican texture of consoling
substantiality. This republican material, though, interleaves places of literal struggle, such as sites of the English Civil War, with a literary topography, such as Rousseau's Switzerland or Godwin's Wales. In the same way,
the Shelleys' English republicanism evokes the presence of absent European
centres and figures of republicanism, from Machiavelli to Sismondi. Such
syntheses must remain, in Rossington's terms, 'counterfactual' histories, but
their idealism powers Percy Shelley's measured response to recent political

oppression. His *Charles the First*, understood within a project of perpetuating English republican politics by other means, mixes historicist dialectics with a pragmatic approach to contemporary radicalism. The play resists the temptation to sacrifice historical grasp to the polemical satisfactions of uncritically monumentalizing an alternative to history's winners.

Getting into the canon, or encouraging reading 'across' the canon broad enough to have yourself included within the new boundaries was clearly important for the children of Dissent. The corresponding updating of Dissent can become the major creative focus of a writing bent on this kind of assimilation. Anne Janowitz's account of Lucy Aikin, niece of Anna Barbauld, records another creative history or historicism: the Aikin family's unusual ability to manipulate their ongoing literary reception. Janowitz is interested and understandably challenged by the part her own commentary is invited to play in this continuing process. Here the past repossesses the present at each stage of reinterpretation; or, less dramatically, we can say that the interactive character of historicism becomes unusually salient when the past is so vociferous in claiming its share of the hermeneutical contract. In this case, the Aikin family's management of its reception is of a piece with their other educational enterprises. The Warrington and Palgrave academies prepared Dissenting students for the learned professions. Their ambition of assimilating non-conformism into polite society through professional competence and civic sense attracted mainstream Anglican support. The gentrification of Dissent increases with its post-Revolutionary mutation from a politically fraught *fraternité* into 'friendship', or a liberal openness to the opinions of others. But the 'severe contentions' of friendship of which Jon Mee writes are still apparent in Janowitz's account of the career of Barbauld's niece, Lucy Aikin, in her updating of the family's literary culture in a shape appropriate to Victorian times. Even her familial memoirs were formally partisan, explicitly combating French hegemony in this genre. Her description of the relation between her father and aunt discloses a considerable literary rivalry and its effects on herself. Historical momentum towards a universal franchise provoked her aggressively to set limits to the liberalism in which Dissent had come to rest. She could feel disgust when remembering the unbridled democratic moment of early Dissenting sympathy for the French Revolution. Janowitz's subtly sympathetic account lets us see how Lucy Aikin's memoirs, literary and familial, repossess her family's past so as to create a central role for the Dissenting heritage to whose polite assimilation she is a participating witness.

Pamela Clemit, in the subsequent essay, re-aligns canonical Romanticism from a different point of view. She does this by applying Butler's remarks about the irreplaceability of scholarly editions to the case of Godwin's letters. To find explanatory contexts in a circle of acquaintance is especially useful where a writer of Godwin's longevity and mobility of opinion is concerned. Changeable on principle, Godwin's views were always meant to originate in the collision of minds and the clash of ideas resulting from public conversation and association. The letters show that in private life too, in the give and take of more intimate social relations, his ideals of sincerity, rationality, and frank communication are put to the test in various comic and tragic ways. Clemit speculates that the private, epistolary tempering of Godwin's notorious intellectualism correlates with a general movement of ideas in the Romantic period from revolutionary rationalism to radical sympathy. The progressive drive is not lost; it is modified by a conciliatory pragmatism that revives sentimentalism as the context for forward thinking. Like everyone else, Godwin has to manage affection and conflict domestically. Sentimental expression is too urgent and democratic a force to wait for the best supporting philosophical argument to emerge. Domestically, in other words, Godwin can be seen to be negotiating in his letters the affective life mostly sidelined by his earlier, purer Enlightenment optimism. Equally, the fact that his still unpublished letters do in fact possess this large-scale resonance revises received views about the sources of his philosophical energy and inventiveness, and reminds us that the Enlightenment was sentimental as well as rationalistic.

Godwin's complex and far from unexamined life, recorded in his letters, provokes a versatility and range of writing that now can be seen to answer philosophical purposes. Rather than abandoning philosophical and political theory, Godwin's later writings, Clemit suggests, confirm his acceptance that Whig practice is required to communicate republican principle: he was prepared, that is, to use orthodox literary resources, in all their generic diversity, to present the case for reform. Clemit goes so far as to claim that Godwin's presentation of his theories through novels, histories, biographies, and meditations critically revises the accepted 'organization' and 'classification' of knowledge. His writing thus keeps alive a project high-minded enough to justify the 'secular career' of a lapsed Dissenting minister. Clemit also demonstrates that this high-mindedness goes with an astute commercial sense for the literary market. A mixture of the two, perhaps, explains Godwin's unusual support for contemporary women writers. Godwin's letters, if published, would confirm Clemit's picture of a thinker whose speculations were always meant to be socially practicable and whose sociability was always principled. His increasingly diverse writings both map the literary resources of the time and suggest his continuing dissent from a straightforward use of them, implying, as in the case of Wollstonecraft, an 'experimental' take on his period that refines our understanding of its historical character.

For many, Marilyn Butler's most considerable editing venture was the edition of Maria Edgeworth she oversaw for Pickering and Chatto. The special case of Edgeworth as a Romantic-period writer unusually alive to the need for a stable establishment open to radical improvements is, of course, bound up with her Irishness. That writerly identity, though, is ideologically fraught, beset by local quarrels over its definition. For some, Edgeworth is a patrician, English provincial, no less interesting for that, but limited in moment and seriousness. For others, she is a responsible Irish partisan who tried to broaden political consciousness to take account of concerns that ought to be on the political agenda. Edgeworth's literary identity typically unpacks itself as a perspective on national issues and on cosmopolitan debates about education and gender. Susan Manly argues that although Maria Edgeworth's early work on education has appeared to some narrowly rationalist, even mechanically so, actually its reasoned opposition to conservative mystification serves in the long term to encourage in pupils a greater imaginative licence and freedom of thought than its competitors. Beginning at the beginning, Manly demonstrates that Edgeworth's pedagogic originality, when considered in the context of her own family, arises through the reforms that her father, Richard, agreed to make in his educational practice which she had endured as a child. She opposes his disciplinarian use of associationism as a kind of Pavlovian instrument of instruction. Her much more liberal treatment of children here fuels a more generous conception of the radical educational dynamic driving Dissenting philosophy as a whole, from Hartley to Godwin and including her father Richard's friends Priestley and Darwin. This indirect contribution towards oppositional thinking, at the time when Burke had successfully cast Dissenting thought as mechanical and inhumane, is another example of the discreet radicalism Marilyn Butler found expressed through reference and allusion rather than by explicit thesis in Edgeworth's other writings.

In Edgeworth's theory, educating children can stand for enfranchisement by refusing domestic support for that authoritarian policing of the larger political establishment that Burke wanted it to provide. In *Practical Education*, written appropriately in collaboration with her father, Edgeworth suggests that children should not be disqualified from but welcomed to conversation with their social betters and seniors as part of a mutual rational development. In its rejection of paternalism this model of education enables individual emancipation and social reform. The authors Edgeworth cites in support of her arguments indirectly constitute a radical provocation: their names are those of the intellectual 'cabal' demonized by such conservatives as Burke and Barruel. Yet if Edgeworthian education is different from Burkean authoritarianism, it is also, Manly suggests, in its openness to the child quietly more radical than Rousseau's attempt to endow education with the exemplary force of natural necessity. Edgeworth invites those politically hostile reviews of *Practical Education* that remain polemically blind to the attempts of a Dissenting culture of education to establish its own theoretical and practical credentials outside established conservative and radical positions.

James Chandler highlights the puzzling combination of specificity and vagueness that Marilyn Butler identified in the topographical writing of the novels of Maria Edgeworth and pursues the insight in a reading of Sir Walter Scott. He refers the paradox not to the Romantic-theory paradigm of the 'concrete universal', beloved of Goethe and Coleridge, but to the contemporaneity these writers wished their novels to possess. He suggests that these writers *repossess* their pasts fictionally in order both to re-stage current negotiations of national identity and to emphasize the genealogical idiom in which this debatable territory keeps appearing. This inventive use of historical example to express different kinds of Romantic self-consciousness – national, political, and cultural – suggests to Chandler an informality and expansiveness of understanding that can be usefully modelled in key notions of Deleuze and Guattari. He focuses on the *agencement* or 'assemblage', whose rhizomatic growth displaces itself through possession and dispossession, territorialization and deterritorialization. Like the 'runner' of a rhizomatic plant, its apparently established growths disguise more definitive subterranean proliferations. The 'vagueness with respect to place' – Butler's puzzling insight into Edgeworth's and Scott's realism – is then theorized as resulting from the undercover historical growth surfacing in locodescription. Chandler further uses a Deleuzean paradigm of deterritorialization, the shift in analytical attention from the body to the face. Deleuze's notorious hatred of interiority ensures that this displacement from body to expression is discussed at the level of codes, the codes of signification that the face, as opposed to sheer corporeal extension, enters. Such change of territory is more clearly described in Deleuze's film-theory, where the 'close-up' abstracts the subject from the spatio-temporal coordinates which, until the face fills the screen, seemed to map it definitively. Chandler sees connections here with moments of sentimental stasis in Romantic historical novels, when techniques and expectations belonging to the novel's generic past exceed the roles they play in temporal narrative and topography. The momentary suppression of these specificities of time and place, though, has the effect of making the novel's incidents feel immediate, of re-coding them, of giving them a 'face' responsive to our different situation, of making them part of the writer's and reader's own *actualité*. But the awareness that this is an effect of coding or convention then tempers the metaphysics of this facial presence with a critical distance.

Chandler's essay expounds Romanticism's repossession of the past in a way that renders present critical readings of it still more self-conscious. His use of contemporary theory helps do this, of course, but he uses theory to rationalize one of Marilyn Butler's free-standing critical insights, and the effect is to show that her work leads to critical futures we are still in the process of achieving. Foucault was sure his century should be known as the 'Deleuzean' century, and Chandler's apt articulation of the intellectual effort of this collection through mainline theory implies the prominence of Butler's thought for the more modest world of Romantic scholars. He shows that the exploration of 'new discursive territory', as he calls it, is an inevitable consequence of Butler's practice.

In this spirit, Paul Hamilton looks at the case of Coleridge, a thinker whose critical esteem was often suspected by Butler, partly because of most of his influential commentators' wilful ignorance of the political character of his transcendentalism. But perhaps the philosophical Coleridge, so eager for assimilation but so difficult for the English critical tradition to swallow, also needs his European and cosmopolitan character appreciated if his uncanny stamina as an authority on critical theory is to be understood. Can 'new discursive territory' any longer be opened up in reading Coleridge? This essay argues that the historical coding in need of deciphering lies in the contemporary German philosophical explanations which are symmetrical with, but then render redundant, theological explanations. Coleridge's devout Christian religiosity attracts him to the German schemes whose examination of our power to reflect on everything forges, he recognizes, the temperament of the modern intellectual. Their apparently theological structures are especially congenial to him, but this very symmetry is what makes possible their secularization of religious experience so troubling to his religious faith. Schelling, Coleridge's interactive philosophical source, in fact undoes what M. H. Abrams famously called 'natural supernaturalism' by making the concept of each logically dependent on the other. But while the theological cast of contemporary logical speculation attracted and repelled him, it also made him more historicist in his search for a way of arguing that an originally religious intuition might still be preserved in its currently philosophical incarnation. Coleridge's admission that revelations originally belonging to one discourse can only be repeated in historically different ones, as the infinite *I am* becomes finite, worried him religiously. But this transformative logic or historical grammar, trumpeted at the end of the first volume of *Biographia Literaria*, ought also to worry us. It undermines any complacent belief that the way we organize knowledge now – calling some things scientific and other things ethical, aesthetic, or political – is anything other than a provisional settlement.

Nigel Leask takes his cue from a Marilyn Butler article that reverses the accustomed positions of background and foreground in the reading of Romantic oriental tales by Byron and Southey. The Eastern setting, rather than the erotic and violent events, becomes the intellectual centre of the poem for the historicist reader. Building on Butler's work and his own influential extension of it, Leask investigates further the reversals possible in colonial writing. In Elizabeth Hamilton's *Translation of the Letters of a Hindoo Rajah* (1796), the turn-around demanded of the reader anticipates a critical stance we now associate with Edward Said's 'orientalism'. The handing-over of the role of critical commentator to the visiting colonial subject turns the usual form of travelogue inside out. Hamilton's use of the trope of colonial reversal (like a Martian poet's defamiliarization, one could say, if Mars were a colony) allows her, like the earlier Enlightenment narratives of Voltaire, Montesquieu, and others, to criticize her society's unselfconscious ethnology, its unexamined Enlightenment. She can only do this, however, by herself uncritically ventriloquizing the colonial characters she has fictionally invested with her own critical authority. Yet one can equally say that the degree to which this cultural appropriation still retains a detailed picture of Hinduism to articulate its self-criticism shows Hamilton's non-sectarian willingness to pursue her Christian ideals in the idiom of another culture. Indeed Leask is fascinated by Hamilton's elusiveness to criticism in terms of expected ideologies and labels – anti-Jacobinism, orientalism, evangelicalism.

What happens, though, when the reversal is transposed, and a colonial subject ventriloquizes those he is visiting at the imperial centre? For an example of this complication and a possible escape from the critical bind just described, Leask turns to the Indian Muslim Abu Taleb Khan's *Travels*, composed 1803–4 and translated probably fairly tendentiously in 1810. Taleb's rich mixture of critique, diplomacy, erotic self-advertisement, and manifesto finally exhibits the cultural flexibility and mobility of the colonial subject whom the colonizers conveniently homogenize. Taleb's Indo-Persian background (his text was originally written in Persian), his opportunistic marriage into Bengali nobility, and his residual nostalgia for the days of the Moguls make for an identity far too individualized ever to be adequately enlisted to Hamilton's Christian progressiveness or any other form of Enlightened, moderate Dissent. The final impression is of the cultural reduction and violence imposed both by colonial administrative efficiency and by high-minded, Enlightened, sympathetic bridge-building. Hamilton's and Taleb's texts cannot, one might say, exist in the same canon, however broadly we read across it; in fact they expose the limitations of canonical thinking.

In a different sort of conversation with Marilyn Butler, Janet Todd picks up on a quite sharp refinement of the idea of the 'middling sort of people' in the early nineteenth century. The influence of the almost exclusively male professions and the wifely behaviour enjoined upon their spouses was, she suggests, increasingly distinguished by Austen and others from commercial pressures. Pure love of brass was increasingly opposed to the truly economical or many-sided management of affairs that Austen constantly emphasized should lie behind all successful households. Refining on Butler's understanding of Austen's conservatism, Todd shows how Austen promotes the professional ethos as conducive to a needful re-conceiving of general social benefit, a theme predictably popular in writing at the time of the rise of many of the professions. The professions, now dubbed the 'liberal professions', were seen as contributing essentially to the gentlemanly standards underpinning civic behaviour. Todd picks out those important moments when Jane Austen explores the crucial role of the professional man's wife in the formulation and regulation of professional standards, especially when men fall short of them. The feminism here is complicated, and far from un-misgiving, as Todd's acute *résumé* of the modulations of this theme throughout Austen's novels reveals. Finally, though, the conclusion is not the anticipated one. Austen, especially at the end of her major novelistic work in *Persuasion*, does not let her fiction lend explicitly romantic and erotic support to a more sophisticated understanding of the compatibilities making for professional partnership. The idea that professionalism in private life can set the pattern for public management is limited by the force of 'total desire'. Todd's Austen, like Porter's Enlightened Dissenters, concedes to 'sentiment' a decisive power in personal relations. Unlike them, though, she does not believe this power displays an obvious and pleasing symmetry with what she wants to happen politically.

In the rhetoric of Jerome McGann's Romantic retrospective, to be for poetry is to be for beauty and against sublimity. Kant's theory making the sublime the authentic expression of our best self is not for him. The sublime is 'sentimental' in Schiller's sense: to find pleasures in contemplating our characteristic ways of knowing compensates for failures to know. Instead McGann ties aesthetic pleasure to our harmony with our world, to beauty. He champions a poetry of beauty in motion, one whose fleeting movement matches our mortality to its continuity. To be against sublimity only appears to be against theory because this apparent refusal of theory is as paradoxical as Schiller's knowing recapture of an impossible naivety. McGann, following Wallace Stevens, wants to replace the monolithic sublime associated with the critical establishment of Hartman and Bloom that preceded his own new historicism. The detail of poetic success, itself possessing sufficient beauty, now obviates the need for further exposition. Byron is McGann's example of a poetic ally who abandons both Wordsworthian sublimity and his own earlier Satanic discontent with a beauty impossible to close on. These earlier poetic manners are replaced by a meticulous art in which syllables can 'assume an absolute condition'. The beauty of this writing 'indexes the medium of which [it] is made'. Unlike the sublime, such beauty is unobliged to any transcendental order: McGann's 'beautiful soul', unlike Schiller's, possesses all the elements of mundanity, irreligious and procreative, 'tellingly mortalized', but really present.

McGann understands modernist convulsions over the definition of beauty as symptomatic of a Romantic future not taken up. He reworks his own influential views on Romantic ideology, which so complemented Butler's early work, in order to foreground Romantic-period writing whose human expression escapes prevailing idealizing or empiricist stereotypes. This Romantic writing dispenses with Platonic traditions of the ideal. It also opposes the contemporary empiricist sensibility often presented as mechanical and unsatisfying in order to justify the difficulties and obscurities resulting from attempts to transcend it in Romantic sublimity. To read against Wordsworth's influence, therefore, is to detach beauty not from 'use' but from the aesthetic uses to which it has so often been put. The true use of beauty for McGann ends up being to imagine a kind of availability that both democratizes aesthetics and makes it stand for our basic, pleasurable connection with the world, our 'contract to live'. As, paradoxically, both sufficient and mortal, beauty prompts the creative efforts by which we truly inhabit the world. McGann's difficult conclusion sketches a repossession of a particular past – the history of beauty – and also implies that repossession is a paradigm of so much else besides.

Marilyn Butler is not one of those critics who have sought to establish a school. Her influence is broader and the example she sets – in its scepticism and constructiveness – is more creative than could be summarized by a single methodological approach. Her personal generosity in encouraging so many scholars is of the same order. Various as they are, none of the essays in this volume could have been written without her. She has opened up new subjects with a criticism alert to the precise historical moment of the texts it seeks to read. This book builds on her work by reviewing the diversification of the forms of Dissenting culture as it grows progressively more secular during the late Enlightenment and early stages of Romanticism. It selects Maria Edgeworth, whose works were the subject of Butler's main editorial venture, as a test-case of this process. Finally, it takes the lesson from its subject matter that our own academy has to register a similar openness to change and development if its critical readings are to remain adequate to the historical mobility of the cultural phenomena they interpret. Easy divisions into canonical and non-canonical, polite and impolite, past and present, the aesthetic and the non-aesthetic create oppositions where sometimes it would be better to recognize that new integrations are required of the reader to understand complex processes of cultural change. A 'war of ideas', as Butler showed in her study of Austen, is just that, a confluence of competing interests with their different takes on central issues. This book for her reaffirms her discovery for us that disenchantment with neatly antithetical explanations matches the actual secular diversification of the Romantic period, vindicating the open-endedness of our modern repossession of it, the generosity of reading we should aim for, and the dialogic opposition that is true friendship.

NOTES

1. Marjorie Levinson, Marilyn Butler, Jerome McGann, and Paul Hamilton, *Rethinking Historicism: Critical Readings in Romantic History* (Oxford: Blackwell, 1989), p. 4.
2. John Barrell, for example, detects in the threatening patterns of London Corresponding Society organization a replication of the monstrous unknowability of much of London to the authorities. See his chapter in James Chandler and Kevin Gilmartin (eds.), *Romantic Metropolis: The Urban Scene in British Romanticism, 1780–1840* (Cambridge: Cambridge University Press, 2005).
3. Jonathan I. Israel, *Radical Enlightenment: Philosophy and the Making of Modernity 1650–1750* (Oxford: Oxford University Press, 2001), p. 11.
4. An interesting and quick way into current versions of this formative opposition would be to compare Kevin Sharpe's Colleyish *Reading Revolutions: The Politics of Reading in Early Modern England* (New Haven, Conn: Yale University Press, 2000) with David Norbrook's *Writing the English Republic: Poetry, Rhetoric and Politics, 1627–1660* (Cambridge: Cambridge University Press, 1999).

5. Linda Colley, *Britons: Forging the Nation, 1707–1837* (London: Pimlico, 1992); J. C. D. Clark, *English Society 1688–1832* (Cambridge: Cambridge University Press, 1985).

6. Wordsworth's secular trumping of Milton in the end of *Home at Grasmere* (also reproduced as the 'Prospectus' to *The Excursion*) relates

> Speaking of nothing more than what we are –
> How exquisitely the individual Mind
> (And the progressive powers perhaps no less
> Of the whole species) to the external world
> Is fitted . . .

7. Roy Porter, *Enlightenment: Britain and the Creation of the Modern World* (Harmondsworth: Penguin Books, 2000), pp. 47, 277, 294. See Paul Langford, *A Polite and Commercial People: England 1727–1783* (Oxford: Oxford University Press, 1989).

8. P. P. Howe (ed.), *The Complete Works of William Hazlitt* (London: Dent, 1930–3), 21 vols., vol. XII, p. 246.

PART I

Dissent and opposition

'Severe contentions of friendship': Barbauld, conversation, and dispute

Jon Mee

My title is taken from the following passage in William Blake's epic poem *Milton*:

> Is this our Femin[in]e Portion the Six-fold Miltonic Female
> Terribly this Portion trembles before thee O awful Man
> Altho' our Human Power can sustain the severe contentions
> Of Friendship, our Sexual cannot: but flies into the Ulro.
> Hence arose all our terrors in Eternity! & now remembrance
> Returns upon us! Are we Contraries O Milton, Thou & I
> O Immortal!¹

This essay is not concerned with Blake directly, but aims to unpick some of the hidden relations behind the hegemonic eighteenth-century idea of the conversation of culture. 'Conversation' is a ubiquitous term in eighteenth-century historiography, but there seems to have been little work done on what constituted conversation as what we might term a literary and verbal technology, or how it stood in relation to ideas of controversy and freedom of speech. In Habermas's account, for instance, conversation is the means by which private opinions come to be transformed into the public sphere, but neither he nor his many followers have looked in much detail at what constituted conversation (as opposed to other kinds of discourse) in and for the period.² What were the contentious others, I want to ask, against which conversation was defined? Is conversation defined as part of a continuum with contention, dispute, and controversy, or is it seen as part of a binary opposition with such terms? Could the 'severe contentions of friendship' claim a place in the conversation of culture construed in broad national terms?

I quote the passage from Blake in full because it usefully refers us to some of the broader issues that inform this paper: issues of gender, tensions between ideas of conversation and controversy, and the nature of the Miltonic inheritance for the eighteenth century in relation to ideas of freedom of speech and religious enquiry. Whereas for some the conversation of culture was predicated on an ideal of harmonious exchange, a seemingly inclusive culture of politeness and mutuality, for others it was constituted by a more vigorous enquiry after truth that did not preclude the clash of differences. This latter *frictive* tradition of verbal and literary exchange runs from the encouragement to 'much arguing, much writing, many opinions' in Milton's *Areopagitica* through to Blake's famous invocation of 'Mental Fight'.[3] I do not wish, however, to be misunderstood as drawing from Milton to Blake any kind of 'strong' male tradition in which women had no part. Quite the contrary, in fact, since I want to suggest that if a feminized notion of polite conversation offered women certain opportunities, then those opportunities often brought with them certain kinds of restraints, restraints which many women, especially from backgrounds in non-conformity, refused in favour of the opportunity for 'the collision of mind with mind'.[4]

The primary focus of this essay is on the varying relations between Anna Laetitia Barbauld and the bluestocking circle associated with Elizabeth Montagu, Elizabeth Carter, Elizabeth Vesey, and, slightly later, Hannah More. During the 1770s the primarily Anglican circle surrounding Montagu made an effort to recruit Barbauld (or, as she was then, Anna Aikin) to their company. This project may have had an influence on Barbauld's ecumenical thinking in the 1770s. Then her desire to distance herself from the perceived uncouthness of her Presbyterian past – shared with other 'liberal' Dissenters of both sexes associated with the Warrington Academy – drew her to the politeness of the supposedly national culture of Anglicanism. No doubt part of the attraction of the bluestockings for Barbauld was the prospect of female solidarity, but this affirmation came at the cost of certain kinds of conformity that eventually she was unwilling to pay. For Montagu and her circle thought of conversation more in terms of the suppression of difference in the name of harmony. Nicole Pohl and Betty A. Schellenberg describe the bluestockings as practising 'a commitment to these ideals as the basis of civic virtue in a liberal society'.[5] 'Liberal' such attitudes might be in one sense, and the Anglican complexion of Montagu's circle did not exclude the appearance of leading Dissenters such as Richard Price, as well as Barbauld herself, but they also inevitably perpetuated the authority of Church and State, even if sometimes under the guise of an inclusive notion of a national culture.[6] Joseph Priestley's critique of Barbauld's essay 'Thoughts on the Devotional Taste' (1775) discussed below may represent a gendered attack on the feminization of culture, but one also has to see that he is challenging what he sees as the recruitment of a talented Dissenting intelligence to the ranks of the establishment. Priestley was a 'liberal' Dissenter himself, but his version of rational religion did not assume that contention and controversy had no place in public discourse. On the contrary, Priestley, like Isaac Watts before him and William Godwin after, thought that the conversation of culture in its broadest sense was predicated on 'the collision of mind with mind', that is, the kind of 'severe contention' that could produce religious and political truths as yet unknown. Barbauld herself did not need Priestley to point this model of conversational discovery out to her. She was always ambiguous about the attractions of the Montagu set, and, especially from the 1780s, when she became more involved with Dissenting circles in London, increasingly insisted on the importance of freedom of enquiry to religious and political truth. By the 1790s, pamphlets such as her *Sins of Government, Sins of the Nation* (1793) were articulating an apocalyptic mode that was very much at odds with the millennial quietism of Montagu's valorization of the paradise of conversation recently discussed by Harriet Guest and Emma Major.[7] The explanation is not just to be found in the radicalization of Dissent in the context of the French Revolution, but also in Barbauld's insistence on a woman's right to a tradition of contention and controversy as the means to religious truth. 'Politeness' as a cultural discourse may have enabled certain kinds of female cultural participation, but it also had implications with regard to the kind and extent of this involvement.

The biography written by Barbauld's niece Lucy Aikin provides a neat contrast that offers a way into this issue:

At the splendid mansion of her early and constant admirer Mrs Montague [sic], Mrs Barbauld beheld in perfection the imposing union of literature and fashion; – under the humbler roof of her friend and publisher, the late worthy Joseph Johnson of St Paul's Church-yard, she tasted, perhaps with higher relish, 'the feast of reason and the flow of soul'.[8]

Teasing out the contrast implied here by Aikin between the bluestockings and the Johnson circle in fact provides the framework for my essay. Let me begin by sketching in some more detail about the bluestockings. For my purposes here the term is used in the narrow sense of the Montagu circle, a group of women who became famous in the 1770s for the influence they wielded at the literary salons staged mostly at the homes of Montagu and Vesey: 'These informal gatherings united men and women primarily of the gentry and upper classes, with the participation of a number of more middle-class professionals, in the pursuit of intellectual improvement, polite sociability, the refinement of the arts through patronage, and national stability through philanthropy'.[9] Many of those involved, including Barbauld, were celebrated together in Mary Scott's poem *The Female Advocate* (1774) and painted in Richard Samuel's *Nine Living Muses of Great Britain* (1778). Samuel's painting was exhibited at the Royal Academy in 1779, but it was mainly known through the engraving distributed with *Johnson's Ladies New and Polite Pocket Memorandum for 1778*. Barbauld and Montagu were celebrated together in a special piece called 'Observations on Female Literature' in the *Westminster Magazine* for June 1776.[10] The 1770s was the key decade in the public recognition of the role of the bluestockings, and it is significant that Joseph Johnson was in at the beginning (he was also the publisher of Scott's poem). Indeed Carter referred to the painting as Johnson's in her correspondence with Montagu:

One thing is perfectly agreeable to my vanity, to say nothing about my heart, that it seems to be a decided point, that you and I are always to figure in the literary world together, and that from the classical poet, the water drinking rhymes, to the highest dispenser of human fame, Mr. Johnson's pocket book, it is perfectly well understood, that we are to make our appearance in the same piece.[11]

The condescending tone in regard to Johnson is worth noting, but for now I want to stress that 'rational conversation' was at the centre of the bluestocking project.[12] Indeed this aspect of their activity was celebrated in Hannah More's poem *The Bas Bleu*, dedicated to Elizabeth Vesey. In her 'Advertisement' to later editions of the poem, More defined the bluestockings as 'composed of persons distinguished, in general, for their rank, talents, or respectable character, who met frequently at Mrs *Vesey's* and at a few other houses, for the sole purpose of conversation, and were different in no respect from other parties, but that the company did not play at cards'.[13] Conversation here was being opposed to frivolous fashionable pursuits that the group, no less than Mary Wollstonecraft later, regarded as a distraction from the proper exercise of women's capabilities. Indeed, in her essay 'Thoughts on Conversation' (1777), which provides something of a preface to the later poem, More insisted:

It has been advised, and by very respectable authorities too, that in conversation women should carefully conceal any knowledge or learning they may happen to possess. I own, with submission, that I do not see either the necessity or propriety of this advice. For if a young lady has that discretion and modesty, without which all knowledge is little worth, she will never make an ostentatious parade of it, because she will rather be intent on acquiring more, than on displaying what she has.[14]

Conversation then for the bluestockings provided a proper medium for the exercise of female talents, especially for More in relation to religious ideas, although, as we shall see, even for More female conversation could paradoxically be defined in terms of silence rather than controversy.

No doubt the possibility that polite discourse might provide an ecumenical platform for the woman intellectual is what attracted Barbauld to the bluestockings, although it was Elizabeth Montagu who first made overtures to her, in the wake of the publication of Barbauld's *Poems* (1773) and (with John Aikin, her brother), *Miscellaneous Pieces in Prose* (1773). On reading the latter Montagu told Barbauld in a letter that her essays had made her 'still more intimately acquainted with the turn of your mind'.[15] Montagu may have been even more delighted to have read another Barbauld essay published soon afterwards, 'Thoughts on the Devotional Taste', which offers 'devotion' as a term that could provide a bridgehead between what were construed as the narrowly sectarian interests of Dissent and the broader national culture associated with the Church of England. Barbauld's 'Thoughts' begins by admitting that there are dangers that religious feeling left to itself may be a conduit of enthusiasm of the most vulgar kind:

> If directed by a melancholy or enthusiastic faith, their workings are often too strong for a weak head, or a delicate frame; and for this reason they [that is, the religious affections] have been almost excluded from religious worship by many persons of real piety.[16]

She imagines with disdain 'some florid declaimer who professes to work upon the passions of the lower class, where they are so debased by noise and nonsense, that it is no wonder if they move disgust in those of elegant and better-informed minds'.[17] The work of self-regulation that she imagines as beyond the Methodist crowd, she believes can be provided by the 'taste' of the person of sensibility. Animating Barbauld's essay is a fear that Dissenters were in danger of recreating what she sees as the 'critical and disputatious spirit' of their seventeenth-century Presbyterian forebears.[18] From this perspective, Dissent was falling into a vulgar enthusiasm when it was tasteless enough to *insist* on its differences from the 'liberal' Anglican culture of politeness, which by virtue of its constitutional status could claim to be truly national.[19] Certainly the mainly Anglican bluestockings with whom Barbauld was beginning to correspond in the 1770s routinely took the view that, as Elizabeth Carter wrote to Mrs Montagu, 'the powers of imagination are annihilated by the violence of ungoverned passions, and must languish when they are most warmed and animated by the social affections of the

heart', especially in relation to 'sentiments of religion when looking at the
sublime in nature', although I shall be suggesting below that we should be
wary of understanding the 'social affections' as a gendered term that can be
translated seamlessly across religious and social differences.[20]

Barbauld's main concern when reflecting on her Dissenting background
is the potentially destructive pressure it could put on the social affections
by too much candour in religious enquiry: 'a sect is never stationary, as
it depends entirely on passions and opinions'.[21] From at least Isaac Watts
and Philip Doddridge onwards, Dissent's attempt to distance itself from
the uncouthness of its Presbyterian past had concerned itself with the difference between the affections and the kind of passion that smacked of
enthusiasm. Watts's sponsorship of Elizabeth Rowe's poetry is an example of precisely this movement. Barbauld celebrated the 'gentle sweetness'
(l. 40) of her precursor in 'Verses on Mrs Rowe'.[22] The Dissenter William
Enfield recognized Barbauld's essay as part of this ongoing project, 'desirous
to remove the disgrace which enthusiasm in its several forms has brought
upon devotion'.[23] These 'several forms' of enthusiasm were not necessarily
solely questions of excess of emotion (as we might imagine). 'Enthusiasm' could designate dogma and controversy as much as the welter of the
emotions.[24]

For most commentators at the time Barbauld was writing and for several
decades thereafter, the chief generator of the factious 'opinion' in Dissenting
circles was believed to be Joseph Priestley, and Priestley certainly identified
himself as the target of Barbauld's critique. There have been several recent
accounts of the disagreement between Barbauld and Priestley on these
matters and I will not rehearse the details again here.[25] Barbauld objects
not primarily to any coldness or dryness in Priestley's brand of Dissent,
but to its extended version of candour as against the kind of feminized
yet also regulated sensibility approved in the Montagu circle. Barbauld
had written to her brother in 1774 that: '*You* are hardly social creatures
till your minds are humanized and subdued by that passion which alone
can tame you to "all the soft civilities of life".'[26] These 'soft civilities' are
precisely what the Montagu circle was deemed by many to have brought
to the discussion of political and religious affairs. Barbauld's account of
Priestley implied that the vigour of his idea of God was too strong for
human capabilities to comprehend, and that this overwhelming power put
the idea of a coherent selfhood in danger. Religious 'devotion' she imagines
at this stage in her career as a much more sociable passion, the feminized
'beautiful' of religion – to use Edmund Burke's binary – to be contrasted
with Priestley's 'sublime'.

Priestley responded to 'Thoughts' as an act of betrayal, and wrote to Barbauld directly in protest, asking her to make changes to future editions, but some care has to be taken in understanding his response. No less than Watts and Doddridge before him, Priestley had also argued for a view of religion not simply as a matter of reason, but as 'an elevated passion, or affection'. What he detects in Barbauld's appeal to 'taste' (rather than some idea of 'feeling' or 'affection' as such) is something different.[27] An aversion to the specifically aesthetic associations of the term 'taste' – smacking to him perhaps of the superstitious contrivances of Anglican ceremony and ritual – seems to be in play for Priestley. Significantly in this respect, having read her poetry and early essays, Elizabeth Montagu's first overture to Barbauld in February 1774 had claimed that 'the genuine effect of polite letters is to inspire candour, a social spirit, and gentle manners'.[28] Priestley would probably have thought the idea of 'candour' promoted here a dubious attenuation of his understanding of the term. Montagu had also claimed that 'to live under the benign empire of the muses, on the conditions of a naturalized subject, who, not having any inherent right to a share of office, credit, or authority, seeks nothing but the protection of the society is all I aim at'.[29] Had Priestley read this letter, its doctrine of non-resistance to 'empire' and depreciation of 'inherent rights' would likely have confirmed all his suspicions of the idea of 'taste' being scouted in Barbauld's 1775 'Thoughts on the Devotional Taste'. Harriet Guest has argued that bluestocking assemblies were much valued (by men) in the 1760s and 1770s 'because they seemed to exclude the factionalisms of politics'.[30] We might also add 'religious controversy'. For Priestley, this kind of 'taste' was inherently invested in the perpetuation of the political and religious status quo. 'Taste' in its artificiality was dampening of religious 'passion' for Priestley, and this concern with mere politeness made an accommodation with the Church possible by turning a blind eye to theological (and political) enquiry. Priestley's letter to Barbauld expresses particular surprise at her positive attitude towards religious establishments, especially her view that 'an establishment will preserve devotion from ever sinking into contempt'.[31] Priestley believed that what Barbauld saw as the disputatious enthusiasm of sects was the astringent means of keeping the road to religious and civic truth open. Her conciliatory language of taste and sensibility, he believed, was a means of making defections from Dissent to the Church of England easier. She was in danger for Priestley of surrendering herself to Montagu's 'empire'.

Returning to bluestocking writings on the subject of conversation, we can see that they firmly dissociated it from any form of disputatiousness.

Indeed it was precisely in damping down such differences that femininity was seen as having a particular role to play in the conversational arts, but if this was a kind of empowerment, then it was of a very particular kind. Let me return to Hannah More's discussion of the subject in her essay 'On Conversation':

How easily and effectually may a well-bred woman promote the most useful and elegant conversation, almost without speaking a word! for the modes of speech are scarcely more variable than the modes of silence . . . A woman, in a company where she has the least influence, may promote any subject by a profound and invariable attention, which shows that she is pleased with it, and by an illuminated countenance, which proves she understands it. This obliging attention is the most flattering encouragement in the world to men of sense and letters, to continue any topic of instruction or entertainment they happen to be engaged in.[32]

Commenting on a newspaper report of a schism in the ranks of the blue-stockings, Montagu wrote to Carter in 1783 to say that 'such an influence has ye good humour and benevolent nature of our Vesey, that Persons of the most contrary dispositions are harmonized if not brought in unison in her Concertos of conversation'.[33] Although More was much more likely than Montagu to court the charge of enthusiasm in the vigour of her concern for religious truth, especially after her turn towards evangelicalism, she was quite clear that the female arts of conversation were not controversial ones. For More, 'of all the qualifications for conversation, humility, if not the most brilliant, is the safest, the most amiable, and the most feminine'.[34] Others, such as Elizabeth Carter, less evangelical in their Anglicanism than More, were more confirmed as to the vulgarity of disputing over religious matters, and saw it as an inherent feature of Dissenting culture that even shockingly extended to female believers in the sects:

There is a new school of oratory set up, where, on a Sunday evening, for the price of sixpence, people may go and hear the discussion of knotty points of divinity. There were five hundred people there on Sunday. The subject was Predestination. The opponent to this doctrine said it was a damnable opinion, on which a gentlewoman (for I am not sure that ladies go to divinity lectures) who was probably on the other side of the question, hissed the speaker. She was rebuked for this by the moderator, and told it was only for serpents to hiss. All the other oratorical institutions will only make people impertinent; but such a method of treating subjects of divinity will certainly help to make them mad.[35]

For her part, Montagu herself was sometimes condescending in her comments on Barbauld to her other bluestocking friends. In November 1774 she had written to Carter: 'I had last night a charming letter from Mrs Barboult. I find she is in a very uncouth neighbourhood, but she speaks of her situation with that resignation I shd expect. I have a more exquisite sense of her superior merit than she has, & I am chagrined at what does not mortify her'.[36] Carter's response has an equally condescending if perhaps less charitable tone: 'Mrs. Barbault's acquiescence is an excellent proof of her good sense and right principles, a consistency which is unhappily not very common in people who have made such a kind of choice. May she never find out that the gratifying one favourite wish, does not necessarily preclude every other'.[37] Montagu and Carter may be commenting on Barbauld's situation at Palgrave, Norfolk, where she ran a school with her husband, a French Dissenting minister. Montagu was no doubt piqued because she had earlier in 1774 proposed to Barbauld that they establish 'a College for young ladies'.[38] The choice referred to by Carter refers either to Barbauld's decision to marry Rochemont Barbauld in June 1774 or more likely to her decision to help at his boarding school rather than take up Montagu's offer. Barbauld had refused Montagu's proposal for reasons that might at first blush seem anti-feminist, especially in the context of following her husband rather than taking up an offer from another intellectual woman:

A kind of Literary Academy for ladies (for that is what you seem to propose), where they are to be taught in a regular systematic manner the various branches of science, appears to me better calculated to form such characters as the '*Precieuses*' or the '*Femmes sçavantes*' of Moliere, than good wives or agreeable companions. Young gentlemen, who are to display their knowledge to the world, should have every motive of emulation, should be formed into regular classes, should read and dispute together, should have all the honours and, if one may so say, the pomp of learning set before them, to call up their ardour: – it is their business, and they should apply to it as such. But young ladies, who ought only to have such a general tincture of knowledge as to make them agreeable companions to a man of sense, and to enable them to find rational entertainment for a solitary hour, should gain these accomplishments in a more quiet and unobserved manner: – subject to a regulation like the ancient Spartans, the thefts of knowledge in our sex are only connived at while carefully concealed, and if displayed, punished with disgrace. The best way for women to acquire knowledge is from conversation with a father, a brother or friend, in the way of family intercourse and easy conversation, and by such a course of reading as they may recommend. If you add to these an attendance upon those masters which are usually provided in schools, and perhaps a set of lectures as Mr Ferguson's, which it is not uncommon for ladies to attend, I think a woman will be in a way to acquire all the learning that can be of use to those who are not to teach or engage in any learned profession. Perhaps you may think, that having myself stepped out of the bounds of female reserve in becoming an author, it is with an ill grace I offer these sentiments: but though this circumstance may destroy the grace, it does not the justice of the remark; and I am full well convinced that to have a too great fondness for books is little favourable to the happiness of a woman, especially one not in affluent circumstances. My situation has been peculiar, and would be no rule for others.[39]

Barbauld's objections would seem anti-feminist if we see them as laying a deferential emphasis on becoming 'agreeable companions to a man of sense' and on the authority of 'a father, a brother or friend'. Barbauld herself had, of course, benefited from such an education at the Warrington Academy, but she had been taught to aspire beyond what were usually thought of as female 'accomplishments'. Indeed Barbauld seems in part to be objecting to a specific idea of an education for 'ladies' as such. The last section of her response, for instance, shows itself to be acutely aware of the social implications of this word, and there is an edge to the reply that barbs her humility:

> But suppose I were tolerably qualified to instruct those of my own rank; – consider, that *these* must be of a class far superior to those I have lived amongst and conversed with. Young ladies of that rank ought to have their education superintended by a woman perfectly well-bred, from whose manner they may catch that ease and gracefulness which can only be learned from the best company; and she should be able to direct them, and judge of their progress in every genteel accomplishment. I could not judge of their music, their dancing; and if I pretended to correct their air, they might be tempted to smile at my own; for I know myself remarkably deficient in gracefulness of person, in my air and manner, and in the easy graces of conversation. Indeed whatever the kind partiality of my friends may think of me, there are few things I know well enough to teach them with any satisfaction, and many I never could learn myself. These deficiencies would soon be remarked when I was introduced to people of fashion; and were it possible that, notwithstanding, I should meet with encouragement, I could never prosecute with any pleasure an undertaking to which I know myself so unequal.[40]

Effectively Barbauld would have been working for a genteel patron and servicing the production of fashionable young ladies whose arts of conversation followed those promoted by More's essay rather than the more disputatious culture of Dissent in which she had unusually been educated at Warrington. This view was the one taken in an interesting if little-known lecture from 1854 on Barbauld by Clara Lucas Balfour (a temperance activist and educationalist):

> Surely the prejudices of society that so often then (may we not add now?) made female education consist in the attainment of mere shewy accomplishments, calculated to make a graceful *artiste* rather than a good and sensible woman, were at the root of her reluctance to enter upon the work of teaching her own sex. She could have taught principles; society demanded a few brilliant results. She could have improved the mind; society was anxious only as to manner.[41]

Balfour's lecture was part of a series for 'Instructors' written in praise of Barbauld's wider contribution to the cause of female education. Barbauld's own letters become increasingly clear as to the kind of culture of conversation being promoted by Montagu. She wrote to her brother in January 1784 to say: 'Mrs Montagu, not content with being the Queen of literature and elegant society, sets up for the Queen of fashion and splendour. She is building a very fine house, . . . and I am afraid will be as much the woman of the world as the philosopher'.[42] Although not necessarily typical of bluestocking gatherings – including, for example, Vesey's, who was lauded for her ability to create harmony from mixed company – Montagu's salon was arranged in an extremely hierarchical manner reflecting the rank of its participants. Others in Dissenting circles also criticized Montagu's regulated version of conversation. Samuel Rogers, a friend of Barbauld's since 1786, reports a discussion at the house of Helen Maria Williams, another woman with a background in religious Dissent, from April 1791, where he and William Seward both agreed that Montagu was 'a composition of art'.[43] When Lucy Aikin uses Pope's image of the 'feast of reason and the flow of soul' to contrast the atmosphere found at Joseph Johnson's with the more staged hierarchies of Montagu's parties, then, she perpetuates the estimation of a previous generation of male and female Dissenters.[44]

For her part, Barbauld herself was not contrasting Montagu as a 'woman of the world' with an ideal of female retirement. Rather she was as alert as Balfour to the ways in which a feminized and aristocratic ideal of politeness could limit the horizons of women's activities. Perhaps it is significant that the early comparison of Barbauld and Montagu in the *Westminster Magazine* saw a 'masculine force' beneath the sentiment of Barbauld's poetry, whereas Montagu is primarily associated with polish and elegance. Barbauld herself came increasingly to see a role for the female intellectual beyond the more quiet idea of companionship that may seem to be scouted in her rejection of Montagu's offer to run the ladies' academy. Certainly she seems to have been at ease in a much more vigorous conversational culture than the polite elegance of Montagu's semi-circles of chat. Once she went to live in Hampstead in 1786, Barbauld began to participate more fully in the more forceful sort of conversation to be enjoyed in the Johnson circle and others associated with religious Dissent in London. The combative abilities of a younger generation, including Helen Maria Williams, Mary Hays, and Mary Wollstonecraft, were encouraged in this milieu. Barbauld writes to her brother: 'Our evenings, particularly at Johnson's, were so truly social and lively, that we protracted them sometimes till . . . But I am not telling tales'.[45] Whereas candour had in the past had to make its compromise with Anglican manners for Barbauld, now there is a much less conciliatory attitude in her writing. The conversation of culture is not one that is predicated on harmony, but instead on bold exchanges. The closing pages of her *Address to the Opposers of the Repeal of the Corporation and Test Acts* (1790), for instance, come close to taking on the kind of apocalyptic tone that Anglicans such as Carter and Montagu tended to see as part of the rough pretentiousness of Dissent:

Whatever is loose must be shaken, whatever is corrupted must be lopt away; whatever is not built on the broad basis of public utility must be thrown to the ground. Obscure murmurs gather, and swell into a tempest; the spirit of Enquiry, like a severe and searching wind, penetrates every part of the great body politic; and whatever is unsound, whatever is infirm, shrinks at the visitation.[46]

Here is the register that led Walpole to describe Barbauld to Hannah More as 'Deborah' after the militant Old Testament prophet. If his friend Hannah More was willing to be more tolerant, urging Walpole to forgive Barbauld's politics for her poetic contributions to abolitionism, he tartly countered: 'her party supported the abolition, and regretted the disappointment as a blow to the good cause: I know this – do not let your piety lead you into the weakness of respecting the bad, only because they hoist the flag of religion, while they carry a stiletto in the flagstaff'.[47] Even Montagu was a little more tolerant than Walpole. Certainly she promised More in 1791 that she would read Barbauld's poem to Wilberforce, although in the previous year she had written to Carter – a subtly different audience, less evangelical than More, she was also much less tolerant of Dissent – to declare herself 'more sorry than surprised, that Mrs Barbauld has exerted her talents in favour of ye Dissenters; & as that Set of people are partial to Republican Government, they approve every attempt, means & measures, to subvert it [Church and State]'.[48] The solidarity that the bluestockings offered Barbauld in the 1770s had been conditional on conformity of a very restricted kind.

If over the rest of her career, which lasted another thirty-five years, Barbauld was forced more and more into retirement by the practical position of Dissenters in a hostile print culture (and, more specifically, the breaking up through death and imprisonment of the circle that surrounded Johnson), there is little sign that she either passively accepted this situation or transmuted it into a romantic idea of a 'higher' freedom of the imagination. She remained in contact with More and in 1799 offered her an idea of a public sphere open to many different kinds of intervention:

I express my ardent wishes that your benevolent intentions towards the rising generation, and your unwearied exertions in every path where good is to be done to your fellow creatures may meet with ample success. The field is large and labourers of every complexion, and who handle their tools very differently, are all called upon to co-operate in the great work. May all who have the good of mankind in view, preserve for each other the esteem and affectionate wishes which virtue owns to virtue, through all those smaller differences which must ever take place between thinking beings seeing through different mediums and subjected to the weakness and imperfection of all human reasoning.[49]

More's first biographer offered a note of laconic disapproval in his foot-note to this letter: 'The differences, however, were by no means small, between Mrs More's and Mrs Barbauld's religious opinions'. One may hear in Barbauld's conciliatory words an awareness that Anglican culture had hardened in its intolerance of Dissent in the context of the 1790s and the reaction against what was perceived as the covert republicanism of her non-conformity, but *The Female Speaker* anthology that Barbauld brought out in 1811 contained an extract from Isaac Watts that illustrates her continuing commitment to an idea of the Dissenting public sphere rather different from the idea of conversation outlined in Hannah More's *Bas Bleu*:

Our souls may be serene in solitude, but not sparkling, though perhaps we are employed in reading the works of the brightest writers. Often has it happened, in free discourse, that new truths are strangely struck out, and the seeds of truth sparkle and blaze through the company, which in calm and silent reading would never have been excited.[50]

Here is the model of conversational exchange that was transmitted through the culture of Dissent to the radicalism of the 1790s, producing Godwin's commitment to 'the collision of mind with mind' in *Political Justice* and the *Enquirer* essays, as well as disputatious women such as Mary Hays and Mary Wollstonecraft. Charlotte Smith (another woman who had associations with Joseph Johnson) wrote to Hays in 1800 to confirm her view of the stultifying effects of the kind of conversation being practised in the Montagu circle:

What you describe, however, in what are called literary meetings, I have more than once felt, & have wonder'd how it happens that when several persons of reputed talents are collected, the conversation is often so little pleasant. I was heretofore to admitted then being a mere novice & much in favor, to the celebrated conversations at Mrs Montagues, & I found that the greatest difficulty I had was to resist a violent inclination to yawn tho I suppose every body talk'd their very best. Since, I have been at other assemblies of literati when I own I have been equally disappointed tho not quite in the same way.[51]

Although More's *Bas Bleu* poem also speaks of conversation's ability to 'strike new light by strong collision' (l. 267), its dominant emphasis is on accommodation rather than friction:

> Hail! Conversation, soothing power,
> Sweet goddess of the social hour!
>
> (ll. 212–13)

Indeed only a prior context of conformity seems a safe context for collision:

> But sparks electric only strike
> On souls electrical alike;
> The flash of Intellect expires,
> Unless it meet congenial fires.
> The language to th'Elect alone
> Is, like the Mason's mystery, known;
> In vain th'unerring sign is made
> To him who is not of the Trade.
> What lively pleasure to divine,
> The thought implied, the hinted line,
> To feel Allusion's artful force,
> And trace the Image to its source!
>
> (ll. 286–99)[52]

Harmony seems to have been guaranteed by the fact that the participants are an 'Elect' pre-selected by a qualifying examination of taste. Barbauld had been praised in More's poem 'Sensibility' (1782) as one of the stars of the bluestocking firmament, but she is a conspicuous absence from the 1786 poem on conversation.[53] Perhaps by this stage Barbauld had already travelled too far from the union of 'literature and fashion' at Mrs Montagu's towards the Dissenting idea of conversation modelled after Milton's 'much arguing, much writing, many opinions'.

I would not want to exaggerate this point. More, for instance, remained relatively open to the 'commerce' of conversation with Dissent compared with either Carter or Montagu, a fact perhaps reflected in Barbauld's 1799 letter to her. Yet whatever the bluestockings, considered as a group, offered by way of female solidarity seems from early on to have been tainted for Barbauld by the idea that its definition of polite femininity brought with it a large measure of conformity to the doxa of Church and State. When Maria Edgeworth suggested they join together to edit *The Lady's Paper* in July 1804, Barbauld replied:

There is no bond of union among literary women, any more than among literary men; different sentiments and different connections separate them much more than the joint interest of their sex would unite them. Mrs Hannah More would not write along with you or me, and we should probably hesitate at joining Miss Hays, or if she were living, Mrs Godwin.

If she remained more reticent than either Hays or Wollstonecraft, she did like them benefit from the intellectual ferment of the Johnson circle and its Dissenting model of conversation that saw sparks of friction as the means to religious and political truth. Barbauld's career contains something of the ambivalence of recent feminist literary criticism on the subjects of politeness and sentiment. Her work sometimes seizes on politeness and sentiment as a validation of feminine participation in the public sphere, but also sees them as a means of restricting the power of women to change the world-as-it-is and imagine the unknown. As she told Edgeworth: 'There is a great difference between a paper written *by* a Lady, and *as* a lady. To write professedly as a female junto seems in some measure to suggest a certain cast of sentiment, and you would write in trammels'.[54] Marilyn Butler has often written of the dynamism of this Dissenting culture extinguished in the counterrevolution of the 1790s.[55] For Barbauld, it seems, as for other, later women writers, such as Helen Maria Williams, Mary Hays, and Mary Wollstonecraft – not to mention Edgeworth, to our knowledge of whom Marilyn Butler has contributed so much – this culture of Dissent appeared to offer more opportunity than the idea of a discourse of sentiment that might restrict the feast of reason and flow of soul for women even as it seemed to provide a means of feminine expression.

NOTES

1. William Blake, *Milton*, plate 41, lines 30–6, in David V. Erdman (ed.), *The Complete Poetry and Prose of William Blake*, revised edition (New York and London: Doubleday, 1982), p. 143.
2. See Jürgen Habermas, *The Structural Transformation of the Public Sphere: An Inquiry into a Category of Bourgeois Society*, trans. Thomas Burger (Cambridge, Mass: MIT Press, 1989).
3. For Milton's phrase, see *Areopagitica* in Ernest Sirluck (ed.), *Complete Prose Works of John Milton*, vol. ii (London: Oxford University Press, 1959), p. 554. Blake's phrase occurs in what we now know as the hymn 'Jerusalem' embedded in the prose 'Preface' to *Milton*. See *Complete Poetry and Prose*, p. 95.
4. The phrase comes from William Godwin's *Enquiry Concerning Political Justice* (1793). See Mark Philp (gen. ed.), *Political and Philosophical Writings of William Godwin*, 6 vols. (London: William Pickering, 1993), vol. iii, p. 15. Pamela Clemit has used it in the title of a short article discussing Godwin's creative relationships with women in the 1790s and beyond: 'Godwin, Women, and "The Collision of Mind with Mind"', *The Wordsworth Circle* 35 (2004), 72–6. Her primary example is Elizabeth Inchbald, not herself a Dissenter, but most of the other women she mentions were either Dissenters like Barbauld or closely allied to Dissent (Amelia Alderson, Mary Hays, Mary Wollstonecraft).

5. Nicole Pohl and Betty A. Schellenberg, 'Introduction: A Bluestocking Historiography', *Huntington Library Quarterly* 65 (2002), p. 2.

6. At a conversation in the home of another non-conformist woman, Helen Maria Williams, Samuel Rogers recalled a conversation in which William Seward complained that Montagu was 'an aristocrat and a friend to the slave trade. But I suspect her of art. She has often diverted me with instances of Dr Price's simplicity.' See Philip Clayden, *The Early Life of Samuel Rogers* (London, 1887), p. 173.

7. See Harriet Guest, 'Bluestocking Feminism', *Huntington Library Quarterly* 65 (2002), and Emma Major, 'The Politics of Sociability: Public Dimensions of the Bluestocking Millennium', *Huntington Library Quarterly* 65 (2002), pp. 175–92, as well as the former's *Small Change: Women, Learning, Patriotism, 1750–1810* (Chicago: Chicago University Press, 2000). I have also benefited from reading Elizabeth Eger's essay '"The Noblest Commerce of Mankind": Conversation and Community in the Bluestocking Circle', in Barbara Taylor and Sarah Knott (eds.), *Women and Enlightenment: A Comparative History* (forthcoming), although I see the bluestockings as operating with a more restricted idea of conversation than the one available to Barbauld within the culture of Dissent.

8. Lucy Aikin (ed.), *The Works of Anna Laetitia Barbauld: With a Memoir*, 2 vols. (London, 1825), vol. I, p. xxxi.

9. Pohl and Schellenberg, 'Introduction', p. 2.

10. See *Westminster Magazine* 4 (1776), pp. 283–5. On Joseph Johnson and Mary Scott, see Helen Braithwaite, *Romanticism, Publishing and Dissent: Joseph Johnson and the Cause of Liberty* (Basingstoke: Palgrave Macmillan, 2003), pp. 38–9.

11. [Montagu Pennington (ed.),] *Letters from Mrs. Elizabeth Carter to Mrs. Montagu between the Years 1755 and 1800, chiefly upon literary and moral subjects*, 3 vols. (London, 1817), vol. III, pp. 47–8.

12. Montagu uses this phrase writing to Carter, 17 [August 1765], 'Montagu correspondence and papers', Henry E. Huntington Library, MO 3151. I am grateful to the Library for permission to quote from these letters and for the fellowship that allowed me to read them in the summer of 2003. Emma Major and Emma Mason gave me invaluable help in locating the letters.

13. The later advertisement can be found in the copy of the poem printed in Hannah More, *Sacred Dramas and Other Poems* (London, 1827), p. 154. I have not found it in any edition before 1800. More may have needed to define the nature of the conversation after 1800 because of scandals surrounding aristocratic women, such as the Faro Ladies, in the 1790s and Wollstonecraft's critique of them, although More's evangelicalism, of course, had aristocratic immorality as one of its targets at the same time. On the Faro Ladies, see Gillian Russell's '"Faro's Daughters": Female Gamesters, Politics, and the Discourse of Finance', *Eighteenth-Century Studies* 33 (2000), 481–504.

14. Hannah More, 'Thoughts on Conversation', in *Essays on Various Subjects, principally designed for Young Ladies* (London, 1777), pp. 37–8.

15. Elizabeth Montagu, '22 February, 1774', in Anna Letitia Le Breton, *Memoir of Mrs. Barbauld* (London, 1874), p. 39.

16. Anna Laetitia Barbauld, 'Thoughts on the Devotional Taste, on Sects, and on Establishments', in *Devotional Pieces, Compiled from the Psalms and the Book of Job* (London, 1775), p. 3.
17. Ibid., p. 4.
18. Ibid., p. 29. For a discussion of this issue and the anxiety about enthusiasm in Barbauld, see my *Romanticism, Enthusiasm, and Regulation: Poetics and the Policing of Culture in the Romantic Period* (Oxford: Oxford University Press, 2003), chap. 4.
19. For a useful discussion of the self-presentation of Anglican women as participating in genuinely national debate by virtue of the Church's role, see Emma Major, 'The Politics of Sociability'. I also benefited greatly from reading Dr Major's thesis in relation to this issue; see Emma Major, 'Rethinking the Private: Religious Femininity and Patriotism, 1750–1789', unpublished DPhil. thesis, University of York (2000).
20. 25 August 1777, *Letters from Elizabeth Carter* (1817), vol. III, p. 35.
21. Barbauld, 'Thoughts', p. 35.
22. On Barbauld in the context of Dissent's attempt to distance itself from an uncouth past, see the discussion in my *Romanticism, Enthusiasm, and Regulation*, pp. 181–2. For her poem on Elizabeth Rowe, see the *Poems of Anna Laetitia Barbauld*, ed. William McCarthy and Elizabeth Kraft (Athens: University of Georgia Press, 1994), pp. 79–80. Watts wrote the preface for Rowe's much reprinted *Devout Exercises of the Heart* (1738).
23. [William Enfield], *Monthly Review* 53 (1775), 419.
24. For a fuller account of the diverse trajectories of this word, see Mee, *Romanticism, Enthusiasm, and Regulation, passim.*
25. See Deirdre Coleman, 'Firebrands, Letters, and Flowers: Mrs. Barbauld and the Priestleys', in Gillian Russell and Clara Tuits (eds.), *Romantic Sociability: Social Networks and Literary Culture in Britain, 1770–1840* (Cambridge: Cambridge University Press, 2002), pp. 82–103; Anne Janowitz, 'Amiable and Radical Sociability: Anna Barbauld's "Free Familiar Conversation"', ibid., pp. 62–81; and Mee, *Romanticism, Enthusiasm, and Regulation*, pp. 177–90.
26. Barbauld, *Works*, ed. Aikin, vol. II, p. 4.
27. Joseph Priestley, 'To Mrs. Barbauld, December 20, 1775', in J. T. Rutt (ed.), *The Theological and Miscellaneous Works of Joseph Priestley*, 25 vols. (1871), vol. I, p. 280.
28. Le Breton, *Memoir*, p. 38.
29. Ibid., pp. 38–9.
30. See Guest, 'Bluestocking Feminism', p. 63.
31. Barbauld, *Works*, ed. Aikin, vol. I, p. 282.
32. More, 'On Conversation', pp. 40–1.
33. Montagu, 'December 15, 1783', 'Montagu correspondence', MO3565.
34. More, 'On Conversation', p. 61.
35. Carter, 'May 8, 1780', *Letters from Elizabeth Carter*, vol. III, p. 129.
36. Montagu, 'November 12 1774', 'Montagu correspondence', MO3350.
37. Carter, 'December 1st, 1774', *Letters*, vol. II, p. 295.

38. Barbauld, *Works*, ed. Aikin, vol. i, p. xvi.

39. Ibid., vol. i, pp. xvii–xix. While this chapter was in press, my attention was drawn to William McCarthy's article: 'Why Anna Letitia Barbauld Refused to Head a Women's College: New Facts, New Story', *Nineteenth-Century Contexts* 23 (2001), 349–59, which describes a transcription of the passages Lucy Aikin claims were addressed to Montagu in the Althorp papers of the Countess Spencer. In this copy, those passages precede remarks addressed to Barbauld's husband defending her decision not to participate in the academy for girls. McCarthy's conjecture is that the passages Lucy Aikin claims were addressed to Montagu were also originally addressed to Barbauld's husband, but without access to the original letter(s) one should be wary of discounting Lucy Aikin's provenance for the remarks. I am indebted to Penelope Bradshaw for drawing my attention to this new material, and for the opportunity to read her own excellent article 'The Limits of Barbauld's Feminism: Re-reading "The Rights of Woman"', *European Romantic Review* 16 (2005), 23–37.

40. Barbauld, *Works*, ed. Aikin, vol. i, pp. xxii–xxiv.

41. Clara Lucas Balfour, *Working Women of the Last Half Century: The Lesson of Their Lives* (London, 1854), p. 96.

42. Le Breton, *Memoir*, p. 55.

43. See Philip Clayden, *The Early Life of Samuel Rogers* (London, 1887), p. 173. Clayden points out in a note that this view of Montagu was not the one generally held at the time, but his examples to the contrary are drawn from Lord Bath, Edmund Burke, and Sir Joshua Reynolds – not exactly figures hostile to hierarchy. Both Helen Maria Williams and Samuel Rogers were part of the world of London Dissent in the 1780s, and the attitudes in conversation transcribed by Clayden reflect as much. Rogers reports Montagu belittling Price, who was an important influence on both Rogers and Williams. Rogers had known Barbauld from the time she moved to Hampstead in 1786. See Clayden, *Life of Samuel Rogers*, p. 35.

44. Much quoted in the eighteenth century, Pope's line is from 'Satire I' of 'Satires of Horace Imitated'; see Alexander Pope, *Works* (London, 1736), vol. ii, p. 116, line 130.

45. Barbauld, '21 January, 1784', in *Works*, ed. Aikin, vol. ii, p. 24.

46. Barbauld, *An Address to the Opposers of the Repeal of the Corporation and Test Acts*, 4th edn (1790), p. 33.

47. Horace Walpole, '29 September 1791', *The Yale Edition of Horace Walpole's Correspondence*, ed. W. S. Lewis, 48 vols. (New Haven: Yale University Press, 1937–83), vol. xxxi, pp. 361–2.

48. See 'Montagu to More, 1791', in William Roberts, *Memoirs of the Life and Correspondence of Mrs Hannah More*, 2nd edn, 4 vols. (London, 1834), vol. ii, pp. 267–9.

49. See Roberts, *Memoirs of More*, vol. iii, pp. 81–2.

50. Barbauld, 'On Conversation from Watts', in *The Female Speaker* (London, 1811), pp. 79–80. The quotation is from Isaac Watts's *Improvement of the Mind* (London, 1741), a book that was in print well into the nineteenth century.

51. Charlotte Smith, '26 July, 1800', *The Collected Letters of Charlotte Smith*, ed. Judith Phillips Stanton (Bloomington and Indianapolis: Indiana University Press, 2003), pp. 349–50. On Smith's association with Johnson, see Braithwaite, *Romanticism*, pp. 174–5.

52. See Hannah More, *Florio: A Tale for Fine Gentlemen and Fine Ladies and The Bas Bleu; or, Conversation: Two Poems* (London, 1786), pp. 84, 80, and 85–6.

53. See More, 'Sensibility: A Poetical Epistle to the Hon. Mrs. Boscawen', in *Sacred Dramas: Chiefly Intended for Young Persons* (1782), p. 272.

54. Barbauld, '30 August, 1804', in Le Breton, *Memoir*, p. 87.

55. See for instance the comments in Marilyn Butler, *Romantics, Rebels and Reactionaries: English Literature and its Background 1760–1830* (Oxford: Oxford University Press, 1981), pp. 13–14, 43–6, and 94–5.

CHAPTER 2

Hazlitt's visionary London

Kevin Gilmartin

Although an aggrieved sense of neglect persists among some of his admirers, William Hazlitt has in fact enjoyed a striking critical revival, to the point where one London reviewer's estimate of his 'soaring' reputation 'as one of the great figures in our literature' seems no more than an enthusiastic overstatement of his emergence from literary minority.[1] In particular, the treatment of Hazlitt as a committed radical essayist has come a long way since Herschel Baker's 1962 critical biography, with its invidious comparison between the 'angry and uneven' volume of *Political Essays* and the subsequent lectures and essays on English literature that are said to secure his reputation.[2] And this was the view of a sympathetic biographer. Other responses in the same period, often guided by an understanding of the English Romantic imagination as a redemptive transcendence of betrayed revolutionary expectation, found little use for a body of political writing that developed under immediate journalistic pressures, and kept an abiding and prosaic faith with the French Revolution – to say nothing of Hazlitt's perverse insistence on associating the Lake school with pensioned apostasy rather than apocalypse by imagination. As in so many other areas of Romantic studies, Marilyn Butler set the terms for Hazlitt's resurgent reputation by decisively recontextualizing the politics of revolution and counterrevolution alike in her 1981 study *Romantics, Rebels, and Reactionaries*, in which Hazlitt figures as engaged radical journalist, persistent sectarian, and keeper of revolutionary faith, and as an emerging 'new professional type, the star journalist'.[3] For Hazlitt studies as such the yield of a historically more nuanced critical framework came in 1988 with Seamus Deane's chapter in *The French Revolution and Enlightenment in England*, an unabashed 'Jacobin Profile' that sought to raise the discussion of Hazlitt's politics up to that of his aesthetics and metaphysics. Yet in many respects the central point for which Deane contended, the consistency of Hazlitt's political opinions,[4] remains the least satisfactorily settled, and recent scholarship continues to elaborate a whole range of political Hazlitts. Thus alongside

Deane's Jacobin profiler of Jacobin disillusionment we have John Kinnaird's steady 'constitutional Whig', Tom Paulin's Irish-accented adherent of a 'Dissenting counter-culture', Simon Bainbridge's 'ambiguous' Bonapartist, and Philip Harling's pragmatic journalist working within the conventions of late-Georgian radicalism – this last a revision of E. P. Thompson's influential early treatment of Hazlitt as an elite radical whose voice was refracted and to some extent compromised by the 'polite culture' of the periodical essayist.[5] If there is now some agreement that Hazlitt can claim a place, after Burke, Paine, and Wollstonecraft perhaps, but along with Godwin, Coleridge, Hannah More, William Cobbett, Leigh Hunt, William Hone, and others in a revised canon of Romantic-period literary politicians, the thrust of his politics remains very much at issue.

In identifying a core political disposition, each of the critics I have cited also acknowledges countervailing tendencies that seem to move Hazlitt's prose in other directions, from mainstream Whig or radical positions to what were, by the early 1820s, the more anachronistic or contrarian fringes of Jacobinism, Bonapartism, and rational Dissent. Beyond his rising reputation, and a new regard for his political journalism, the most striking convergence in recent Hazlitt criticism may be the interest in a dynamic and improvisational prose style that accommodates competing perspectives within an ideological framework more firmly secured by what it refuses than by what it affirms. The result is a consistency in resistance, and the fierce animosity that Hazlitt himself identified with 'the pleasure of hating'.[6] Imperfectly managed contradiction becomes the unifying theme in critical discussions of a restless body of prose that extended from philosophical enquiry and literary, dramatic, and fine arts criticism to familiar essays, biography, confessional autobiography, political journalism, and travel writing. In perhaps the most careful version of the case for contradiction as an enabling feature of Hazlitt's prose, David Bromwich draws 'a weapon of criticism' from the philosophical critique of personal identity that was advanced in Hazlitt's first book, *An Essay on the Principles of Human Action* (1805). He then develops a portrait of a critic converging on the theory of imaginative disinterestedness, who possessed 'the faculty of holding two opposed ideas in his mind at the same time', and who distinguished himself from Coleridge by refusing to reconcile opposites in experience and aesthetic expression.[7] Conflict, contradiction, paradox, tension, ambivalence, motion, energy – this has become the shared vocabulary of Hazlitt criticism.[8]

Now I am not inclined to challenge this sense of a literary achievement animated by paradox and contradiction,[9] in part because the accommodation of competing perspectives has not come at the expense of productive

disagreement about matters of emphasis and priority. Yet if the willingness
to acknowledge contradiction encourages a healthy critical pluralism, it
entails some risks as well, particularly where it obscures a more synthetic
and even utopian strain in Hazlitt's political writing. While philosophically oriented critics like Bromwich and Uttara Natarajan find important
unifying concerns in metaphysics, Hazlitt's political writing has tended
to remain a more fragmentary field, or, worse, his political passions have
been felt to distort otherwise valuable literary and aesthetic judgements.[10]
Without wanting to privilege Hazlitt's specifically *political* articulation of a
consistency-in-contradiction, I do think it is worth bringing into focus
a visionary and apocalyptic strain of political affirmation in his prose,
which survived and was in many ways even enabled by his notoriously
venomous expressions of post-Revolutionary disenchantment, and which
proved compatible with his contradictory energies. The culture of rational Dissent was a key vector for Hazlitt's political vision, and the tone of
eulogy that surrounds his reverential tributes to the life and memory of
his father (a Unitarian minister) can be understood to have fused regret
for a passing legacy with a vivid sense of achieved community.[11] But in
this essay I want to focus instead on Hazlitt's treatment of a potentially
shared experience of life in London, which was powerfully inflected by his
own public commitments as a radical journalist, and which offered perhaps
the most compelling counterweight he could find to the feared post-war
consummation of 'Legitimacy' that was his political nightmare.[12]

   In a compelling discussion that ought to reframe Hazlitt's politics for
Romantic literary studies, the historian Philip Harling has shown that,
far from being a 'freakish iconoclast of Romantic letters', Hazlitt produced a body of oppositional writing that fell squarely 'within the conventions of late-Georgian radical journalism', particularly in its attack on the
hypocrisy and repressiveness of established powers, and its engagement with
British constitutional history. Radical journalism was, to be sure, an uneven
field, and Hazlitt negotiated it selectively. In tracing correspondences with
more plebeian journalists like T. J. Wooler and John Wade, Harling allows
that the oppositional and radical periodicals in which Hazlitt published –
Jeffrey's *Edinburgh Review*, Scott's *Champion*, the Hunt brothers' *Examiner* – were 'chiefly aimed at well-educated and reform-minded members
of the urban "middling sort"'.[13] Furthermore, in substantially restricting his
own public engagement to writing (and arguably lecturing as well), he stood
at a further remove from the day-to-day energies of political organization
than Wooler or Cobbett, or even Leigh Hunt and William Hone, who as
editors and publishers set their weekly periodicals in the service of specific

Parliamentary candidates, political organizations, and petition campaigns, with the result that they were far more vulnerable to government prosecution. At the same time, E. P. Thompson's pointed assessment of Hazlitt as a writer whose style, 'with its sustained and controlled rhythms, and its antithetical movements, belongs to the polite culture of the essayist', and who even in his 'most engaged Radical journalism' aimed his polemic 'not towards the popular, but towards the polite culture of his time',[14] may cut in more than one direction. For this was a period in which the elusive possibility of an integrated radical front, linking elite leadership (Sir Francis Burdett, John Cartwright) and middle-class protest strategies (Parliamentary petition campaigns, pamphlet warfare) with emerging working-class agency and issues (mass meetings, labour organization, universal manhood suffrage), was palpably expressed in the formal properties of radical discourse. The vernacular weekly periodical format that developed in the era of the Napoleonic Wars served to join the polemically motivated and synthetic form of the political pamphlet with the more fragmentary news content of the daily press, and with the polite rhythms of the monthly magazine and periodical review. William Cobbett himself used the term 'essay' to identify the format's distinctive opening editorials, and this central strand of expression only grew in prominence through a post-war phase of economic dislocation and popular unrest, as radical discourse converged on an increasingly vigorous and synthetic analysis of material dispossession and systematic political corruption.[15] When in late 1816 Cobbett circumvented taxes meant to limit the diffusion of political argument and information by supplementing his stamped *Register*, priced at a shilling halfpenny, with a cheaper unstamped edition, the new 'Two-Penny Trash' was restricted from printing news content, and therefore appeared first as a single unstamped sheet and then as an octavo pamphlet devoted substantially to the lead editorial essay. As the unstamped weekly format was picked up and modified in T. J. Wooler's *Black Dwarf* (1817–24), Hone's *Reformist Register* (1817), Sherwin's *Weekly Political Register* (1817–19), John Wade's *Gorgon* (1818–19), John Hunt's *Yellow Dwarf* (1818), and Richard Carlile's *Republican* (1819–26), it incorporated a range of political, satirical, and miscellaneous content, with the lead essay remaining central. Coleridge explicitly worked from and against Cobbett's weekly model in his first periodical version of *The Friend*,[16] and Southey was arguably as engaged with Cobbett as he was with the *Edinburgh Review* in his most expansive and programmatic post-war essays for the *Quarterly Review*. In this sense, then, the political development of the periodical essay was itself an opportunity for engagement, and in a career as a political writer that opened with the *Weekly Register* letters on

Malthus, and culminated in the pages of the *Yellow Dwarf*, Hazlitt was able
to play the polite manner and structured rhythms identified by Thompson
off against the more topical, fragmentary, contested, and even apocalyptic
rhythms of the popular radical press.

   To align Hazlitt with contemporary radical discourse is inevitably to
trace the movement through his prose of specific arguments and idioms
bearing upon the experience of post-war economic distress and political
dispossession under the unreformed English constitution. There is, for
example, his endorsement of universal suffrage rather than representation
of property (xix: 308), his defence of 'combinations among labourers for the
rise of wages' (xix: 309), the sharp distinction he drew between 'productive
and unproductive labour' (vii: 106), and his complaint that, even beyond
its immediate devastation, warfare compounded unproductive labour (xix:
294–6), fostering a swarm of profiteers, pensioners, and placemen who were
maintained by the labour of others, a point on which he cited both Cobbett
and Paine (vii: 276). In style and strategy, there was his insistent assault
on the familiar radical demons of the era (Malthus, Burke, Ricardo, Pitt,
Canning, Castlereagh, Ellenborough, Stoddard, Gifford), and his concern
to replace subtle Ricardian analysis or Malthusian calculation with a more
elementary, unforgiving, and populist arithmetic of exploitation:

The case on the part of the people is . . . self-evident. There is but a limited earth
and a limited fertility to supply the demands both of Government and people; and
what the one gains in the division of the spoil, beyond its average proportion, the
other must needs go without . . . If the Government take a fourth of the produce
of the poor man's labour, they will be rich, and he will be in want. If they can
contrive to take one half of it by legal means, or by a stretch of arbitrary power,
they will be just twice as rich, twice as insolent and tyrannical, and he will be twice
as poor, twice as miserable and oppressed, in a mathematical ratio to the end of the
chapter, that is, till the one can extort and the other endure no more. (vii: 263–4)

To conduct this kind of argument, in an essay ('What Is the People?')
that was published serially in both the *Champion* and the *Yellow Dwarf*
in conjunction with weekly news accounts of popular distress and corrupt
government expenditure, was to follow Cobbett, John Wade, and others in a
materially grounded and vernacular discourse, demystifying in its bluntness
rather than dazzling in its mastery of paradox and contradiction. Given
Hazlitt's wariness about radical speculation, and his concern that reformers
were temperamentally prone to being distracted from the 'solid and certain'
ground of 'that *which is*' by the allure of 'that *which may be* or *ought to be*'
(vii: 13), it is worth observing how closely his own polemical materialism
could follow the contours of popular radical argument. At the same time,

'the end of the chapter' in a ratio of exploitation was not for Hazlitt, as it was for so many post-war radical journalists and editors, an occasion for apocalyptic expectations about the catastrophic demise of a system of corruption and exploitation.[17] Just as the visual spectacle and personal vanity of monarchy seemed to him to play into an inherent weakness in the human imagination,[18] so a system of economic exploitation and dispossession showed an alarming capacity to sustain and regenerate its own untenable premises.

It is striking that where Hazlitt did allow his populist radicalism to assume visionary and even apocalyptic dimensions as an urban social body, he tended to depart from the economic and agricultural terms of 'a limited earth and a limited fertility', and from the strictly binary, even Manichaean terms that typically framed the popular radical conception of a politicized labouring body (production/consumption, wealth/poverty, fertility/barrenness, war/peace). Romantic studies has long observed Hazlitt's endorsement of life in London in large part because it figures so prominently in his critical response to Wordsworth, notably in an 1814 *Examiner* review of *The Excursion*. Conceding the achievement of an impressive poetic landscape, Hazlitt goes on to interrogate more sceptically Wordsworth's idealization of rural life, and his own shift to unreserved assault hinges on the caustic observation, 'All country people hate each other' (xix: 9, 20–1). David Simpson has trenchantly cast this response as 'the result of an "urban" political economy' that is 'precisely opposite' to the 'ideal of agrarian civic virtue' advanced and modified by Wordsworth over the course of his career.[19] While this ideological affiliation is crucial to understanding Hazlitt's politics of resistance, the opposition with Wordsworth and with agrarian virtue is not always precise, so that in pursuing the radical dimensions of Hazlitt's civic sensibility some preliminary qualifications are in order. As with Dissenting character and community, the urban political body that takes shape in his prose, often by way of response to Wordsworth, is too rhetorically flexible to be mistaken for the end-point in a programme of radical reform. Writing as he did in the long shadow of Edmund Burke's decisive post-Revolutionary reworking of Whig civic humanist traditions in the *Reflections on the Revolution in France*,[20] Hazlitt was (no less than Wordsworth) compelled to negotiate the period's revisions and cross-fertilizations of agrarian classical republican and commercial humanist political idioms that were once more straightforwardly opposed. His engagement with a contemporary radical attack on court and ministerial corruption was invariably conditioned by the political language of eighteenth-century Country party opposition, as well as by a characteristic Dissenting austerity. This was evident for example in *A Reply to the Essay on Population*, where Malthus's treatment of 'vice and misery as the necessary consequences of an abstract principle' was refuted by a very different account of 'the real and determining causes of the decay of manners': 'If I must give a short answer, I should say, – Great towns, great schools, dress, and novels' (1: 280).

While an agrarian radical disposition certainly diminished over the course of his career, it survived above all in this willingness to entertain the morally destructive influence of metropolitan refinement. In the essay 'On the Literary Character', the analysis of 'the weaknesses and vices that arise from a constant intercourse with books' is reminiscent of nothing more than Wordsworth's own diagnosis of urban modernity, without the latter's sense of a redemptive literary imagination:

[Literature] creates a fictitious restlessness and craving after variety, by creating a fictitious world around us, and by hurrying us, not only through all the mimic scenes of life, but by plunging us into the endless labyrinths of imagination. Thus the common indifference produced by the distraction of successive amusements, is superseded by a general indifference to surrounding objects, to real persons and things, occasioned by the disparity between the world of our imagination and that without us. (IV: 133)

After its first appearance in the *Morning Chronicle*, the essay was collected in the *Round Table* volume along with the *Excursion* review, and this proximity of a critical treatment of urban and rural life, taken together with Hazlitt's high regard for the moral influence of books, theatres, shops, streets, and metropolitan life generally, reminds us that any distinction between country and city takes shape within a fluid and often contradictory field of polemical claims. The *Examiner* review of *The Excursion* vividly signals this by assembling an urban response to the poem's idealized 'northern Arcadians' not as a positive construct, nor as a close counter-Wordsworthian account of the salutary moral influence of city life upon the human imagination, but instead as a merely serial and morally ambiguous catalogue of deprivation: 'There are no shops, no taverns, no theatres, no opera, no concerts, no pictures, no public-buildings, no crowded streets, no noise of coaches, or of courts of law, – neither courtiers nor courtesans, no literary parties, no fashionable routs, no society, no books, no knowledge of books. Vanity and luxury are the civilizers of the world, and sweeteners of human life' (XIX: 22). Through sheer extension, this negative cartography may challenge the oppressive sublimity of a late-Wordsworthian blank verse dominated by 'the gigantic and eternal forms of Nature' (XIX: 9), but it does little in the way of advancing an alternative, nor does it come to terms with

Hazlitt's own pessimistic recognition of the corrosive moral influence of 'vanity and luxury'. This is the city considered as critical instrument and topical antidote rather than grand spectacle or modern phenomenology, and in this sense the argument appropriately yields a comic cure for rural deprivation, in Hazlitt's suggestion that 'a company of tragedians' might 'be established at the public expense, in every village or hundred, as a better mode of education than either Bell's or Lancaster's' (xix: 22).

A more constructive though still internally contested account of urban experience can be found in the 1823 essay 'On Londoners and Country People', first published in the *New Monthly Magazine* and reprinted in perhaps the most belletristic of Hazlitt's essay collections, *The Plain Speaker*. The abrupt opening to the essay takes issue with a now famous episode in Romantic-period reviewing: 'I do not agree with Mr *Blackwood* in his definition of the word *Cockney*. He means by it a person who has happened at any time to live in London, and who is not a Tory – I mean by it a person who has never lived out of London, and who has got all his ideas from it' (xii: 66).[21] Yet as a response to the *Blackwood's* attacks, what follows is far from being a straightforward celebration of the inhabitants of London. In a sensitive reading of the essay's interest in a phenomenology of urban life, framed by Hazlitt's preoccupation in the same period with the conditions for periodical journalism, Greg Dart has teased out the positive and negative implications here of a whole range of Cockney characteristics (vanity, vulgarity, abstraction, sympathy, prejudice, complacency, egalitarianism), to suggest that these features unfold as an overlapping rather than antithetical sequence of identifications and evaluations that remain 'porous to one another'.[22] In its final paragraphs, the essay vividly stages the difficulty of delivering this kind of mixed and fluid representation, as a problem of literary form and as a problem of critical engagement with the likes of Wordsworth and Lockhart. The already differentiated account of the 'true Cockney' is at this point further complicated as Hazlitt belatedly comes round to the title's implied contrast with country life, and the mannered antithesis of his transition – 'If familiarity in cities breeds contempt, ignorance in the country breeds aversion and dislike' – quickly falls away into a more one-sided indictment of rural 'sullenness, coldness, and misanthropy'. He then refers the reader to the 'picture of country-life', as sheer absence of urbanity, that he drew in the review of *The Excursion*, openly conceding that such an account was perhaps a 'caricature' (xii: 75–6), and more covertly intimating that it involved the autobiographical entanglements of the Keswick episode, in which he was reported to have been driven out of a country village for his sexual advances or even assault upon a local girl.[23]

From here, the restless effort to manage an overlapping sequence of antithetical representations and assessments continues. 'If these then are the faults and vices of the inhabitants of town or of the country, where should a man go to live, so as to escape from them?' (XII: 76). Dart identifies this as the 'more pressing question', to which the essayist eagerly advances after he has discharged country life with an allusion to an earlier review.[24] Yet Hazlitt's answer, such as it is, seems more calculated to expose the limits of a whole line of polite enquiry that advances inexorably towards compromise and enervating resolution: 'It appears to me that there is an amiable mixture of these two opposite characters in a person who chances to have past his youth in London, and who has retired into the country for the rest of his life. We may find in such a one a social polish, a pastoral simplicity. He rusticates agreeably, and vegetates with a degree of sentiment' (XII: 76). Should there be any doubt that this is the stuff of remote commonplace, Shakespeare's 'Mr Justice Shallow' is identified as one who 'answered in some sort to this description of a retired Cockney and indigenous country gentleman' (XII: 76).

If there is, as I suspect, a kind of internal resistance here to the antithetical procedures of the familiar essay, the measured satire has a constructive role in the development of the essay, since it serves to introduce by way of disjunction a long final paragraph that could never be reached through antithesis and compromise, nor through any of the other movements (comparison, discrimination, recollection, perambulation) that have structured the course of 'On Londoners and Country People' up to this point.[25] To set up this extraordinary coda, the essay reverts to the polemical bearings of its opening, with Mr Wordsworth rather than Mr Blackwood as the antagonist. The movement is complex, since the essay has so far proceeded through the flaws and virtues of both country and city life. The refutation of *The Excursion*'s prefatory account of 'men in cities as so many wild beasts or evil spirits, shut up in cells of ignorance, without natural affections' is accompanied by a no less aggressive endorsement of a stray remark from Burke's *Letter to a Noble Lord*:

Man in London becomes, as Mr Burke has it, a sort of 'public creature.' He lives in the eye of the world, and the world in his. If he witnesses less of the details of private life, he has better opportunities of observing its larger masses and varied movements. He sees the stream of human life pouring along the streets – its comforts and embellishments piled up in the shops – the houses are proofs of the industry, the public buildings of the art and magnificence of man; while the public amusements and places of resort are a centre and support for social feeling. A playhouse alone is a school of humanity, where all eyes are fixed on the same gay or solemn scene, where smiles or tears are spread from face to face, and where a thousand hearts beat in unison! Look at the company in a country-theatre (in comparison) and see the coldness, the sullenness, the want of sympathy, and the way in which they turn round to scan and scrutinise one another. In London there is a *public*; and each man is part of it. We are gregarious, and affect the kind. We have a sort of abstract existence; and a community of ideas and knowledge (rather than local proximity) is the bond of society and good-fellowship. This is one great cause of the tone of political feeling in large and populous cities. There is here a visible body-politic, a type and image of that huge Leviathan the State. We comprehend that vast denomination, *the People*, of which we see a tenth part daily moving before us; and by having our imaginations emancipated from petty interests and personal dependence, we learn to venerate ourselves as men, and to respect the rights of human nature. Therefore it is that the citizens and freemen of London and Westminster are patriots by prescription, philosophers and politicians by the right of their birth-place. In the country, men are no better than a herd of cattle or scattered deer. They have no idea but of individuals, none of rights or principles – and a king, as the greatest individual, is the highest idea they can form. He is a 'species alone,' and as superior to any single peasant as the latter is to the peasant's dog, or to a crow flying over his head. In London the king is but as one to a million (numerically speaking), is seldom seen, and then distinguished only from others by the superior graces of his person. A country squire or a lord of the manor is a greater man in his village or hundred! (xii: 76–7)

Dart has shrewdly noticed the way in which this affirmative gathering together and escalation of a whole range of urban characteristics works to incorporate the very flaws and limitations that were witheringly analysed through the first phase of the essay, with Cockney levelling ('he fancies he is as good as any body else'), Cockney vanity ('London is the first city on the habitable globe; and therefore he must be superior to every one who lives out of it'), and sheer Cockney delusion ('he sees hundreds and thousands of gay, well-dressed people pass – an endless phantasmagoria – and enjoys their liberty and gaudy fluttering pride') suddenly recuperated and trans-formed into democratic citizenship through a vivid apprehension of the regenerative potential of urban modernity. Again, however, the movement of the essay through to this coda involves disjunction rather than accu-mulation or antithesis: the preening Cockney of popular caricature must first be expressed and explored, before its utopian counterpart can be fully conjured.

One of the pivotal revaluations at work in the surprising emergence of an enfranchised 'public creature' involves a capacity for abstraction, a cru-cial term in Hazlitt's writing about mind and imagination. For the same cognitive process that first condemns the impoverished Cockney to a pri-vate delusion – 'he is a citizen of London; and this abstraction leads his imagination [on] the finest dance in the world' (XII: 68) – is then in this final paragraph said to sustain the conditions for an ideal urban community: 'In London . . . we are gregarious, and affect the kind. We have a sort of abstract existence; and a community of ideas and knowledge (rather than local proximity) is the bond of society and good-fellowship.' Hazlitt was not, as some critics have suggested, a uniform enemy of abstraction, and the movement here is consistent with a distinction that David Bromwich (following Dewey) has made between a 'vicious' abstraction that neglects the primary experiential unity role of detached fragments, and a more 'liberating' abstraction that freely brings objects into new relations with one another.[26] Yet the most striking feature of the essay's final movement towards a vision of urban community may not have to do with how the Cockney has 'got all his ideas' (XII: 66), to borrow Hazlitt's deliberate vernacular. For we are also offered the remarkable Hobbesian figure of embodiment, and the distinctive 'political feeling' said to be conditioned by the daily presence of 'a visible body politic, a type and image of that huge Leviathan the State'. The psychological egoism of Hobbes was a crucial point of contact in Hazlitt's early philosophical arguments on behalf of the imagination as a faculty that potentially led beyond self to others.[27] In this sense, the refiguring of the Leviathan in the essay 'On Londoners and Country People' pursues a lifelong argument, by investing the capacity for sympathy and fellow feeling in a distinctively Hobbesian figure, and by subverting the sublime terrors of royal sovereignty in favour of a collective public body that could by itself form and sustain civic identity and obligation: 'the citizens and freemen of London and Westminster are patriots by prescription, philosophers and politicians by the right of their birth-place.' Given his eagerness throughout his late prose to contest Legitimacy by insisting upon the revolutionary heritage of the British crown, Hazlitt's interest in this canonical figure for absolute power was no doubt informed by a sense of Hobbes's *Leviathan, or the Matter, Form, and Power of a Commonwealth, Ecclesiastical and Civil* (1651) as a text conditioned by England's own century of revolution. The Hobbesian necessity for absolute monarchy yields to the possibility, though not the inevitability, of popular right. And in this sense, though Hazlitt was capable of remarking coolly on 'the scaly finger of Mr Hobbes' Leviathan' (XIX: 311), it is worth observing that the first of his 1812 lectures on English philosophy closed with a brief but suggestive treatment of Hobbes's politics, in which the supposed 'despotic tendency' of the work was mitigated (and an alignment with Rousseau intimated) on the grounds that any 'absolute submission' to the laws was offset by the presumptive consent of the governed (II: 145).

The figure of the urban Leviathan, and it is emphatically 'a type and image', becomes the climactic phase in an ongoing problem of embodiment and representation that absorbs the final movements of the essay, from the passing of the rusticated Londoner into vegetable retirement, through Wordsworth's prefatory representation of men in cities as 'so many wild beasts or evil spirits' and the calculated counter-statement of London's 'visible body politic', to the final diminishment of the king's sovereign body 'as one to a million' in the endless flow of urban humanity. In this sense, the essay 'Of Londoners and Country People' completes the case against *The Excursion*, both in its positive rendering of an earlier catalogue of rural deprivation (streets, shops, theatres, public buildings, works of art), and in its advancement of the Leviathan as a collective and spectacularly magnified embodiment of 'the stream of human life pouring along the streets'. Hazlitt was prepared to concede that 'there is little mention of mountainous scenery in Mr. Wordsworth's poetry' (he did not know *The Prelude*), but insisted that 'by internal evidence one might be almost sure it was written in a mountainous country, from its bareness, its simplicity, its loftiness and its depth' (xi: 90).[28] And the virtues he was prepared to grant the verse were not extended to 'the inhabitants of the mountainous districts described by Mr Wordsworth': 'The immensity of their mountains makes the human form appear little and insignificant. Men are seen crawling between heaven and earth, like insects to their graves. Nor do they regard one another more than flies on a wall' (xix: 23–4). If the popular Leviathan registers Hazlitt's sense of the very different conception of human nature fostered among the works of human hands, it turns out that such a conception was not confined to urban life. The record of his own experience of mountainous scenery in *Notes of a Journey through France and Italy* (1826) yielded a distinction between those who felt their own vanity 'chilled, mortified, shrunk up' by the vastness of the Alps, and those who were by contrast 'raised in their own thoughts and in the scale of being by the immensity of other things' – and here Hazlitt's own self-aggrandizing response leads inevitably to Napoleon, who alone 'seemed a match for the elements' (x: 191) in any confrontation with natural sublimity.[29] On the obligatory visit to Mont Blanc there was once again 'an end . . . of vanity and littleness', and perhaps intimations of Shelley's poem 'Mont Blanc', in Hazlitt's response to the mountain as at once 'a huge dumb heap of matter' and a meaningful 'image of immensity and eternity': 'You stand, as it were, in the presence of the Spirit of the Universe, before the majesty of Nature, with her chief elements about you; cloud and air, and rock, and stream, and mountain are brought into immediate contact with primeval Chaos and the great First Cause' (x: 291–2). If Hazlitt seems more willing than Shelley to accommodate theism, he was normally guarded about his faith,[30] and the distinctive feature of his response to Mont Blanc may finally be the extent to which it pivots on a human response: 'You stand . . .' The same point informed his most direct intervention in a literary controversy over the theological implications of Alpine sublimity, found not in the *Journey through France and Italy* but rather in the essay 'On the Jealousy and Spleen of Party', as an elliptical footnote to some acerbic remarks on the 'shivering-fit of morality' contracted by 'some of our fashionables' in crossing the Alps. Against the assertion by Thomas Moore in his *Rhymes on the Road* that Mont Blanc was 'As sure a sign of Deity / As e'er to mortal gaze was given',[31] Hazlitt let the divinity signified remain uncertain, but dramatically changed the identification of the 'sign': 'The poet himself, standing at the bottom of it, however diminutive in appearance, was a much greater proof of his own argument than a huge, shapeless lump of ice' (XII: 368).[32] Taken together, the magnificent observer of Mont Blanc and the popular Leviathan of London trace the lineaments of Hazlitt's version of a Blakean 'human form divine', issued in response to the diminished sense of human potential he detected in the politics and theology of *The Excursion* and in the entire movement of British society since the 1790s.

With Blake and sectarian radical tradition in mind, we ought to take seriously the apocalyptic implications of a claim to have discovered in 1823 in the streets of London 'a visible body-politic, a type and image of that huge Leviathan the State'. As far as Hazlitt was willing to indulge it in the prosaic confines of a *New Monthly Magazine* essay, this was a form of apocalyptic writing. And in relation to romanticist interpretive traditions, it answers precisely to the objection that Fredric Jameson has advanced against Northrop Frye's reworking, under Blakean auspices, of a Christian fourfold scheme of allegorical interpretation in ways that privilege the individual rather than the collective or social. In Jameson's analysis, Frye's identification of a final anagogic level of literary meaning beyond community, in the giant form of the human body, represents 'a significant strategic and ideological move, in which political imagery is transformed into a mere relay in some ultimately privatizing celebration of the category of individual experience': 'The image of the cosmic body cannot stand for anything further, for anything other than itself. Its figural and political momentum is broken, and the collective content of the image has been reprivatized in the henceforth purely individual terms of the isolated body.'[33] Without acceding to Frye's account of Blake, it is worth insisting on at least the potential for collective trajectories in Hazlitt's prose. While he often sets out from some vivid personal claim,[34] this does not mean that a subsequent movement towards collective social forms is broken by fantasies of individual fulfilment. As a socially embedded condition for popular right, Hazlitt's politically invested 'public creature' dictates a movement from 'petty interests and personal dependence' to 'the bond of society and good-fellowship'.

It is clear too that the achievement of apocalyptic vision here does not require a transcendence of engaged radical journalism. Even as 'the stream of human life' flows into the giant form and typological idiom of the popular Leviathan, Hazlitt continues to enumerate and specify – London as a 'tenth part' of the nation, the king as 'one to a million'. The involvement of visionary expectation with the more mundane representational language of the Parliamentary reform movement is evident too in an earlier conjuring of the popular Leviathan in the essay 'What Is the People?' First published serially in the *Champion* in October 1817 and in the *Yellow Dwarf* in March 1818, and then collected in the *Political Essays*, this is not only among the most brilliant and complex of Hazlitt's political essays,[35] but also the most compacted, bringing together in a slashing and vividly dialogic performance the major problems and antagonists with which he wrestled throughout his political career. Coleridge, Burke, Stoddart, Malthus, and Gifford all come in for abuse, but for my purposes here Southey is the crucial antagonist, as Hazlitt derives the political refrain of his essay from a 'rhapsody against the old maxim, *vox populi vox Dei*' in the Poet Laureate's 1816 *Quarterly Review* diatribe against Parliamentary reform.[36] The voice of the people, the voice of God: once again the apocalyptic form of the political Leviathan emerges for Hazlitt at a contested nexus of expression and embodiment. As if to anticipate the contest with Southey and others, the essay opens with an abrupt, even disorienting interrogation of the question posed by the title: '– And who are you that ask the question? One of the people. And yet you would be something! Then you would not have the People nothing.' The rhetorical gesture plays out the embeddedness of the *Yellow Dwarf* and *Champion* versions of the essay in an extended phase of acute periodical controversy over Parliamentary reform, and Hazlitt's response to what turns out to be a conservative interlocutor insists upon a viscerally embodied populace: 'For what is the People? Millions of men, like you, with hearts beating in their bosoms, with thoughts stirring in their minds, with blood circulating in their veins, with wants and appetites, and passions and anxious cares, and busy purposes and affections for others' (VII: 259). With this claim in place, the disjointed early movements of the essay conduct a restless search for some way to set 'the hand, heart, and head of

the whole community acting to one purpose', against the destructive interests of legitimate monarchy, court opinion, and ministerial corruption. The
popular Leviathan promises a point of resolution:

Vox populi vox Dei, is the rule of all good Government: for in that voice, truly
collected and freely expressed (not made the servile echo of a corrupt Court, or a
designing Minister), we have all the sincerity and all the wisdom of the community.
If we could suppose society to be transformed into one great animal (like Hobbes's
Leviathan), each member of which had an intimate connexion with the head or
Government, so that every individual in it could be made known and have its due
weight, the State would have the same consciousness of its own wants and feelings,
and the same interest in providing for them, as an individual has with respect to his
own welfare. Can any one doubt that such a state of society in which the greatest
knowledge of its interests was thus combined with the greatest sympathy with its
wants, would realize the idea of a perfect Commonwealth? But such a Government
would be the precise idea of a truly popular or *representative* Government. The
opposite extreme is the purely hereditary and despotic form of Government, where
the people are an inert, torpid mass, without the power, scarcely with the will, to
make its wants or wishes known: and where the feelings of those who are at the
head of the State centre in their own exclusive interests, pride, passions, prejudices;
and all their thoughts are employed in defeating the happiness and undermining
the liberties of a country. (VII: 267–8)

If this version of the figure is more closely informed by matters of Parliamentary representation, it is also more explicitly utopian, and more condition-
ally expressed. In 'On Londoners and Country People', Hazlitt managed
to develop the Leviathan simultaneously as figure ('type and image') and as
available urban experience ('in London there is'), in part through a sleight
of hand in the development of an essay that first scrupulously exposed the
distortions and exaggerations of Cockney fantasy but then left the essayist's own final act of imagination unexamined. By contrast, in disclosing
for the reader 'the precise idea of a truly popular or *representative* Government', and insisting on its identity with the more utopian 'idea of a
perfect Commonwealth', the essay 'What Is the People?' insistently betrays
its own representational devices, serially qualifying a figure that unfolds as
the similitude ('like') of an assumption ('suppose') that may not be within
reach ('If we could . . . '). Even the final antithesis, while sharply defined,
manages to convey within its verbal forms the disturbing difference between
radical possibility ('would be . . . a truly popular or *representative* Government') and oppressive fact ('is the purely hereditary and despotic form of
Government'). And throughout the essay, the radical desire that issues in
the figure of popular embodiment is blocked and obscured by the 'bloated

hideous form' of Legitimacy, a 'detestable fiction' perhaps, but a political reality that cannot be denied (VII: 259, 269).

In advancing the popular Leviathan as a qualified figure for representative government, Hazlitt is noticeably reticent about universal suffrage or any of the specific electoral mechanisms that were at issue in contemporary reform agitation. On economic matters having to do with 'war and taxes' and 'our high-flying sinecurists and pensioners', the essay does consistently mobilize the idioms of popular radicalism, even citing Cobbett's 'two penny Registers' on wartime finances. But a language of political representation is more generalized, returning through Paine and Rousseau to the broad foundations of the European Enlightenment: 'The will of the people necessarily tends to the general good as its end'; 'For a people to be free, it is sufficient that they will to be free' (VII: 267, 275).[37] This is not to say that 'What Is the People?' stumbles as a piece of committed post-war radical journalism, nor that Hazlitt's visionary impulses involve the kind of material disengagement once associated with a Romantic apocalypse by imagination. On the contrary, the pattern of embodiment that is viscerally posed in the essay's opening sentences, and then revisited in relation to political representation through the figure of the Leviathan, involves some of Hazlitt's most explosive claims. Against Burke's 'profoundly metaphysical or highly poetical' redactions of state power, and against Southey's claim that popular discontent was the work of a few reckless demagogues, Hazlitt treats the body of the people as a potent figure for material deprivation and resistance. 'The people are not subject to fanciful wants, speculative longings, or hypochondriacal complaints. Their disorders are real, their complaints substantial and well-founded. Their grumblings are in general seditions of the belly' (VII: 275). And perhaps the only matter upon which he was prepared to agree with Southey was that insurrection was a real and present threat. To be sure, his point in attending to 'the agonizing cry of human nature raised . . . against intolerable oppression' (VII: 278) was to recommend immediate reform as a way of averting violence, but this was itself consistent with mainstream post-war radical argument, and should not by itself be taken as evidence of a polite nervousness about political violence. In fact, Hazlitt's idiosyncratic insistence on keeping faith with the French Revolution meant that he was unusually willing to advocate preventative reform as part of the brief *for* revolution in all its recent historical forms: 'The American Revolution produced no horrors, because its enemies could not succeed in sowing the seeds of terror, hatred, mutual treachery, and universal dismay in the hearts of the people. The French Revolution, under the auspices of Mr Burke, and other friends of social order, was tolerably prolific of these horrors. But that should not be charged as the fault of the Revolution or of the people'. It was in this revolutionary framework that 'Timely Reforms' were recommended as 'the best preventatives of violent Revolutions' (VII: 279–80).

As a figure for 'truly popular or *representative* Government' in the absence of specific electoral arrangements, the popular Leviathan seems to throw us back upon the work of the writer, evident in this essay's complex network of figures, suppositions, and enquiries, and in its host of polemical engagements. This should not be surprising, since for Hazlitt as for other contemporary radical journalists the case for 'seditions of the belly' became ameliorative rather than catastrophic only through a conception of the press as a provisional alternative to Parliamentary representation, and as a way of mediating some of the vexed fissures entailed in Hazlitt's 'precise idea of a truly popular or *representative* Government' – between individual and community, mind and body, private interest and common sympathy. Here Coleridge was the crucial antagonist, and Hazlitt alludes to the attack on the very idea of a 'reading public' in *The Statesman's Manual* (1816) as a way of recasting his own title so as to foreground the role of the press in any scheme of representation: 'To put this question in a different light, we might ask, What is the public?' (VII: 273).[38] The spiritual and educational concerns of the two Lay Sermons remain antagonistically present as Hazlitt contends with this new question, rejecting the notion of the Bible as 'political palliative' and 'all the fuss and bustle and cant about Bell and Lancaster's plans, Bible and Missionary, Auxiliary and Cheap Tract Societies' (VII: 273). And while 'What Is the People?' contains no clear intimation of a counter-clerisy, along the lines suggested by the Dissenting ministry's habits of communication, mobility, and transmission in 'My First Acquaintance with Poets' (XVII: 107), Hazlitt does look to the press for a more secular and less rigidly established and hierarchical solution to the problems of leadership, education, and organization that were at stake in Coleridge's counterrevolutionary theory of the clerisy, fully developed in *On the Constitution of the Church and State* (1829) but already incipient in the Lay Sermons. In both periodical versions of the essay, the figure of the representative public body comes immediately before the first break in the essay, and is followed by yet another question that extends the pursuit of Coleridge: 'Where are we to find the intellect of the people?' The idealist rather than materialist strains of Hazlitt's searching enquiry here are sustained in his preliminary answer, that 'public opinion expresses not only the collective sense of the whole people, but of all ages and nations', and therefore includes within itself 'all the greatest poets, sages, heroes' as advocates of popular right rather than legitimate privilege. But a second and not wholly distinct response, which insists upon the popular derivation of genius, engages more directly with the concrete matter of political representation left open by the popular Leviathan. For the claim that 'all discoveries and all improvements in arts, in science, in legislation, in civilization' have been 'gained for themselves by the people' challenges established powers, with 'the Bench of Bishops', the courts of law, and even 'the House of Commons' all found wanting, and only 'the press' left with a credible claim that it 'has done every thing for the people' (vii: 269–70). Now Hazlitt was under no illusions about the adequacy of print protest to the cause of reform, nor about the reliability of the press as a liberal or radical institution. He distinguishes sharply in this essay between 'government-writers' and 'writers on the popular side of the question', and bitterly observes that state apologists finally answer a popular 'appeal to the pen' not in kind but rather at 'the point of the bayonet': 'They quote Burke, but rely on the Attorney-General. They hold Universal Suffrage to be the most dreadful of all things, and a Standing Army the best representatives of the people abroad and at home. They think Church-and-King mobs good things, for the same reason that they are alarmed at a meeting to petition for a Reform of Parliament' (vii: 270–1). Yet if the tentative alignment of the wisdom of the ages with radical reform and the immediate instrumentality of the press does not compromise Hazlitt's commitment to political warfare, it does sort out the mind–body problem embedded in the Leviathan figure so as to distinguish the whole body of the people from the 'enlightened and disinterested part' (vii: 270) that conducts its defence. This registers the sense of meritocratic privilege that shaped Hazlitt's democratic commitments throughout his career, and also suggests that his political conceptions partook of the elitism that John Barrell and John Whale have found more vividly registered in literature and the fine arts.[39]

There is nothing like the tone of eulogy that characterizes Hazlitt's writing on Dissent to mark this visionary popular Leviathan as something other than an end-point in a programme of political reform. Yet the democratic popular body is fully engaged in a politics of contradiction, shot through with Hazlitt's particular arguments against Southey, Coleridge, Burke, and others, and offset by a sober scepticism about the liberating potential of popular mobilization. The case for elite direction within a levelling republic of letters bears closely upon Hazlitt's willingness (by way of contradiction) to come to terms with debased and destructive versions of the urban crowd. The glancing reference in 'What Is the People?' to the Church-and-King mob as an instrument of state repression is itself a bitter Dissenting memory, and Hazlitt first entered upon public writing at the age of thirteen with a letter to the editor of the *Shrewsbury Chronicle* protesting against the July 1791 attack on Joseph Priestley's house and laboratory in Birmingham.[40] Later in life he continued to write and reflect critically upon what he took to be corrupt versions of popular assembly. In his comic-grotesque treatment of the 1821 coronation of George IV in the essay 'On the Spirit of Monarchy', the distended body of the king is fully met and mirrored by the deluded body of the urban populace: 'the crowd presses on, the metropolis heaves like a sea in restless motion, the air is thick with loyalty's quick pants in its monarch's arms' (XIX: 263–4). And as far as he was concerned the public fervour of 1823 in support of Queen Caroline was not redeemed by its radical inflection: 'The Queen's trial gave a deathblow to the hopes of all reflecting persons with respect to the springs and issues of public spirit and opinion. It kept the town in a ferment for several weeks: it agitated the country to the remotest corner. It spread like wildfire over the kingdom; the public mind was electrical. So it should be on other occasions; so it was only on this' (XX: 136). It is worth noting that while these *negative* accounts of the mob are grounded in specific circumstance, the *positive* urban Leviathan is developed as supposition or as apocalyptic 'type and image'. Again, while it is important to recognize such antithetical considerations, it would be wrong to assume that they uniformly distinguish a polite essayist from vernacular radicalism. On the contrary, in his 1821 *Political Dictionary*, the radical pressman John Wade sympathetically cited Hazlitt for a contemptuous definition of the mob.[41] In this sense, Hazlitt's contradictions are not his alone, and the cross-currents in his prose of politics and aesthetics, democracy and privilege, hope and despair offer insight into the complex organization of British political culture in the early nineteenth century as well as into the literary and rhetorical structure of his distinctive critical commentary on it.

NOTES

1. Michael Foot, *Daily Telegraph* review, cited on the dust jacket of Tom Paulin, *The Day-Star of Liberty: William Hazlitt's Radical Style* (London: Faber and Faber, 1998).
2. Herschel Baker, *William Hazlitt* (Cambridge, Mass.: Belknap Press of Harvard University Press, 1962), pp. 204, 320.
3. Marilyn Butler, *Romantics, Rebels, and Reactionaries: English Literature and Its Background, 1760–1830* (Oxford: Oxford University Press, 1981), pp. 144, 159–60, 169–71.

4. Seamus Deane, *The French Revolution and Enlightenment in England, 1789–1832* (Cambridge, Mass.: Harvard University Press, 1988), p. 130.

5. John Kinnaird, *William Hazlitt: Critic of Power* (New York: Columbia University Press, 1978), pp. 107–8; Paulin, *The Day-Star of Liberty*, pp. 2, 67–8, 131; Simon Bainbridge, *Napoleon and English Romanticism* (Cambridge: Cambridge University Press, 1995), p. 199; Philip Harling, 'William Hazlitt and Radical Journalism', *Romanticism* 3 (1997), 54; E. P. Thompson, *The Making of the English Working Class*, revised edition (Harmondsworth: Penguin, 1980), pp. 821–2.

6. The phrase was of course the title and (relentlessly) the subject of his late essay for *The Plain Speaker*, in P. P. Howe (ed.), *The Complete Works of William Hazlitt*, 21 vols. (London: J. M. Dent, 1930–4), vol. XII, pp. 127–36. Further references to Hazlitt are to this edition, and will be included in the text in the form (XII: 127–36).

7. David Bromwich, *Hazlitt: The Mind of a Critic* (New York and Oxford: Oxford University Press, 1983), pp. 22, 56, 233–4.

8. For some characteristic treatments of contradiction and mobility in Hazlitt's prose, see Kinnaird, *William Hazlitt: Critic of Power*, pp. 304, 322; James Chandler, *England in 1819: The Politics of Literary Culture and the Case of Romantic Historicism* (Chicago: University of Chicago Press, 1998), pp. 181–5; Annette Wheeler Cafarelli, *Prose in the Age of Poets: Romanticism and Biographical Narrative from Johnson to De Quincey* (Philadelphia: University of Pennsylvania Press, 1990), pp. 131–6; James Mulvihill, 'Hazlitt and "First Principles"', *Studies in Romanticism* 29 (1990), 245, 254–5; John Whale, 'Hazlitt on Burke: The Ambivalent Position of a Radical Essayist', *Studies in Romanticism* 35 (1986), 465–81; John Whale, *Imagination under Pressure, 1789–1832: Aesthetics, Politics, and Utility* (Cambridge: Cambridge University Press, 2000), p. 110.

9. The approach informs my own treatment of Hazlitt as both an effective practitioner and critic of radical opposition in the afterword to my book, *Print Politics: The Press and Radical Opposition in Early Nineteenth-Century England* (Cambridge: Cambridge University Press, 1996), pp. 227–33.

10. See for example Kinnaird, *William Hazlitt: Critic of Power*, p. 199, and Baker, *William Hazlitt*, p. 355. For Uttara Natarajan's compelling case for Hazlitt as the proponent of a hybrid 'British idealism' fused from contrarian elements within the British empirical tradition, see her *Hazlitt and the Reach of Sense: Criticism, Morals, and the Metaphysics of Power* (Oxford: Clarendon Press, 1998), pp. 1–4.

11. For the legacy of Dissent in Hazlitt's life and prose, see Baker, *William Hazlitt*, pp. 3–36; Kinnaird, *William Hazlitt: Critic of Power*, pp. 1–36; Butler, *Romantics, Rebels, and Reactionaries*, pp. 169–70; and Paulin's discussion throughout *The Day-Star of Liberty*.

12. For Hazlitt, 'Legitimacy' named the oppressive reinstitution of divine-right monarchy and eradication of political dissent in the aftermath of the defeat of Napoleon Bonaparte. For a discussion of the contested political development of the term in radical discourse, which considers Hazlitt's contributions, see

Stuart Semmel, 'British Radicals and "Legitimacy": Napoleon in the Mirror of History', *Past and Present* 167 (2000), 140–75.

13. Harling, 'William Hazlitt and Radical Journalism', p. 54. By contrast, in *Hazlitt: A Life* (Oxford: Oxford University Press, 1991), pp. 240–2, Stanley Jones provides evidence of some negative responses to Hazlitt from other radical journalists and leaders; these are, as Jones suggests, evidence of fractious tendencies within popular radical culture in the period, and Harling's larger point holds.

14. Thompson, *Making of the English Working Class*, pp. 821–2.

15. The discussion here summarizes elements of my argument about the radical weekly form in *Print Politics*, pp. 65–113. For Cobbett's reference to 'these Essays of mine', see *Cobbett's Weekly Political Register* 28 (1815), 71.

16. See the introductory discussion by Barbara E. Rooke in Samuel Taylor Coleridge, *The Friend*, ed. Barbara E. Rooke, 2 vols. (Princeton: Princeton University Press, 1969), vol. 1, pp. xlii–xliii.

17. Where Hazlitt did sometimes entertain a more apocalyptic rhetoric, it was in his treatment of the war against Napoleon Bonaparte; see for example VII: 71–5.

18. See Harling, 'William Hazlitt and Radical Journalism', pp. 55–6.

19. David Simpson, *Wordsworth's Historical Imagination* (New York: Methuen, 1987), pp. 56, 188. The review first appeared in the *Examiner* in three parts in August and October 1814, and was then reprinted in modified form in 1817 in the *Round Table*; see IV: 111–25, XIX: 9–25.

20. For Burke's revision of the Whig commercial tradition in the *Reflections*, see J. G. A. Pocock, 'The Political Economy of Burke's Analysis of the French Revolution', in *Virtue, Commerce, and History* (Cambridge: Cambridge University Press, 1985), pp. 193–212.

21. For a compelling treatment of the *Blackwood's* attacks in relation to collective literary formations, see Jeffrey N. Cox, *Poetry and Politics in the Cockney School: Keats, Shelley, Hunt, and Their Circle* (Cambridge: Cambridge University Press, 1988).

22. Gregory Dart, 'Romantic Cockneyism: Hazlitt and the Periodical Press', *Romanticism* 6 (2000), 153, 157–9.

23. For the episode and its aftermath in his literary relations with Coleridge and Wordsworth, see Baker, *William Hazlitt*, pp. 134–9, and Jones, *Hazlitt: A Life*, pp. 49, 158–60, 176–7, 298–300.

24. Dart, 'Romantic Cockneyism', 157.

25. For a suggestive treatment of Hazlitt's eccentric handling of closure in 'My First Acquaintance with Poets', see Jeffrey C. Robinson, 'Hazlitt's "My First Acquaintance with Poets": The Autobiography of a Cultural Critic', *Romanticism* 6 (2000), 182–3.

26. Bromwich, *Hazlitt: The Mind of a Critic*, pp. 27–8, 413–14.

27. See Bromwich, *Hazlitt: The Mind of a Critic*, pp. 46–8, and Baker, *William Hazlitt*, pp. 143–4.

28. See Bromwich, *Hazlitt: The Mind of a Critic*, p. 183, for the intriguing suggestion that, in identifying Wordsworth as a poet of the sublime proportions of the self, Hazlitt 'found a way to review *The Prelude* before its time'.

29. The *Journey* first appeared serially in the *Morning Chronicle* between September 1824 and November 1825. For a thoughtful treatment of this passage in relation to the ambiguities of Hazlitt's writing about egotism and personal power, see Bromwich, *Hazlitt: The Mind of a Critic*, p. 323.

30. In *The Day-Star of Liberty*, Paulin casually announces that Hazlitt was 'an unbeliever' (273). Baker is more cautious in *William Hazlitt* when he suggests that while Hazlitt 'writes much about the follies and vulgarities of organized religion he has almost nothing to say about what he himself believed' (p. 35).

31. Thomas Moore, *The Poetical Works of Thomas Moore* (Paris: A. and W. Galignani, 1829), p. 173.

32. The central text for critical discussions of a later Romantic controversy over the theological and political implications of Alpine sublimity has been Shelley's 'Mont Blanc', often considered as a response to Coleridge's 'Hymn Before Sun-Rise, in the Vale of Chamouni'. See for example Gavin de Beer, 'An "Atheist" in the Alps', *Keats-Shelley Memorial Bulletin* 9 (1958), 1–15; Harold Bloom, *Shelley's Mythmaking* (Ithaca, N.Y.: Cornell University Press, 1959), pp. 11–19; Butler, *Romantics, Rebels, and Reactionaries*, pp. 141–2; John Rieder, 'Shelley's "Mont Blanc": Landscape and the Ideology of the Sacred Text', *ELH* 48 (1981), 778–98; Jerrold E. Hogle, *Shelley's Process: Radical Transference and the Development of His Major Works* (New York: Oxford University Press, 1988), pp. 79–86; Robert Ryan, *The Romantic Reformation: Religious Politics in English Literature, 1789–1824* (Cambridge: Cambridge University Press, 1997), pp. 196–202; Stuart Peterfreund, 'Two Romantic Poets and Two Romantic Scientists "on" Mont Blanc', *Wordsworth Circle* 29 (1988), 152–61; and Robert M. Maniquis, 'Filling Up and Emptying Out the Sublime: Terror in British Radical Culture', *Huntington Library Quarterly* 63 (2000), 369–405.

33. Fredric Jameson, *The Political Unconscious: Narrative as a Socially Symbolic Act* (Ithaca, N.Y.: Cornell University Press, 1981), pp. 70–4. For the relevant discussion in Frye, see *Anatomy of Criticism: Four Essays* (Princeton: Princeton University Press, 1957), pp. 118–19.

34. See for example the vividly embodied resistance to corruption in the 'Preface' to *Political Essays*, VII: 10, which then advances to the individual figure of Napoleon Bonaparte.

35. Though Baker found evidence here of the 'nonstop diatribes' that compromise Hazlitt's political prose, evaluations of the essay have risen with Hazlitt's reputation as a political writer, and Whale follows Kinnaird in judging it Hazlitt's finest political essay; see Baker, *William Hazlitt*, p. 321; Whale, *Imagination under Pressure*, p. 111; and Kinnaird, *William Hazlitt: Critic of Power*, p. 123.

36. Robert Southey, 'Parliamentary Reform', *Quarterly Review* 16 (1816), 276.

37. Hazlitt's phrase may echo the title of Hume's 'Idea of a Perfect Commonwealth', an essay principally engaged with Harrington's *Commonwealth of Oceana*. See David Hume, 'Idea of a Perfect Commonwealth', in *Essays: Moral, Political, and Literary*, ed. Eugene F. Miller (Indianapolis: Liberty Classics, 1985), pp. 512–29.

38. See Samuel Taylor Coleridge, *Lay Sermons*, ed. R. J. White (Princeton: Princeton University Press, 1972), pp. 36–7, and Hazlitt's review, XVI: 99–114.

39. John Barrell, *The Political Theory of Painting from Reynolds to Hazlitt: 'The Body of the Public'* (New Haven and London: Yale University Press, 1986), pp. 335–7, and Whale, *Imagination under Pressure*, pp. 115–16, 123, 129.

40. Herschel Moreland Sikes, Willard Hallam Bonner, and Gerald Lahey (eds.), *The Letters of William Hazlitt* (New York: New York University Press, 1978), pp. 57–9. See also Paulin, *The Day-Star of Liberty*, pp. 9–10.

41. John Wade, *A Political Dictionary; or, Pocket Companion* (London: T. Dolby, 1821), p. 61.

CHAPTER 3

Shelley's republics

Michael Rossington

For Shelley, the stay at Marlow in 1817 was unforgettable, but perplexingly so. In April 1818, recently arrived in Milan, he wrote to Thomas Love Peacock about the tenacity of his memories of the place:

> I often revisit Marlow in thought. The curse of this life is that whatever is once known can never be unknown. You inhabit a spot which before you inhabit it is as indifferent to you as any other spot upon the earth, & when, persuaded by some necessity you think to leave it, you leave it not, – it clings to you & with memories of things which in your experience of them gave no such promise, revenges your desertion. Time flows on, places are changed, friends who were with us are no longer with us, but what has been, seems yet to be, but barren & stript of life. See, I have sent you a study for Night Mare Abbey.[1]

That final allusion to the satire Peacock had just begun shows Shelley's self-mocking awareness of the Gothic possibilities of this melancholy meditation. But the passage also demonstrates his characteristic alertness to the unpredictable ways in which the past appears to possess the present even as the desire to repossess that past absolutely is frustrated. The eerie hold upon the mind of a previously inhabited place evidences the impossibility of 'unknowing' but, with equal force, temporal continuity is exposed as an empty illusion: 'what has been, seems yet to be, but barren & stript of life'. Such revisiting takes an openly nostalgic turn a few months later: 'my thoughts for ever cling to Windsor Forest, and the copses of Marlow, like the clouds which hang upon the woods of the mountains, low trailing, and though they pass away, leave their best dew when they themselves have faded'.[2] Within this economy the environment of Marlow exercises a gravitational pull upon Shelley's thoughts and becomes the repository of 'their best dew', the place where their distillation is imagined to be most productive. Earlier, in a reply to a lost letter of Shelley's from Bagni di Lucca, Peacock had articulated this exchange between England and Tuscany in the same literary vein: 'I am glad that your thoughts revert to the Thames with so much kind remembrance even from the poetical Arno.'[3] Shelley's 'writing back' to the republican moment of Marlow from a continental European vantage-point is the subject of this essay.

Shelley wrote little about the English Revolution directly in 1817 but in retrospect Marlow may be seen to have clung to him as the territory out of which grew the groundwork of his uncompleted *Charles the First*, a drama that, in the words of Timothy Morton and Nigel Smith, 'demonstrates the attempt by radical writers in the later period to reassess and reappropriate the radicalism of their revolutionary past'.[4] The sobriquet, 'The Hermit of Marlow', on the title-pages of *A Proposal to Put Reform to the Vote* and *An Address to the People on the Death of the Princess Charlotte* published in February and November 1817 respectively, belies wittily the oppositional writing and alternative living all the more dangerous to the hostile reviewers of the *Quarterly* and *Blackwood's* because it was collective. Peacock's epitome of life at Marlow – 'Perhaps a due mixture of tea Greek & pedestrianism constitute the summum bonum' – playfully subverts Hobbes's view (which had recently been summarized by Coleridge) that the Ciceronian *summum bonum* is 'absolute tranquility and implicit obedience'.[5] Peacock's triumvirate amounts to another innocuous formulation that disguises the formidably productive conversation, exercise, excursions, reading (often aloud), correspondence, political and literary journalism, and the planning or writing of poetry and novels by, variously, Claire Clairmont, William Godwin, Thomas Jefferson Hogg, Leigh Hunt, Mary Shelley, Percy Shelley, and himself that went on. In this respect the character of Marlow and its function, while distinctively constituted, has elements in common with the Geneva circle in the summer of 1816, and both may be seen to anticipate the projected circle at Lerici, unrealized because of Shelley's death, that was to have combined the key figures in each of the earlier sites, Byron and Hunt. Within such a trajectory Marlow may seem to have a transitional status, as the interlude of an English place between two more creatively momentous continental venues where Byron's presence was crucial. But, following Marilyn Butler's insight that 'What happened at Marlow in 1817 was the counterpart to what happened at Alfoxden between Wordsworth and Coleridge in 1797',[6] the process of redressing the vagaries of a literary history that would promote Byron's significance to Shelley at the cost of occluding that of Godwin, Hunt, and Peacock – or indeed prioritize the centrality of Shelley over Hunt to the Marlow circle – is now well under way.[7] Marlow's minority amongst English Romantic coteries is emphatically no longer admissible. But it is another dimension of the parallel with Wordsworth and Coleridge at Alfoxden that I propose to address here. For

Marlow, like Alfoxden, marks a working-out of Shelley's differences from Godwin and Hunt, as well as the reinforcement of lasting bonds, that may explain the dividedness registered in the letter to Peacock from Milan. Shelley's flight to Europe in March 1818 may be seen as an attempt to accelerate his identity as, in Butler's phrase, one of the 'conscious internationalists' amongst the Romantic poets, along with Blake, Byron, and Southey.[8] And Europe helped him towards what may be denoted as a 'post-religious' or philosophical analysis of the origins of the English Civil War.

In his circumspect memoir of Shelley, Peacock recalled one of their pastimes at Marlow:

We took many walks in all directions from Marlow, and saw everything worth seeing within a radius of sixteen miles. This comprehended, among other notable places, Windsor Castle and Forest, Virginia Water, and the spots which were consecrated by the memories of Cromwell, Hampden and Milton, in the Chiltern district of Buckinghamshire.[9]

This deliberate retracing of the contours of seventeenth-century English history in the landscape of Buckinghamshire makes clear that part of what became memorable about Marlow to this circle was the collective acts of memorializing that occurred there. The habit of visiting places associated with the fictions of such writers as Godwin and Rousseau is familiar from Shelley's visits to Wales in 1812 and Switzerland in 1814 and 1816. And, as they are by Peacock, the meliorative effects of the silent contemplation of sites associated with seventeenth-century English heroes are noted by the tormented son of a Genevan Syndic, Victor Frankenstein, in his account of a tour with Clerval of Great Hampden and Chalgrove: 'We visited the tomb of the illustrious Hampden, and the field on which that patriot fell. For a moment my soul was elevated from its debasing and miserable fears to contemplate the divine ideas of liberty and self-sacrifice, of which these sights were the monuments and the remembrancers.'[10] Mary Shelley drafted this passage in October 1817[11] probably after her visit to the tomb with Godwin as part of his ongoing excavation of the lives of the Commonwealthmen from the *Essay on Sepulchres* (1809) to the *History of the Commonwealth of England* (1824–8) – whose purpose was 'to attend to the neglected, to remember the forgotten'[12] – via an oblique biography of Milton, *The Lives of Edward and John Phillips* (1815), and a novel whose narrator is born in the year (1638) in which Charles obtained his judgement against Hampden in the Ship Money trial, *Mandeville: A Tale of the Seventeenth Century in England*, begun in May 1816 and published on 1 December 1817.[13] There were precedents for contemplating Hampden's death, but of a different stamp, in

the poetry of the 1790s. Whereas the Calvinist Frankenstein is exalted – with
sure irony – by 'divine ideas of liberty and self-sacrifice' in contemplating
(the Calvinist) Hampden, 'For a Column at Newbury', the second poem in
Southey's 'Inscriptions' sequence of 1797, purposively conflates the battle-
fields of Newbury and Chalgrove.[14] This imaginary inscription enjoins the
true patriot to consider the deaths of the royalist Falkland (Lucius Cary)
and Hampden as a lamentable travesty of their virtue:

> Art thou a Patriot Traveller? on this field
> Did FALKLAND fall the blameless and the brave
> Beneath a Tyrant's banners: dost thou boast
> Of loyal ardor? HAMBDEN perish'd here,
> The rebel HAMBDEN, at whose glorious name
> The heart of every honest Englishman
> Beats high with conscious pride. Both uncorrupt,
> Friends to their common country both, they fought,
> They died in adverse armies. Traveller!
> If with thy neighbour thou should'st not accord,
> In charity remember these good men,
> And quell each angry and injurious thought.[15]

As in Godwin's *Essay on Sepulchres*, the Hampden-Falkland pairing is here a
means to remember civil war as a tragic contestation to the death of distinct
versions of love of one's country.[16]

Thus the 'spots' around Marlow to which Peacock refers allow for a
grieving over thwarted aspirations in the nation's past, or, to put it another
way, provide grounds for recognizing alternatives both to the monological
(and monotheistic) teleology enforced by European Restoration culture
and, more broadly, to the 1688 settlement. And, in a further perspective on
the Alfoxden-Marlow conjunction, the promotion of the visibility of these
spots by this circle in 1817 may be set alongside the burial of one, recent,
republican history associated with Robespierre, through the recovery of
others – Rousseavian as well as English, according to Gregory Dart – that
Wordsworth began to undertake in the articulation of his autobiographical
'spots of time' after 1797.[17] In this way the Marlovian 'spots' are not *lieux de
mémoire* as defined by the contemporary French historian Pierre Nora,
that is, 'sites' commemorated elegiacally within – even by – a nation-
state.[18] The grounds of Perry Anderson's hostility towards Nora's vast *Les
Lieux de mémoire* project is what he sees as its 'creation of an *union sucrée*
in which the divisions and discords of French society would melt away
in the fond rituals of postmodern remembrance'. Anderson's scepticism
towards a circumscribing enterprise 'to define the acceptable meanings of

the country's past and the permissible bounds of its present' is suggestive in terms of debates in eighteenth-century Britain.[19] For the consecrated places described by Peacock invoke traditions of patriotism that resist such 'acceptable meanings', traditions which J. G. A. Pocock has identified in analysing Catharine Macaulay's politics:

In more than one European language of the eighteenth century, 'patriot' had a measurably subversive significance. It meant in the first instance one who loved his or her country more than its ruling family or even its institutions, and might be found rebelling against the king in the king's name, as had happened in the English Civil Wars, or against the monarchy in the name of the nation or the people . . . The patriot was one whose *patria* was a common possession, easily identified with those who possessed it; the commonweal or commonwealth, the *res publica* or republic; and this is the sense in which Catharine Macaulay could be and was described as both a 'patriot' and a 'republican'.[20]

Although the degree of its impact has been disputed, Macaulay's *History of England* (1763–81), which Shelley read in the summer of 1820, undoubtedly contributed to the making of *Charles the First*.[21] This may constitute affirmation of Pocock's double-edged assertion that by the mid 1780s 'Patriotism, in the sense in which one uses the term of Macaulay, was a lost cause [but i]t did not disappear; it persisted as part of the rhetoric of the next fifty years'.[22]

Hogg conceded that Shelley 'was upon paper and in discourse a sturdy commonwealth-man'[23] and 'Real Whig' elements, possibly deriving in part from his ancestry,[24] may be discerned in a letter Shelley wrote from Dublin in February 1812:

I cannot bear to hear people talk of the glorious Revolution of 1688. – was that period glorious when with a presumption only equalled by their stupidity, and a shortsightedness incomme[n]surable but with the blindest egotism Parliament affected to pass an act delivering over themselves and their posterity to the remotest period of time to Mary and William and their posterity. I saw this Act yesterday for the first time: and my blood boils to think that Sidney's and Hampden's blood was wasted thus, that even the defenders of liberty as they are called were sunk thus low, and thus attempt[ed] to arrest the perfectibility of human nature.[25]

But even the genealogy of this impetuous statement seems typically sophisticated. On the one hand, the youthful Shelley sounds like a Country-party republican of the mid eighteenth century (a Catharine Macaulay), and emphatically not of that variety of early-nineteenth-century Whig, like Francis Jeffrey for whom, regrettably, the period of anti-Jacobin reaction in the 1790s was one in which 'The Revolution of 1688, it was agreed, could

not be mentioned with praise without giving some indirect encouragement
to the Revolution of 1789; and it was thought as well to say nothing in favour
of Hampden or Russell or Sidney, for fear it might give spirits to Robespierre, Danton or Marat.'[26] On the other, this recent correspondent of
Godwin's, and a perfectibilarian, seems to make the connection between
the utopianism of the 1790s and the 1650s noted in the *British Review and
London Critical Journal* a few years later: 'The civil troubles of Charles the
First's reign called forth the "Oceana" of Harrington . . . This crisis [the
revolution in France] produced in England "The Political Justice".'[27] Yet
another variety of Hampden entertained by the young Shelley must have
been that of Thomson's *Summer* and Gray's 'Elegy', the works of poets
whose influence upon his early poetry has perhaps been underestimated.
But Shelley's republicanism later becomes increasingly inflected by European traditions from Plato to Sismondi via Machiavelli and Rousseau. His
journeys to Geneva and Tuscany from England in 1816 and 1818 symbolize
this shift and represent an intellectual untethering that takes him not only
beyond the Godwinian tradition of rational dissent or the genial liberalism of Hunt's *Examiner* but, following Blair Worden's reminder that, 'It
was in France that William Wordsworth developed, under the influence of
his friends among the Girondins, his enthusiasm for Sidney, Harrington
and "others who called Milton friend"',[28] towards recognition that congenial aspects of English republicanism might be more easily found on the
banks of the Arno than of the Thames. The way that English and European republican thought had been deeply imbued with one another since
the mid seventeenth century may be instanced by the invocation of Harrington in Sismondi's *Histoire des républiques italiennes* (1818) which the
Shelleys began to read in January 1819.[29] To explore this 'Europeanizing' of
the English Revolution, I suggest in what follows that the scene in *Charles
the First* comprising the dialogue between Hampden and Sir Henry Vane
the Younger evidences that emphasis on the *patria* as 'a common possession',
a secure *res publica* beyond the boundaries of monarchical and institutional
definitions of the state that Pocock has described. But it also shows that this
ideal republic, America being its earthly type, is threatened by a religious
idiom of purity.

An awareness of the singular appropriateness of their having just taken up
residence in Marlow to the unfolding political crisis in the opening months
of 1817 was noted by Mary Shelley. Marlow was close to the Buckinghamshire seat of Wendover that Hampden had represented in Parliament,
and in a letter to Hunt in London she records the Ship Money case being

re-enacted in Peacock's mother's house where they were staying before moving into Albion House:

Shelley & Peacock have started a question which I do not esteem myself wise enough to decide upon – and yet as they seem determined to act on it I wish them to have the *best advise*. As a prelude to this you must be reminded that Hambden was of Bucks and our two worthies want to be his successors for which reason they intend to refuse to pay the taxes as illegally imposed – What effect will this have & ought they to do it is the question? Pray let me know your opinion.[30]

Hampden's position had been defended in the first edition of *Political Justice* as an example of how 'it was perhaps fair to resist [a] tax, even supposing it to be abstractedly a good one, upon account of the authority imposing it'.[31] Such passive resistance epitomized political justice. In 'Friends of Revolution – Taxation', the leading article in *The Examiner* of 23 February 1817 that seems to have prompted the invocation of Hampden's precedent by Peacock and Shelley, Hunt remarked that the government had 'created a taxation, which has spread physical and moral desolation all around', and that 'the Friends to Revolution' were not those who advocated reform of the franchise (as Shelley had done in his *Proposal*) but those who had created 'a Debt so overwhelming, that it has become literally impossible to pay the interest of it at present, and a pure speculation whether taxation can be made to cover it'.[32] That resistance to taxation had explosive dramatic potential at this time is registered by Peacock's comment a year later on reading Francis Midon's *The History of the Rise and Fall of Masaniello, the Fisherman of Naples* (1729): 'An excellent subject for a tragedy: but of course would not be licensed as it turns on *resistance of taxes*.'[33] The humble Neapolitan's success in inciting a revolution because of the Spanish imposition of a tax on fruit makes him, albeit temporarily, in Midon's words, 'the Dread of the Spaniards, the Avenger of Publick Oppressions, and the Saviour of his desolate Country'.[34] Though his status and context do not make Masaniello precisely a Hampden, both mid-seventeenth-century men, in their principled opposition to a tax, are amenable to being made martyrs whose fates may assume a tragical cast.[35] Godwin had cited Hampden's example in 1793 as a means of showing how an unfolding revolution might achieve its goals philosophically. Hunt's reformist agenda in early 1817 requires Hampden – albeit obliquely[36] – not only as a reminder of an alternative, more measured resistance to such recent episodes as the Spa-Fields riots and the stoning of the Regent's carriage but as a source of inspiration, a means of affirming that Restorations in Europe have been temporary, terminally undermined by the residual force of the revolutionary moments to which they react:

> The authors of grievances are therefore the authors of revolution, not the people who can no longer bear them. Such was the case in vilified France; such the operation under CHARLES I. This is so true, that the restored STUARTS, acting as before, were *again* expelled from the country, as will the BOURBONS from France, if they resemble them. It is easy to see that France cannot again be made what she was; nor, thanks to the PITT politicians, not the Jacobins, – England remain what she is.[37]

Charles the First may be said to look back to the winter of discontent of 1816–17 in which Shelley's intervention in *A Proposal* was to avert one kind of revolution in the cause of furthering another.

The most celebrated phase of Hampden's political career coincides almost exactly with the chronological compass of what Shelley had written and conceived of *Charles the First* before his death, the period from 1633 to 1641. In *Political Justice* Godwin saw this as the successful, relatively peaceful early phase of the English Revolution: 'The original design of [Charles's] opponents was that of confining his power within narrow and palpable limits. This object, after a struggle of many years, was fully accomplished by the parliament of 1640, without bloodshed (except indeed in the single instance of lord Strafford) and without commotion.'[38] Hampden in Shelley's play represents the possibilities of this moment prior to civil war. He plays out a counterfactual history in which his dramatic function is, according to one critic, 'to represent republican (and thus Romantic) idealism',[39] in contrast to the problematical actuality of his cousin Cromwell's career. But Shelley's resolve 'to write a play, in the spirit of human nature, without prejudice or passion',[40] suggests that it is the disturbing because religious foundations of mid-seventeenth-century republican (and not necessarily 'Romantic') idealism which it is the object of his 'Historical Tragedy'[41] to scrutinize. Myths of Hampden in the long eighteenth century may be summarized in the contrast between Clarendon's royalist verdict that he was possessed of Satanic guile ('his Affections seem'd so publickly guided, that no corrupt, or private ends could byass them'),[42] and the republican idiom of Catharine Macaulay's rejoinder that this was 'the testimony of an enemy to virtues possessed only by the foremost rank of men', and that in debate he joined 'the art of Socrates with the graces of Cicero'.[43] It was within this terrain that Godwin was to adjudicate in his *History*. But the focus on Hampden in *Charles the First* is less upon his political aptitude than on the nature of his idealism.

As R. B. Woodings first noted,[44] amongst the earliest of his surviving research notes, from Hume's *History* and Whitlocke's *Memorials*, there is evidence that Shelley conceived of the first scene of his play as depicting the attempted emigration to America of Hampden and others: 'Hazelrig Hambden Pym &/ Cromwell, are restrained from embarking/ for America, & following the political/ & religious puritans, who had there/ already laid the foundation of a free/ government; – First scene/ (date unknown).'[45] Nora Crook has even suggested the possibility that 'Hampden/Vane' may have been the first scene to have been composed, at the same time as these notes were written,[46] during the summer of 1821 and probably by 25 September.[47] As part of what has become entitled the 'Abstract' of the opening two acts, probably written in January 1822,[48] the position of the scene is altered to the third and final scene of the first act and its content sketched thus: 'Pym Hazelrig/ Cromwell, young Sir H. Vane,/ Hampden &c. – their characters/ & intentions – a pursuivant/ comes with an order of/ council to prevent their/ embarkation – Cromwell's/ speech on that occasion – / high commissions pursuivants.'[49] The following scene, the first of the second act, was to depict the 'Chiefs of the Popular Party,/ Hampden's trial & its effects'.[50] The purpose of this juxtaposition of the failed bid to emigrate to America and the Ship Money trial is to reinforce the dramatic irony of the foreclosure of this utopian moment by royal proclamation, captured by Hume thus:

Eight ships, lying in the Thames, and ready to sail, were detained by order of the council; and in these were embarked Sir Arthur Hazelrig, John Hambden, John Pym, and Oliver Cromwel, who had resolved for ever to abandon their native country, and fly to the other extremity of the globe; where they might enjoy lectures and discourses of any length or form which pleased them. The king had afterwards full leisure to repent this exercise of his authority.[51]

It is worth pausing to note Hume's gloss on this event: 'Can any one doubt, that the ensuing quarrel was almost entirely theological not political? What might be expected of the populace, when such was the character of the most enlightened leaders?'[52] It seems certain that Shelley would have relished this acute diagnosis of the infusion of the politics of the 'Popular Party' by religion. Traces of Hume's vocabulary are apparent in the way the Abstract distinguishes the 'rational and logical' resistance to Ship Money of Hampden from the 'impetuous and enthusiastic' reasons of

Vane.[53] They are also evident in part of Hampden's speech in the earlier 'Hampden/Vane' scene based here on Crook's pioneering editorial work on the text of *Charles the First*:

> O light us to the isles of the Evening land.
> Like floating Edens cradled in the glimmer
> Of dew, touched by departing hope they gleam.
> Where Power's poor dupes & victims yet have never
> Propitiated the savage fear of Kings
> With purest blood of noblest hearts; whose dew
> Is yet unstained with tears of those who wake
> To weep, each day, the wrongs on which it dawns,
> Whose sacred silent air owns yet no echo
> Of formal blasphemies, nor impious rites
> Wrest man's free worship from the God who loves
> Towards the worm who envies us his love.[54]

In this aetherializing of America as a refuge, the high language of purity and sanctity eschews monarchs and priests but also perhaps carries a painful awareness of the impossibility of a peopled paradise. Hampden's idealizing is enraptured but, in light of Shelley's reading of Hume, such republican rapture is potentially hazardous. So, while the neglect of Macaulay as a source for *Charles the First* has been redressed valuably by Kenneth Neill Cameron and Greg Kucich, the attack on Whig history from another angle by Hume is not, in itself, as we have seen, a reason why Shelley would have found it unpalatable. The politics of Hume's *History*, too easily assumed to be antipathetic because of its 'Tory' appropriation, was less important to him than what Karen O'Brien has identified as its 'cosmopolitan nature', a eurocentrism that may be felt in Shelley's practice of reading Hume's *History* aloud most evenings throughout the *ménage*'s first summer in Italy in 1818.[55] In O'Brien's words, 'Hume's endeavour was to take the political and constitutional materials of British history . . . and insert them into a social, national and ultimately European fabric of causation.'[56] This is exemplified in his comment in respect of the early part of Charles's reign that, 'of all European nations, the British were at that time, and till long after, the most under the influence of that religious spirit, which tends rather to inflame bigotry than encrease peace and mutual charity'.[57] Hume's treatment of Hampden's trial is poised between an endorsement of his position and a sense of its vulnerability to enthusiastic exploitation. It provides a way of seeing *Charles the First* as a tragedy in which Hampden and Charles are both helpless in the face of essentially religious forces unleashed by the trial's outcome:

What though the personal character of the king, amidst all his misguided counsels, might merit indulgence, or even praise? He was but one man; and the privileges of the people, the inheritance of millions, were too valuable to be sacrificed to his prejudices and mistakes. Such, or more severe, were the sentiments promoted by a great party in the nation: No excuse on the king's part, or alleviation, how reasonable soever, could be harkened to or admitted: And to redress these grievances, a parliament was impatiently longed for; or any other incident, however calamitous, that might secure the people against those oppressions, which they felt, or the greater ills, which they apprehended, from the combined encroachments of church and state.[58]

Mary Shelley's comment that her husband was attracted to a subject involving 'contrasted character' enables us to see that the play intended to portray not just contested judgements over Charles but over Hampden too.[59] Its premature announcement in *The London Magazine* in January 1821, probably a public-relations stunt to try to secure a publisher, commented on 'Mr Shelley's determination . . . to exclude from his work all prejudice, political as well as moral'.[60] This assessment suggests Shelley's effort at moving beyond the heroic memorializing of Hampden that motivated Southey's 'Inscription' poem and Godwin's *History* towards an analytical understanding of the roots of English republicanism.

In response to John Taylor Coleridge's brutal offensive on Shelley's private life in a review of *The Revolt of Islam* in the *Quarterly*,[61] Hunt in *The Examiner* recalled his three-month residence at Albion House in the summer of 1817: 'we never lived with a man who gave so complete an idea of an ardent and principled aspirant in philosophy as Percy Shelley; and . . . we believe him, from the bottom of our hearts, to be one of the noblest hearts as well as heads which the world has seen for a long time'.[62] In this memoir Marlow was a place where patriotism was reclaimed. Hunt's praise for Shelley as an 'ardent and principled aspirant in philosophy' revalues a word that Southey had recently deployed contemptuously in the *Quarterly* as a means of associating utopians of the 1790s (Godwin must have been in his sights) with extreme seventeenth-century Dissent:

the French revolution, acting upon political enthusiasm, produced a set of speculators as wild as the old fifth-monarchy men. They announced the advent of a political millenium, – which was to be not the kingdom of the saints, – saints and kingdoms being with them alike out of fashion, – but the commonwealth of philosophers.[63]

The commonplace conflation of the two revolutionary moments here is less significant than the placing of 'philosophy' in contradistinction to religion. Hunt countered Coleridge by recalling the authentic acts of charity that made up Shelley's daily routine as he, 'visited (if necessary) "the sick and the fatherless," whom others gave Bibles to and no help'.[64] There was, then, an absolute consistency between the alternative to orthodox Christianity advanced in the poem Shelley wrote at Marlow, *Laon and Cythna* – which, for Hunt, demonstrated that 'the moral spirit of his philosophy approaches infinitely nearer to that Christian benevolence, so much preached and so little practised, than any the most orthodox dogmas ever published' – and his life.[65] Mary Shelley was later to affirm his regard for the 'very poor population' of Marlow: 'this minute and active sympathy with his fellow-creatures gives a thousand-fold interest to his speculations, and stamps with reality his pleadings for the human race'.[66] That both Hunt and Mary Shelley all but identify Shelley with Christ is continuous with his writings of 1817. In the fragmentary prose draft now called 'On Christianity', written at Marlow, Christ is dressed in the language of republicanism – 'A man of ardent genius, and impatient virtue perishes in stern and resolute opposition to tyranny, injustice and superstition'[67] – and, in historicizing vein, is seen as a critic of the failures of the late Roman empire, that is as a genuine patriot. It is Plato and Rousseau, singled out as the proper interpreters of Christ's revolutionary practice, who help us to see that 'The only perfect and genuine republic is that which comprehends every living being.'[68] In late May 1817, on a visit to her father's house in Skinner Street, Mary Shelley, in re-reading *Childe Harold Canto the Third*, fondly remembered Shelley first reading it to her in manuscript at Chapuis on the shores of Lake Geneva the previous summer: 'Dear Lake! I shall ever love thee. How a powerful mind can sanctify past scenes and recollections – His is a powerful mind.'[69] Shelley's writing at Marlow returns to Europe, to these memories of Byron at Geneva with its Rousseauvian associations, but also looks forward to the Tuscany of Machiavelli and Sismondi that awaited him. In this way Marlow may be seen as a place of exile from which he needed to retreat back to the continent of Europe where he had the necessary perspective to comprehend the English Revolution.

NOTES

1. Shelley to Peacock, 20 April 1818, in Frederick L. Jones (ed.), *The Letters of Percy Bysshe Shelley*, 2 vols. (Oxford: Clarendon Press, 1964), vol. II, p. 6.
2. Shelley to Peacock, 26 July 1818, in Jones (ed.), *Shelley Letters*, vol. II, pp. 26–7.
3. Peacock to Shelley, 5 July 1818, in Nicholas A. Joukovsky (ed.), *The Letters of Thomas Love Peacock*, 2 vols. (Oxford: Clarendon Press, 2001), vol. I, pp. 131 and 133 n. 30.

4. Timothy Morton and Nigel Smith, 'Introduction', in Morton and Smith (eds.), *Radicalism in British Literary Culture, 1650–1830: From Revolution to Revolution* (Cambridge: Cambridge University Press, 2002), p. 6.

5. Peacock to Thomas Jefferson Hogg, 26 September 1817, in Joukovsky (ed.), *Peacock Letters*, vol. I, p. 116.

6. Marilyn Butler, *Romantics, Rebels, and Reactionaries: English Literature and Its Background, 1760–1830* (Oxford: Oxford University Press, 1981), p. 128.

7. See Jeffrey N. Cox's reorientation in *Poetry and Politics in the Cockney School: Keats, Shelley, Hunt, and Their Circle* (Cambridge: Cambridge University Press, 1998): 'While Butler centers her discussion on the group gathered in 1817 at Marlowe [sic], particularly Shelley and Peacock, I would see this meeting as an offshoot of the larger and earlier Hunt circle' (p. 110).

8. Marilyn Butler, *Literature as a Heritage: Or Reading Other Ways* (Cambridge: Cambridge University Press, 1988), p. 21.

9. Thomas Love Peacock, 'Memoirs of Percy Bysshe Shelley. Part II', *Fraser's Magazine* 61 (January 1860), 101. It seems possible that Peacock forgets that some of these places were visited from Marlow in 1818 not 1817: 'Hogg is coming down on Wednesday and we are going together up the river to Oxford. We think, too, of walking to Chalgrove field, where Hampden was killed, and to Chequers, the seat of Cromwell in the Chiltern Hills' (Peacock to Shelley, 14 June 1818, in Joukovsky (ed.), *Peacock Letters*, vol. I, p. 126).

10. Mary Shelley, *Frankenstein: or The Modern Prometheus*, the 1818 Text, ed. Marilyn Butler (Oxford: Oxford University Press, 1994), p. 133.

11. See Charles E. Robinson's notes to his edition of *The Frankenstein Notebooks*, 'The Manuscripts of the Younger Romantics: Mary Wollstonecraft Shelley', 2 vols. (New York: Garland, 1996), vol. II, pp. 458–9.

12. William Godwin, *The History of the Commonwealth of England*, 4 vols. (London, 1824–8), vol. I, Preface, p. vi. John Morrow notes that the motto 'came from Edmund Burke's eulogy on John Howard's visit to European prisons'. See his 'Republicanism and Public Virtue in William Godwin's *History of the Commonwealth of England*', *The Historical Journal* 34.3 (1991), 645–64 (648) and his Introduction to Godwin's *History of the Commonwealth* (Bristol: Thoemmes Press, and Tokyo: Editions Synapse, 2003), pp. v–xxxiv (p. xv).

13. For Mary's excursion with Godwin to Hampden's monument, see Paula R. Feldman and Diana Scott-Kilvert (eds.), *The Journals of Mary Shelley 1814–1844* (Baltimore: Johns Hopkins University Press, 1995), p. 181. On the circumstances of *Mandeville*'s composition and publication, see Pamela Clemit's 'Introductory Note' to her edition in *The Collected Novels and Memoirs of William Godwin*, general editor Mark Philp, 8 vols. (London: Pickering and Chatto, 1992), vol. VI, pp. v–viii.

14. On Hampden's Calvinist origins, see Conrad Russell, 'Hampden, John (1595–1643)', *Oxford Dictionary of National Biography* (Oxford: Oxford University Press, 2004), http://www.oxforddnb.com/view/article/12169, accessed 3 July 2005.

15. Robert Southey, *Poetical Works 1793–1810*, ed. Lynda Pratt, 5 vols. (London: Pickering and Chatto, 2004), vol. v, p. 63.

16. 'The scenes of the grand contest for our liberties under the Long Parliament, the fields where Falkland expired, and Hambden bled, hold a language of another sort.' William Godwin, *Essay on Sepulchres*, in *The Political and Philosophical Writings of William Godwin*, general editor Mark Philp, 7 vols. (London: Pickering and Chatto, 1993), vol. vi, p. 21.

17. See Gregory Dart, '"The virtue of one paramount mind": Wordsworth and the politics of the mountain', in his *Rousseau, Robespierre and English Romanticism* (Cambridge: Cambridge University Press, 1999), pp. 163–208 (pp. 200–8).

18. Pierre Nora, 'Between Memory and History: *Les Lieux de mémoire*', trans. Marc Roudebush, *Representations* 26 (Spring 1989), 7–25. This essay was first published in French in 1984 under the title 'Entre mémoire et histoire: la problématique des lieux'.

19. Perry Anderson, 'Union Sucrée', *London Review of Books*, 26.18 (23 September 2004), http://www.lrb.co.uk/v26/n18/print/ande01_.html, accessed 10 October 2004.

20. J. G. A. Pocock, 'Catharine Macaulay: Patriot Historian', in Hilda L. Smith (ed.), *Women Writers and the Early Modern British Political Tradition* (Cambridge: Cambridge University Press, 1998), pp. 243–58 (p. 246).

21. For Shelley's reading of Macaulay's *History* between 18 July and 4 September 1820, see Feldman and Scott-Kilvert (eds.), *Mary Shelley Journals*, pp. 326–31. On the significance of Macaulay for *Charles the First*, see Kenneth Neill Cameron, 'Shelley's Use of Source Material in *Charles I*', *MLQ* 6 (1945), 197–210; Cameron, *Shelley: The Golden Years* (Cambridge, Mass.: Harvard University Press, 1974), pp. 411–21; Greg Kucich, '"This Horrid Theatre of Human Sufferings": Gendering the Stages of History in Catharine Macaulay and Percy Bysshe Shelley', in Thomas Pfau and Robert F. Gleckner (eds.), *Lessons of Romanticism* (Durham, N.C. and London: Duke University Press, 1998), pp. 448–65. In 'Shelley's Sources for "Charles the First"', *MLR* 64 (1969), 267–75, R. B. Woodings downplays her influence.

22. Pocock, 'Catharine Macaulay', p. 257.

23. Thomas Jefferson Hogg, *The Life of Percy Bysshe Shelley*, introd. by Edward Dowden (London: George Routledge and Sons, 1906), p. 133.

24. For an excellent account of the Shelley family's Whig affiliations and property interests in Sussex, see Susan C. Djabri, with Annabelle F. Hughes and Jeremy Knight, *The Shelleys of Field Place: The Story of the Family and Their Estates* (Horsham: Horsham Museum Society for Horsham Museum, 2000), especially Part II. The classic account of Whiggisms is J. G. A. Pocock, 'The Varieties of Whiggism from Exclusion to Reform: A History of Ideology and Discourse', in *Virtue, Commerce, and History: Essays on Political Thought and History, Chiefly in the Eighteenth Century* (Cambridge: Cambridge University Press, 1985), pp. 215–310.

25. Shelley to Elizabeth Hitchener, 27 February 1812, in Jones (ed.), *Shelley Letters*, vol. i, p. 264.

26. Francis Jeffrey in the *Edinburgh Review* (1808), cited in Blair Worden, *Roundhead Reputations: The English Civil Wars and the Passions of Posterity* (London: Penguin, 2001), p. 208.

27. Review of *The Lives of Edward and John Philips* (1815), *British Review and London Critical Journal* 7 (1816), in Kenneth W. Graham, *William Godwin Reviewed: A Reception History 1783–1834* (New York: AMS Press, 2001), p. 322.

28. Worden, *Roundhead Reputations*, p. 207.

29. J. C. L. Simonde de Sismondi, *Histoire des républiques italiennes du moyen âge*, 2nd edn, 16 vols. (Paris, 1818), vol. I, p. 58. On European elements in English republicanism in the early modern period, see Blair Worden, 'English Republicanism', in J. H. Burns (ed.), *The Cambridge History of Political Thought, 1450–1700* (Cambridge: Cambridge University Press, 1991), pp. 443–75. On European dimensions of republican thought in Romanticism, see Paul Hamilton, 'Afterword: The Republican Prompt: Connections in English Radical Culture', in Morton and Smith (eds.), *Radicalism in British Literary Culture*, pp. 201–15.

30. Mary Shelley to Leigh Hunt, 2 March 1817, in Betty T. Bennett (ed.), *The Letters of Mary Wollstonecraft Shelley*, 3 vols. (Baltimore and London: Johns Hopkins University Press, 1980–8), vol. I, p. 29.

31. William Godwin, *An Enquiry Concerning Political Justice* (1793 edition), in Godwin, *Political and Philosophical Writings*, vol. III, p. 93.

32. Leigh Hunt, 'Friends of Revolution – Taxation', *The Examiner* 478 (23 February 1817), 113, 114.

33. Peacock, 'Marlow Journal', 28 July 1818, in Joukovsky (ed.) *Peacock Letters*, vol. I, pp. 136–7.

34. Francis Midon, *The History of the Rise and Fall of Masaniello, the Fisherman of Naples* (London, 1729), p. 198. For an assessment of the mainly royalist and monitory usages to which Masaniello's tale was put, see Silvana D'Alessio, 'Masaniello's Revolt: A "Remedy" for the English Body Politic', *Restoration and 18th-Century Theatre Research* 17, Parts 1–2 (2002), 10–19.

35. The insight of Morton and Smith (itself indebted to Nora Crook) that 'Shelley's play might appropriately have been entitled *Sir Henry Vane*' is relevant here (Morton and Smith, 'Introduction', p. 6).

36. Hampden is referred to directly in the subsequent issue of the *Examiner*: 'FELLOW-COUNTRYMEN, Inheritors of Magna Charta and the Bill of Rights, Demanders of Constitutional Reform, Demanders of decent and commonly capable Ministers, Descendants of the ALFREDS, the RUSSELLS, the HAMPDENS, the SHAKSPEARES;-'. Leigh Hunt, 'On the Proposed Suspension of the Habeas Corpus Act: To the English People', *Examiner* 479 (2 March 1817), 129–31, rpt. in Robert Morrison and Michael Eberle-Sinatra (eds.), *Selected Writings of Leigh Hunt*, 6 vols. (London: Pickering and Chatto, 2003), vol. II, pp. 100–5 (100). The latitude of such appropriations of Hampden in the Romantic period is considered in Worden, *Roundhead Reputations*, Chapter 7, 'The Patriots', pp. 181–214.

37. Hunt, 'Friends of Revolution – Taxation', *Examiner* 478 (23 February 1817), 113.

38. Godwin, *Political Justice*, vol. III, pp. III–12.

39. Peter J. Kitson, "'Not a Reforming Patriot but an Ambitious Tyrant'": Representations of Cromwell and the English Republic in the Late Eighteenth and Early Nineteenth Centuries', in Morton and Smith (eds.), *Radicalism in British Literary Culture*, pp. 183–200 (p. 195).

40. Shelley to Thomas Medwin, 20 July 1820, in Jones (ed.), *Shelley Letters*, vol. II, pp. 219–20.

41. Shelley to Charles Ollier, 11 January 1822, in Jones (ed.), *Shelley Letters*, vol. II, p. 372.

42. Edward, Earl of Clarendon, *The History of the Rebellion and the Civil Wars in England*, 3 vols. (Oxford, 1720), vol. II, Part I, p. 266. Shelley read Clarendon's *History* between 9 September and 7 November 1819 (see Feldman and Scott-Kilvert (eds.), *Mary Shelley Journals*, pp. 298–301).

43. Catharine Macaulay, *History of England*, 3rd edn, 5 vols. (London, 1769), vol. III, pp. 429–30.

44. R. B. Woodings, "'A Devil of a Nut to Crack'": Shelley's *Charles the First*, *Studia Neophilologica* 40 (1968), 216–37 (229).

45. Bodleian MS. Shelley adds. e. 7, p. 249 rev. The source of this transcription is *The Hellas Notebook: Bodleian MS. Shelley adds. e. 7*, ed. Donald H. Reiman and Michael J. Neth, vol. XVI of 'The Bodleian Shelley Manuscripts' (New York: Garland, 1994), p. 233.

46. Nora Crook, Introduction, in Crook (ed.), *The 'Charles the First' Draft Notebook: A Facsimile of Bodleian MS. Shelley adds. e. 17*, ed. Nora Crook, vol. XII of 'The Bodleian Shelley Manuscripts' (New York: Garland, 1991), p. xlv.

47. See Donald Reiman and Michael Neth, Introduction, in Reiman and Neth (eds.), *The Hellas Notebook*, p. xxx.

48. Mary A. Quinn, Introduction, in Quinn (ed.), *Shelley's 1821–1822 Huntington Notebook: A Facsimile of Huntington MS. HM 2111*, ed. by Mary A. Quinn, vol. VII of 'The Manuscripts of the Younger Romantics, Percy Bysshe Shelley' (New York: Garland, 1996), p. xxxiv.

49. HM 2111, ff. *1ᵛ–*2ʳ [rev]. Source of transcription: Quinn (ed.), *Shelley's 1821–1822 Huntington Notebook*, pp. 336, 334.

50. HM 2111, f. *3ʳ [rev]. Source of transcription: Quinn (ed.), *Shelley's 1821–1822 Huntington Notebook*, p. 330.

51. David Hume, *The History of England from the Invasion of Julius Caesar to the Revolution in 1688*, 6 vols. (1778; Indianapolis: Liberty Fund, 1983), vol. V, pp. 241–2. Compare the pithy account in Godwin's history for children, [Edward Baldwin], *The History of England* (London, 1807): 'Three years before the meeting of parliament in 1640, Hambden and Oliver Cromwell went on board ship, with a resolution to spend the remainder of their days in America: Charles the First ordered their voyage to be stopped, and thus unthinkingly sealed his own destruction' (p. 147). The source of Shelley's 1821 notes in Bod. MS. Shelley adds. e. 17 is the 1819 'Regent's Edition' of Hume's *History*, which

included Smollett's continuation. This was first noted by R. B. Woodings, 'Shelley's Sources for "Charles the First"', *MLR* 64 (1969), 267–75 (269).

52. Hume, *History*, vol. v, p. 241n.
53. HM 2111, f. *3ʳ [rev]. Source of transcription: Quinn (ed.), *Shelley's 1821–1822 Huntington Notebook*, p. 330.
54. Bod. MS. Shelley adds. e. 17, pp. 45–6. My text is based on Crook's diplomatic transcription in *The 'Charles the First' Draft Notebook*, pp. 95–6.
55. See the entries for 19 June–15 August 1818 in Feldman and Scott-Kilvert (eds.), *Mary Shelley Journals*, pp. 215–23.
56. Karen O'Brien, *Narratives of Enlightenment: Cosmopolitan History from Voltaire to Gibbon* (Cambridge: Cambridge University Press, 1997), Chapter 3, 'European Contexts in Hume's *History of England*', pp. 56–92 (p. 57).
57. Hume, *History*, vol. v, p. 164.
58. Ibid., vol. v, p. 248.
59. Mary Shelley (ed.), *The Poetical Works of Percy Bysshe Shelley*, 4 vols. (London, 1839), vol. iv, p. 227.
60. For the text of the announcement and the suggestion that his cousin Thomas Medwin was responsible for it, see Kenneth Neill Cameron, *Shelley: The Golden Years* (Cambridge, Mass.: Harvard University Press, 1974), p. 640 n. 45.
61. John Taylor Coleridge, Review of *The Revolt of Islam*, *Quarterly Review* 21 (April 1819), 460–71.
62. Leigh Hunt, 'The Quarterly Review, and Revolt of Islam', *Examiner* 615 (10 October 1819), 653.
63. Robert Southey, Review of Colquhoun, *Propositions for Ameliorating the Condition of the Poor*, *Quarterly Review* 8 (December 1812), 319–56 (321).
64. Hunt, 'The Quarterly Review, and Revolt of Islam', *Examiner* 615 (10 October 1819), 653.
65. Hunt, 'The Quarterly Review, and Revolt of Islam', *Examiner* 614 (3 October 1819), 636.
66. Mary Shelley (ed.), *Poetical Works of Percy Bysshe Shelley*, vol. i, p. 377.
67. Percy Shelley, 'On Christianity', in E. B. Murray (ed.), *The Prose Works of Percy Bysshe Shelley* (Oxford: Clarendon Press, 1993), vol. i, p. 247.
68. See the section headed 'Equality of Mankind' in 'On Christianity', in Murray (ed.) *Prose Works of Shelley*, vol. i, pp. 263–6 (p. 264).
69. Feldman and Scott-Kilvert (eds.), *Mary Shelley Journals*, p. 172.

CHAPTER 4

Memoirs of a dutiful niece: Lucy Aikin and literary reputation

Anne Janowitz

AN AUTHORIZING FAMILY

The remarks that follow address a question that arose when I was working on a comparative study of the poetics of Anna Barbauld and Mary Robinson: I was struck by the way in which Mary Robinson's self-publicity as a woman of letters served as a form of self-protection against her notoriety as a courtesan and actress, while Anna Barbauld's eminence was shaped and burnished by a reputation machine, part of an intergenerational claim for the importance of her family within British culture as the embodiment of moral conviction from the seventeenth-century period of religious controversy to the liberal politics of the nineteenth.

Readers of Romantic poetry are now familiar with the poetry of Anna Laetitia Barbauld, whose two great poems, 'A Summer Evening's Meditation' and 'Eighteen Hundred and Eleven', bind a fifty-year life in writing that began in gladness and ended, if not in madness, in a share of despondency and sadness, as Barbauld felt herself marginalized by age and intellectual temperament in a new world of sentimental respectability.[1] Unlike other Romantic-age poets, Barbauld is not considered to be a poet isolate; even her most startling poems belong to a fabric of assumptions and a level of confidence unimaginable for the deracinated Mary Robinson. And unlike Wordsworth and Coleridge and Southey, whose reputations were made, along with Mary Robinson's, through the contemporary periodical and newspaper press and from both collegial support and publicity (for example, the *Biographia Literaria* as an extended advertisement for Wordsworth's poetry), Anna Aikin's fame as a poet was part of the cultural work of a public family formation, elaborated and maintained through religious networks, periodicals, newspapers, educational institutions, and through a series of family memoirs. For about a hundred years this family observed itself and wrote about itself and did an impressive job of redescribing itself in response to earlier versions of their family's religious, social, and literary commitments. The chief sources for this ongoing self-assessment are contemporary memoirs written by members of the Aikin family and their set, including ones by and about the Dissenting minister John Aikin, his son John Aikin, M. D., Anna Barbauld, her niece Lucy Aikin, her grand-niece Anna Laetitia Le Breton and Anna Le Breton's husband, Philip Hemery Le Breton, and, as recently as 1958, another Aikin descendant, Betsy Rodgers, in *Georgian Chronicle: Mrs. Barbauld and Her Family*.[2] It was when I was putting together the bibliography for my study that I understood how seriously micromanaged I had been by the Aikin family, whose multiple memoirs create and satisfy the taste for knowing about them. Which isn't to say that they refrain from criticism of themselves and others; for example, mediated through the psychologically revealing memoirs of his dutiful daughter, Lucy, John Aikin is unexpectedly presented as a neglected poet and martyr to the talents of his sister Anna Barbauld. The point I will illustrate over the next pages is that the Aikins were representative of a style of living and thinking as literary liberals that they narrated as being founded in and developed through their own exemplary history.

Anna Barbauld's father, the Rev. John Aikin (1713–80), was at one time a strong radical Dissenter of the 'low Arminian' heresy, well before the ameliorative religious politics of Unitarianism, and his friends and relations were central in establishing the ethos and reputation of the Dissenting Academy at Warrington, an institution that influenced a generation of liberal thought – in natural philosophy, in history, and in political thinking. The Warrington Academy was famous for its enlightened values and methods, and for its free-thinking tutors such as Joseph Priestley and the wonderfully irascible Gilbert Wakefield, an unrepentant radical even after his friends and relations, the Aikins, had settled down in the last years of the 1790s. The institutional network of the Warrington Dissenters resulted in marriages and children: Anna Aikin married a Huguenot Warrington student, Rochemont Barbauld; her brother John Aikin married their cousin Martha Jennings; and John and Martha's son John married Gilbert Wakefield's daughter. Among the younger generation of Warrington Aikins, Anna's brother John, after a short period of radicalism, was known as a reforming 'man of letters'; Anna's influential writings while running the boys' school at Palgrave led to her reputation as the 'pedagogue of the nineteenth century'; in the third generation, John and Martha Aikin's daughter Lucy Aikin was a poet and biographer and their son Arthur, a literary editor.

Anna's brother John Aikin, M. D. (1747–1822) edited the *Monthly Magazine* and took an important step in founding the journalism of the liberal intelligentsia by not offering much in the way of religious controversies

and instead purveying the knowledge created by the Dissenting community and adapting to the more anodyne Unitarian goal of the nineteenth
century. Arthur Aikin, John's son, continued that pathway in the *Annual
Review*, which he edited from 1802 to 1806. In 1813, the *Monthly Repository*,
which Isobel Armstrong has shown to have been a decisive cultural influence in Victorian society under the editorship of W. J. Fox, published a
year-long history of the Warrington Academy by William Turner, who had
been educated there.[3] In 1822, the Aikins were described in the *Monthly
Repository*, which had by then become the organ of the liberal intelligentsia,
as 'a family which has perhaps done more than any other family in England
for the promotion of knowledge and the gratification of the literary taste'.[4]
Within that capacious category of 'literary taste' were tastes for domestic
reform, democratic poetics, liberalism, and religious latitude.

Key to the developing public reputation of the Aikin family was their
close religious, social, and business connection with Joseph Johnson, the
publisher of most of the work of John Aikin, his children, and their children
as well. Johnson supported the writing of the Aikin/ Barbaulds for more
than forty years, publishing their sermons, polemics, geography books,
medical books, poems, philosophical essays, and children's texts, as well as
the widely disseminated *Monthly Magazine*, edited by Anna's brother John
Aikin, M. D. Joseph Johnson was the agent and distributor of the Aikins'
self-publicity. Johnson's role as a radical publisher will be familiar to any-
one interested in the work of Thomas Paine, Mary Wollstonecraft, and
William Godwin, the outré radical intellectuals of the late 1780s and 1790s.
The years of John Aikin's editorship of the *Monthly Magazine* overlapped
with one of Joseph Johnson's other periodicals, the *Analytical Review*, in
which Mary Wollstonecraft first published her work as a St. Paul's Yard
literary drudge, writing reviews and political essays, and which also featured the work of Fuseli, John Aikin, Lucy Aikin, Anna Barbauld, William
Enfield, and William Cowper. And it is worth considering that though
the Aikins were just as active and public as the Godwin-Wollstonecraft-
Shelleys, they were far less well known as *personalities* than their Godwin
and Wollstonecraft and Shelley contemporaries and acquaintances, whose
extraordinary poetry and fiction and polemical writing was coupled with
their often bizarre and certainly publicly outrageous attempts to explain
themselves and each other: it is impossible to forget William Godwin amiably, naively, but tragically exposing Mary Wollstonecraft's sexual life in his
Memoir of the Author of 'A Vindication of the Rights of Woman'.[5]

The Aikin family, by contrast, were far less naive as they shaped themselves through public writing as an important strand of first polite and

then respectable society. In their poems and essays of the 1770s, the Aikin family presented their own aims and those of the Warrington Academy as inextricably interconnected, blurring the distinction between institution and family. Their renown depended upon personal as well as public reports of their 'free, familiar conversation' – their polite sociability, recounted, for example, in the sermon William Enfield delivered at Anna's father's funeral. Warrington tutors aimed to incarnate an ideal of social intercourse conceived of as informal and amiable, teaching the virtues of what Anna Barbauld called 'candid manners' and an 'active mind'.

The Dissenting Academy at Warrington was founded as one of a series of establishments to train non-conformist clergy, who had been excluded from public life from the time of Charles II's Corporation and Test Acts of 1661 and 1673, legislation that rendered non-conformists second-class citizens until 1828. The strength of the Warrington institution was chiefly in science and letters: there was a strong secular strain to the curriculum, and it drew from a wide social base of sons of planters, professionals, and manufacturers, including families who belonged to the Established Church, but who felt their sons would get a better education in the intellectually advanced and apparently more disciplined Dissenting educational milieu.[6]

Dissenting education influenced the social fields it wished to conquer. The English Enlightenment, as it absorbed and developed ideas from both Europe and Scotland, was strengthened in the Dissenting intelligentsia. Joseph Priestley was an important influence on the Warrington Academy's curriculum while he served there as the Modern Languages tutor from 1761 until 1767. Priestley introduced lectures on politically useful subjects that ran in tandem with the religious teaching on which the Academy was founded; these included 'History and General Policy', 'Laws and Constitutions of England', and the 'History of England'. He later recalled:

This I did in consequence of observing that, though most of our pupils were young men designed for situations in civil and active life, every article in the plan of their Education was adapted to the learned professions.[7]

Priestley advocated the kind of learning that would service the new citizen-managers of a growing industrial and governmental apparatus. Although Dissenters were still kept out of public office in the 1770s, men such as Priestley believed this would not be the case for long. What appeared to be the clear and steady path towards integration, however, was interrupted during the period of the wars with France (1793–1815), as it appeared to many people that the causes of Dissent and of revolutionary ardour were too closely linked. At the same time, as families outside the Dissenting community also sent their sons to Warrington for its emphasis on civil society, the connections grew ever stronger between political insiders and the Dissenting intellectual and scientific outsiders.

After the Academy's closure in 1786, Warrington's reputation served as an emblem of what liberal pedagogy might rise to, 'distinguished by sound learning, just and liberal principles, and virtuous manners'.[8] The appearance of Anna Aikin's first volume of *Poems* in 1773 was as consequential for the Warrington Academy as an institution as it was for Anna Aikin as a poet. William Woodfall's discussion of the *Poems* in the *Monthly Review* reminds its readers of Aikin's place within the informal familial-pedagogic network of Dissenting intellectuals, suggesting her indebtedness to her social circle: 'The pupils of that very useful seminar [Warrington] . . . celebrated her genius, and diffused her praises far and wide; and some of her compositions have been read and admired by persons of the first taste and judgment in the republic of letters.'[9] The volume signalled a step away from the world of the private circulation of poems into a public print culture. But if Warrington gave fame to Anna Aikin the volume also promoted the Academy. One of the best poems of the volume, 'The Invitation', serves as an advertisement for the institution, describing its pedagogic aims: 'Beneath [the Mersey's] willows rove th'inquiring youth, / And court the fair majestic forms of truth', picturing its pleasant surrounds: 'Here bath'd by frequent show'rs cool vales are seen, / Cloath'd with fresh verdure, and eternal green'; and enacting its polite rhetoric: 'Where science smiles, the Muses join the train; / And gentlest arts and purest manners reign.'[10] John Guillory has shown how Anna Aikin's landscape poetry participates (however unself-consciously) in the project of cultural advancement by Dissenters through taking on and forward 'polite vernacular discourse', suggesting that 'cultural capital can be acquired like property'.[11] That is, while the aristocracy claimed its position by antiquity and entitlement, the bourgeoisie might buy it, and not only as a welter of objects but also through education, taste, and sensibility. It was good publicity for the Academy that in the 1775 *Annual Register* David Garrick had noted that Anna Aikin 'lately sung the sweetest lay'.[12]

But publicity is one thing, lived experience another, and against Anna Aikin's prospectus for Warrington we need to place the hints from the Academy's papers that life there was actually very fraught. Henry Bright, a nineteenth-century Lancashire historian, found documents amongst the papers of the Academy's founder John Seddon that attest to ongoing emotional and financial tumult. Love affairs begun with the daughters of tutors, rowdy nights in local taverns, and bad behaviour by students who could not be properly disciplined because the Academy feared losing their fees, meant that the Warrington Academy was in a continual state of psychological and financial difficulty. Aikin's amusing portraits of the flirtatious Rigby girls make a strong counterpoint to the report that: 'The beautiful Miss Rigbys made wild work with the students' hearts; and the trustees had to insist that they must be removed from the house if any students stayed there.' A memorandum from Gilbert Wakefield suggests the problem: 'The Academy is neither school nor college; it is without the supervision exercised in the one, and it wants the influence and authority of the other, – the students are treated as men, while they are but a set of wild and reckless boys.'[13] So, when William Woodfall in the *Monthly Review* criticized Anna Aikin's *Poems* of 1773 for lacking 'passion', he may have identified not a poetic fault but a clan strategy.[14] The problem is not that Barbauld's poetic is unfeminine, and 'cold', as Coleridge would scurrilously declare many years later; but that the amiable sociability upon which Warrington was built had to be made rhetorically firm, so as not to call attention to the troubles of a small community that had no 'real sanctions against bad behaviour, except expulsion' which it was financially difficult to enforce.[15] In a genealogy of literary sociability, we might locate in Warrington a precursor to the Bloomsbury intelligentsia of the early twentieth century, whose convergence of male Cambridge education with the Stephens daughters' accomplishments and talents also strove towards a rigorous intellectual life, both polite and informal. Virginia Woolf was the daughter of the Editor of the *Dictionary of National Biography*, sister of a post-impressionist painter, and part of a milieu that she first archly complained of: 'the dominion Bloomsbury exercises over the sane & insane alike seems to be sufficient to turn the brains of the most robust'; then amiably continued in her diary entry, 'Happily, I'm "Bloomsbury" myself, and thus immune.'[16]

In the series of memoirs written by the Aikins, they present themselves as a model intellectual family, and as the educators of the great men of the nineteenth century: Malthus and Lord Denham, among others, form part of a national network of Warrington-educated public persons. And when there was a scandal in the family – the publication of Anna Barbauld's *Eighteen Hundred and Eleven* – her family manned the inkstands to defend the piece. Her niece Lucy wrote a long and passionate apologia for the poem: 'She like Cassandra, was the prophetess of woe; at the time, she was heard perhaps with less incredulity, but the event has happily discredited her vaticination in every point . . . [Who would doubt] for a moment that this strain was dictated by the heart of a true patriot, a heart which feared because it fondly loved.'[17]

The different paths of the Aikins and the Wollstonecraft-Godwin-Shelleys mark out different lines in the cultural politics of radicalism and liberalism, as they emerged from the polymorphously perverse world of the 1780s and 1790s. The Aikins' liberalism was rooted deeply in and bounded by their religious convictions, within a social order underwritten by the economic implantation of Dissenters as well as by the pedagogic and scientific work they undertook outside Oxbridge. The Godwin-Shelleys' radicalism burst the bounds of piety and convention, and they didn't look back.

Though not great friends, Anna Barbauld and Mary Wollstonecraft were both in the circle published by and dining at Joseph Johnson's in London in the early 1790s. Thirty years later, in the 1820s, Lucy Aikin was on occasion present in the same houses as the recently widowed Mary Godwin Shelley, but now they were divided by the tundra of respectability. Amongst the Aikin memoirists, the anti-Wollstonecraft tendency was remembered as a family inheritance: in 1834, Lucy Aikin wrote that 'It was [Godwin's] misfortune or folly to adopt, with other debasing views of the French school, their contempt of chastity in women.'[18] Thirty years later still, in 1867, Anna Laetitia LeBreton wrote that 'The ladies of my family [that is her great-aunt Anna Barbauld and her aunt Lucy Aikin], though great admirers of Mrs Godwin's writings, were too correct in their conduct to visit her, and the same objection was felt to Mrs Shelley.'[19] 'When my aunt Lucy was at a large party . . . Mrs Daniel Gaskell . . . brought up Mrs Shelley to introduce her to my aunt [that is, Lucy Aikin] . . . my aunt, however, resolutely turned her back on the fair widow.'[20] The declension of the Aikins' radicalism seems to have been accompanied by a rise in their moral delicacy. By 1831, Lucy Aikin treats Godwin more judiciously:

You will read, I think with interest, and in part with great satisfaction, Godwin's new volume, entitled *Thoughts on Man*. Probably, it will prove the last fruit of his mind, for he is now rather nearer eighty than seventy, and I believe declining. With all his extravagances of opinion, some which in the early part of his career did considerable mischief and threatened more, I have always entertained a respect for some parts of his character, as well as a high admiration of his powers; and felt sincere pity for the long misfortunes in which partly his own errors, but still more that proscription of society, have involved him.[21]

But in the late 1780s and early 1790s, Barbauld and Mary Wollstonecraft occupied cognate places in reputation.

Anna Barbauld, like Godwin and other London writers, moved in more than one metropolitan social circle. She often dined at the Portman Square house of Elizabeth Montagu, where she observed 'the imposing union of literature and fashion'; but it was while 'under the humbler roof' of her friend and publisher, Joseph Johnson, that she saw 'a chosen knot of lettered equals'.[22] There is no doubt but that Johnson's circle was lively, daring, artistic as well as politically radical, and that it exerted a powerful influence on rationalist women such as Wollstonecraft and Mary Hays. In Johnson's dining room Fuseli hung his painting *The Nightmare*, so Johnson's dining club of discursive rationality was overseen by the Romantic passions of that frightening and compelling dreamscape.[23] Barbauld, along with her brother John, turned her hand to the public issues of religious toleration, the slave trade, and the French Revolution, and made passionate claims for them in both poetry and prose. Walpole called her the 'virago Barbauld'; and in 1791 she had become a 'poissoniere', a 'prophetess' ready to exercise her 'talons'.[24]

She made a significant intervention into the pamphlet war around the proposed repeal of the Corporation and Test Acts. Barbauld's *Address to the Opposers of the Repeal of the Corporation and Test Acts* was reprinted by Johnson twice in 1790. Her pamphlet explicitly linked the domestic political questions of religious toleration that had originated in the English Revolution of the 1640s with the international ones of 1789. Condemning the opposition to the repeal, she reminds her readers: 'England, who has held the torch [to illuminate France] is mortified to see it blaze brighter in [France's] hands.'[25] Johnson's pamphlet press offered anonymity – he published over fifty pamphlets on the issue of toleration – and this anonymity cut across the sexual division of intellectual labour that Barbauld had endorsed whilst at Warrington.[26] Dissenters such as Barbauld felt that events in France would help the domestic struggle for civic entitlement. The result was, however, quite the opposite: as Dissenters pressed their case, they were maligned in the press as threats to national security. Barbauld's polemic was printed within endpapers advertising other republican Dissenting pamphleteers, including the Warrington tutors Gilbert Wakefield and Joseph Priestley. Before the year was out, Barbauld's address had itself become the object of a set of 'strictures' by William Keate, rector of Laverton.[27] She was thus fully engaged in the public debate, as a 'citizen' rather than as an 'Authoress'. In her address, Barbauld articulates the enlightened rationality that aims for a universal constituency: 'We wish to bury every name of distinction in the common appellation of Citizen.' This address is grounded in a sense of intellectual entitlement, as Barbauld claims her right to speak of a 'certain, sure operation of increasing light and knowledge'.[28] Barbauld passionately insists that 'Truth is of a very intolerant spirit. She will not make any compromise with Error.'[29] She had brought with her from her Warrington education her focus on the universal and the rational, and from her Palgrave pedagogy the importance of language that is vibrant and emotional, but now her style was ignited by the excitement of current events. By the later 1780s and 1790s, much of the Aikin family and the Warrington community had dispersed throughout the metropolitan area, and they caught the new, more emotional language of reform. While Rochemont and Anna Barbauld lived in Church Row, Joseph Priestley and Gilbert Wakefield were living in Hackney, and John Aikin moved to London in 1792, after being hounded out of Norfolk for his political positions after the defeat of the 1790 bill for the repeal of the Corporation and Test Acts.

DUTIFUL DAUGHTER, DUTIFUL NIECE

The reputation of the Aikin-Barbaulds moved through three distinct periods: firstly, the more intimate period of radical Dissenters, or, as Lucy Aikin calls it, Free Dissent, when the still-marginal life of sectarian Dissenters produced an internal community based on a humanistic doctrine; secondly, the period of domestic reform, when Free Dissenters became increasingly committed to exploring the link between the French Revolution and Dissent, mediated through the domestic reform movements. This pathway became notorious when the Hackney Dissenters welcomed the French Revolution. The third period leads up to the passage of the first Reform Bill of 1832, when the Aikins foregrounded themselves as, most important, a literary family. Of course, many of the radical Dissenters had been broken by the radical years. The Aikins' great friend and publisher, Joseph Johnson, was tried and imprisoned for publishing Gilbert Wakefield's excoriation of the Bishop of Llandaff.[30] Wakefield, long an interlocutor and friend of the Aikin family, also spent a year in prison and died soon after in 1801. Just after Wakefield's release, John Aikin wrote and published in the *Monthly Magazine* a poem to him in the temper of defeated Jacobinism, in which he invited Wakefield to 'Cease then, my Friend, thy generous hopeless aim', put aside his politics, and return to a more amiable muse:

> Take serene
> The tranquil blessings that thy lot affords,
> And in the soothing voice of friendship drown
> The groans and shouts, and triumphs of the world.

The passionate radical and internationalist aim of '*fraternité*' was turning into the more local and familiar idea of friendship, a modified version of Warrington 'conversation' imbued with an elegiac sentimentalism. The stalwart Wakefield replied in a poem, also published in the *Monthly Magazine*, in which he refused to take that route, vowing still to 'Front the grim visage of despotic power, / Lawless, self-will'd, fierce, merciless, corrupt'. By 1800 the vocabulary of passionate reformism sounds old. Wakefield died before the end of 1801.[31] The following year John Aikin declared: 'I am cured of all theoretical ideas of reform.'[32] John Aikin then moves from radicalism to liberality in religion and politics and promotes the *Monthly Magazine* as a benign diffusion and redirection of the family's commitments. Literature shifts from being the vehicle of principles to being the principle of liberality itself.

In that cause memoir writing became as central to the family's vocation as were their public reform causes. To my reckoning, the most interesting of the Aikin memoirists is Anna Barbauld's niece Lucy Aikin. She has a very lively personal voice which makes her an excellent writer of the social genres of private lives: biography, memoir, and letter. And Lucy Aikin's voice is formidably nineteenth century: she is respectable and proud and snobbish, but she also bears traces of her family's liberality as a defender of women's rights: 'When I was a little girl', she writes, 'I used to battle with boys about the Rights of Woman.'[33] She has Benthamite leanings – 'I confess that the "greatest good of the greatest number" is what alone is entitled to consideration' – but admits her feelings cannot be made to match up to what she calls that 'incontrovertible theory', 'when I reflect on the blindness, the ignorance, the gross selfishness of that majority – that headlong majority'. She sounds very different, indeed, from the generation of her father and her aunt, on whom nonetheless she is dependent as a literary legatee.

Lucy Aikin takes on two related tasks in her memoirs of her father and her aunt Barbauld: to establish the family's importance as literary rather than political; and to vindicate her father's rather poorer performance in the literary vocation than his sister, Anna Barbauld. But Lucy Aikin's memorial work was also a way of developing her own literary vocation. Her attempts to enter the literary world as a poet and fiction writer herself were not, in fact, very successful. In 1810, at a time when Anna Barbauld had been silent poetically for some years, Lucy published a volume of *Epistles on Women* (1810) – a survey of women's conditions over time – which was neither widely nor positively reviewed, and the miscellaneous poems attached were described in the *Critical Review* as 'being stuffed with epithets and receding only from prose in the obscurity of their ideas and the strutting pomp of their diction'.[34] Anna Barbauld's *Eighteen Hundred and Eleven*, her 'westward the course of empire' poem of British decay and American advancement, written the year after Lucy's volume appeared, is an oddly visionary and empirical view of the fortunes of empire through the historical genre of the ruin poem. 'Thy world, Columbus, shall be free', she writes.[35] Barbauld is able to imagine and even welcome the supercession of the British Empire – something that makes her kin to other liberal writers such as Constantin-François Volney and Percy Bysshe Shelley. We cannot know precisely what gave her the confidence to offer her polemic; in part it may have been the psychological privilege of advancing age. It is true that she had written in 1804 that 'it is equally true of books as of their authors, that one generation passeth away and another cometh', but her niece's volume was criticized, not for its politics, but for its bad poetry. But Barbauld's poem was formally anachronistic in 1812, and it embraced those Enlightenment principles of internationalism that could have no appeal to a public that had been almost continuously at war since 1793. Linked to the optimistic fatalism of her internationalism was Anna Barbauld's political boldness, which elicited even more aggressive reviews than did Lucy's fairly anodyne *Epistles*. Shortly thereafter Lucy wrote a painfully clichéd novel, *Lorimer*, whose hero, wrote the *Critical Review*, 'Miss Aikin launches, at the outset, into such depth of mystery as would inflame our interest on behalf of the most insignificant grub, that ever wore a pair of breeches and a stick.' Lucy's reviews, though devastating, nonetheless welcomed the newly published Aikin as part of the dynasty:

Upon the whole, however, we think very highly of Miss Aikin's talents. Her mind is evidently well cultivated, and stored with elegant and useful information: she has all the good sense and justness of thinking on moral and political subjects which we should expect in the daughter of Dr Aikin, and though her poetical powers are not of the higher order, she is fully entitled to the praise of an elegant and accomplished versifier.[36]

Not only did the Aikin family present themselves as a literary family, but their work was read as part of an intergenerational literary project.

Lucy Aikin was, however, a talented historical writer. Her 1818 *Memoirs of the Court of Queen Elizabeth* were widely read and reprinted throughout the nineteenth century, going through six editions by 1874. She went on to write *Memoirs of the Court of James I* (1822) and of *Charles I* (1833). And she argued that there was a dearth of the *kind* of writing 'in that class which forms the glory of French literature – memoir'. She was not aiming to produce history, but to capture 'the biography, the literature, and the manners of the period'.[37] With this confidence and sense of what a memoir might accomplish, she began writing family reminiscences that stressed the literary inheritance. Her memoir of her father begins with a description of how he was 'imbued indelibly with that love of letters which became at once the ornament and safeguard of his youth, and the occupation and solace of every succeeding period of his life'.[38] She quite extraordinarily fashions him as a precursor to the landscape poetry of her own period: 'Many causes were secretly conspiring to excite that passion for natural scenery, and all the objects connected with rural life, by which Englishmen are now distinguished above the members of any other civilised community . . . Mr Aikin, among others, proved a prosperous missionary in the cause.'[39] In fact, John Aikin's *Poems* (1791) make a poor showing in this respect. Few of them make use of the landscape at all, and those that do betray nothing of a sympathetic relation between observer and objects observed, nor do they suggest a relationship between the speaking identity and the natural world, so characteristic of the poetry of sensibility and Romanticism.[40] Lucy Aikin also writes of Anna Barbauld's poetic on the model of Wordsworth, updating her aunt's poetic voice for the world of the 1820s: '[Barbauld's] active imagination', she writes, 'represented all objects tinged with hues "unborrowed from the eye".'[41]

One recurring motif in her memoirs of both her father and Anna Barbauld is Lucy's suggestion that John Aikin has been undervalued in a world that spends too much time crediting his sister, Anna Barbauld. Philip Le Breton's memoir of Lucy Aikin reveals that Lucy herself felt defeated by her aunt Barbauld's judgements: 'She called me "Little Dunce"; the reproach sank deep, and its effect was certainly unfavourable . . . it filled me with a sense of incurable deficiency.'[42]

The story circulated for some time of Charles James Fox complimenting John Aikin on the essays of his joint venture with Anna, *Evenings at Home*. Each time Fox mentioned a particular essay, John Aikin was forced to answer 'That [one] is my sister's', until, Samuel Rogers writes in his *Table-Talk*, 'Fox thought it best to say no more about the book'.[43] Lucy Aikin writes that Mrs Barbauld 'also supplied some valuable contributions to Dr Aikin's popular book for children, *Evenings at Home*, the first volume of which appeared in 1792: but her share in this work has generally been supposed much greater than in fact it was: of the ninety-nine pieces of which it consisted, fourteen only are hers'.[44]

There is something strangely artless about the way Lucy presents the chip on her father's shoulder as if it were a medal. It becomes clear that John

Aikin doesn't think he has gotten himself a good place in society: he retains an awareness of 'the indisputable fact [that] he had not yet risen to his just level in society'.[45] It's easy to see how difficult it might have been for him, given the professional success of his father and the literary success of his sister. So, in 1784, John Aikin went to Leyden and took his medical degree. At the end of that year he and his family went off to Yarmouth. But Lucy is keenly aware that this was a bad placement in 'a commercial town of the second rank'.[46] In 1785 John Aikin decided to move to London, but after only four months he was called back to Yarmouth, since one of the older doctors in town had given up his practice. Lucy quotes from a letter he wrote which, she tells the reader, is written in a 'tone of habitual contentedness, and also affords some interesting notices of the pursuits and habits of the writer': 'I should now and then feel a little disappointment at the loss of the brilliant and lively prospects ["my London expedition"] afforded, did I not immediately call to mind the circumstances of midwifery, – rivalship, – intrigue, – meanness, – hazard, – and family sickness, which must have accompanied them; and then I perfectly acquiesce in the change.'[47] The aftermath of the rejection of the law to repeal the Test and Corporation Acts in 1790 led him to become increasingly an intellectual activist. Yarmouth polite society turned against him, and in 1792 the family moved to Broad Street, London. The London family circle was established, which included Anna and Rochemont, Priestley and Wakefield. John Aikin was clearly anxious about his status in the world: 'Yet what man of forty-five can cast his part anew in life, – and after mediocrity and literary leisure have been my darling objects so long, how can I ever change them for their opposites?'[48] In 1793, John Aikin and Anna Barbauld produced *Evenings at Home*: 'The volumes of this work appeared successively during several subsequent years, and amounted at length to six; Mrs Barbauld contributing in the whole about half a volume to the collection, and my father supplying the rest.'[49]

John Aikin published two sets of *Letters from a Father to His Son*, volume I written in 1792 and 1793, and volume II in 1798 and 1799, published in 1796 and 1800 respectively, by Joseph Johnson. In volume II, Aikin gives a perfectly Romantic introduction to his state of mind in *this* state of the state.

The agreeable spectacle of rural nature has, indeed, at a peculiarly seasonable time engaged my attention, when otherwise I could scarcely have avoided fixing my mind too earnestly on the desolating prospects which the late train of human affairs has presented to the lover of mankind. What disappointment of elevated hopes! What heart-rending scenes of public and private calamity! What audacity of crime! What triumph of violence and injustice![50]

In 1796, his literary ambitions were re-channelled by taking on the *Monthly Magazine*.

The long and rivalrous relationship between Anna Barbauld and John Aikin, mediated through Lucy's depiction of them both, provides a useful counter-example to the brother–sister relationship between Dorothy and William Wordsworth, which for some time has been emblematic of the dominance of the brother poet in Romanticism. Here the roles are reversed, and the disappointed brother cannot redirect his envy into sentimental love. Lucy approvingly cites John Aikin's 1793 sonnet to his sister, in which he ventriloquizes Anna's muse: 'Did I, Laetitia, lend my choicest lays, / And crown thy youthful head with freshest bays, / That all th' expectance of thy full-grown year / Should lie inert and fruitless'?[51] Lucy Aikin's memoir interestingly reveals and conceals her own ambivalence about her father's and her aunt's literary vocations.

Lucy Aikin's writing is also interesting for the window she opens onto the lead-up to, the passage through, and the let-down after the Reform Bill of 1832, giving us a personal view of how reform looked to a liberal middle-class Lady of Letters. Lucy was a descendant of the Free Dissenters, yet the *DNB* (old style) dryly points out that her own experiences as a Unitarian 'gave her a liberal, but by no means tolerant, political creed'.[52] In her long correspondence with William Ellery Channing, she follows the movement of the Reform Bill with a combination of pride and horror. Reading her expostulations against what she calls the 'low and ignorant, the selfish, and on the whole, not moral classes of whom these associations of trades unions are formed' and her fear of the poor – 'lazy, luxurious, discontented, lying and worthless', made me realize that while Anna Aikin would have dealt with servants in her various households, she never had to confront the possibility of the labouring poor becoming enfranchised along with Dissenters and Catholics. Of course that didn't happen in Lucy Aikin's time either, but as the pressure for a Parliamentary bill became greater, and as liberal orators relied on the power of city and country labourers to carry the reform, her fear rises and overcomes her liberality. She rails against workers and frame-brakers, hates slavery and its injustices but sees no parallel with the labouring poor: 'Shall I begin tea-drinking with my maudlin washerwoman?' she asks Channing. 'Will you invite to your table the bow-legged snip who made your coat? How soon, alas! at this rate would the rivulet of refinement be swallowed up in the ocean of vulgarity.'[53]

Is this just a sad tale of radicalism becoming respectability? Well . . . yes it is, as most nineteenth-century stories are – for example, polite sociability as a wing of reform in the Warrington generation does, in the context of the nineteenth-century labour movement's claims for autonomy, at least for Lucy Aikin, become a barrier or bulwark of refinement against the ungainly majority; and what is idealized as the free exchange of conversation in the generation of Barbauld and Wollstonecraft looks like rudeness and immorality to the next:

> My youth was spent among the disciples or fellow-labourers of Price or Priestley, the descendants of Dr John Taylor, the Arian, or in the society of that most amiable of men, Dr Enfield. Amongst these there was no rigorism. Dancing, cards, the theatre, were all held lawful in moderation; in *manners* the free dissenters, as they were called, came much nearer the Church than to their own stricter brethren, yet in *doctrine no* sect departed so far from the Establishment. At the period of the French Revolution, and especially after the Birmingham riots, this sect distinguished itself by the vehemence of its democratical spirit, and becoming in a manner a faction, as well as a sect, political as well as religious animosity became arrayed against it, and I now remember with disgust, not without compunction, the violent contempt and hatred in which, in common with almost all the young, and not a few of the more mature of that set, I conceived it meritorious to indulge towards the Church and the aristocrats.[54]

Yet Lucy's memoirs do bestow immortality upon the generation of her parents, and in memorializing them she makes them and their coterie worthy of the same admiration and cultural study as the glittering courts of Elizabeth I and Charles I – the dutiful niece dragging the radical Dissenters from the republic into the aristocracy of letters.

The notoriety of the Godwin-Wollstonecraft-Shelley family was sustained through the power of their political, philosophical, and poetic arguments with the world and themselves. The Aikins' publicity performed quite different functions, for themselves and for their world. Unlike the Godwin-Shelleys, who inhabited and enjoyed an 'outsider' position, the Aikins aimed to produce themselves as a 'central' family within middle-class English society. Their intellectual focus shifts from religion to reform politics to 'literature' as a form of liberal discourse with changing civic liberty for Dissenters and with the changing function of the periodical press, and puts the third generation in a centrally respectable liberal position. There is some very good poetry in Barbauld's oeuvre, and although Lucy Aikin's poetry isn't very good, her memoirs of English royalty are interesting. And while they didn't give us *Frankenstein*, the Aikin family did publish a lot of other writers' work, including that of Coleridge and Southey and Lamb, along with reviews of Wollstonecraft and Robinson. Through their self-publicity the Aikins also facilitated other and often stronger writers and liberal politicians. In 1832, Lucy Aikin provides an anecdote of how

Anna Barbauld's influence has permeated the unconscious of even the great men of government: Thomas Denman, Lord Chancellor in 1832, 'cherishes her memory most religiously. In a great public entertainment where I saw him last year', Barbauld's niece Lucy writes in her memoirs, 'he came up and said with a look of delight, "I dreamed of Mrs Barbauld only last night"!'[55]

NOTES

1. Recent interest and work on Barbauld has included: Isobel Armstrong, 'The Gush of the Feminine: How Can We Read Women's Poetry of the Romantic Period?', in Paula Feldman and Theresa M. Kelley (eds.), *Romantic Women Writers: Voices and Countervoices* (Hanover, N.H.: University of New England Press, 1995), pp. 13–32; William McCarthy, '"We Hoped the Woman was Going to Appear": Repression, Desire, and Gender in Anna Laetitia Barbauld's Early Poems', in Feldman and Kelley (eds.), *Romantic Women Writers*, pp. 113–37; Eleanor Ty, 'Engendering a Female Subject: Mary Robinson's (Re)Presentations of the Self', *English Studies in Canada* 21 (1995), 407–33; William Keach, 'A Regency Prophecy and the End of Anna Barbauld's Career', *Studies in Romanticism* 33 (1994), 569–77; William Keach, 'Barbauld, Romanticism, and the Survival of Dissent', in Anne Janowitz (ed.), *Romanticism and Gender* (Leicester: English Association, 1998), pp. 44–61; John Guillory, 'The English Common Place: Lineages of the Topographical Genre', *Critical Quarterly* 33 (1991), 3–27; Anne Janowitz, 'Amiable and Radical Sociability: Anna Barbauld's "Free Familiar Conversation"', in Gillian Russell and Clara Tuite (eds.), *Romantic Sociability: Social Networks and Literary Culture in Britain, 1770–1840* (Cambridge: Cambridge University Press, 2003), pp. 62–81; Anne Janowitz, *Women Romantic Poets: Anna Barbauld and Mary Robinson* (Plymouth: Writers and Their Works, 2004).
2. Gilbert Wakefield, *Memoirs* (London: Hodson, 1792); Lucy Aikin, *Memoir of John Aikin, M.D.*, 2 vols. (London: Baldwin, Craddock, and Joy, 1823); Lucy Aikin and Anna Laetitia Barbauld, *The Works of Anna Laetitia Barbauld, with a Memoir by Lucy Aikin*, 2 vols. (London: Longman, 1825); Anna Le Breton, *Memoirs of Mrs. Barbauld* (London: G. Bell, 1874); Betsy Rodgers, *A Georgian Chronicle: Mrs. Barbauld and Her Family* (London: Methuen, 1958); Gilbert Wakefield, *Memoirs* (London: Hodson, 1792).
3. Isobel Armstrong, *Victorian Poetry: Poetry, Poetics, and Politics* (London: Routledge, 1993), pp. 29–33.
4. *Monthly Repository* 17 (1822), 771.
5. William Godwin, *Memoir of the Author of 'A Vindication of the Rights of Woman'* (London: Johnson, 1798).
6. H. McLachlan, *Warrington Academy: Its History and Influence* (Manchester: Chetham Society, 1943), p. 23.
7. Joseph Priestley, *Memoirs* (Bath: Adams and Dart, 1970), p. 88.

8. William Enfield, *A Funeral Sermon, Occasioned by the Death of the Late Rev. John Aikin, D.D.* (Warrington: W. Eyres, for J. Johnson London, 1781), p. 18.

9. William Woodfall, *Monthly Review* 48 (1773), 54–9, 133–7 (133).

10. Anna Laetitia Barbauld, *Selected Poetry and Prose*, ed. William McCarthy and Elizabeth Kraft (Ontario, Canada: Broadview Press, 2002), pp. 53, ll. 95–6, 109–10 (p. 51, ii. 55–6).

11. John Guillory, 'The English Common Place: Lineages of the Topographical Genre', *Critical Quarterly* 33 (1991), 8.

12. David Garrick, *Annual Register* 18 (1775), cited in Rodgers, *Georgian Chronicle*, p. 61.

13. Gilbert Wakefield's memorandum is cited in Henry A. Bright, 'A Historical Sketch of Warrington Academy', *Transactions of the Historic Society of Lancashire and Cheshire* 11 (1859), 22, 28.

14. Woodfall, *Monthly Review* 48 (1773), 133.

15. Samuel Taylor Coleridge, *Table Talk*, ed. Carl Woodring, 2 vols. (Princeton: Princeton University Press, 1990), vol. 1, pp. 564–5; Bright, 'Historical Sketch', p. 21.

16. Virginia Woolf, *Diary*, ed. Anne Olivier Bell, vol. 1, 1915–19 (London: Penguin, 1979), p. 106.

17. Lucy Aikin, *Works of Anna Barbauld, with a Memoir*, vol. 1, p. 1.

18. Philip Hemery Le Breton (ed.), *Memoirs, Miscellanies and Letters of the Late Lucy Aikin* (London: Longman Green, 1864), p. 298.

19. Anna Le Breton, *Memoirs of Mrs. Barbauld* (London: G. Bell, 1874), p. 81.

20. Rodgers, *Georgian Chronicle*, p. 189.

21. Le Breton (ed.), *Memoirs of Lucy Aikin*, p. 226.

22. Lucy Aikin, *Works of Anna Barbauld*, vol. 1, pp. xxxii–xxxiii.

23. Leslie F. Chard, 'Joseph Johnson: Father of the Book Trade', *Bulletin of the New York Public Library* 79 (1975), 51–82 (63).

24. W. S. Lewis (ed.), *Horace Walpole's Correspondence* (New Haven: Yale University Press, 1937–), vol. XI, pp. 169, 320.

25. Anna Barbauld, *Selected Poetry and Prose*, ed. William McCarthy and Elizabeth Kraft (Ontario: Broadview Press, 2002), p. 279.

26. Gerald P. Tyson, *Joseph Johnson* (Iowa City: University of Iowa Press, 1979), p. 93.

27. William Keate, *A Free Examination of Dr. Price's and Dr. Priestley's Sermons, with a post-script containing some strictures upon 'An Address to the Opposers of the Repeal of the Corporation and Test Acts'* (London: Dodsley, 1790), pp. 55–64.

28. Barbauld, *Selected Poetry and Prose*, p. 276.

29. Ibid., p. 269.

30. Tyson, *Johnson*, p. 163; see also Jane Worthington Smyser, 'The Trial and Imprisonment of Joseph Johnson, Bookseller', *Bulletin of the New York Public Library* 77 (1974), 418–35, and Chard, 'Joseph Johnson', pp. 51–82.

31. John Aikin, 'To Gilbert Wakefield, A.B. on His Liberation from Prison', *Monthly Magazine* (June 1801), 422; Gilbert Wakefield, 'To John Aikin,

M. D.', *Monthly Magazine* (July 1801), 513. See also Lucy Aikin, 'To the Memory of Gilbert Wakefield', *Monthly Magazine* (October 1801), 220–1.

32. Lucy Aikin, *John Aikin*, vol. 1, p. 247.
33. Le Breton (ed.), *Memoirs of Lucy Aikin*, p. 25.
34. *Critical Review*, series 3, 23 (1811), 426.
35. Barbauld, *Selected Poetry and Prose*, p. 173.
36. *Critical Review*, s3, 23 (1811), 418–26.
37. Lucy Aikin, *Memoirs of the Court of Queen Elizabeth*, 2 vols. (London: Longman Hurst, 1818), vol. 1, pp. ii, vii.
38. Lucy Aikin, *John Aikin*, vol. 1, p. 4.
39. Ibid., vol. 1, p. 3.
40. John Aikin, *Poems* (London: Johnson, 1791).
41. Lucy Aikin, *Works of Anna Barbauld*, vol. 1, p. x.
42. Le Breton (ed.), *Memoirs of Lucy Aikin*, p. x.
43. Samuel Rogers, *Table-Talk*, ed. Rev. Alexander Dyce (London: Rogers, 1887), p. 82.
44. Lucy Aikin, *Works of Anna Barbauld*, vol. 1, p. xxxvi.
45. Lucy Aikin, *John Aikin*, vol. 1, p. 63.
46. Ibid., vol. 1, p. 100.
47. Ibid., vol. 1, p. 114.
48. Ibid., vol. 1, p. 153.
49. Ibid., vol. 1, p. 157.
50. John Aikin, *Letters from a Father to His Son*, 2 vols. (London: Johnson, 1796–1800), vol. 11, p. 3.
51. John Aikin, *Poems*, p. 75.
52. Leslie Stephen (ed.), *Dictionary of National Biography*, 67 vols. (London: Smith Elder, 1885–1903), vol. 1, p. 187.
53. Le Breton (ed.), *Memoirs of Lucy Aikin*, pp. 307, 234.
54. Ibid., p. 196.
55. Ibid., p. 274.

CHAPTER 5

Holding Proteus: William Godwin in his letters

Pamela Clemit

The 1980s and 1990s saw a transformation in the reading of prose literature of the eighteenth and early nineteenth centuries. This transformation
was pioneered by enterprising academic editors, working closely with the
forward-thinking London publishing house Pickering and Chatto, and
began with the publication of a series of multi-volume scholarly editions of
prose writers eminent in their own day, but largely unavailable to modern
readers. For students of literature and history, a key event was the publication in 1989 of *The Works of Mary Wollstonecraft*, which brought together
Wollstonecraft's entire oeuvre for the first time.[1] This edition was closely
followed by *The Collected Novels and Memoirs of William Godwin, The Novels and Selected Works of Mary Shelley, The Works of Maria Edgeworth, The
Works of Thomas De Quincey*, and many others.[2] Further landmark editions
are in progress – notably *The Works of Charlotte Smith*.[3] Large-scale editions
such as these, each 'dedicated to an archaeological task of recovery',[4] have
provided the foundations for much of the rehistoricizing of authors, texts,
and contexts that has distinguished recent critical and interpretative study
of the Romantic era.

Marilyn Butler was in at the start of this new phase in Romantic editing,
and its present expansiveness owes much to her timely recognition of the
need for annotated, high-quality editions as a prerequisite to any critical
repossession of the literary past. As co-editor of the works of Wollstonecraft,
co-author of the critical introduction to Godwin's collected novels, and,
especially, general editor of Edgeworth's works, she has played a major role
in changing our preconceptions about Romantic prose in all its forms.
Significantly, Butler's editorial achievements have not been confined to
major scholarly editions: she has edited a number of paperback editions for
classroom use – one of which, *Burke, Paine, Godwin, and the Revolution
Controversy*, has opened up an entire field to further editorial and critical
exploration.[5] This wealth of editorial experience has given Butler a keen

sense of the advantages special to the genre. As she wrote in 1995: 'We must have true scholarly editions . . . not only to grasp the internal dynamics of an individual career, but to understand its group dynamics, its inter-relations with society and history.'[6] Scholarly editions are important, Butler argues, not just because they establish definitive or near-definitive texts, but because of their capacity to open up the text's range of external reference: through apparatus such as explanatory notes, introductions, and collations, they provide the biographical, literary, historical, and inter-textual information necessary for a properly contextualized reading. A scholarly edition alone, in Butler's view, can perform all these functions.

Nowhere is the transformative potential of editorial repossession more evident than in the case of the radical philosopher, novelist, and social thinker William Godwin. Only a few of his works, until recently, were available to modern critical scrutiny. The publication in 1992 of the Pickering Masters edition of his novels, together with his major political, philosophical, and educational works, helped to re-establish Godwin as a central presence in the literary and historical culture of the Romantic era. In collecting for the first time all six of his full-length novels, this edition highlighted Godwin's innovative use of the novel 'to write an alternative form of history, a history of mentalities' and offered special insights into a key Romantic literary grouping, which included his first wife Mary Wollstonecraft, his daughter Mary Shelley, and his son-in-law Percy Bysshe Shelley.[7] However, the inclusion in volume 1 of a few items from Godwin's massive archive of correspondence – five letters of moral and intellectual advice to Shelley, written in 1812 – made the absence of any scholarly edition of his letters even more striking.[8]

Some 1,200 of Godwin's outgoing letters survive, but only a small number has been published. A selection (with unreliable texts) appeared in C. Kegan Paul's *William Godwin: His Friends and Contemporaries* (1876), a 'life and letters' study commissioned by Godwin's grandson, Sir Percy Florence Shelley, and his wife Jane, Lady Shelley, as part of their efforts to safeguard the reputations of their controversial forebears. The twelve-month correspondence between Godwin and Wollstonecraft was published in *Godwin & Mary: Letters of William Godwin and Mary Wollstonecraft* (1967), edited by Ralph M. Wardle. A selection of Godwin's other letters may be found in *Shelley and His Circle*.[9] As Stuart Curran observed in a review of Godwin's *Collected Novels*, these disparate publications suggest what might be constituted if Godwin's letters were available in their entirety: 'an intellectual record of the age commensurate with that of Coleridge's letters, which have been long accessible in six fat volumes'.[10]

A full edition of Godwin's letters is now under way.[11] No other scholarly
genre can take us so intimately into a writer's personal and creative life, or
his historical and cultural milieu. This genre is especially suited to a literary
figure of such versatility and range as Godwin. Although Godwin is often
treated as if he were a contemporary of Wordsworth and Coleridge, he was
almost the same age as Blake, and he outlived all the major Romantic writers,
apart from Wordsworth. His letters, as a record of his maturity as well as of
his origins and formation, have a special richness. They document a larger
shift in cultural sensibility, from the uncompromising rationalism of the
French revolutionary era to a Romantic emphasis on sympathy and feeling,
as reflected through the changing consciousness of one individual. Kelvin
Everest, in his annotations to the Longman edition of Shelley's poems,
discerned a fleeting, playful identification between Godwin and 'Proteus
old' in *Prometheus Unbound* (1820).[12] Proteus was the ancient, prophetic
sea-god who eluded questioners by assuming many different shapes. If
he were held fast, throughout his struggles, eventually he would resume
his original state and yield his wisdom. Holding Proteus, through all his
changing forms, seems a fitting image for the project of editing the letters
of Godwin, that consummate Romantic shape-shifter, who regarded the
change of opinion as a moral duty, in cases of further enlightenment, and
who prided himself, above all, on his intellectual mobility.

'Do you not feel how very inadequately epistolary communication supplies
the place of oral discussion?', wrote Godwin at the end of a brief letter
to his new friend Thomas Wedgwood, dated 7 November 1795.[13] Such a
question reflects Godwin's early belief in colloquial discussion – what he
called in *An Enquiry concerning Political Justice* (1793) 'the collision of mind
with mind' – as the best means by which social and moral improvement
could be achieved.[14] This belief in the reformist power of social interchange
was a central feature of the culture of English Rational Dissent in which
Godwin was educated. In Richard Price's words, 'It is only . . . by diligent
enquiry, by free discussion and the collision of different sentiments, that
knowledge can be increased, truth struck out, and the dignity of our species
promoted.'[15] The Rational Dissenters did not hold to a unified doctrinal
position, but they shared the ideal of a free public sphere, in which all were
able to think, debate, and publish without State interference.[16] Although
Rational Dissent went into decline by the end of the 1790s, as many of
its leaders retired, died, or went into exile, Godwin maintained a lifelong
commitment to the ideal of like-minded citizens assisting each other in the
pursuit of truth.

Despite his throwaway remark to Wedgwood, Godwin prized epistolary communication at least as highly as oral exchange. His education in
the traditions of Rational Dissent had given him a keen understanding
of the link between written records and a sense of communal identity,
together with a lifelong habit of personal account-keeping. So important
was epistolary communication to Godwin that by the end of November
1795 he had begun to make use of a portable letter-copying machine, a
gift from Wedgwood, inaugurating a lifelong habit of keeping duplicates,
either mechanical or scribal, of his outgoing letters.[17] By 1798, Godwin
had further modified his view of the 'inadequacies' of letter-writing. In a
letter to an unknown correspondent, dated 10 January, he admitted that
epistolary communication afforded scope for both philosophical discussion
and exploration of feeling: 'I am pleased with the style of writing we have
lately employed. I have more taste . . . for letters & conversations of feeling, than of discussion.'[18] By 1805, fresh from the completion of his third
full-length novel, *Fleetwood; or, The New Man of Feeling*, Godwin's views
had undergone a further shift. He positively welcomed the opportunity to
write what he called, in a letter to his second wife Mary Jane Godwin, dated
2 April, 'a little journal of my impressions & sensations'.[19] As the author
of books in the epistolary mode, Godwin knew that letters could never be
transparent windows into the soul – however much he might wish them to
be – but were always, to a greater or lesser extent, compositions, designed
for the particular audience that the writer has in mind. In documenting
the processes of thinking and feeling, letters offered him scope for a special
kind of self-presentation. As a record of his shaping of his 'impressions &
sensations' over three generations, Godwin's letters tell a story unmatched
by any of his other autobiographical documents.

Godwin's extant letters begin in 1782 with a draft to an unknown correspondent concerning a church dispute, which led to his expulsion from
the post of Dissenting minister at Stowmarket in April of that year.[20] The
latest letter so far identified, to John Hobart Caunter, is dated 18 March
1836, less than three weeks before Godwin's death, and concerns the publication of Mary Shelley's last novel, *Falkner* (1837).[21] In between, the letters
record the nuances of Godwin's intellectual, emotional, and psychological
development from his origins in provincial Dissent, through a decade of
metropolitan fame and notoriety as a radical philosopher, to his later years
as a prolific author, businessman, and father of an extraordinary literary
family. In a limited space it is possible only to suggest the multiple perspectives on Godwin's life, works, and times afforded by the letters. The
'private talk'[22] of this protean intellectual not only adds to our knowledge

of his individual career, but also increases our understanding of British social and cultural networks in the late eighteenth and early nineteenth centuries.

To begin with, Godwin's letters add a new dimension to his intellectual history. They document his efforts to live a life based on his advanced principles, charting his responses, more or less considered, to situations in which his key philosophical commitments – to unfettered enquiry, to disinterested benevolence, to unreserved social communication – were put to the test. In displaying the processes of thinking, as represented to different recipients, they reveal the contradictions, tensions, and ambiguities which became the substance of his creative writings. For example, following his marriage to Mary Wollstonecraft on 29 March 1797, Godwin's recognition that he had acted in opposition to his philosophical doctrines led him to justify his conduct in letters to friends. He wrote to Thomas Wedgwood on 19 April:

> Some persons have found an inconsistency between my practice in this instance & my doctrines. But I cannot see it. The do[ctrine] in my Political Justice is, that an attachment in some [degree per]manent, between two persons of opposite sexes is right, but that marriage, as practised in European countries, is wrong. I still adhere to that opinion. Nothing but a regard for the happiness of the individual, which I had no right to injure, could have induced me to submit to an institution, which I wish to see abolished, & which I would recommend to my fellow men never to practise, but with the greatest caution. Having done what I thought necessary for the peace & respectability of the individual, I hold myself no otherwise bound than I was before the ceremony took place.[23]

Here Godwin rehearses for Wedgwood's benefit the process by which the dictates of pure theory had been modified in the crucible of experience. Godwin's principled opposition to marriage gives way to what he perceives as the superior claim of his duty to promote the peace and respectability of an individual, that is, his love for Wollstonecraft – even if he has not yet found a vocabulary in which to express it. This super-subtle reasoning adumbrates a characteristic feature of Godwin's thought, showing that the distinction between theory and practice drawn in his philosophical writings extended to private as well as publicly political matters.

Yet Godwin's response to intractable daily experience was not always so measured. For example, his zealous pursuit of frankness and sincerity, as a means of moral enlightenment, appears fraught with contradictions. Godwin's commitment to unreserved communication is especially evident in letters to the many talented younger men to whom he became a substitute father and intellectual guide, and with whom he sought to create a rational community based on the ideal of collective moral supervision advocated in *Political Justice*.[24] In the early 1790s, this group included Thomas Abthorpe Cooper, his second cousin and a future star of the American stage, who lived in Godwin's household from the ages of twelve to sixteen, and George Dyson, one of Godwin's 'prime favourites',[25] a translator and amateur painter, who was a few years older than Cooper. When in March 1792 these two young men quarrelled, and Dyson struck Cooper, Godwin seized the opportunity to advance moral progress by writing a letter of reproof to Dyson:

> You say, you struck him from a feeling uncorrected by philosophy, & supported by an opinion that such modes of reproof were necessary for minds like his . . . & what good did you intend to his mind by striking him? . . . A blessed government will this be of philosophers who are to deal their blows whenever it shall please their high mightinesses to be in a passion. You have already perhaps done an irreparable injury to T's mind, who like all young people is very apt to judge of philosophy or any set of principles by the conduct of those who profess them. Ought we to beat our fellow mortals for our own sakes or for theirs? If for theirs, we ought at least maturely to deliberate in each instance whether beating be precisely the best mode of reforming their characters & meliorating their minds. The doctrine of beating is a very comfortable one, because it indulges all our indolent propensities . . . Not to add that as in your case it teaches us to indulge our passions, & persuades us that there is no reason for us to be very anxious to subdue the brutality of our nature.[26]

This letter shows the dilemmas which arose when Godwin's role as self-appointed arbiter of one young man's moral conduct was complicated by the presence of another. As well as demonstrating the high admonitory tone he often adopted in pursuit of the philosophical ideal of sincerity, it reveals his unphilosophical anger towards Dyson and his fierce protectiveness of Cooper. In addition, the sole surviving text of the letter is preserved in a draft in Cooper's hand, with Godwin's autograph corrections, suggesting that it was probably dictated to the person who forms its subject. This indicates that Godwin wished Cooper as well as Dyson to be instructed – and perhaps reassured – by his intervention. That Godwin was on occasions prepared to manipulate the doctrine of sincerity to serve his own ends is confirmed by a postscript: 'M[r] Holcroft has read what I have written[;] perhaps it would be of use to you to converse with him while the impression is fresh on his mind.' This statement is entirely consistent with Godwin's belief in collective moral supervision, but it also makes it hard for Dyson to do anything but admit he was in the wrong. In the dust and heat of lived experience, the exercise of frankness appears anything but disinterested.

As well as helping us to grasp the dynamics of Godwin's volatile household, the letters transform our understanding of his character as a family man. Ever since conservative reviewers caricatured the author of *Political Justice* as an embodiment of abstract reason, Godwin has been depicted as intellectually detached and stoically unemotional. As a result, we have little sense of his interiority: he is nearly always portrayed from the outside, whether being satirized by conservatives (Elizabeth Hamilton's 'Mr Vapour'), ridiculed by former admirers ('oh, most abominable nose!'), or dismissed by casual visitors ('Godwin's great head full of cold brains').[27] Yet many of Godwin's letters to friends and family reveal a man who, to reverse Wordsworth's formulation, not only thought long and deeply but also had powerful feelings. For example, when Wollstonecraft died on 10 September 1797, ten days after the birth of their daughter Mary, Godwin was too upset to attend the funeral. Instead he took refuge at the house of his old friend James Marshal, where he wrote a letter to Anthony Carlisle, the doctor who had nursed her to the end:

I am here sitting alone in Mr Marshal's lodgings during my wife's funeral. My mind is extremely sunk & languid. But I husband my thoughts, & shall do very well. I have been but once since you saw me, in a train of thought that gave me alarm. One of my wife's books now lies near me, but I avoid opening it. I took up a book on the education of children, but that impressed me too forcibly with my forlorn & disabled state with respect to the two poor animals left under my protection, & I threw it aside.

Nothing could be more soothing to my mind than to dwell in a long letter upon her virtues & accomplishments, & our mutual happiness past & in prospect. But the attractions of this subject are delusive, & I dare not trust myself with it.

. . . I may say to you on paper what I observed to you in our last interview, that I never, in the whole course of my life, met with the union of so clear & capacious an understanding, with so much goodness of heart & sweetness of manners.[28]

Letters such as this reveal a voice that has rarely been heard in British Romanticism: Godwin's vulnerable interior voice, registering the moment when his theories had come smack against the rock of experience; grappling with powerful emotions of love and loss; composing an image of Wollstonecraft in order to compose himself. Nine days later, he began work on *Memoirs of the Author of A Vindication of the Rights of Woman* (1798).

To his young friend Amelia Alderson (later Opie), Godwin candidly represented his worries about Wollstonecraft's two children: 'They have no mother, & I am afraid I am scarcely worth having as a father. I feel as if I were the most unfit person in the world for the business of education. She was the best qualified of any person I ever saw.'[29] Yet, judging by his letters,

Godwin was unnecessarily pessimistic in his low estimate of his ability to bring up Fanny Imlay, then aged three, and his new-born daughter Mary. When he visited Ireland in July and August 1800, he wrote regular letters home to Marshal, in whose care he left the children, anxiously requesting news about their daily activities: 'Every minute particular that you will be so good as to write to me respecting them, will be highly gratifying.'[30] Moreover, the letters included long passages written expressly for Fanny and Mary. For example, he wrote on 2–3 August:

Ah, poor Fanny, here is another letter from papa & what do you think he says about the little girls in it. Let me see! Would pretty little Mary . . . be offended if I did not put in her name? Look at the map! This is Sunday, that I am now writing. Before next Sunday I shall have crossed that place there that you see marked as sea, between Ireland & England, & shall hope indeed to be half way home. That is not a very long while now, is it? Perhaps I shall be upon the sea in a ship, the very moment Marshal is reading the letter to you. There is about going in a ship in mrs Barbauld's book. But I shall write another letter that will come two or three days after this, & then I shall be in England. And in a day or two after that I shall hope to see Fanny & Marshal & Mary sitting on the trunks of the trees.[31]

This passage not only reveals Godwin's tenderness towards the children, but also shows him thinking his way into their situation and answering their unstated concerns. To engage their interest, he adopts an accessible style, using simple concepts, vocabulary, and sentence structures – an idiom that was to be developed further in his experimental children's books.[32] As well as seeking to foster their 'appropriate portion of independence',[33] he reassures them of his love and thoughts, distracting them from his absence by focusing on his return – down to the concrete particulars of the view he would like to see from the coach-window as it arrived at Camden Town.

Godwin was not only an attentive father, but also a loving son – and husband. When his mother died, following a long illness, on 13 August 1809, he wrote a long letter to his second wife Mary Jane Godwin describing his feelings when he returned home alone after the funeral:

That night I slept in the chamber you used, & where my mother's corpse reposed the night before . . . I have had strange feelings arising from the present occasion. I was brought up in great tenderness, & though my mind was pr[one] to independence, I was never led to much independence of feeling. While my mother lived, I always felt to a certain degree as if I had somebody who was my superior, & who exercised a mysterious protection over me. I belonged to something; I hung to something; there is nothing that has so much reverence & religion in it as affection to parents. The knot is now severed, & I am for the first time, at more than fifty years of age, alone.[34]

This passage reads as a Godwinian 'spot of time', recalling the moments of moral and imaginative growth in *The Prelude* (1805). The mundane details of the funeral drop away as Godwin, alone at night, recollects in tranquillity his childhood feelings of security; this process of meditative reflection leads to a heightened perception of the world of psychological and moral certainties he has lost. Moreover, that he expressed himself so openly to Mary Jane Godwin, often caricatured by those who disliked her, suggests that his second marriage was much more of a fulfilling partnership than is often thought. Such letters not only challenge the received biographical image of Godwin, shedding light on the different stages of his eventful domestic life, but also bear witness to significant changes in his ethical views. As he noted privately in July 1801: 'My writings hitherto . . . have exhibited a view of half only of the human mind, there remain the feelings, & the imagination considered as the instrument of feeling.'[35] This formulation was characteristically belated: Godwin's letters record his development of a 'new language' of feeling from 1796 onwards, when he and Wollstonecraft began to 'woo philosophy' together.[36] After losing her, he worked to re-establish an equally loving domestic bond, based on intellectual and sexual equality, with Mary Jane Godwin.

Godwin's letters also reveal his lasting importance as a cultural commentator, refuting the traditional view that he was a man in retreat, both politically and intellectually, from around 1800. On the contrary, he continued to engage with contemporary politics, both at home and abroad, to assist younger authors seeking to establish themselves in the literary marketplace, and to pursue his own project of moral and political enlightenment through writing and discussion. Above all, Godwin's commitment to gradual political reform did not diminish in his later years. He welcomed the 1820 Spanish Revolution, with a characteristic mixture of approval and caution.[37] He applauded the 'generous magnanimity and forbearance' displayed by the leaders of the 1830 July Revolution in France.[38] At home, when the Reform Bill was rejected by the House of Lords in October 1831, Godwin (then aged seventy-five) wrote to Earl Grey, the Whig prime minister, offering to draft a formal protest to the king on behalf of the House of Commons.[39] To the end he remained, as he declared to Lady Caroline Lamb in 1819, 'in principle a republican, but in practice a Whig'.[40]

Moreover, Godwin continued to take an active interest in the contemporary literary scene – even if he did not like all that he saw. The poetry of Walter Scott, he wrote to his son William, then away at school, is 'very pretty . . . as good as a second rate novel'. Byron, on the other hand, 'is in the true sense of the word a poet': 'His energy is real energy; his language is truly felicitous . . . All that I have to object against him, is the narrow range of his talent.'[41] Shelley's poetry, as might be expected, provoked an even more divided response. Godwin wrote to Mary Shelley on 30 March 1820: 'I have read the tragedy of Cenci, & am glad to see Shelley at last descending to what really passes among human creatures. The story is certainly an unfortunate one; but the execution gives me a new idea of Shelley's powers.'[42] By the early nineteenth century, however, Godwin's real literary preferences lay in the Renaissance era, as he admitted to Shelley: 'These were the times when Authors thought: every line is pregnant with sense & the reader is inevitably put to the expense of thinking likewise.'[43] Above all, Godwin revered Milton, whose testimony to his sense of personal calling in book II of *The Reason of Church Government* he appropriated to describe his own. '"I have long taken it"', he wrote to an unknown correspondent on 3 August 1811, 'as Milton says, "by an inward prompting which daily grew upon me, to be my portion in this life", to be a communicator of truth.'[44]

This paraphrase of Milton's celebrated vocational reflections is by no means the only indication of Godwin's fundamental belief in the civic responsibilities of authorship. In one of his earliest surviving letters, to his mother, he explains his abandonment of the Dissenting ministry in favour of secular authorship: 'I know of nothing worth living for but usefulness & the service of my fellow creatures . . . And as I derive every thing from God, I hope the situation in which I am now placed is that in which I am most likely to be useful.'[45] Godwin's emphasis on moral responsibility owes much to the Calvinist belief that each individual is a steward of talents placed in his or her possession by God, and will eventually be called to account for how such gifts have been used.[46] His letters reveal the dilemmas of conscience which arose, from time to time, when this belief in individual moral responsibility came into conflict with the practical demands of earning a living. Even so, he continued to represent himself as a writer dedicated to public welfare. Writing on 15 April 1830 to Mary Shelley, he instructed her how to describe to the publisher John Murray his latest work, *Thoughts on Man* (1831), then in progress. Tell Murray, he wrote, 'Whether it is published during my life, or after my death, it is a light that cannot be extinguished – "the precious life-blood of a discerning spirit, embalmed and treasured up on purpose to a life beyond life".'[47] This invocation of Milton's view of books as active agents of reform is more than an impressive sales pitch: it bears witness to Godwin's lifelong quest for a secular justification of his career as an author.

Godwin's letters also provide a wealth of practical information about his career as a professional author. Over the six decades of his writing life, he corresponded with most of the leading publishers of the day – including William Blackwood, Henry Colburn, Archibald Constable, Richard Phillips, and George Robinson, as well as Murray. These letters shed light on his methods of researching and composing his published works, and enable us to track the development of works in progress – as in, for example, the growth of *History of the Commonwealth of England* (1824–8) from two volumes to four.[48] As well as adding to our knowledge of his completed works, they provide unique evidence of unexecuted literary plans. For example, on 29 March 1793, whilst writing volume 1 of *Caleb Williams* (1794), he wrote to Robinson formally proposing in three quarto volumes 'a Roman History from the building of the city by Romulus to the battle of Actium'.[49] Although this plan came to nothing, it shows how easily his career might have taken a different path. In later life, he sketched plans for a series of large-scale projects concerning the classification and organization of knowledge, including a literary history of England, a history of the Protestant Reformation, and a multi-volume 'Lives of the English Poets'. Again, these projects never materialized – unless we consider *Life of Chaucer* (1803) as the first instalment of 'Lives of the English Poets' – but they underscore Godwin's ambitions as a purveyor of knowledge and a bringer of enlightenment.

Yet Godwin was not just an English *philosophe*, seeking to change the world through the intellectual medium of books: he was also a practical man with a keen eye for what would sell. His letters to publishers deal with not only contracts and deadlines, but also proofs, titles, and advance publicity, showing how closely he was involved in all aspects of book production. For example, a letter of 2 January 1798 to Joseph Johnson reveals Godwin responding to, and sometimes resisting, changes which the publisher suggested to the proof of *Memoirs*: 'The only reason why I do not approve your pencil alterations in page 9', wrote Godwin, 'is because I think they bear harder upon Mary's father than the passage as it stands. Severities, if it does [not] mean blows, means whipping, & this would be the obvious meaning, taken with the context. You therefore seem to make him threaten his wife with a whipping.'[50] Such a degree of interaction between author and publisher might seem exceptional – especially in view of Johnson's close friendship with Wollstonecraft – but letters to Phillips, Colburn, and others convey a similar attentiveness to detail. Moreover, for twenty years of his life Godwin was himself a publisher and bookseller. His letters concerning the Juvenile Library, which he owned and managed with Mary Jane Godwin from 1805 to 1825, provide a comprehensive record of his business dealings: from the commissioning of authors and illustrators, through the various stages of sponsorship, financing, publication, and distribution. These letters form a compendium of knowledge about publishing practices in the early nineteenth century, mapping the overlapping economies of literary patronage and the marketplace, and revealing the dilemmas of an author who frequently got caught between the two.

Godwin's letters do not merely tell the story of his own development, but also shed light on the workings of the intricate literary and social communities he inhabited. As a record of his epistolary 'collisions of mind' with many literary, political, dramatic, and artistic figures of note, his letters enrich our understanding of the major radical networks of the late eighteenth and early nineteenth centuries. Above all, the letters uncover Godwin's role in promoting the work of women writers. One of his most creative epistolary dialogues was with his daughter, Mary Shelley, to whom he offered practical help and constructive criticism when she sought to establish herself as a professional writer after Shelley's death in 1822.[51] This practice of actively supporting women writers began in the decade following the French Revolution, when Godwin, then at the height of his fame amongst educated radicals, acted as literary adviser to several women intellectuals sympathetic to the cause of reform, who sought to further their public ambitions by forming alliances with helpful men. In addition to Wollstonecraft, these figures included Amelia Alderson, Mary Hays, and Mary Robinson. A study of this entire network of literary and social relations would be the subject of another essay. The richest example is Godwin's epistolary dialogue with Elizabeth Inchbald, with whom he corresponded, at intervals, for more than twenty-five years.[52]

Unlike most of Godwin's women acquaintances, Inchbald did not share his Dissenting background, but, as a Roman Catholic, she shared his experience of belonging to a marginalized social and religious community.[53] When the pair met on 29 October 1792, she, three years his senior, had retired from her first career as an actress and was already a successful dramatist and novelist; he, after a decade of anonymous publications in an extraordinary diversity of genres, was writing the final books of *Political Justice*. Although it has been suggested that Godwin proposed marriage to Inchbald, there is little evidence to support this idea.[54] The surviving data suggests that their mutual personal regard found its main expression in their frank admiration of each other's literary abilities, and in their equally unreserved criticisms of each other's perceived faults.

Godwin's letters reveal that he acted as a valued source of professional advice to Inchbald in the early 1790s. Mindful of the growing climate of government repression, which followed the Proclamation against Seditious

Writings and Publications of 21 May 1792, he advised her against publication on politically inflammatory subjects. On their first meeting, they discussed her play *The Massacre*, a tragedy based on the St Bartholomew Massacre of 1572, which contained pointed allusions to the killing of 1,000 royalist prisoners in Paris in September 1792.[55] When, after the visit, Godwin wrote advising her to withdraw the play from the press, Inchbald replied on 3 November 1792 that she found 'so much tenderness mixed with the justice of [his] criticism' that she was willing to agree.[56] Again, Godwin regularly assisted Inchbald, who was acutely conscious of her lack of formal education, in preparing her manuscripts for publication. As well as revising her hugely popular comedy *Every One Has His Fault* (1793), he corrected a draft of her second novel, *Nature and Art* (1796), in response to her characteristically direct instructions, given in a letter of 24 January 1794: 'Pray mark bad spelling and grammar, obscurities, tediousness &c &c | and pray don't preach.'[57] Above all, Godwin encouraged her to persevere with the novel, which took her two years to write. When she sent him a tentative sketch, he provided affirmative feedback:

I perceive in this sketch the same sureness of aim and steadiness of hand, which first told me what you were capable of, in the 'Simple Story'. It seems to me that the drama puts shackles upon you, and that the compression it requires prevents your genius from expanding itself . . . I know not what is to come, but what I have already seen leads me confidently to hope the same mastery in the execution of the remainder of your plan. Do not, I conjure you . . . desert a beginning that promises so much instruction and delight!58

When she finished the manuscript, Godwin was again on hand to respond. According to his diary, he read it twice in December 1795, evidently approving it, since the following month Inchbald sold it to Robinson for £150.[59]

Yet the flow of advice between the two writers was by no means one-way. That Godwin learned as much as he taught is suggested by a letter to Inchbald, dated 1 December 1817, in which he recollected 'with some emotion the sort of intercourse that passed between us when Caleb Williams was in his non-age, and in the vigor of his age. Particularly, I have looked a hundred times with great delight at the little marginal notes and annotations with which you adorned the pages of my writings of that period.'[60] These annotations have not survived, but Inchbald also gave her opinion of *Caleb Williams*, which she read just prior to publication, in several undated letters. After reading the first thirty pages, she wrote excitedly to Godwin, 'Nobody is so pleased when they find anything new as I am. | I found your style different from what I have ever yet met . . . I have to add to your praises, that of a most <u>minute</u> and yet most <u>concise</u> method of delineating human sensations.'[61] Significantly, this first critical reaction was one of recognition as well as discovery: in singling out Godwin's economical depiction of psychological states, Inchbald highlighted what he had learned from her own methods of dramatic revelation of character in *A Simple Story* (1791) – a work he re-read frequently as a source of inspiration for his own.[62] When she had finished, she gave a more considered verdict: 'Your first volume is far inferior to the two Last. | Your 2^d is sublimely horrible – captivatingly Frightful. | Your 3rd is all a great genius can do to delight a great genius . . . | It is my opinion that fine Ladies, milliners, mantuamakers, and boarding school Girls will Love to tremble over it – and that men of taste and judgement will admire the superior talents, the *incessant* energy of mind you have evinced.'[63] As well as correctly predicting the novel's appeal to all classes, Inchbald cautioned Godwin against politically outspoken remarks, 'and these particularly marked for the reader's attention by the purport of your preface'. It is not known whether or not Godwin toned down his political criticisms as a result of this advice, but when the novel appeared on 26 May 1794, the preface was withheld.

This frank, mutually beneficial epistolary interchange adds further depth and context to Godwin's social circles, revealing the extent to which women were regarded as the discursive and professional equals of men: Godwin treated Inchbald no differently from close male friends, such as Thomas Holcroft and William Nicholson, with whom he engaged in regular political and philosophical discussions. In this community of reform-minded individuals, literary composition was not a solitary process, but a shared, even collaborative activity between men and women, supported by a network of literary and social relations. Godwin's letters document a lasting commitment to egalitarian professional relationships between the sexes, helping to explain why he continued to act as a magnet for women intellectuals and social reformers in later life, when he was sought out by Madame de Staël, Frances Wright, and Harriet Martineau, amongst others.

Each separate letter mentioned above is significant for the contribution it makes to our understanding of the minute particulars of Godwin's personal and professional development. Viewed collectively, these person-to-person exchanges create a whole that is greater than and different from the parts. They offer a revaluation of the career of an Enlightenment intellectual for whom, as Ruth Benedict wrote of Wollstonecraft, 'life had no axioms; its geometry was all experimental',[64] and provide an insider's view of the diverse communities which constituted the radical intelligentsia of his times. As an historical as well as a personal record, they bear witness to aesthetic, social, and political upheavals across three generations: from the Dutch Patriot Revolution through the French Revolution and the Napoleonic Wars to the largely bloodless reforms of the 1830s. To scrutinize Godwin's letters in their entirety is to engage with different values from those traditionally associated with the Romantic past: sociability as well as solitary contemplation, political savoir-faire as well as political idealism, stoical detachment as well as heartfelt emotion – together with a lifelong commitment to the ideals of the Commonwealth era. Godwin's voice – analytical, forthright, cerebral – provides a new element in the conversation of British Romanticism. His letters, as witnesses to the interior life of a vanguard thinker who borrowed every changing shape to find expression, provide a searching reappraisal of an extended revolutionary era.

NOTES

1. Janet Todd and Marilyn Butler (eds.), *The Works of Mary Wollstonecraft*, 7 vols. (London: Pickering and Chatto, 1989).
2. Mark Philp (gen. ed.), *The Collected Novels and Memoirs of William Godwin*, 8 vols. (London: Pickering and Chatto, 1992); Nora Crook with Pamela Clemit (gen. eds.), *The Novels and Selected Works of Mary Shelley*, 8 vols. (London: Pickering and Chatto, 1996); Grevel Lindop (gen. ed.), *The Works of Thomas De Quincey*, 21 vols. (London: Pickering and Chatto, 2000–3); Marilyn Butler (gen. ed.), *The Works of Maria Edgeworth*, 12 vols. (London: Pickering and Chatto, 1999–2003).
3. Stuart Curran (gen. ed.), *The Works of Charlotte Smith*, 14 vols. in progress (London: Pickering and Chatto, 2005–).
4. Marilyn Butler, 'Editing Women', *Studies in the Novel* 27 (1995), 281.
5. Marilyn Butler (ed.), *Burke, Paine, Godwin, and the Revolution Controversy* (Cambridge: Cambridge University Press, 1984). See also Jane Austen, *Emma*, introd. Butler (London: Everyman's Library, 1991); Maria Edgeworth, *'Castle Rackrent' and 'Ennui'*, ed. Butler (Harmondsworth: Penguin, 1992); Mary Shelley, *Frankenstein; or, The Modern Prometheus: The 1818 Text*, ed. Butler (London: Pickering and Chatto, 1993; rpt. Oxford: Oxford University Press, 1994); Jane Austen, *Northanger Abbey*, ed. Butler (Harmondsworth: Penguin, 1995); Jane Austen, *Mansfield Park*, ed. James Kinsley, introd. Butler (Oxford: Oxford University Press, 1990).
6. Butler, 'Editing Women', p. 274.
7. Marilyn Butler and Mark Philp, 'Introduction', in Godwin, *Collected Novels*, vol. 1, p. 42.
8. 'Godwin–Shelley Correspondence', in Godwin, *Collected Novels*, vol. 1, pp. 69–82.

9. Kenneth Neill Cameron, Donald H. Reiman, and Doucet Devin Fischer (eds.), *Shelley and His Circle, 1773–1822*, 10 vols. to date (Cambridge, Mass.: Harvard University Press, 1961–).

10. Stuart Curran, review of Godwin, *Collected Novels*, *Eighteenth-Century Fiction* 5.4 (July 1993), 383.

11. Pamela Clemit (ed.), *The Letters of William Godwin*, 6 vols., to be published by Oxford University Press.

12. Percy Bysshe Shelley, *Prometheus Unbound*, 3. 3. 64–8 (l. 65), in Kelvin Everest and Geoffrey Matthews (eds.), *The Poems of Shelley*, 3 vols. in progress (London: Longman, 1989–), vol. II, pp. 589–90.

13. Bodleian [Abinger] Dep. b. 228/3. I am grateful to the Bodleian Library, University of Oxford, for permission to publish materials from the Abinger papers (hereafter '[Ab.] Dep.').

14. William Godwin, *An Enquiry concerning Political Justice*, in Mark Philp (gen. ed.), *The Political and Philosophical Writings of William Godwin*, 7 vols. (London: Pickering and Chatto, 1993), vol. III, p. 15.

15. Richard Price, *The Evidence for a Future Period of Improvement in the State of Mankind* (1787), in D. O. Thomas (ed.), *Richard Price: Political Writings* (Cambridge: Cambridge University Press, 1991), pp. 163–4.

16. See esp. John Seed, 'Gentlemen Dissenters: The Social and Political Meanings of Rational Dissent in the 1770s and 1780s', *Historical Journal* 28.2 (1985), 317, and John Seed, '"A Set of Men Powerful Enough in Many Things": Rational Dissent and Political Opposition in England, 1770–1790', in Knud Haakonssen (ed.), *Enlightenment and Religion: Rational Dissent in Eighteenth-Century Britain* (Cambridge: Cambridge University Press, 1996), pp. 158–9.

17. See Pamela Clemit, 'William Godwin and James Watt's Copying Machine: Wet-transfer Copies in the Abinger Papers', *Bodleian Library Record* 18.5 (April 2005), 532–60.

18. [Ab.] Dep. b. 215/5.

19. [Ab.] Dep. c. 523.

20. Cameron et al. (eds.), *Shelley and his Circle*, vol. I, pp. 26–34.

21. G-145, The Carl H. Pforzheimer Collection of Shelley and His Circle, The New York Public Library, Astor, Lenox, and Tilden Foundations.

22. Wordsworth, *The Prelude* (1805), x. 372, in Jonathan Wordsworth, M. H. Abrams, and Stephen Gill (eds.), *The Prelude, 1799, 1805, 1850* (New York: W. W. Norton, 1979), p. 378.

23. [Ab.] Dep. b. 227/2(a).

24. Godwin, *Political Justice*, in Godwin, *Political and Philosophical Writings*, vol. III, pp. 448–9, 456.

25. Godwin to Dyson, date-stamped 26 Sept. [1795], [Ab.] Dep. b. 214/9.

26. Godwin to [Dyson], 21 Mar. 1792, [Ab.] Dep. c. 607/3. The addressee of this letter can now be identified from Godwin's unpublished diary ([Ab.] Dep. e. 199) (hereafter 'GD').

27. Elizabeth Hamilton, *Translation of the Letters of a Hindoo Rajah; Written Previous to, and During the Period of His Residence in England*, 2 vols. (London:

G. G. and J. Robinson, 1796), vol. II, pp. 210–15; Robert Southey to Joseph Cottle, 13 Mar. 1797, in Charles Cuthbert Southey (ed.), *The Life and Correspondence of the Late Robert Southey*, 6 vols. (London: Longman, Brown, Green & Longman, 1849–50), vol. I, p. 306; George Stillman Hillard (ed.), *Life, Letters, and Journals of George Ticknor*, 2 vols. (Boston: James R. Osgood, 1876), vol. I, p. 294.

28. Godwin to Anthony Carlisle, 15 Sept. 1797, [Ab.] Dep. b. 215/2.

29. Godwin to [Amelia Alderson], 23 Oct. 1797, [Ab] Dep. b. 227/8, fol. 68.

30. Godwin to Marshal, 11 July 1800, [Ab.] Dep. b. 214/5.

31. [Ab.] Dep. b. 214/5.

32. See Pamela Clemit, 'Philosophical Anarchism in the Schoolroom: William Godwin's Juvenile Library, 1805–25', *Biblion: The Bulletin of the New York Public Library* 9.1/2 (Fall 2000/Spring 2001), 44–70.

33. Godwin, 'Of Cohabitation', *The Enquirer* (1797), in Philp (ed.), *Philosophical Writings*, vol. V, p. 119.

34. Godwin to Mary Jane Godwin, date-stamped 21 Aug. 1809, [Ab.] Dep. c. 523.

35. Godwin, undated note, [Ab.] Dep. b. 227/5. This note can now be identified as 'Notes of Essays', written 18 July 1801 (GD, [Ab.] Dep. e. 205).

36. Godwin, *Memoirs of the Author of A Vindication of the Rights of Woman*, in Godwin, *Collected Novels*, vol. I, p. 118; Wollstonecraft to Godwin, [15 Sept. 1796], in Ralph M. Wardle (ed.), *Godwin & Mary: Letters of William Godwin and Mary Wollstonecraft* (Lincoln: University of Nebraska Press, and London: Constable, 1967), p. 35.

37. Godwin to Henry Rosser, 27 Mar. 1820, [Ab.] Dep. c. 532/1.

38. Godwin to W. Cross, 4 Jan. 1831, [Ab.] Dep. b. 215/2.

39. Godwin to [Earl Grey], 11 Oct. 1831, [Ab.] Dep. c. 607/1.

40. Godwin to Lady Caroline Lamb, 25 Feb. 1819, [Ab.] Dep. c. 529.

41. Godwin to William Godwin, Jun., n.d., [Ab.] Dep. b. 227/3(b).

42. [Ab.] Dep. c. 524.

43. Godwin to Shelley, 10 Dec. 1812, [Ab.] Dep. c. 524.

44. [Ab.] Dep. b. 228/7; cf. Milton, *The Reason of Church-Government Urg'd against Prelaty*, in Don M. Wolfe (gen. ed.), *The Complete Prose Works of John Milton*, 8 vols. (New Haven and London: Yale University Press, 1953–82), vol. I, p. 810.

45. Godwin to Ann Godwin, n.d., [Ab.] Dep. c. 526.

46. See D. O. Thomas, *The Honest Mind: The Thought and Work of Richard Price* (Oxford: Clarendon Press, 1977), p. 68.

47. [Ab.] Dep. b. 524; cf. Milton, *Areopagitica; A Speech . . . for the Liberty of Unlicenc'd Printing*, in Wolfe (gen. ed.), *Complete Prose Works*, vol. II, p. 493.

48. See correspondence of Godwin with Henry Colburn, Forster 48.E.3, National Art Library, Victoria & Albert Museum.

49. [Ab.] Dep. c. 227/2(a). This project found limited expression in Godwin's *The History of Rome . . . For the Use of Schools and Young Persons* (1809), published under the pseudonym of 'Edward Baldwin, Esq.'

50. [Ab.] Dep. b. 227/8, fol. 88. The printed text reads 'blows' (Godwin, *Collected Novels*, vol. I, p. 89).

51. See Pamela Clemit, 'Mary Shelley and William Godwin, a Literary-Political Partnership, 1823–36', *Women's Writing* 6.3 (1999), 285–95.

52. For a fuller statement of the argument developed in the rest of this essay, see Pamela Clemit, 'Godwin, Women, and "The Collision of Mind with Mind"', *Wordsworth Circle* 35.2 (Spring 2004), 72–6.

53. For a comparison between the historical experience of Roman Catholics and other nonconformists, see John Bossy, *The English Catholic Community, 1570–1850* (London: Darton, Longman, and Todd, 1975), pp. 391–401.

54. Gary Kelly, *The English Jacobin Novel, 1780–1805* (Oxford: Clarendon Press, 1976), p. 91 n., cites Godwin's note of a conversation with Inchbald on 'marriage' (GD, 16 Sept. 1793, [Ab.] Dep. e. 201) as indicative of a proposal, but this is more likely to refer to criticisms of the institution of marriage in book eight of *Political Justice*.

55. James Boaden, *Memoirs of Mrs. Inchbald: Including Her Familiar Correspondence with the Most Distinguished Persons of Her Time*, 2 vols. (London: Richard Bentley, 1833), vol. i, p. 365 n.

56. [Ab.] Dep. c. 509.

57. [Ab.] Dep. c. 509; Godwin revised 'Mrs Inchbald's comedy' from 26 to 28 Nov. 1792 and read 'Inchbald's Romance, ms' from 27 to 30 Jan. 1794 (GD, [Ab.] Dep. e. 200, e. 201).

58. Godwin to Inchbald, [Dec. 1795], in Boaden, *Memoirs of Mrs. Inchbald*, vol. ii, p. 354.

59. Godwin read 'Inchbald', 331 pages, from 24 to 26 Dec., and again from 27 to 30 Dec. 1795 (GD, [Ab.] Dep. e. 202); see Boaden, *Memoirs of Mrs. Inchbald*, vol. ii, p. 3.

60. Boaden, *Memoirs of Mrs. Inchbald*, vol. ii, p. 221.

61. [Ab.] Dep. c. 509.

62. Godwin read *A Simple Story* from 12 to 16 Sept. 1793, whilst writing *Caleb Williams*; from 16 to 27 Sept. 1799, whilst writing *St Leon* (1799); from 19 Oct. to 11 Nov. 1804, whilst writing *Fleetwood*; and from 18 to 20 Aug. 1831, whilst writing *Deloraine* (1833) (GD, [Ab.] Dep. e. 201, e. 204, e. 207, e. 225).

63. [Ab.] Dep. c. 509.

64. Ruth Benedict, 'Mary Wollstonecraft', in Margaret Mead (ed.), *An Anthropologist at Work: Writings of Ruth Benedict* (London: Secker and Warburg, 1959), p. 491.

PART II

Reopening the case of Edgeworth

Edgeworth and Scott: the literature of reterritorialization

James Chandler

Few scholars have done as much as Marilyn Butler has to re-energize and reorient studies in the novel of the Romantic period. Even if she had never written, say, *Jane Austen and the War of Ideas* or *Rebels, Romantics and Reactionaries*, her work on Maria Edgeworth would constitute an enormously influential legacy in itself. It is work that stretches over four decades from Butler's early biography of the Anglo-Irish novelist into the invaluably annotated Pickering and Chatto edition, and beyond. Her insistence on taking Edgeworth seriously has not only made it possible to recover a neglected body of extraordinary writing. It has also had great impact on sub-fields for which Edgeworth was historically central: studies in post-Union Irish literature, for example, or in the relation between nineteenth-century literature and education, or in feminist accounts of Romantic literary history, or indeed in the Romantic novel more broadly, a field that has probably never been more keenly engaged than it is now. More particularly, understanding Edgeworth better, having a better sense of her place in literary history, makes a distinct difference for studies in Jane Austen and Sir Walter Scott, two of the authors for whom Edgeworth, in very different ways, set the stage. Butler herself has done much to show what Edgeworth meant to Austen's transformation of the domestic novel. Here I will be more interested in Edgeworth's relation to Scott's work in transforming – some would say 'inventing' – the historical novel.

In addition to being much indebted to Butler's scholarship in Romanticism generally and in Edgeworth especially, the following chapter departs most immediately from one of Butler's offhand remarks apropos of the 1814 novel *Patronage* – her observation about what she calls 'an odd vagueness with respect to place' in Edgeworth's fiction.[1] The larger question at issue has to do with how fiction at this crucial juncture in the early nineteenth century represents location – how it contextualizes action and character, negotiates boundaries, and contests territory. This question in turn has had a certain urgency for literary and cultural studies more broadly in recent years, an urgency associated with larger issues about borders and territories, citizenship and subjection, empire and globalization in our time – with debates about the 'postcolony', for example, or 'the new Europe'. In the context of these larger interests, literary studies have turned to the Romantic novel as never before, and especially to the circumstances of the 'historical novel's' emergence. These are circumstances in which Edgeworth became a crucial agent.

My argument in this chapter, to preview it briefly, is that what since Georg Lukács we tend to call the 'realism' of the historical novel – its mode of attending to actual specificities of time and place – is compromised in ways that merit fresh scrutiny.[2] This 'realism' is compromised, I will suggest, not only by the sorts of typological function that Lukács himself acknowledged ('mediocre heroes' and 'world historical individuals'), but also by a contest of genres that the historical novel stages within itself, especially *vis-à-vis* the sentimental novel. Putting the matter in the starkest possible form, I will be suggesting that the central category of historical *place* in the fiction of Edgeworth and Scott is itself at key moments displaced by a particular kind of attention to the expressive qualities of the sentimentalized *face*.

I am well aware that other genres come into play in the Edgeworth-influenced historical novel, including the travel narrative and survey, as Ina Ferris has stressed.[3] I am also aware that there are distinctions to be made between the 'national tale', and the historical novel. My concern here is with a shared interest in ethnographic and topological specificity in Edgeworth's Irish tales and Scott's Scottish novels, and with a curious tendency in each novelist to complicate or undercut it. The discussion will fall into three parts: first a laying out of the problem of how, broadly speaking, sites, or 'lands', come to be multiply 'debatable' in this body of fiction;[4] second an effort to develop a conceptual framework for addressing it, one which will involve some grappling with the work of Gilles Deleuze and even a foray across a disciplinary border into cinema theory; and finally a return to Edgeworth and Scott in the light of these concepts.

I am by no means sure that Marilyn Butler will agree with either my conclusions or my way of proceeding, which involves a degree of, let us say, methodological anachronism. I take some consolation, however, in recollecting certain other memorable observations she has made – more typically in conversation than in print: her analysis of Johanna Bailie's dramaturgy of the passions in terms of Harold Pinter's theatre of menace, or, staying with Edgeworth, her suggestive account of class consciousness and narrational indirection in *Castle Rackrent* as producing for Edgeworth's moment what Kazuo Ishiguro produces for his (and ours) in *The Remains of the Day*.

For in such comments, relaxing her customary historicist rigour, Butler acknowledges that sometimes what comes after can be used to illuminate what comes before.

The historical novel would seem to be a particularly privileged site for the problem of contested territory and literary representation, since it was Sir Walter Scott himself who extended the sense of 'debatable lands' from its initial, narrowly legal sense to the broader associations that enable it to serve so well for us here. Indeed, the Waverley novels offer a range of variations on the theme of 'debatable lands', an array of territorial conflicts carried out sometimes at the level of the estate, sometimes at the level of the region, sometimes at the level of the nation. In a novel of the (notoriously contested) Scottish borders like *The Bride of Lammermoor*, all three levels – estate, region, and nation – evidently come into play. Lukács, we recall, claimed that the emergent realism he saw in the Waverley novels is explained by Scott's willingness to re-stage the actual conflicts around which Britain negotiated its historical destiny: the Civil War, the Cameronian skirmishes, the '15, the Act of Union, the Porteous Riots, the '45. For Lukács, the specificities of locale and language, custom and manners, all figure as they do because the dramatic action of the fiction is historically derived. Topographical and ethnographical depictions in the Waverley novels need to be at once so detailed and so accurate, in other words, because the stakes are so real. And there is merit in Lukács's view, at the very least to the degree that it helps to make sense of the enormous mass of sheer description in the Waverley novels, a feature that was much noted in their first reception and then carried to even greater lengths in Scott's many imitators. We need think only of the long descriptive passages that mark Cooper's efforts to work out the Scott formula in novels about the debatable lands of upstate New York in the late eighteenth century, or in Balzac's similar adaptation of Scott to the French 1790s in *Les Chouans*.

At the same time, however, there is something in the Waverley novels that clouds this clarity about their various settings. The point can be made in relatively straightforward terms if we compare Scott's descriptions of places with the 'originals' towards which he sometimes pointed his readers in his notes and prefaces. Scott said that the land most immediately under debate in *The Bride of Lammermoor*, that of the declining noble family of Ravenswood, was based on Holdfast Castle in East Lothian, just where the North Sea coast turns into the Firth of Forth. But any pilgrim who has made the trek down the long dirt road from the little working farmhouse to see the unmarked ruins of Holdfast Castle must be disappointed at what a tiny and rather paltry affair this edifice by the sea must have been even in its best days, how unlike the seat of grace and power that Scott would have us imagine it before its decline. This sense of misrecognition or dislocation, though available only to those who know the local scene, is compounded by the novel's notorious vagueness of *temporal* setting, well documented by scholars such as Fiona Robertson and Peter Garside, in relation to that much debated settlement, the 1707 Act of Union.[5]

Or again, just to stay with familiar texts, we might think of *Waverley* itself, and the property issues that develop around the Baron Bradwardine's estate at Tully-Veolan. This estate, we recall, is described in great detail on three separate occasions in the book, each marking a different stage in the legal and physical disposition of the house and its lands. Wolfram Schmidgen has convincingly shown how one might map the entire action of *Waverley* according to the sequenced depictions of Tully Veolan's shifting status: first, on the occasion of Edward Waverley's arrival there early in the novel; then, after its occupation and sacking by Cumberland's army in the wake of Culloden; and finally, its eventual restoration, when its title documents have been laundered, as it were, through the agency of Colonel Talbot and the property has been turned over to Edward Waverley and Rose Bradwardine.[6]

It surely raises a question about Scott's practice, however, that the acknowledged model for Tully-Veolan – down to the celebrated Bear-gates and the long lonely 'Avenue' leading to the manor house beyond them – is one of the best-known estates in Scott's own neighbourhood: the establishment known as Traquair, which to this day maintains its claim to be the oldest continuously inhabited residence in Britain. What does it mean that the debated lands so central to this novel about the last violent conflict over Scotland itself can simply be relocated from the south bank of the Tweed on the edge of the Scottish Borders to the foothills of the Perthshire Highlands, those sublime forms that loom mightily over Edward Waverley's first glimpse of the Bradwardines' family seat? Ought not a relocation from one side of the Kingdom of Fife to the other to carry some significance for a novel in which even small regional differences ostensibly matter so much?

One might well object at this point: well, this is fiction, and fiction will have its licence, even if it purports to be historical fiction, realist fiction, or what have you. Perhaps, but the suspicion that something else is going on here is reinforced in the novels of Edgeworth, Scott's acknowledged teacher in the practice of ethnographic realism. Everyone knows the story of the manuscript left in the drawer with the fishing tackle until the author of *Waverley* happened on Edgeworth's *The Absentee* and decided he wanted to 'emulate' her work, to do something for his own country in the manner in which she had done something for hers.[7] Ferris reminds us in her discussion of Edgeworth's reception history that Scott joined others in esteeming the 'accuracy' of her portraits of Ireland.[8]

Scott must also have been struck by Edgeworth's avowedly Scottish-Enlightenment influenced method for approaching questions of ethnography and topography. It is, after all, a method that becomes programmatic at a level internal to the action of her Irish tales. In *The Absentee*, for example, it gradually becomes clear as the narrative unfolds that Lord Colambre, the worthy scion of the absentee family, has embarked on a kind of metaproject beyond his primary mission of sorting out his family's messy affairs. The metaproject is to develop a systematic approach to understanding the land of Ireland and its people, and thus not only to avoid the casual errors of bigotry and prejudice that the novel represents as already rife enough, but also to correct the deliberate misinformation circulated by characters like Lady Dashfort and Nicholas Garraghty, who benefit when Ireland and the Irish are presented in a bad light. 'I have seen, compared, and judged', Colambre tells Nicholas Garraghty, the dishonest agent who's been running things in the family's absence, and that threefold principle for establishing accuracy in representation is enshrined as an explicit principle in the novel.[9] This method and that principle constitute, I suggest, a large part of its claim to 'realism'. Though Edgeworth is never mentioned in Lukács's account of Scott – an absence pertly documented by Katie Trumpener among others[10] – he certainly learned much from the Irish novelist in relation to the claim for accuracy.

And yet in Edgeworth as in Scott, there are undercurrents that seem to run against the claim to realist accuracy even as the novels assert it most urgently. This is that feature that Marilyn Butler calls 'an odd vagueness about place' in her novels. For Butler, this vagueness has to do with Edgeworth's onomastic practices, and particularly with her well-nigh-systematic tendencies to blend names from different literary sources, historical periods, and, above all, geographical locales. And for Butler, this coded mix of allusive reference 'puts the action on to a theoretical abstract plane'.[11] Thus, in *The Absentee*, in addition to the quasi-scientific and proto-ethnographic aspiration – what I've described as its internally dramatized method of observation, comparison, and careful analysis – we *also* find an extraordinary mix of what might be called external framing references: references to Edgeworth's family history, to Longford regional history, to Irish history, to

British history, to European history, to local folklore (including the quasi-legendary figure of Grace Nugent), and to world literary history (e.g. to *The Odyssey*). And all this is grafted onto a narrative structured like a kind of Moebius strip, in which the story of a character named Grace Nugent – heroine of a well-known eighteenth-century aisling collected for the 1792 Belfast Harp Festival – can be resolved in a finale that shows Irish villagers around the Clonbrony estate, celebrating her promised nuptials with Lord Colambre to the tune of that very same aisling, 'Grace Nugent'. What, we may legitimately ask, are we to make of the 'realism' in a novel so constructed?

How such questions about Edgeworth's coded allusion and irony matter to the issues of geography and property conflict – to debatable lands – becomes clearer when we turn to *Patronage*, a novel published just over a year later than *The Absentee*, and out of which *The Absentee* itself evolved. *Patronage*, begun much earlier, grew too long, and so its substantial Irish subplot was merged with a private drama Edgeworth wrote in the summer of 1811 to produce *The Absentee* in order to fill out the second series of *Tales of Fashionable Life*, published in 1812. Though only a couple of Irish characters remain in the four-volume published form of *Patronage* – and though for all the world it seems to be a novel about English characters, English patronage, English virtues, and indeed English land disputes – Butler suggests that it is true 'only on the face of it' that the novel is set in England.[12] The case she makes, which draws on the work of W. J. McCormack even as Claire Connolly has subsequently built on hers, is based partly on the fact that, like Edgeworth's straightforwardly Irish tales, *Patronage*'s narrative is fashioned out of source materials that come from Irish contexts.[13] These contexts inevitably include a seventeenth-century family-land dispute well documented in the stormy annals of the Edgeworth family. Further, argues Butler, this novel, like many in the Edgeworth canon, places a particular emphasis on language. This is not just about language as territorial in an ethnographic sense – the coding of 'manners' – but also about various forms of onomastic coding that come into play in this novel, just as they do in, say, *The Absentee* or, later, in *Ormond*. And they do so in a way that becomes, as Butler emphasizes, acutely self-conscious in the experience of the novel by virtue of Edgeworth's having made the practice of coding and deciphering so central to the novel's plot on all levels. The action of *Patronage* actually begins with a shipwreck near the estate of the virtuous central family, the Percys, the patriarch of which happens to be skilled in the art of decipherment. The shipwreck maroons a French spy on the Percy estate. This spy and his misplaced papers, written in complex cipher, generate both the political and the domestic territorial issues that are played out in the rest of the novel. In spite of the specificities of the territorial issues – the sense that the book must be about, say, the English land and the English patronage system if it is to be intelligible at all – I find persuasive Butler's suggestion that the book is simultaneously coding other places, other scenes.

How, then, do we make sense of the Edgeworth-Scott moment in the history of British fiction as, on the one hand, the point of emergence of ethnographical/topographical realism in the treatment of (say) land conflicts and, on the other, the conjuncture in which all such particulars seem to dissolve into the airy thinness of coded abstraction and geographical fungibility? How is it that the new novel in the Edgeworth-Scott mould seems to be both about the geographical and cultural specificity of territories *and* about their non-specificity at the same time?

DETERRITORIALIZATION AND THE CLOSE-UP

To address this puzzle, I propose that we substitute for the simple and static notion of a territory the more dynamic notion of 'territorialization', along with its associated concepts of 'deterritorialization' and 'reterritorialization'. They are terms that suggest a sort of processual or discursive dimension, a movement between levels of analysis, that seems truer to the spirit of an interest in 'debatable lands'. To be sure, unlike 'debatable lands' itself, these are the terms of our time rather than Edgeworth's, but this need not in itself reflect adversely on their utility. We certainly see their utility for our own contemporary issues in the work of Etienne Balibar, to which Celeste Langan has directed our attention, especially in what he calls his 'reflections on transnational citizenship' in *We, the People of Europe*. Late in that book, addressing the implication of a globalized economy for the question of state sovereignty, Balibar offers the following clarification:

The issue here is . . . a certain relation between a people and a territory. Control of the territory on which economic activity occurred and, in particular, on which capital and labor power 'met' was what allowed the state to intervene at a certain moment as 'mediator' between the two. But this presupposes that economic processes are fundamentally 'territorialized'. [And] we all know that this is . . . no longer so within the same borders, the same sort of borders. Economic processes are all the less 'territorialized' insofar as they include, on a massive scale, not only processes of production and distribution of consumer goods, but processes of [for example] the economy of information and knowledge . . . The question posed is thus whether . . . a [re]territorialization of the transnational economy is possible without a rethinking of the way in which communities and human groups are attached to their 'territory'.[14]

I cite this passage not to broach the vexed questions of the European Constitution (on which Balibar has declared himself a naysayer), but to illustrate how the notion of territorialization has entered contemporary political and cultural discourse, especially around questions of political economy. As Balibar makes clear earlier in his own discussion, this terminology derives from the work of French philosopher and polymath Gilles Deleuze. There it forms part of a difficult array of concepts – 'stratification', 'abstract machines', 'plane of consistency', 'assemblages', 'bodies without organs', and the like – whose connections Deleuze worked out over some years but which is most fully set forth in *A Thousand Plateaus* (1980), co-authored with Felix Guattari. It is to some of these elaborations that I want to turn for help with our puzzle. And I should simply note here that it is only part of the claim of this work on those of us working on Romantic writers of the so-called Celtic fringe that territoriality is a notion that Deleuze and Guattari elaborated alongside their seminal notion of 'minority usage' in language, literature, and culture, a notion that David Lloyd and others have brought to bear on Irish studies.[15]

One can glimpse the formidable difficulty of Deleuze's work, and perhaps its potential relevance for our puzzle, in one of the earliest of several discussions of 'territorialization' in *A Thousand Plateaus*, where Deleuze and Guattari attempt to distinguish 'forms' from 'substances' in relation to what they call 'strata':

Forms related to codes and processes of coding and decoding in the parastrata; substances, being formed matters, related to territorialities and movements of deterritorialization and reterritorialization on the epistrata. In truth, the epistrata are just as inseparable from the movements that constitute them as the parastrata are from their processes. Nomadic waves or flows of deterritorialization go from the central layer to the periphery, then from the new center to the new periphery . . . The organization of the epistrata moves in the direction of increasing deterritorialization on their own stratum and between strata.[16]

I will not attempt a paraphrase, but I will suggest that part of the enormous difficulty of this theoretical project has to do with its ambition – its attempt to produce a discourse, a framework of analysis, that will function across the three great primary strata that Deleuze and Guattari address in what they call their 'geology of morals'. These three strata correspond broadly to the traditional tripartite distinctions among the physical, biological, and human sciences. At each of these levels, what is being 'territorialized' is in no sense to be seen as a simple material ground, so to speak, but always includes both material relations and forms of 'expression'. This is true even on the level of the physical stratum, the geological stratum as such. Indeed, the passage I have just cited pertains to that physical or geological level: it is actually about rocks.

It is when Deleuze and Guattari turn to the second stratum, the 'organic', on which thinking about 'populations' becomes inevitable in the wake of Malthus and Darwin, that the figures of 'coding' and 'expression' are easier to recognize – easier on account of their relation to gene coding and gene expression, a topic that Deleuze and Guattari discuss at some length. It is only in the shift to the third great stratum (the anthropomorphic or allocentric), as they explain, that 'the form of expression becomes linguistic rather than genetic; in other words, it operates with symbols that are comprehensible, translatable, and modifiable from the outside' (p. 60). And it is for the analysis of this third stratum that Deleuze and Guattari develop their complex notion of the 'assemblage', which provides terms more immediately apposite for the tasks of literary and cultural analysis. Here are some 'general conclusions' they offer on 'the nature of Assemblages':

On a first, horizontal axis, an assemblage comprises two segments, one of content, the other of expression. On the one hand it is *a machinic assemblage* of bodies, of actions and passions, an intermingling of bodies reacting to one another; on the other hand it is a *collective assemblage* of enunciation, of acts and statements, of incorporeal transformations attributed to bodies. Then on a vertical axis, the assemblage has both territorial sides, or reterritorialized sides, which stabilize it, and cutting edges of deterritorialization, which carry it away. (p. 88)

To provide a concrete illustration of what they call this tetravalence of the assemblage, Deleuze and Guattari offer the feudal assemblage as a case in point. Along one axis, they point first to 'the interminglings of bodies defining feudalism: the body of the earth and the social body; the body of the overlord, vassal, and serf; the body of the knight and the horse and their new relation to the stirrup; the weapons and tools assuring a symbiosis of bodies – the whole machine assemblage' (p. 89). But then they explain that they 'would also have to consider statements, expressions, the juridical regime of heraldry, all of the incorporeal transformations, in particular, oaths and their variables (the oath of obedience, but also the oath of love; etc) – the collective assemblage of enunciation' (p. 89). Deleuze and Guattari's attention to oaths, it should be noted, has to do with their emphasis on *order-words*, or special performatives, which for them break down the distinction between semantic and pragmatic considerations of language, between acts of speech and the contexts in which they occur. The challenge to such distinctions is crucial to the concept of the assemblage as they elaborate it. On the other axis, then, completing the schematic sketch, they suggest that one must 'consider feudal territorializations and reterritorializations, and at the same time the line of deterritorialization that carries away both the knight and his mount, statement and acts. We would have to consider how all this combines in the Crusades' (p. 89).

Here we come yet a little closer to the context of the historical novel and to its theorizations not only of the feudal and commercial stages of society but also of the shift from one to the other. In his important essays on Chivalry and Romance, after all, Scott offered an account of the feudal assemblage in not too dissimilar terms. He emphasized, we might say, the rhizomatic movements between subjects and codes, disciplinary manners and modes of symbolic representation. For Scott, the chivalric romance was not a world apart, a mere mimesis of the social order of the European middle ages, but rather an instrument of that very disciplinary process of intermingling bodies and things that constituted, for example, the chivalric code as a fact of life. Might we not say that, with Scott, the very possibility of displaying this dynamic becomes a step in its deterritorialization? It seems to me fair enough to suggest, at the least, that the historical novel is built on some such notion as 'the assemblage' – something that might loosely be called the concept of culture or cultural hegemony. Indeed it seems to me that Scott scholars have been considering the implications of such a view of his work for some years now.[17]

I have provided only a woefully superficial sketch of the larger contours of the analysis in *A Thousand Plateaus*, but perhaps it is enough to enable us to turn now to the feature of the territorialization analysis in Deleuze that proves most apposite to our present purposes. It is a part of the argument that I believe had its origins in Deleuze's longstanding interest in the philosophy of cinema, an interest that in fact issued in two major books on the subject close on the heels of *A Thousand Plateaus* in the early 1980s – *The Movement Image* (1983) and *The Time Image* (1985). The feature I have in mind is the work on what Deleuze calls 'visagéité' – faciality – and on its relation, first, to the theory of the close-up in cinema, then, to certain techniques in the novel from which it was derived, and finally to the concept of territoriality.

Deleuze and Guattari premise their discussion of the subject on the apparently well-attested claim that the face is not the anthropological universal we sometimes take it to be. '"Primitives" [they put the word in scare quotes] may have the most human of heads, the most beautiful and the most spectral, but they have no face and need none' (p. 176). This point becomes crucial to their account because of their insistence that 'the head is included in the body, but the face is not'. The face, in short, effects a deterritorialization of the body:

The face is a surface: facial traits, lines, wrinkles; long face, square face, triangular face; the face is a map . . . even when it surrounds and borders cavities that are now no more than holes. The head, even the human head, is not necessarily a face. The face is produced only when the head ceases to be coded by the body . . . when the body, head included, has been decoded and has to be *overcoded* by something that we shall call the Face. (p. 170)

For Deleuze and Guattari the shift from the body-head system to the face system has a special place among the various possible 'movements of deterritorialization' that they sketch in that it represents for them an 'absolute deterritorialization' (p. 172). It is, they suggest, 'no longer relative because it removes the head from the stratum of the organism, human or animal, and connects it to other strata, such as significance and subjectification' (p. 172). The Face is, for them, a white-screen / black-hole figure in which the screen offers the promise of significance and the black hole the imagined interiority of subjectification.

Like much else in *A Thousand Plateaus*, these claims are fascinatingly elusive, provokingly incomplete – both heady, one might say, and in your face at the same time. But in the subsequent cinema books, singly authored by Deleuze, the working out of these issues is a good deal more perspicuous and the conclusions more immediately compelling. This is partly because Deleuze does not attempt to rehearse the entire frame of reference in Rhizomes, Strata, Bodies Without Organs, and so on. Instead, he relates the question of deterritorialization to a familiar and concrete concern in the history of cinema – that of the close-up. This discussion is not without its own philosophical embeddedness – in this case deriving from the work of Henri Bergson, on whose work Deleuze's two cinema books form an explicit and extended commentary. Deleuze's contention is that cinema incarnates the new theory of the movement-image that Bergson was striving for. In particular, the close-up is discussed in relation to the aspect of the movement-image that he calls 'the affection-image', because it occupies the Bergsonian 'interval' between the linked processes of perception and action, a suspension or translation between movement in and movement out: the afferent and efferent movements of the nervous system. Deleuze supplements Bergson's account with the idea that the face (as it were) 'figures' the affection-image because it is the seat of the perceptual organs that *register* movement but lacks the locomotive organs for *executing* movement. In the interval of suspension both movements are translated into the sheer expressiveness of the facial features.[18] What Deleuze then adds to this facialized account of Bergson's affection-image is an understanding of the close-up that he borrows from three early theorists of cinema, each of whom offered crucial commentary on the relation of the *gros plan*, as the French call it, to the face: Béla Balázs, Jean Epstein, and Serge Eisenstein. In doing so, he produces the following equations: 'the face is in itself the close-up, the close-up is by itself face, both are affect, affection-image' (*Movement Image*, p. 88).

How might these equations matter to the notion of 'deterritorialization' and ultimately to the Edgeworth-Scott moment in fiction? The answer begins to come into focus with the recognition that, just as the facialized affection-image opens an interval of suspension or reflection in the spatio-temporal field defined by the linked process of perception and affection, so the close-up opens a new dimension in the course of a film narrative, a movement into a domain of expression, a 'line of flight' from the territory of the framed action. Closely following Balázs in particular, Deleuze argues that 'the close-up does *not* tear away its object from a set of which it would form a part, of which it would be a part, but on the contrary it abstracts it from all spatio-temporal coordinates' (*Movement Image*, p. 96). This difficult distinction is crucial to the concept and its application.

In two seminal books – *The Visible Man* [*Der Sichtbare Mensch*] (1924), and *Theory of the Film* (1945) – Balázs, childhood friend of fellow Hungarian Georg Lukács, as it happens, had urged the development of a radical new criticism, a new theory of seeing, to answer the needs of a post-print-cultural society. Keen to explain our practices of coding and decoding of the human figure, Balázs pressed for nothing less than a new grammar of the language, of (in particular) facial expression and gesture.[19] And in a passage actually cited by Deleuze, Balázs writes of the face – the expression of the face as it emerges in the film close-up – in the following highly suggestive terms:

The facial expression . . . is complete and comprehensible in itself and therefore we need not think of it as existing in space and time. Even if we had just seen the same face in the middle of a crowd and the close-up merely separated it from the others, we would still feel that we have suddenly been left alone with this one face to the exclusion of the rest of the world. Even if we have just seen the owner of the face in a long shot, when we look into the eyes in a close-up, we no longer think of that wide space, because the expression and significance of the face has no relation to space and no connection with it. Facing an isolated face takes us out of space, our consciousness of space is cut out and we find ourselves in another dimension: that of physiognomy. The fact that the features of the face can be seen side by side, i.e., in space – that the eyes are at the top, the ears at the sides and the mouth lower down – loses all reference to space when we see, not a figure of flesh and bone, but an expression, or in other words when we see emotions, moods, intentions and thoughts, things which although our eyes can see them, are not in space.[20]

As I indicated above, other versions of this influential argument were available to Deleuze – indeed they are referenced by him – with Epstein in France and Eisenstein in the Soviet Union. All three theorists, furthermore, took their points of bearing in silent cinema from Griffith to Carl Dreier, whose 1927 *The Passion of Joan of Arc* is a locus classicus for claims of this sort, including some of the claims made by Deleuze himself. To return to Dreier in the light of them is indeed a revelation, though one not limited to Dreier's work. With these arguments and this revelation, in any case, we arrive at what might just be the heart of the matter for the deterritorialization thesis: the notion of the facial close-up as opening a new dimension alongside a constituted spatial domain, and one not to be understood as transcendent of that domain.

READING COUNTENANCES IN SCOTT AND EDGEWORTH

Did Deleuze actually derive his notions of deterritorialization as a back-formation from the theory and practice of the facialized close-up in early cinema? That's a question I don't know enough about to answer with confidence. Certainly cinema was a lifelong passion for Deleuze, and just as certainly the references to the cinematic close-up are already fully explicit in the pages of *A Thousand Plateaus*. I can only say that, for me, the cinematic example of the close-up, especially as it is worked out in *The Movement Image* book, provides the clearest and most compelling example of how these two elusive categories work, both separately and together. Moreover, in *A Thousand Plateaus*, which cites Eisenstein's celebrated essay on Griffith and Dickens in some detail, Deleuze and Guattari, following Eisenstein's lead, accept the notion that the novel seems to have anticipated the practice of early cinema in its use of the facialized close-up. It will be recalled that the larger burden of Eisenstein's great essay of 1944 was to show how far the cinema of Griffith and his followers was indebted to the literary past in general and to Dickens in particular. In this sense, too, the theory of faciality in *A Thousand Plateaus*, where Eisenstein's specific uses of Dickens's 'The Cricket and the Hearth' are well noted, also anticipates the connection of the face's work of deterritorialization with the domain of the affections – indeed with the sentimental mode in British fiction.[21]

We can now return to Scott and Edgeworth, and to the puzzle of that 'odd vagueness about place' in their ethnographic fiction. As should be clear by now, I want to suggest that a possible key to understanding this puzzle lies in the sentimental role that faces play at this particular conjuncture in the history of the novel. So, remembering Deleuze and Guattari's example of the feudal assemblage, let us recall an exemplary scene in Scott's *Ivanhoe* that takes place in the debatable lands of the forest around Torquilstone Castle, an exchange between Ivanhoe, still disguised as the Black or Sluggish Knight, and a woodsman who seeks his help with the rescue of Cedric and Rowena, who are imprisoned in the Castle itself. When the woodsman tells the Knight he is only 'a nameless man; but the friend of my country, my country's friends', the Knight replies: 'I willingly believe it . . . I have been accustomed to study men's countenances, and I can read in thine honesty and resolution. I will therefore ask thee no further questions, but aid thee'.[22] Or, coming back to the Borders, we might consider that moment in *The Bride of Lammermoor* when Lucy Ashton and her father encounter Blind Alice, in a rather different terrain:

> it was her expression of countenance which chiefly struck the spectator, and induced most persons to address her with a degree of deference and civility very inconsistent with the miserable state of her dwelling, and which, nevertheless, she received with that easy composure which showed she felt it to be her due . . . It scarce seemed possible that a face, deprived of the advantage of sight, could have expressed character so strongly; her eyes, which were almost totally closed, did not, by the display of their sightless orbs, mar the countenance to which they could add nothing.[23]

Like innumerable other such passages in Scott's fiction, these two demonstrate how the Balázs / Deleuze notion of the face's detachment from its world is anticipated in fiction, indeed in pre-Dickensian fiction. The countenances here described – again, many others could be cited – make their appearance, to be sure, in the time and space of their respective narratives. They are nominally a part of bodies that stand ground, give ground, emerge victorious or defeated on the contested terrain of the action. But in each case they seem to open up another dimension in the narrative, a dimension where a different order of things can make an entry: meanings, qualities, abstractions, values, sentiments, thoughts. In an idealist account, the shift of dimensions might be considered a transcendental movement. Refusing on philosophical principle to regard this domain as transcendent, Deleuze invites us to think of it in materialist terms as a deterritorializing movement instead.

Often, in Scott's fiction, the course of a novel's action will turn in a subtle but decisive way on just such a moment when the meaning or quality of a countenance is registered by another character – the kind of plot event that Aristotle described as the convergence of recognition with reversal or peripeteia. In *Waverley*, for example, we find this sort of convergence in the first phase of the novel's denouement. It is the moment that begins to transform this great saga of debatable lands from the solemn tragedy of the state executions in Carlisle to the comic marriage of Edward Waverley and Rose Bradwardine recounted in the final pages. In the scene in question, Waverley has just seen Fergus McIvor led away to the place of execution:

The courtyard was now totally empty, but Waverley still stood there as if stupefied, his eyes fixed upon the dark pass where he had so lately seen the last glimpse of his friend. At length, a female servant of the governor's, struck with compassion at the stupefied misery which his countenance expressed, asked him if he would not walk into her master's house and sit down?[24]

The impending fate of the Scottish rebel occasions the stupefied misery on the part of the rehabilitated British officer, which now in turn becomes the occasion of compassion on the part of a servant to the very governor who passed the death sentence on Fergus in the first place. Fergus is not even dead yet, but in this instance of facial deterritorialization, the recognized expression of a countenance has already inaugurated the sentimental resolution of his fate, as sensations of pain and horror are softened into a workable emotional basis for Union.

It is at moments like these that one can begin to understand the debt of the historical novel to the sentimental novel, with its differently configured chronotope, one shaped around the principle of virtual face-to-face sympathy that I have elsewhere, apropos of Sterne's fiction, called 'sentimental probability'.[25] In the sentimental chronotope, I have argued, the whole game is to make territoriality a non-issue by making it impossible at all points to distinguish between the literal and figurative, actual and virtual, medium and message, land and commerce, sentiment in travel and travel in sentiment. The sentimental vehicle, apotheosized by Sterne and Abraham Tucker, is a device of perpetual deterritorialization. Scott was certainly about other business. Yet, at certain points in his novels, for all his claims to the establishment of a new 'realism', debated lands seem to dissolve, by way of the face-to-face exchange, into the flow of sentiments. At such points, in short, one realizes that it was not for nothing that the author of *Waverley* dedicated his first great novel to Henry Mackenzie, the author of *The Man of Feeling*.

Maria Edgeworth was of course no Sternean or Mackenzian sentimentalist. She spent some of her considerable energy writing against the sentimentalism, as she saw it, of Lady Morgan, whose *Wild Irish Girl* brings to bear the full range of sentimental tactics, including the techniques of faciality, on a plot in which debatable lands in Ireland are seriously at stake. At the same time, Edgeworth was from an early age a great student of Adam Smith, and she seems to have learned at least as much from the *Theory of Moral Sentiments* as from the *Wealth of Nations*. Like Smith's, her version of the dynamics of sympathetic exchange – the commerce of feelings – has a more stoic cast than, say, the version we find in Laurence Sterne (though Sterne, to be sure, has his stoic moments). Certainly the resort to the face as a device of narrative deterritorialization is something that one finds all over Edgeworth's work, though we must confine our attention here just to *The Absentee* and to *Patronage*, the novel from which *The Absentee* was spun off.

In *The Absentee*, to take one moment from among many to consider in that novel, we can note that it is an early close encounter by Lord Colambre with the countenance of Grace Nugent, seen as if anew, that establishes her as the leading candidate for his heart and hand, this in spite of the cloud of St Omar family shame that seems at this point to hang over her:

He marked the superior intelligence, the animation, the eloquence of her countenance, its variety . . . [Eventually] it was necessary to remove his eyes from that countenance on which he had gazed unobserved . . . [The] whole train of Lord Colambre's thoughts was . . . completely deranged.[26]

Indeed, through the subsequent course of the novel, much of the communion and communication between Colambre and Grace Nugent is established by means of this sort of facialized close-up – an engagement between countenance and countenance. At times, this deterritorialized ground of their relation becomes explicit, as when, at his mother's garish gala, Grace counsels Clonbrony not to look so like a chafed lion: 'Others may read your countenance as well as I do.'[27]

But the capacity to see the face, to recognize what it means, to move into a new dimension that the face-to-face encounter opens up within the territory of the body and the territory to which the body belongs – this is a talent not equally possessed by all. The possibilities of face-to-face recognition codified in the modern commercial order of things seem not only to permit a practice of decoding but also to require what Deleuze calls a kind of recoding or overcoding. Here is where the older sense of countenance as composure or self-constraint seems to merge with Edgeworth's neo-stoic sense of the moral life. To read a countenance one must have countenance, as Grace and (eventually) Clonbrony both conspicuously do.

The positing of this kind of stoic coding indeed seems crucial to the way in which Edgeworth imagines fictional worlds in which the specificities of debatable lands and local codes can become, in Butler's phrase, oddly vague. Nowhere does all this become more evident than in *Patronage*, preoccupied as it is with both land debates and forms of decipherment. At four volumes, it is a sprawling novel, but if there is a single character around whom it is formalized, that character is surely Caroline Percy, the wise, intelligent, and beautiful first daughter of the worthy family who refuse to play the game of patronage and who suffer (and ultimately triumph) accordingly.

Caroline Percy stands out among all the characters for her way with countenances, and this in a novel where such a capacity constitutes the most fundamental of the universal languages it makes a part of its topic. Caroline's virtuous father, the decipherer of the spy's documents, has a hobbyhorsical interest in universal-language theories. Indeed, knowing how to show and see countenances is arguably the most important ability imaginable in the world of this novel, in both the political and personal spheres of its action. When Commissioner Falconer, ill-fated player and pawn in the patronage system, is confronted by his own patron, Lord Oldborough, about the malfeasance of his son, it is 'the astonishment and horror'[28] that Oldborough sees on Falconer's countenance that convinces him of his innocence. When Lord Oldborough appears before his own patron, the king, he is careful to 'place himself so as to give the King the advantage of the light, which he did not fear to have fall on his own countenance'.[29] But, as I have suggested, the ability to see a countenance itself requires countenance – self-containment – and this quality is what Caroline Percy's character most fundamentally demonstrates throughout the novel.

One episode late in the novel seems to have been composed for the express purpose of rendering this demonstration unmistakable. Caroline Percy, in love with a German Count who has suddenly and inexplicably broken off relations with her, is encouraged by a well-intentioned older friend, Lady Grenville, to accept the attentions of an English nobleman, Lord William, a character Edgeworth has, in a very un-Austen-like manner, introduced when the novel's action is very far advanced. Lord William is described as a man of substance and merit, but his one character flaw is a form of 'timidity' that causes his looks to be out of line with his inner nature:

He was subject to that nightmare of the soul, who sits herself upon the human breast . . . and . . . pronounces: 'Henceforward you shall never appear in your natural character. – Innocent, you shall look guilty. Wise, you shall look silly.'[30]

Inwardly insulted by those women who imagine they flatter him by praising the outward man he knows he is not, Lord William turns to Caroline Percy, whose 'penetration' allows her to see him for what he is and to esteem him. But whereas he seeks her hand in marriage, for her the limit is friendship. As the relation develops, thus asymmetrically, Lady Grenville urges Caroline *not* to discourage a proposal from Lord William, not to refuse an offer she has not yet been made. This matter of extreme delicacy requires a discussion about composing and interpreting countenances that stretches over several pages of the novel. The chapter comes to a head in an exquisitely sensitive exchange between Caroline and Lord William that follows upon Lady Grenville's having aggressively broached the question in conversation with them both: 'Would it not be strange, indeed, if a lady were to reject a gentleman before she was asked?' To which Caroline carefully replies: 'she might, without any premature or rude rejection, simply by a certain ease of manner, which every man of sense knows how to interpret, mark the difference between esteem and the tenderer sentiments'. At the next available exchange, after failing to draw 'some encouraging omen from her countenance', Lord William screws up his courage and tries his luck with the remark that in spite of Caroline's evident 'ease of manner' with him he thinks it impossible 'that with your penetration, you can be in any doubt as to my sentiments'. Longing, yet fearing, 'to see that look, and hear that word', Lord William is delivered the following response: 'And I think it impossible, that, with your Lordship's penetration, you should mistake mine.'[31]

I want to suggest that episodes like this show a strong connection between countenance as coded expression and countenance as coded discipline – each a universalizable principle of deterritorialization in a Smithian, neo-stoic scheme. This sort of code is not, for Edgeworth, to be confused with the facile cosmopolitan theatre of the emotions practised by another character, Lady Angelica, whom we see engaged in an 'exhibition of the passions'[32] in a series of *tableaux vivants* after the manner of Emma Hamilton. For such a theatre betrays only the most superficial sort of self-command, as Edgeworth emphasizes by giving us a scene quick on the heels of the *tableaux* when Lady Angelica is caught off guard and 'many conflicting passions appeared in [her] countenance'.[33] Lady Angelica's kind of artifice is shown in the end to belong to the same system that destroys the Falconers: the local politics of patronage that is fuelled by ungoverned passions and interests. Edgeworth's code, by contrast, belongs to what Dr Johnson (who is cited approvingly in *Patronage*) once called 'general nature', a deterritorialization of the politics of 'place', in *all* the resonant senses of that term.[34]

More generally, then, my suggestion has been that the fiction that Edgeworth and Scott developed between them, founded as it is on the principles of exchange that govern both goods and sentiments, reframed the very debate on contested territory, 'debatable lands', and opened up new discursive territory that we may only just be beginning to explore. The fact that the quasi-science of 'physiognomy' emerged into full recognition in this period, for example, is a matter that would have to be considered in any further consideration of the relation of the face and the place in the new novel taking shape in the hands of Edgeworth and Scott.[35] The fundamental role played by reading of countenances and the centrality of the affective code according to which the countenance is constituted and deciphered, these are topics worthy of further examination not only in the sentimental novel but also in the fiction that maintains a clear connection to it. Pursuit of such topics may help us to understand better why Edgeworth's Irish tales were referred to as 'portraits' in their initial reception, and why the sentimental resolution of the first Waverley novel famously brings its reader's gaze to rest not on a view of any of the places that supply its dramatic settings but on the newly painted portrait of its protagonist.

NOTES

1. Marilyn Butler, 'Introductory Note' to *Patronage*, in Marilyn Butler and Mitzi Myers (eds.), *The Novels and Selected Works of Maria Edgeworth*, 12 vols. (London: Pickering and Chatto, 1999), vol. VI, p. xviii.
2. Georg Lukács, *The Historical Novel*, trans. Hannah and Stanley Mitchell (London: Merlin Press, 1962), pp. 19–30.
3. Ina Ferris, *The Romantic National Tale and the Question of Ireland* (Cambridge: Cambridge University Press, 2002), pp. 18–45.
4. I take the term 'debatable lands' from Claire Lamont and Michael Rossington, who themselves borrowed it (via Walter Scott) from British legal history, where it names contested territory. This essay was initially composed as a plenary lecture for the BARS conference they organized on the subject, and I am indebted to those who offered helpful responses on that occasion. I would like to acknowledge Noelle Gallagher and Mollie Godfrey for their assistance in preparing this chapter for publication, and to thank Claire Connolly for steering me toward *Patronage* in the first place.
5. Fiona Robertson, 'Note on the Text' for Sir Walter Scott, *The Bride of Lammermoor* (Oxford and New York: Oxford University Press, 1991), pp. xxxiv–xxxv;

Peter Garside, 'Union and the *Bride of Lammermoor*', *Studies in Scottish Literature* 14 (1984), 85–9.

6. Wolfram Schmidgen, *Eighteenth-Century Fiction and the Law of Property* (Cambridge: Cambridge University Press, 2002), pp. 186–213.

7. Sir Walter Scott, 'General Preface to the Waverley Novels, 1829', in his *Waverley* (New York: Penguin Books, 1988), pp. 522–4.

8. Ferris, *Romantic National Tale*, p. 13; Ferris points out that this sense of 'accuracy' was qualified by a further sense that Edgeworth's 'portraits' sought sympathy for their subjects. This anticipates some of what I'll be arguing below in respect to the reading of countenances in Edgeworth and Scott.

9. Edgeworth, *Novels and Selected Works*, vol. v, p. 134.

10. Katie Trumpener, *Bardic Nationalism: The Romantic Novel and the British Empire* (Princeton: Princeton University Press, 1997), pp. 128–37.

11. Butler, 'Introductory Note', p. xviii.

12. Ibid., p. xvii.

13. W. J. McCormack, 'The Tedium of History: An Approach to Maria Edgeworth's *Patronage* (1814)', in Ciaran Brady (ed.), *Ideology and the Historians* (Dublin: Lilliput Press, 1991), pp. 77–98; Claire Connolly, '"A Big Book about England"? Public and Private Meanings in Maria Edgeworth's *Patronage*', in *Ireland and the Novel in the Nineteenth Century* (Four Courts Press and Syracuse University Press, forthcoming). Connolly's perceptive essay points to gender as the category that complicates public–private issues in *Patronage*, arguing that certain domestic 'spaces' in the novel are in fact theatres of enormous political implication. She also sees the book as staging a contest among various narrative genres, though her emphasis runs in directions rather different from mine.

14. Etienne Balibar, *We, the People of Europe* (New York: Columbia University Press, 2004), p. 200. Balibar may be drawing more immediately here on the comments about globalization and deterritorialization in Michael Hardt and Antonio Negri, *Empire* (Cambridge, Mass.: Harvard University Press, 2000), pp. 123–4, 294–7. See also Celeste Langan, 'Coup de Tête: Napoleon's Supposed Epilepsy', *European Romantic Review* 11.2 (April–June 2005), 246–7.

15. David Lloyd, *Nationalism and Minor Literature: James Clarence Mangan and the Emergence of Irish Cultural Nationalism* (Berkeley: University of California Press, 1987).

16. Gilles Deleuze and Felix Guattari, *A Thousand Plateaus: Capitalism and Schizophrenia*, trans. Brian Massumi (Minneapolis: University of Minnesota Press, 1987), p. 53. Subsequent references to this book are given parenthetically in the text.

17. See my *England in 1819: The Politics of Literary Culture and the Case of Romantic Historicism* (Chicago: University of Chicago Press, 1998), pp. 127–51; Ian Duncan, *Modern Romance* (New York: Cambridge University Press, 1992), pp. 51–105; James Buzard, *Disorienting Fiction: The Autoethnographic Work of Nineteenth-Century British Novels* (Princeton: Princeton University Press, 2005), pp. 63–104.

18. Gilles Deleuze, *The Movement Image*, trans. Hugh Tomlinson and Barbara Habberjam (Minneapolis: University of Minnesota Press, 1986), pp. 87–122. Subsequent references are given parenthetically in the text.

19. Béla Balázs, *Theory of the Film: Character and Growth of a New Art*, trans. Edith Bone (New York: Dover, 1970), p. 44.

20. Balázs, *Theory of the Film*, p. 61; quoted in large part in Delueze, *Movement Image*, p. 96.

21. Serge Eisenstein, 'Dickens, Griffith and the Film Today', in *Film Form*, trans. Jay Leyda (New York: Harcourt Brace, 1949), pp. 195–256. Cf. Jean Epstein, 'Magnification and Other Writings', trans. Stuart Liebman, *October* 3 (Spring 1977), 9–25. For an overview of these positions, see Mary Ann Doane, 'The Close-Up: Scale and Detail in the Cinema', *Differences* 14 (Fall 2003), 89–111.

22. Scott, *Ivanhoe* (New York: Penguin Books, 1984), pp. 212–13.

23. Scott, *Bride of Lammermoor*, pp. 48–9.

24. Scott, *Waverley*, p. 476.

25. James Chandler, 'The Emergence of Sentimental Probability', in *The Age of Cultural Revolutions* (Berkeley: University of California Press, 2002), pp. 137–70.

26. Maria Edgeworth, *The Absentee*, in Butler and Myers (eds.), *Novels and Selected Works of Maria Edgeworth*, vol. v, p. 15.

27. Ibid., vol. v, p. 34.

28. Maria Edgeworth, *Patronage*, in Butler and Myers (eds.), *Novels and Selected Works of Maria Edgeworth*, vol. vii, p. 179.

29. Ibid., vol. vii, p. 170.

30. Ibid., vol. vii, p. 131.

31. Ibid., vol. vii, pp. 136–7.

32. Ibid., vol. vi, p. 158.

33. Ibid., vol. vi, p. 159.

34. Johnson's most celebrated instance of the phrase appears in his endorsement of the norm of 'just representations of general nature' in the Preface to Shakespeare (1765).

35. Thomas Holcroft's influential translation of J. C. Lavater's *Essay on Physiognomy*, for example, appeared in 1804.

CHAPTER 7

Maria Edgeworth and 'the light of nature': artifice, autonomy, and anti-sectarianism in Practical Education (1798)

Susan Manly

In an influential account of Romantic-era writing for and about children, Alan Richardson suggests that Edgeworthian education, as elaborated in her *Practical Education* (1798), was fundamentally coercive and prescriptive, and sought to 'harness' children's 'deconstructive energies . . . to the pursuit of experimental knowledge', making 'the love of nature' secondary to the 'love of science'. Claiming that the Edgeworthian intention is always to foster rationality and a coldly reductive analytical bent, Richardson criticizes the 'mechanical character of the Edgeworths' conception of psychic development', and alleges that this conception of the child's mind blocked sublime experience and inhibited imagination: 'little ideas were precisely what the Edgeworths found appropriate for little minds'. He does, however, subsequently complicate this rather damning analysis, noting that '[t]he questions of children's imaginative reading and their religious training were more closely related in the early nineteenth century than is generally remarked', and that it was often politically conservative and religiously orthodox educational commentators who took exception to rationalist doubts about the value of magical tales and fantastical tricks and stories.[1] Marilyn Butler has, indeed, illuminated the extent to which Maria Edgeworth's works deliberately evoke, sometimes only via allusion, but often by explicit reference, a network of radical and variously anti-authoritarian thinkers and writers.[2] *Practical Education* is no exception, and this chapter will show that, far from being coercive and prescriptive, Maria Edgeworth's first major published work was in fact, in its own time, considered offensive partly because of the way in which it rejected the fearful awe of and submission to power – divine and otherwise – that conservative contemporaries thought early education should instil.

Jan'y 11th 1780. Little Lovell was ask'd to spell ga go gi which he spelt very well. When he was ask'd, to spell gu, he wd not tell the first letter – nobody told him how to spell it, but after his Father had given him several hard stroaks with a whip he told it. What does obstinacy in children arise from? Is there no danger of making them cowards by beating them? Is it not pain or fear of pain, that makes them yeild to the person who is stronger than themselves? . . . Will not then the child think, I am weak now & am forced to submit, to those that are stronger – but when I am older & stronger I will make others submit to me – What is it that makes a servile, base disposition? being govern'd alone by fear of bodily pain – What would you think of a man who was restrain'd from committing murder only by the fear of being hang'd?[3]

As this extract from the 'child register' kept by Honora Sneyd Edgeworth shows, Edgeworthian education was not, at its inception, always as happy as *Practical Education*, published in 1798, suggests. Although it was Honora who instigated the experimental, practical, and observation-based approach to children's learning which was to form the foundation of, and source-book for, the 1798 publication, her preoccupation with morality and obedience stands in stark contrast to the later work's intention: to create children with active, inventive minds, confident self-command and 'benevolent affections'.[4] The second wife of Richard Lovell Edgeworth, and Maria Edgeworth's first stepmother (two more were to follow), Honora was a stern – if sometimes troubled – disciplinarian, who held that 'almost everything that education can give, is to be given before the age of 5 or 6 – therefore I think great attention & strictness should be shewn before that age; particularly, if there is anything refractory or rebellious in the disposition, that is the time to repress it, & to substitute good habits, obedience, attention, & respect towards superiors.'[5] Richard Lovell Edgeworth's response to his wife's misgivings about severe physical punishments – which in the manuscript of 1780 quoted above is written in Honora's notebook, just after her troubled self-questionings – reveals no remorse over the severity of his punishment of Lovell, although it does show the imprint of the Hartleyan associationism which was another of the formative influences on *Practical Education*, particularly in its aim to foster a psychologically informed understanding of children's ideas and motivations. Lovell, his father reflects, 'was a very feeble infant; and felt great pain from attempting to walk: so much as to prevent him from going to his food for many hours if it were put at a distance from him. His Nurse ambitious that he should walk early by harsh words & threats made him walk without giving him pleasure when he had done – hence, I apprehend, arose his dislike to obedience.'[6] His explanation of his son's obstinacy notwithstanding, Richard Lovell Edgeworth is contented, in 1780, to dismiss Honora's doubts about the wisdom of harsh discipline.

By 1798, however, when Maria Edgeworth was setting down the Edge-worth family experiment in education, the use of force and of artificial experiences such as the placing of food at a distance were regarded as clear signs of failure in adult preceptors, not as means of discipline or charac-ter formation required by the innate obstinacy and waywardness of young children: Edgeworth indeed emphasizes (citing the radical educationalist David Williams in support) that 'punishments are *the abrupt, brutal resource of ignorance, frequently*, to cure the effects of former negligence' on the part of adult carers and teachers; 'the language of blows need seldom be used to reasonable creatures'.[7] Coleridge's famous comment that the Edgeworth children had been 'most miserable . . . & yet the Father, *in his book*, is ever vapouring about their *Happiness*', is clearly, in part, well founded.[8] Certainly it seems that the children of Richard Lovell Edgeworth's first two marriages were treated with severity and strictness, as the exchange quoted above demonstrates.

But the 1798 volume is far more concerned with making learning an active pleasure rather than a source of pain or shame, with liberating children's minds, including them in the conversation and interests of the family, and thus, through practical example rather than moral harangue or punishment, inspiring them with 'benevolent affections' and a desire to benefit society at large.[9] Practical education, as conceived and explained by Edgeworth, was to be easy, enjoyable, and based on activity and experience, rather than rule and rote, so that independent discovery and experiment were to be valued more highly than dictation and authority, and affection, rather than fear, was to be the motive: Edgeworth stresses the importance of allowing children to make their own choices, and learn 'from their own experience a just confidence in their own powers'.[10] In other words, this was an education intended to create a cohesive society, but one in which variety of opinion and enquiry were valued, as opposed to one which enforced conformity.

When *Practical Education* first came out in 1798, it emerged in the midst of an urgent debate about 'useful knowledge' and its effects on social sta-bility and health. Eight years previously, Richard Price had rejoiced at the French Revolution, seeing it as a sign of a 'diffusion of knowledge which has undermined superstition and error'. He had called on his fellow 'friends of freedom, and writers in its defence' to behold 'the light you have struck out, after setting AMERICA free, reflected to FRANCE and there kindled into a blaze that lays despotism in ashes, and warms and illuminates EUROPE', and to applaud a 'general amendment . . . in human affairs' which was 'catch-ing and spreading', presaging an era of 'increasing light and liberality'.[11] Edmund Burke, on the other hand, had celebrated what he saw as the

English nation's natural firebreak or lightning-rod – a 'sullen resistance to innovation'; and declared: 'We know that *we* have made no discoveries; and we think that no discoveries are to be made, in morality; nor many in the great principles of government, nor in the ideas of liberty, which were understood long before we were born, altogether as well as they will be after . . . the silent tomb shall have imposed its law upon our pert loquacity'.[12] This debate about innovation, inflammatory experiments, and the moral value of the 'diffusion of knowledge' is not simply a feature of explicitly political and public declarations for, or declamations against, the 'rights of man'. As Price's discussion of patriotism and enlightened fellow-feeling had suggested, education – the diffusion of knowledge – was increasingly to seem a matter of public and political importance in the 1790s. Burke had famously enlisted the domestic sphere against the innovators, rhetorically yoking together 'our state' and 'our hearths', and arguing that aristocratic and monarchical authority possessed natural claims equal to the private affections of home and family.[13] Writers on education such as Priestley, Wollstonecraft, and the Edgeworths countered this by showing how the apparently private realm of child-rearing and early education might become a source of social transformation and of challenge to established authorities.[14]

The quiet challenge to authoritarianism posed by *Practical Education* is discernible in many places, but is perhaps clearest in the discussion of 'memory and invention' in Chapter 21. With its attention firmly fixed on the merits of experimentation, observation, adaptation of existing knowledge, and the encouragement of rational enquiry, Edgeworth's critical exploration of the value placed on children's ability to memorize and learn by rote implicitly challenges the conservative Burkean respect for precedents, 'wise prejudice', and the sanctity of custom, and consistently shows more respect for the 'living' world of innovative thinkers than for the 'dead' world of adherence to the established rules and understandings of the natural and human orders. For Burke, the French regard for 'false lights' had led France into a quagmire of 'muddy understandings' and 'cold hearts', and he represents these anti-authoritarian questionings of the old order as a kind of bad science, evoking Lunar experiments with air. The innovations of the revolutionaries had triggered, he argued, a dangerous and unpredictable chemical reaction, in which 'the wild *gas*, the fixed air is plainly broken loose', leaving 'the agitation of a troubled and frothy surface'. Burke goes on to assert that, contrary to this pernicious knowledge, British education is 'in a manner wholly in the hands of ecclesiastics, . . . in all stages from infancy to manhood'.[15] Burke's idea of education as the creator and supporter of orthodoxy is, as we shall see, quite contrary to Edgeworth's notion of education as based on enquiry, observation, and experiment.

Edgeworth, in fact, takes Burke's valuation of prejudice, 'antient usage', and habit and quietly overturns it.[16] Suggesting that it is only '[t]hose who are governed in their opinions by precedent and authority' who believe that rote learning is valuable in and of itself, Edgeworth highlights the suspension of critical thought involved in such feats of memory: 'Whilst we repeat, we exclude all thought from the mind, we form a habit of saying certain sounds in a certain order.' Such habitual behaviour can in fact, she suggests, have lasting injurious effects: 'no one can reason clearly, whose memory has these foolish habits; the ill matched ideas are inseparably joined, and hence they imagine that there is some natural connexion between them. Hence arise those obstinate prejudices, which no arguments can vanquish.'[17] Rational memory, on the other hand, in which ideas are thoroughly tested and subjected by the child to 'philosophic arrangement', is a kind of scientific endeavour which may involve thinking that is 'foreign to [a] customary course of associated ideas'.[18] The communication of knowledge from adult to child is not to be conceived of as a direct imprint of adult categories onto the child's undeveloped but receptive mind, Edgeworth cautions; instead, she recommends that when something is explained, the child should be asked to run through the explanation for him- or herself, not necessarily using the same words: 'In such repetitions as these the mind is active, therefore it will strengthen and improve.'[19] Crucially, Edgeworth suggests that it is children's full inclusion in rational society that helps to create new knowledge: in a 'large and literary family' where there is continual conversation and dialogue, especially if children are 'encouraged to take a reasonable share in conversation' and permitted to 'talk freely of what they read', curiosity will feed the memory at the same time as invention is nurtured.[20] Writing in the manuscript child register about an immersion *en famille* in the study of chemistry in 1796, Edgeworth suggests that such intellectual endeavour, in which adults and children are joined, is the best and most stimulating environment for all, since '[a] large family may send out antennae for knowledge to different regions'. This egalitarian collaborative effort creates an appetite for knowledge, as well as keeping learning pleasurable; for example, elsewhere in the same manuscript account of the family study of chemistry, Edgeworth describes

[a] new chemical masque – To imprint upon our memories the names of the acids and alkalies by their different affinities we gave to each person in the family the name of an acid or an alkali – This diverted us all & we got them by heart with

ease . . . This exhibition not only diverted us but fixed the names of the mixtures on our minds – In the Evening the Children were all upon the gravel walk and they began a chemical dance – When Lovell called to any of the couples & asked what they were they readily told him & each acid & alkali gradually learned to distinguish all their proper partners.[21]

Children, like adults, argues Edgeworth, have more motivation for absorbing ideas when they feel that they can make use of them 'in some future invention': this hope gives more incentive to remember data than when 'they merely learn by rote, because they are commanded to do so by the voice of authority'. The 'habit of inventing' is one, Edgeworth observes, that 'increases the wish for knowledge, and increases the interest men take in a number of ideas, which are indifferent to uncultivated and indolent people. It is the same with children'. She urges: 'Let their useful curiosity be encouraged; let them make a part of the general society of the family, instead of being treated as if they had neither senses nor understanding. When any thing is to be done, let them be asked to invent the best way of doing it.'[22]

In this emphasis on social integration and practicality, as well as on the liberation of children's inventive powers, *Practical Education* shows how different the Edgeworth family's outlook was from Rousseau's. Although frequently cited in *Practical Education*, Rousseau's system, as laid down in *Emile*, had limited appeal for Maria Edgeworth. He had in *Emile* described a relationship in which, from the very beginning, the child's experiences were strictly monitored, and sometimes invented, by the preceptor-figure: 'There is no subjection so complete as that which preserves the forms of freedom . . . Are you not master of his whole environment so far as it affects him?' Rousseau recommends that this mastery should always be invisible to the child: 'Give him no orders at all, absolutely none . . . Let him know only that he is weak and you are strong . . . let this be perceived, learned, and felt . . . let the curb be force, not authority. If there is something he should not do, do not forbid him, but prevent him, without explanation or reasoning.'[23] Echoing this emphasis on control as an ostensible means of creating freedom, in 1797 Tom Wedgwood – one of the sons of Josiah Wedgwood, a Lunar Society man and a friend of Richard Lovell Edgeworth – proposed an experiment in education still more extreme than Rousseau's. Wedgwood wanted to involve Wordsworth, Coleridge, Godwin, Beddoes, Holcroft, and Horne Tooke in the rearing of a child from infancy under strictly maintained conditions: 'The gradual explication of Nature would be attended with great difficulty; the child must never go out of doors or leave his own apartment.'[24] Although the intention must have been to raise a child free of the corruption and compromise of the real world, Wedgwood's proposed scheme paradoxically reproduced the situation prevailing in British society in 1797 – in which 'sedition' was prevented using surveillance, restriction of freedom of expression, and imprisonment without charge – a strange replication of what several of Wedgwood's ideal preceptors had themselves experienced in the 1794 Treason Trials.

Edgeworthian education, by contrast with Rousseau's and Wedgwood's schemes, was sociable, playful, and encouraged children to interrogate the assumptions and reasonings of those who were supposedly superiors. Edgeworth asserts that

> if we compare [children's] method of reasoning with the reasonings of the learned, we shall sometimes be surprised. They have no prejudices, therefore they have the complete use of all their senses; they have few ideas, but those few are distinct; they can be analysed and compared with ease; children, therefore, judge and invent better *in proportion to their knowledge* than most grown-up people.[25]

As so often in Edgeworth's writing, her allusion, in this case to Robert Hooke, in support of this assertion amplifies the point that she seems to undercut with her cautious italicization. Hooke's discussion of scientific experiment and innovation seeks to counter the influence of prejudice and of loyalty to authoritative precedents. Again, there are implicitly anti-Burkean overtones here for the post-1790 reader. Hooke notes, for instance, that philosophy's progress is inhibited if men conform to 'a Prejudice against the search of Truth elsewhere, than in Books thereby chained up by the imbib'd Principles and Dictates of their Teachers', and allow themselves to be 'habituated to a loathing of any thing that offered it self as a Novelty or new Discovery'. He associates this with a mistaken loyalty to orthodoxies which leads to distortion of truth, where those making experiments feel obliged 'to wrest over all the Observations they chance to stumble upon, and make them correspondent with their already believ'd Theory; instead of an indeavour to rectify and regulate those so receiv'd Theories by those Intimations, which careful and accurate Observations would afford'.[26] It is interesting to notice here how Hooke values 'stumbling' in the pursuit of truth: like Edgeworth, he suggests that it is the unprejudiced observer, willing to attend to the evidence of the senses and to reason from this evidence, who will advance knowledge: truly damaging errors come rather from the assumptions and conscious knowledgeability of 'wise' experts than from ignorance.

Edgeworth's account of the family practice of 'conversation-lessons' in the *Memoirs of Richard Lovell Edgeworth* is also suggestive of the kind of openness to enquiry and tolerance of error that Hooke recommends. Of her father's attitude to intellectual enquiry, Edgeworth remembered that, '[i]n trying experiments he always shewed, that he was intent upon learning the truth, not upon supporting his opinion'. The same dialogic openness was evident in his desire to include children in adult pursuits, and in his attitude towards children's efforts to solve problems: 'when he was building or carrying on experiments, or work of any sort, he constantly explained to his children whatever was doing or to be done; and by questions adapted to their several ages and capacities, exercised their powers of observation, reasoning and invention'. This had an electric effect on the children's interest in knowledge, as Edgeworth comments: 'The animation spread through the house by connecting children with all that is going on, and allowing them to join in thought or conversation with the grown-up people of the family, was highly useful . . . thus both sympathy and emulation excited mental exertion in the most agreeable manner.' The Edgeworthian method and attitude allowed the child to make mistakes, in the belief that the process of acquiring understanding and knowledge required error in order to build the power to make right judgements. Her father, Edgeworth records, 'would sit quietly while a child was thinking of the answer to a question, without interrupting, or suffering it to be interrupted, and would let the pupil touch and quit the point repeatedly; and without a leading observation or exclamation, he would wait till the shape of reasoning and invention were gone through, and were converted into certainties'. Through this patient willingness to listen, Maria Edgeworth argues, '[t]he pupil's mind became secure, not only of the point in question, but steady in the confidence of its future powers'.[27] We might compare this with Wollstonecraft's assertion in her *Vindication of the Rights of Woman* (cited with approval very early on in *Practical Education*) that men have 'superiour judgment, and more fortitude than women' because 'they . . . by more frequently going astray enlarge their minds'.[28] Error itself is valued in Wollstonecraft's moral schema as a means of acquiring robust understanding, implicitly running counter to the Miltonic schema in which error and unauthorized knowledge are presented as fatal to innocence.

Error is indeed conceived by Edgeworth as crucial to the child's learning and his relationship with the parent or teacher. She advises: 'Let him try his own experiments, then he will be ready to try yours; and if yours succeed better than his own, you will secure his confidence'. Note that 'if': adult superiority is not a given, and respect is enjoined for the child's own attempts to discover truth. It is assumed that the child has a right to pursue his own investigations and test his own ideas, even if they prove erroneous.

A good example of this tolerance of error appears in Chapter 2 of *Practical Education*, when Edgeworth is discussing the notion of play as a form of serious endeavour. It is worth quoting this passage at length, since it tells us much about the kind of tacit anti-authoritarianism which later brought Edgeworth's moral integrity into disrepute:

S – , a little boy of nine years old, was standing without any book in his hand, and seemingly idle; he was amusing himself with looking at what he called a rainbow upon the floor: He begged his sister M – to look at it; then he said he wondered what could make it; how it came there. The sun shone bright through the window; the boy moved several things in the room, so as to place them sometimes between the light and the colours which he saw upon the floor, and sometimes in a corner of the room where the sun did not shine. As he moved the things he said, 'This is not it;' 'Nor this;' 'This hasn't any thing to do with it.' At last he found, that when he moved a tumbler of water out of the place where it stood, his rainbow vanished. Some violets were in the tumbler; S – thought they might be the cause of the colours which he saw upon the floor, or, as he expressed it, 'Perhaps these may be the thing.' He took the violets out of the water; the colours remained upon the floor. He then thought that 'it might be the water.' He emptied the glass; the colours remained, but they were fainter. S – immediately observed, that it was the water and glass together that made the rainbow. 'But,' said he, 'there is no glass in the sky, yet there is a rainbow, so that I think the water alone would do, if we could but hold it together without the glass. Oh, I know how I can manage.' He poured the water slowly out of the tumbler into a bason, which he placed where the sun shone, and he saw the colours on the floor twinkling behind the water as it fell; this delighted him much . . . He then said he thought the different thickness of the glass was the cause of the variety of colours: afterwards he said he thought that the clearness or muddiness of the different drops of water was the cause of the different colours.[29]

What is striking here is the way in which the child is allowed to play and experiment with the glass of water, without the adults who are listening attempting to direct his reasoning, to correct his errors, or to forestall his enquiry.[30] The conclusions drawn show the adults, in fact, learning something from the child, that is, as Edgeworth immediately notes, how mistaken 'rigid preceptors' would be in supposing the child 'idle whilst he was meditating upon the rainbow on the floor', when it would be apparent to any observer 'free from prejudices' that 'his attention was fixed; he was reasoning, he was trying experiments'. The child exploring the mystery of the rainbow is then compared to Descartes and Buffon; their scientific thought, Edgeworth points out, was equally rooted in 'pleased attention', Descartes pleased and instructed by an experiment with a glass globe to investigate the phenomenon of the rainbow explored here by Edgeworth's half-brother Sneyd with his glass of water, and Buffon diverted by, and then learning from, his observation that the shadows of trees falling on a white wall were green.[31] Edgeworth is concerned above all to show that, notwithstanding his errors, Sneyd was engaged in philosophical work – or play – equal in seriousness to that of Antonio de Dominis, Descartes, or Buffon: something that 'rigid preceptors', such as Blake's Nurse in *Songs of Experience*, might miss. Such observers, remarks Edgeworth, might have condemned the child 'for wasting his time at play' – a phrase that cannot help but recall the thoughts of the Nurse in Blake's Song, who, unlike the permissive Nurse of *Songs of Innocence*, has no confidence in children's self-governance: 'Your spring & your day, are wasted in play / And your winter and night in disguise' (ll. 7–8).[32] Instead, Edgeworth suggests that the child's efforts are not to be considered as different in kind from those of scientists such as de Dominis, 'however high sounding the name', since 'he could have exerted only his utmost attention upon the theory of the rainbow, and the child did the same'.[33] As so often with Edgeworth's allusions, one wonders about the citation of de Dominis, sometime Archbishop of Spalato, pioneer of optical science, and controversial theologian: de Dominis notoriously challenged the authority both of the Papacy and of Protestant England, and ended by having his body burnt, together with his books, by the Inquisition in Rome in 1624 – although he was scarcely any more popular with the Protestant authorities of his time. While not, of course, explicitly advocating such perilous flouting of authority in her child experimentalists, Edgeworth consistently emphasizes throughout *Practical Education* the importance of allowing children the opportunity of judging according to their own experience and observations: 'We should have little hopes of those who swallow every thing they read in a book; we are always pleased to see a child hesitate and doubt, and require positive proof before he believes.'[34]

Edgeworth's subtle, often allusively coded challenge to authority is picked up in the chapter on 'Taste and Imagination', where she urges that children should be encouraged to develop an 'enlarged toleration of mind', attending 'to their own feelings', so as 'to ascertain the truth by experiments upon themselves'. Rather than seeking to influence children's own responses, Edgeworth suggests: 'We should let children see things as they really are, and we should not prejudice them either by our exclamations of rapture, or by our affected disgust.' Again, it is interesting that among the tastes she identifies as injurious when transmitted by unthinking adults to unquestioning children is the taste for high rank or office. Following Erasmus Darwin, who had suggested that ambition was a form of insanity,

Edgeworth warns that these false tastes are easily established in childhood, in 'early mistaken associations. A feather, or a crown, or an alderman's chain, or a cardinal's hat, or a purse of yellow counters, are unluckily associated in the minds of some men with the idea of happiness, and without staying to deliberate, these unfortunate persons hunt through life the phantasms of a disordered imagination.' Such erroneous wrong-headedness, foisted on children by adults, may at first seem insignificant, but it has larger repercussions. Children, though naturally ignorant of and therefore originally indifferent to the attractions of worldly power, can be corrupted by adults who introduce the idea of ambition, and who thus 'instil error and prejudice, without the smallest degree of compunction': Edgeworth therefore expresses disapproval of the kind of 'nonsensical conversation' in which adults probe children as to whether they want to be a king, bishop, judge, general, or admiral when they grow up; by comparison, Edgeworth sees children's ignorance as a form of wisdom: 'Children, who have not learned by rote the expected answers to such interrogations, stand in amazed silence upon these occasions . . . We have often thought, in listening to the conversations of grown up people with children, that the children reasoned infinitely better than their opponents.'[35]

Similarly, it is always urged in *Practical Education* that children should think and feel for themselves, and 'exercise their invention upon all subjects', from fictional plots to poetry, translation, historical events, and scientific technology.[36] (Theology, or scriptural study, is never mentioned.) Even those authors largely approved of by the Edgeworths, such as Buffon and Darwin, are to be considered as authorities which can and should be challenged where children identify faults in their arguments: 'no names of high authority should ever preclude an author's arguments from examination'.[37] Even when it is done with the best intentions, Edgeworth is critical of the kind of reasoning often practised by adults on children, in which '[p]eople arrange questions artfully, so as to bring them to whatever conclusion they please'; the consequence is that the child becomes cunning and timid, fearful of giving the wrong answer, and determined to 'evade the snare that is laid for him'. This kind of artificial exchange, far from promoting an attachment to truth, actually suppresses honest enquiry, according to Edgeworth, and she several times in *Practical Education* compares this subtly authoritarian mode of interrogation with the thwarted exchanges between landowners and peasants, or masters and slaves. The perversion of truthfulness in these situations, and in children governed by fear, is explicitly linked to the project of education. In the case of Irish peasants, Edgeworth identifies the reluctance to give straight answers to straight questions as the result of oppression: peasants are in effect instructed in deception by those in authority, 'from that apprehension of injustice which [they have] been *taught* to feel by hard experience' [my italics]. Slaves are likewise fearful of answering questions: 'Oppression and terror necessarily produce meanness and deceit in all climates, and in all ages; and wherever fear is the governing motive in education, we must expect to find in children a propensity to dissimulation, if not confirmed habits of falsehood.'[38]

This wariness of the potential perversion of truthfulness by authority pervades Edgeworth's approach to children's natural responses. In the chapter on books, for instance, she warns readers about the national stereotypes propagated in some geography textbooks, and urges adults not to dismiss the questions children may ask about the opinions they find in books, which all too often try to impose the authors' own 'moral reflections, and easy explanations of political events' on young readers: 'These reflections and explanations do much harm', warns Edgeworth; 'they instil prejudice, and they accustom the young unsuspicious reader to swallow absurd reasoning, merely because it is often presented to them.' In particular, she values the strong reactions that children have to cruelty and suffering, commenting:

The simple morality of childhood is continually puzzled and shocked at the representation of the crimes and the virtues of historic heroes. History, when divested of the graces of eloquence, and of that veil which the imagination is taught to throw over antiquity, presents a disgusting, terrible list of crimes and calamities; murders, assassinations, battles, revolutions, are the memorable events of history. The love of glory atones for military barbarity; treachery and fraud are often dignified with the names of prudence and policy; and the historian, desirous to appear moral and sentimental, yet compelled to produce facts, makes out an inconsistent, ambiguous system of morality.[39]

Burke had characterized France as an untaught child, suggesting that the French should have had their imaginations directed by a 'pious predilection for [your] ancestors', rather than acting 'as if you had never been moulded into civil society, and had every thing to begin anew'.[40] Edgeworth, by contrast, values the honest and instinctive reactions of the child against the deceitful veil that children are 'taught' to throw over the 'memorable events of history'. Consistently hostile to subterfuge and artifice as a means of directing children's thoughts and observations, Edgeworth thus distances herself from the 'pious predilections' that Burke thinks right, identifying this unquestioning fidelity to authority with a perpetuation of violence and unhappiness. Rather, she believes, parents or teachers 'should never force any system upon the belief of children; but [should] wait until they can understand all the arguments on each side of the question'; likewise, she advises: 'When the young reader pauses to think, allow him time to think, and suffer him to question the assertions which he meets with in books with freedom, and that minute accuracy which is only tiresome to those who cannot reason.'[41]

It was, however, this resolute emphasis on free thinking and free enquiry which later brought *Practical Education* into disrepute. Although celebrated in France, Switzerland, and America, *Practical Education* in Britain was, in the years following its publication, to be closely associated with an unambiguous hostility to established authority and religion, signalled, according to an increasingly reactionary press, in its author's firm determination to remain 'silent' on religion and politics, 'because [as Edgeworth declared in her Preface] we have no ambition to gain partizans, or to make proselytes'.[42] Sarah Trimmer, for instance, saw *Practical Education* as implicitly Jacobinical in its tacit hostility to religion, evident in Edgeworth's neglect of opportunities for religious instruction. What Edgeworth meant by equipping children to receive 'lasting impressions concerning things of the utmost importance to their present and future happiness'[43] was not that they should dwell on religious matters, but that they should be able to make themselves happy using rationality, judgement, and independent reasoning. Trimmer rejects this as a '*false* PHILOSOPHY, which has no foundation in truth or reason', and attacks those who advocate deferring religious instruction until a time when '*young people might . . . with unprejudiced minds chuse a religion for themselves, when (it was imagined) they would be capable of discriminating betwixt truth and error*'.[44] In a series of articles criticizing Edgeworthian notions of utility and truth, Trimmer denies that children need to study anything but 'what is already known': 'all that is necessary is, to *follow an old and beaten track*', not to strive to initiate children in scientific discovery or to encourage them to invent, since, she argues, '*experimental knowledge . . .* ought not to supersede the most important of all knowledge'. Trimmer finds fault, for instance, with the story of Sneyd and the rainbow, contending that his attention should have been called to the rainbow as 'the appointed token of God's everlasting covenant with man'.[45] Rather than having his attention drawn to the fact of human sinfulness, which had necessitated the punishment of the flood and had confirmed God's authority as lawgiver and judge, Sneyd, she alleged, had been deliberately left in ignorance, and a prime opportunity for his spiritual enlightenment had been missed. In contrast with Edgeworth's interest in analysing the corrupting influence of unquestionable authority on truthfulness, Trimmer urges that implanting 'the desire of obtaining the favour of the SUPREME BEING' is the best spur to the 'love and practice of truth and integrity', and laments that this salutary *'fear of* GOD*'* is never mentioned by Edgeworth, partly because of her neglect of religious texts in favour of writings by scientists and radicals: 'for instructions how to excite this fear, the BIBLE will prove a better *text book* than the sophistical writings of a *Williams* and a *Rousseau*', or the 'charming eloquence of a *Godwin*.'[46]

What Trimmer suggests as integral to moral education, the inculcation of fear, is in fact akin to the artificial courses of experience which Edge-worth several times explicitly condemns in *Practical Education*. Whereas Sneyd's investigation of the rainbow could have been annexed to the cause of religious instruction and the emotional manipulation of the child's own observation, according to Trimmer, Edgeworth is more interested in the opportunity to review adult preconceptions afforded by such incidents. Although artificial courses of experience had been explicitly recommended by writers such as Rousseau and Genlis, both frequently cited in *Practical Education*, Edgeworth had her doubts about such underhand devices. Genlis, for instance, recommends that children should be tested by adults, who should invent experiences for them as a necessary part of their training in virtue; this constitutes a species of moral manipulation which Genlis considers more effective than mere harangues, because children have the impression that they are forming their conclusions for themselves: 'Produisez donc des événements, offrez [à l'élève] des tentations, multipliez les épreuves, redoublez-en l'attrait à mesure que la raison se fortifie.'[47] Edge-worth on the other hand warns against 'tormenting' children with 'artificial trials of temper' and other tests imposed by adults on children, declaring: 'We may safely allow children to be as happy as they possibly can be without sacrificing the future to the present', and returns to this theme as she summarizes her book in its concluding chapter: 'We have reprobated the artifices sometimes used by preceptors towards their pupils; we have shewn that all confidence is destroyed by these deceptions. May they never more be attempted! May parents unite in honest detestation of these practices! Children are not fools, and they are not to be governed like fools.'[48]

But this neglect of opportunities to inculcate religious belief, in which experiments in natural philosophy might be turned by parents or preceptors into artful openings for the reinscription of dogma, was among the faults identified by those who saw *Practical Education* as immoral. The freedom from moral 'declamation'[49] that Edgeworth thought so important in the raising of unprejudiced, enquiring children and citizens suggested only impiety and treason to readers anxious about the vast experiment in politics still under way in revolutionary France. This could only have been exacerbated by the publication of two works in 1797–8 which alleged close links between the educators and intellectuals of Prussia and France, and the French Revolution: Barruel's *Memoirs illustrating the History of Jacobinism*, and John Robison's *Proofs of a Conspiracy against all the Religions and Governments of Europe, Carried on in the Secret Meetings of Free Masons, Illuminati, and Reading Societies*. Barruel, for instance, represents the Revolution as the outcome of a perverted education: 'the French Revolution has been a true child to its parent sect; . . . those black deeds and atrocious acts [were] the natural sequel of the principles and systems that gave it birth'. Indeed, Barruel implicates many of the intellectual figures cited in *Practical Education*: Voltaire, Marmontel, D'Alembert, Condillac, d'Argenson, and Buffon, suggesting that all were involved in a conspiracy designed to spread atheism and anarchy, while they pretended only to value 'toleration, reason and humanity', and blaming them for a false philosophy 'reject[ing] . . . every authority that is not derived from the light of nature'.[50]

Where Edgeworth had, in 1798, focused on children's ability to make themselves happy, their aspiration to invent useful solutions to the problems they encountered, and their confidence in their own powers of reason and observation, religious anti-Jacobins such as Sarah Trimmer and the Abbé Barruel would interpret this as a misapplication of enlightenment, contrasting it with the education which would have created a very different set of 'hopes of futurity'. For such critics, Edgeworthian education would remain an unhappy affair. But in its attempt to promote the love of science and to encourage children to bring the 'light of nature' to bear on problems and mysteries, rather than exhibiting a Burkean 'sullen resistance to innovation', *Practical Education* undoubtedly had in view the 'love of mankind' that critics such as Richardson consider inimical to its project.[51]

NOTES

1. Alan Richardson, *Literature, Education, and Romanticism: Reading as Social Practice 1780–1832* (Cambridge: Cambridge University Press, 1994), pp. 53, 55, 56, 59.
2. See, for instance, Marilyn Butler, 'Irish Culture and Scottish Enlightenment: Maria Edgeworth's Histories of the Future', in Stefan Collini, Richard Whatmore, and Brian Young (eds.), *Economy, Polity, and Society: British Intellectual History 1750–1950* (Cambridge: Cambridge University Press, 2000), pp. 158–80 (p. 159). Edgeworth's allusive, often codedly subversive way of suggesting arguments and ideas has also been one of the discoveries that has emerged from the Pickering Masters *The Works of Maria Edgeworth*, 12 vols., general editors Marilyn Butler and Mitzi Myers; consulting editor W. J. McCormack (London: Pickering and Chatto, 1999–2003).

3. All spellings and punctuation as in MS. Lovell, Maria Edgeworth's half-brother, would at this time have been four years old. The extract is taken from Honora's notebook, MS. Eng.misc.c.895, fol.76, Papers of Maria Edgeworth and the Edgeworth Family, Bodleian Library, Oxford. Lovell later set up a school in Edgeworthstown for children of various ranks and religious affiliations, in which they would instigate their studies by learning to read and write without 'a complicated apparatus of severe or preposterous punishment, or by rewards – that foster hurtful propensities' (Richard Lovell Edgeworth, letter of 1816 to the Erasmus Smith Trust, cited in E. F. Burton, *The Contribution to Education of Richard Lovell Edgeworth (1744–1817)*, unpublished Ph.D. thesis, University of Manchester, 1979, p. 319).

4. Maria Edgeworth, *Practical Education* (1798), ed. Susan Manly, vol. XI in *The Novels and Selected Works of Maria Edgeworth*, p. 6. This edition is used throughout this essay. In her General Introduction to the *Novels and Selected Works*, Butler notes that Edgeworth's early stories of around 1792 – including 'Dog Trusty', 'The Orange-Man', and 'The Cherry-Tree' – still threaten children with corporal punishment or with other forms of discipline, but that her later stories 'steadily shift into other registers, typically sympathising with a child who does wrong because she is unhappy', and teaching through empathy (vol. I, p. xiv).

5. Cited in Marilyn Butler, *Maria Edgeworth: A Literary Biography* (Oxford: Clarendon Press, 1972), p. 47.

6. MS. Eng.misc.c.895, fol.78. It seems possible that Maria Edgeworth is thinking back to this exchange when she criticizes 'ill-timed restraints' and 'injudicious incitements' in the treatment of infants in Chapter 1 of *Practical Education* and shows her disapproval of interrupting the child when its attention is elsewhere and peremptorily 'insist[ing] upon it pronouncing the scanty vocabulary which we have compelled it to learn' (p. 15).

7. Edgeworth, *Practical Education*, pp. 138, 148. Williams was the author of *Lectures on Education* (1789). For an expression of Edgeworth's disapproval of 'artificial courses of experience', see *Practical Education*, p. 114.

8. Coleridge assumes that *Practical Education* is the work of Richard Lovell Edgeworth, rather than of his daughter, Maria Edgeworth. (The quotation is from a letter to Coleridge's wife, dated 19 September 1798; in Earl Leslie Griggs (ed.), *Collected Letters of Samuel Taylor Coleridge* 6 vols. (Oxford: Clarendon Press, 1956–71), vol. I, p. 458.) Both names appear as co-authors on the title-page, but it was Maria Edgeworth who actually wrote the book, availing herself of the child registers kept by Honora Sneyd Edgeworth, and of the notes she herself took about children's observations, experiments, and comments in 1796–7: many of these records of conversations and anecdotes appear in the Appendix to *Practical Education*, and occur regularly throughout the main text. Edgeworth's philosophy of education is based principally upon her father's practice, and that of his second and third wives (and of herself) with their children, and secondarily on educational practice and theory drawn from a very wide range of authors, including Rousseau, Wollstonecraft, Kames, Locke, David

Williams, Priestley, Condillac, Barbauld, and Erasmus Darwin; but the organization of the book and nearly all the material is her own. For more on this, see Mitzi Myers, '"Anecdotes from the Nursery" in Maria Edgeworth's *Practical Education* (1798): Learning from Children "Abroad and at Home"', *Princeton Library Chronicle* 60.2 (Winter 1999), 220–50, and Manly, Introductory Note, in Edgeworth, *Practical Education*, p. vii.

9. Edgeworth, *Practical Education*, p. 6.
10. Ibid., p. 29.
11. Richard Price, *A Discourse on the Love of our Country* (London: George Stafford, for T. Cadell, 1789), pp. 41–2.
12. Edmund Burke, *Reflections on the Revolution in France*, ed. Conor Cruise O'Brien (London: Penguin Books, 1968; 1986), pp. 181, 182.
13. Burke, *Reflections*, p. 120.
14. Marilyn Butler argues that Edgeworth in fact 'went further than Wollstonecraft in giving significance and status to the personal, domestic or local sphere of woman, by pioneering an unsentimental and original exploration of our first knowledge of the world, within the home and family' ('General Introduction', in Butler and Myers (eds.), *Novels and Selected Works of Maria Edgeworth*, vol. I, p. viii). For more on the politicization of children's books, especially in relation to Sarah Trimmer, see Matthew O. Grenby, 'Politicizing the Nursery: British Children's Literature and the French Revolution', *The Lion and the Unicorn* 27.1 (2003), 1–26. See also Penny Brown, *The Captured World: The Child and Childhood in Nineteenth-Century Women's Writing in England* (New York and London: Harvester Wheatsheaf, 1993), which notes *Practical Education*'s importance for a 'secularist' tradition of education, picked up by later writers such as Harriet Martineau. For an important discussion of how Edgeworthian education and writing for children relates to enlightenment, see Mitzi Myers, 'Aufklärung für Kinder? Maria Edgeworth and the Genders of Knowledge Genres; Or, "The Genius of Nonsense" and "The Grand Panjandrum Himself"', *Women's Writing* 2.2 (1995), 113–40; see also her 'Romancing the Moral Tale: Maria Edgeworth and the Problematics of Pedagogy', which shows how Edgeworth's moral tales for children, far from cancelling imagination in favour of a dour fidelity to the real and mundane, 'elude the dichotomy of "fantastic visions" and "useful knowledge"', in James Holt McGavran, Jr. (ed.), *Romanticism and Children's Literature in Nineteenth-Century England* (Athens, Ga.: University of Georgia Press, 1991), pp. 96–128 (p. 105).
15. Burke, *Reflections*, pp. 194, 124, 171, 90, 198.
16. Ibid., p. 276.
17. Edgeworth, *Practical Education*, pp. 313, 318, 326.
18. Ibid., pp. 318, 317. An example of this emphasis on the child's own 'philosophic arrangement' as the building-blocks of a 'rational memory' is given in 'Frank', in Edgeworth's *Early Lessons* (London: Joseph Johnson, 1801) – a collection of stories for young children – in which Frank, the child of the title, wishes to learn some lines from Erasmus Darwin's *The Botanic Garden, Part II: The Loves of the Plants* (Canto I, ll. 21–30) by heart to please his father, but does not

attempt this until he has understood all the imagery of the poem by seeking out moths, glow-worms, honey-combs etc, learning something of natural history and respect for animals as he fathoms the meaning of each reference, and thereby prepares his memory while not excluding thought from his mind.

19. Edgeworth, *Practical Education*, p. 327. There is an impressive example of this in Edgeworth's own child register, when she records Henry and Sneyd (then aged about fourteen and ten) being asked, after a series of lectures given by Lovell based on Joseph Black's lectures on chemistry, to give an oral account of all they had learnt. The two acquit themselves well (MS. Eng.misc.c.895, fols. 91–6).

20. Edgeworth, *Practical Education*, p. 328.

21. Edgeworth MSS, 23 August 1796, MS. Eng.misc.c.895, fol. 90. For more on the communal educative process favoured by the Edgeworth family, see Mitzi Myers, 'Reading Rosamund Reading: Maria Edgeworth's "Wee-Wee Stories" Interrogate the Canon', in Elizabeth Goodenough, Mark A. Heberle, and Naomi Sokoloff (eds.), *Infant Tongues: The Voice of the Child in Literature* (Detroit: Wayne State University Press, 1994), pp. 57–79; and Myers, '"Anecdotes from the Nursery" in Maria Edgeworth's *Practical Education* (1798)'.

22. Edgeworth, *Practical Education*, pp. 328–9, 331. Both *Practical Education* and the child register kept by Maria Edgeworth in 1796–7, on which she drew extensively for the 1798 work, record incidents in which children succeeded in offering inventions to solve household problems. For instance, an entry dated 22 July 1796 records what happened when Sneyd, Edgeworth's half-brother, then aged nine or ten, was asked to invent a means of opening a skylight located over a stairwell, and came up with a solution similar to the mechanism used to open the dome of an observatory. *Practical Education* gives several other instances of children's inventions: see, for instance, the anecdote on pp. 333–4, which reveals the talent of Edgeworth's half-sister, Charlotte, then twelve, for mechanical invention.

23. Jean-Jacques Rousseau, *Emile, or Education* (1762), trans. and ed. Barbara Foxley (London and Toronto: J. M. Dent and Sons, 1911), pp. 84, 55. Catherine Toal shows the extent to which Rousseau's philosophy of education differs from Edgeworth's: see her 'Control Experiment: Maria Edgeworth's Critique of Rousseau's Educational System', in Heidi Kaufman and Chris Fauske (eds.), *An Uncomfortable Authority: Maria Edgeworth and Her Contexts* (Newark: University of Delaware Press, 2004), pp. 212–31.

24. Cited in Stephen Gill, *William Wordsworth: A Life* (Oxford: Oxford University Press, 1989), p. 131. The quotation is from Wedgwood's letter to Godwin, 31 July 1797.

25. Edgeworth, *Practical Education*, p. 335.

26. Robert Hooke, *The Posthumous Works of Robert Hooke* (London: Samuel Smith and Benjamin Walford, 1705), pp. 4, 5.

27. Maria and Richard Lovell Edgeworth, *Memoirs of Richard Lovell Edgeworth, esq., begun by himself and concluded by his Daughter, Maria Edgeworth*, 2 vols. (London: R. Hunter, 1820), vol. ii, pp. 181, 182; see also pp. 180–90.

28. Mary Wollstonecraft, *A Vindication of the Rights of Men with A Vindication of the Rights of Woman*, ed. Sylvana Tomaselli (Cambridge: Cambridge University Press, 1995), p. 193. Edgeworth closely paraphrases Wollstonecraft's remarks about needlework and girls' education, but without naming her directly: see *Practical Education*, p. 12, n. 3.

29. Edgeworth, *Practical Education*, pp. 65, 41.

30. Alan Richardson claims that this passage shows 'an enterprising pupil break[ing] down the mystery of the rainbow into its component principles' and hints that this is a good example of the 'records of and recipes for practical experiments' with which the Edgeworths 'pack their work' (*Literature, Education, and Romanticism*, p. 53). The language of Richardson's description misrepresents what really interests Edgeworth in this anecdote: she wants to show that those who dismiss children's play as meaningless and idle are less thoughtful than the children they denigrate.

31. Edgeworth, *Practical Education*, p. 41.

32. See also Edgeworth's respectful treatment of the 'philosophic state of doubt' of a three-year-old, drawing out how a naive question posed by the child is in fact evidence of his powers of observation, ibid., p. 366.

33. Ibid., p. 42.

34. Ibid., pp. 378–9.

35. Ibid., pp. 341, 342, 353, 364. For Erasmus Darwin on ambition, see his *Zoonomia; Or, the Laws of Organic Life*, 2 vols. (London: Joseph Johnson, 1794, 1796), vol. II, pp. 369–70.

36. Edgeworth, *Practical Education*, p. 421.

37. Ibid., p. 372. Edgeworth gives several examples of children questioning the logic they find in books, including an instance where Henry, aged fourteen, and Sneyd, aged ten, questioned Buffon's suggestion that the stripes of the wasp are signs of its viciousness, just as those of the tiger announce its ferocity (p. 372), and another where Sneyd criticizes Darwin's observations about birdsong (p. 424). The child's logic in both cases surpasses the adult authors' logic.

38. Ibid., pp. 374, 124, 125.

39. Ibid., p. 202.

40. Burke, *Reflections*, p. 122.

41. Edgeworth, *Practical Education*, pp. 421, 202.

42. Ibid., p. 6. For an example of a hostile review see the *British Critic* 15 (February 1800), 210; other responses which expressed disapproval of the lack of religious instruction in Edgeworthian education include Marc-Auguste Pictet's account in *Bibliothèque Britannique* XII (1800), p. 283, and XV (1801), pp. 464–5, and Abraham Rees's articles on 'Intellectual Education' and 'Moral Education' in *The Cyclopaedia; or, Universal Dictionary of Arts, Sciences, and Literature*, 39 vols. (London: Longman, Hurst, Rees, Orme, and Brown, 1802–19), vols. XIX and XXIV (no page numbers given). More on the reception of *Practical Education* can be found in an earlier version of this essay, in *Corvey Women Writers on the Web (CW3 Journal)*

(Summer 2005): http://www2.shu.ac.uk/corvey/cw3journal/general%20issues/listofissues.html.

43. The phrase is from Mrs [Sarah] Trimmer, *Reflections upon the Education of Children in Charity Schools; With the Outline of a Plan of Appropriate Instruction for the Children of the Poor* (London: T. Longman and J. and F. Rivington, 1792), p. 34.

44. [Sarah Trimmer], *Guardian of Education* 1 (1802), 10. (The *Guardian of Education* was a periodical publication by Sarah Trimmer, published by J. Hatchard, that appeared in five volumes between 1802 and 1806.) Compare Edgeworth, *Practical Education*, p. 421: 'We should never force any system upon the belief of children; but [should] wait until they can understand all the arguments on each side of the question.' Trimmer's review of *Practical Education* appears serially in *Guardian of Education* 1 (December 1802), 490–8; 2 (January 1803), 30–43; 2 (February 1803), 92–101; 2 (March 1803), 163–71.

45. [Trimmer], *Guardian of Education* 1 (December 1802), 494; 2 (January 1803), 35, 39.

46. [Trimmer], *Guardian of Education* 2 (February 1803), 100–1.

47. 'Produce events, expose [your pupil] to temptation, multiply the number of tests, and make them more and more attractive as the child's reasoning powers grow stronger.' Stéphanie Félicité de Genlis, *Adèle et Théodore*, 3 vols. (Maestricht: J. E. Dufour et P. H. Roux, 1782), vol. 1, p. 358. For instances of Rousseau's advocacy of artificial experiences as a means of controlling children, see his story about Emile and the melon seeds, and the story of the wilful child who insisted on venturing alone into the streets of Paris. Rousseau, *Emile*, pp. 62–3, 87–9.

48. Edgeworth, *Practical Education*, pp. 103, 399.

49. Ibid., p. 6.

50. Abbé [Augustin] Barruel, *Memoirs Illustrating the History of Jacobinism*, 4 vols., [trans. Robert Clifford] (London: T. Burton/E. Booker for R. Clifford, 1797–8), vol. 1, pp. xvi, 150, 4.

51. Richardson, *Literature, Education, and Romanticism*, p. 53.

PART III

Different directions

CHAPTER 8

Coleridge's stamina

Paul Hamilton

When Marilyn Butler's *Romantics, Rebels, and Reactionaries* was published
in 1981, I had to rewrite my own work on Coleridge to make it intellectually
respectable. Her astute sense of the politics behind Coleridge's philosophical addresses to his reading public made it impossible to write about him
purely in the manner of a history of ideas. Suddenly a practice deriving from Lovejoy and Wellek appeared inadequate, or at least grievously
incomplete. In addition to the ability to read the code of historical commentary embedded in ostensibly pure philosophical speculation, Butler
reasonably asked for an acknowledgement in Coleridge scholarship of the
European context in which Coleridge consciously wrote. The furore caused
by the French Revolution was only the start of Coleridgean involvement; he
had an equally complex stance towards the religious revival supporting the
Bourbon restoration and the reconceiving of the role of the intellectual in
the wake of accusations, from Napoleon onwards, of an earlier *trahison des
clercs*. Chateaubriand might help in deciphering the pattern of his conservatism as much as Schelling helped uncover his philosophical techniques.
Above all, while always insisting on the significance of 'coterie' for interpretation, Butler argued that, in the words of one of her reviews, we should
not 'keep it in the family' where either Coleridge or Wordsworth were concerned. The question, then, that this chapter tries to answer affirmatively is:
can Coleridge's philosophy be profitably placed in a European context that
restores credibility to his philosophical activities? The aim is not to establish
the uniqueness in Coleridge's thought to which his defenders often seem
disablingly committed. On the other hand, to exhibit Coleridge's fluency
in the largely German theoretical idiom of his day, and the philosophical
importance of some of the questions most frequently discussed within that
tradition, might answer the charge of plagiarism and help account for his
lasting speculative interest. He was part of a philosophical conversation,
and all conversations make more sense when both sides are heard.

Coleridge remains English literary history's most instinctive intellectual. The advantages of this position ought to be self-evident. In a culture, however, which of all European cultures has remained the most distrustful of theory, Coleridge's distinction incriminates him. His chequered publishing history, full of missed appointments, unacknowledged appropriations, and failed promises, is often connected with his intellectualism: his inveterate habits of reflection and his metaphysical fascinations live so far from the practical pleasures of the English empiricism against which he rebelled. Had not theory, in any case, been persuasively associated, since Swift and Pope, with an experimental licence at odds with literary humanism? This prejudice replaced Dryden's easy bestriding of two 'royal' cultures, monarchy and the 'Royal Society', in 'Annus Mirabilis' and was refuelled by Burke's polemics against speculators and projectors in his *Reflections*. Did Coleridge himself not join Burke's side when he conceded, after all, that 'abstruse research' had offered a means of denaturalizing himself? The place of this opinion within the drama of the poem, 'Dejection: An Ode', in which it appears, is arguably to diagnose, not to succumb to, the distortions of a temperament which uses abstraction in that way. This role, though, is forgotten in the simpler biographical reading in which the poet, agonizing over his forbidden love for Sara Hutchinson, is made to confess that his intellectualism was a substitute for something better, something more psychologically indigenous, more generous, loving, and creative.

The partial reading of 'Dejection' is supported by a stock portrait of Coleridge. In that familiar depiction, too abstract a mind and too speculative a sensibility leave Coleridge playing the part of Hamlet in a play in which what is valued is achievement, grasp of reality, and mature self-knowledge. This drama is allowed to override the dramas of Coleridge's own thought. But in these dramas, Leavisite values are not absolutes but relative to the various philosophical stories in which they feature. For Coleridge, self-knowledge was a vanishing-point, an ideal convergence never to be achieved. In any case, the reflection of a subject by its objective existence modelled for Coleridge the pattern of all creation, a paradigm that must remain mysterious. Self-knowledge in the fullest sense belonged to an Otherness into whose care Coleridge sought to consign himself with doctrinal Christian anxiety. The coincidence of Coleridge's desperate desire for religious consolation with the contemporary form of ultimate philosophical inquiry accounts, I believe, for the unignorable affective power in Coleridgean speculation.

This dynamic, in turn, helps explain his stamina: the lasting attraction and intrigue of his ideas despite their highly variable output. Equally, though, Coleridge's 'stamina' draws out the word's other etymological options. (The stamen is the male seed-bearer of the flower, and also, metaphorically, the warp of a loom, an axis of textual production.) Despite his capriciousness, Coleridge undeniably wrote a massive amount, now collected in the magnificent new Bollingen edition. He was vastly and indiscriminately fertile. Furthermore, the basic unit of intellectual activity as he understood it figured his own kind of productivity. Ideas, for Coleridge, invoked an 'infinite power of semination'. These mental stamina vitalized the many discourses his thought invaded. Once the mobile rather than fixed character of originality was conceded, then the exercise of intellect need not be defined by its conclusions, but could be recognized by its motility, its impulsiveness, its furthering of the principle behind what it has discovered. And, as (Anglophone) appreciation of Coleridge's German philosophical sources becomes more idiomatic, more a fluency in a way of thinking and less a search for sources, and he becomes recognizably addicted to a common European Romantic habit of reflection, other corroborations of Coleridge's intellectual manner appear.

From Kant to Hegel, philosophy repeatedly strives in dialectical fashion to identify 'the rules of the imagination' with 'the very powers of growth and production'.[1] I. A. Richards's favourite Coleridgean formula in fact describes that crucial move which, in different ways, clinched the philosophies of Kant, Fichte, Schelling, and Hegel. Introspection turns out to require, with varying strength of prescription, an unconscious collaborative ground. Driven underground in this way, Leibniz's 'pre-established harmony', guaranteeing the fastening of our ideas upon a corresponding world, can become a troubling affiliation. It can, certainly, continue its underwriting of Enlightenment or the validity of knowledge; but it may also become more like an alarming return upon our spiritual selves of apparently alien material. A world instinct with spirit can reconcile subject and object with consoling or with spectral forms. I. A. Richards need not have seen himself as a materialist sympathizing with an idealist if idealism of Coleridge's kind could only make sense of itself if it was corroborated by a like-minded (as it were) material world. As suggested, the materialisms of Leibniz's successors vary. Fichte's 'not-I', without which each act of self-consciousness would have nothing to discriminate itself from, is subsumed in the objectivity of Hegelian 'reason'. Hegelian reason's progress is finished only when its power to be commensurable with reality has turned into the power to be commensurate with itself (not-I again becoming I in an entirely universal sense). Just as strongly, though, the post-Kantian most influential upon Coleridge, Schelling, resists the notion of such ultimate programming, and retains the sense of a fortuitous, voluntary coincidence between our own intellectual dispensation and something anterior to it. Coleridge's predominantly Christian expression of this good fortune cannot obscure the historical moment in philosophical history that makes it possible for him to think in this way.

Eschewing the Hegelian goal of absolute self-transparency, the Schelling / Coleridge moment is always open to mystery and obscurity. To be adequate, the presentation of what is lucid must be shadowed by what could have been different. The positive is haunted by an imponderable alternative. Coleridge's Christianity has no monopoly on the theological idioms thus brought into play. Michael Rosen succinctly describes the movement from

> an Absolute which is simultaneously *self-revealing* and *self-concealing* (Schelling's doctrine) to a position in which the manifestation of transcendence is at most an *interruption* or *hiatus* in the course of the finite (as in Hölderlin). Romantics, therefore, often seem to hover between affirmative and negative theology.[2]

Revealing by concealing and concealing by revealing foster a variety of entry-points into the discourses with which we construct our world. Some of Coleridge's poems, it is easy to claim, give us a version of Hölderlin's discourse of interruption. The interference that the person from Porlock figures is not arbitrary. His interruption of the writing of *Kubla Khan*, within Coleridge's calculated framing of the poem, authorizes its form and content. Formally, it is a Romantic fragment poem; materially, it speaks a hiatus between the absolute authority to decree that something happens, and the condition of simulation to which we are bound when we envision that authenticity. According to the poem's preface, the poet's immediate intimacy with his inspiration is interrupted and so turns into a task of reconstruction at second hand. But this is what the narrator of the poem does, and, on reflection, what Kubla has done with the natural forces at his disposal; the poem makes its arbitrariness into its own content. The truest version of what is, the poem says, is gained through revelation; but revelation is always an appearance, an epiphany, a mixed prophecy of good and ill. The poem does not say, in a postmodern formulation tempting to us now, that the real has been displaced by the greater solidity of our representations of it – although Coleridge famously evoked his experience of poetic possession with the claim that 'the images rose up before him as *things*'. The real is still what assures our representations of their purchase on something. But this grasp evinces the sense of a willed tractability characteristic of our 'real', a sense of election, a sense by which our foundation in the world feels like a gift. It feels gratuitous, spontaneous, free, voluntary, and accommodating because at other important levels of explanation it also is causeless, unwarranted, and arbitrary. The mysteriousness of the poem's fountain and its eponymous hero's fiat mimes an ultimate inscrutability only got at through an uncertain repetition, through the wonderment that what is, is.

Epiphany, in our necessarily Joycean take on it, reveals a certain world in contrast to a delusory one deprived of God's ontological backing. It also implies that this revelation can make us know more painfully our frequent out-of-placeness, our lack of fit in the discovered world (like, say, the adolescent boy in *Dubliners*), our alienation from an environment that gives us our standards of welcome and reciprocity. The discovery that 'Nature never did betray / The heart that loved her' was surely the common ground of Coleridge's and Wordsworth's temporary poetic collaboration? Yet, in Satanic or Byronic fashion, our incongruity can bolster a negative theology, as Rosen allows. What is represented by this negative theology is not an alternative to divine order, but the same order as it must extend beyond our reach into areas not constrained to fit our purposes. These inimical environments have been evacuated by the God who supports us, but to explore them is perversely to register still more of the Godhead, more of the possibilities he charitably did not adopt. The unassimilable too becomes the sacred or dreadful, the visionary, uncontrolled poet at the end of *Kubla Khan*: 'For he on honey-dew hath fed / And drunk the milk of Paradise'. In a familiar anthropological trope, the abjected achieves inviolable status. What makes it exceptionable also renders it exceptional – a type of the divine precisely by virtue of its alien character. With a shudder the community congratulates itself on being favoured by a God who has not taken this other road.

Clearly, this theology is far from being systematic. It is also highly economical. Coleridge does not try uselessly and verbosely to describe what lies outside his own sphere of possibility. But he describes, as we shall see in more detail later, this inside *as* an inside. In its larger shapes, certainly, Coleridge would no doubt be keen to trace the outline of Christian dispensation. But in local detail, what the theology says is far more indiscriminate, something interchangeable even with ontology. Theology then tends to look like the personification of our dilemma when, deprived of a standpoint of scientific evaluation, we try to account for the fact that science works. We have languages in which to express the vocational character of our experience, and theology appears to add unnecessarily to or mythologize an expressiveness it should find adequate. Coleridge, by implication, applies Occam's razor to theology most dramatically in his poetry. The symbiosis of Geraldine and Christabel, snake and dove entwined and univocal, that is to say equivocal because one has suborned the other, condenses an image of extraordinary compression, a conceptually unmanageable repetition. The nervousness of the poem's Gothic, fragmentary expression maybe derives both from its arrogation to itself of theological sufficiency, and from the way that sufficiency reveals our fragile luck. What if the 'Lord of thy utterance' that you were obliged to repeat were a Geraldine?

But Coleridge conjures comparable effects, if much less conspicuously, in every other discourse or form of words he employs. His descriptive performances, when aptly closing on something, whether a pot of urine in his Notebooks, a landscape, a philosophy, a person, or an historical event, seem powered by the conviction that to defamiliarize is theology enough. Primary imagination, as formulated in *Biographia Literaria*, is indeed primary here, but by virtue of being a repetition. Because it repeats an originally divine contraction – 'a repetition in the finite mind of the infinite I am' – it can define what is absolute *for us*. To say our absolutes are relative is nonsense: how could they remain absolute? But it makes sense to say that precisely because they are relative to God shows that God has chosen them with us in mind. Remove the God-term, and, again, you are left with a repetition carrying the awareness that our differentiations float on an ontology that could have been mapped in other ways, although this ontology is only disclosed in the fact that this Otherness did not happen, is not accessible. Kierkegaard's thought can plausibly be viewed as an extended attempt to retain a uniquely theological explanation of this repetition; and the Christian Coleridge's problem often seems to be that he naturally adopts philosophical explanations, structurally symmetrical, for which this religious affiliation is not strictly necessary. To perceive fully – to employ the 'prime agent of human perception', the Primary imagination – is by philosophical implication to affirm some absolute contraction from a range of other possibilities into the world we find so attuned to our senses. We grasp this congruence as if it were the declaration of another self, an infinite 'I am', to whose assertion of its individuality we can relate. We are sure of our world as if it were someone speaking to us. But when Coleridge's theology is not systematically superimposed on this explanation, then the 'as if' is sufficient.

Awareness of the fact that this hypothetical mundane speech might have been couched in another epistemological language, one tailored to the capacities of another audience altogether, defamiliarizes the world and renews our nervousness or apprehensiveness of it. I prefer to call it 'apprehensiveness' (drawing on Charles Lamb's positive response to Wordsworth's *Excursion*: 'how apprehensive! How imaginative! How religious!'[3]) to try to catch in one word the twin meanings of heightened consciousness of something and fearful awareness of the limitations this sharpened sense of outline lends. By definition, we can have nothing to say about the ineffable alternatives. The charged repetition we are left with is the staple of Kantian aesthetics, the philosophical tradition Coleridge strove to inherit. To some, this restriction of philosophical speculation to its own inside, aesthetically intensifying descriptions of what exists as a substitute for theological comparison, has looked impoverished. The fate of this art, as Jay Bernstein puts it, following Benjamin, is to induce a kind of mourning.[4] We mourn the plenitude denied us, and this, redoubling our lament, is the only idea we can have of that fullness of which our experience is a part. Already in Coleridge's time, though, aesthetic repetition was being unpacked to reveal more than the failure to signify something bigger. Schelling's voluntarism, the *Sehnsucht* of his Absolute, would increasingly abandon this synecdochal understanding. On his view, it makes little sense to think of the different person one might have been, if genuinely enfranchised by the aesthetic into a complete existence, as a complementary self, one of two halves making up a whole. For the Schelling of the *Freiheitschrift*, the very notion of a self would disappear or be annihilated in the difference contemplated. Benjamin characteristically developed the Jena departure from Kant of which Schelling's essay was perhaps another delayed result. Outflanking the subject/object dichotomy, the defining progressiveness of the Jena art-work suggests a new ontology in which what an art-work is increases with each reception and reworking. The art-work changes with its history. Its repetitions – each time it is read, performed, interpreted – become reproductive. It provokes new versions of itself beyond the scope of its author's conscious intention and beyond the power of any of its historical audiences to curtail. This fact leads to a cognitive theory of art, one like Gadamer's, where the aesthetic suggests new and different continuances by which something is brought into play without ever being objectified. The art-work, we might say, offers a benchmark for philosophical stamina.

The aesthetic of Kant's third *Critique*, so rich a resource, may prefigure but never formulates these escapes from melancholy underachievement. The beautiful and the sublime survive our loss of cognitive interest through their power to produce pleasure. This feeling, scientifically inarticulate, describes an irreplaceable sense of wonder. More recently, Peter de Bolla has re-examined and elucidated the wonder in which aesthetic experience trades.[5] Above all it is mute, leaving us with two options. One option is to

take its refusal of paraphrase or exposition to be an advantage, one tied to
the irreplaceability of art which Coleridge believed in down to the order
of words in a Shakespearean sentence. In Richard Wollheim's formulation,
'it is not clear that we have any other way of talking about the objects
themselves. Or, to put the same point in non-linguistic terms, it is not
always the case that things that we see as expressive, we can or could see
in any other way'.[6] If you want the feeling, you have to quote the lines,
observe the painting, listen to the music. The particularity of aesthetic
judgement insisted on by Kant, the paradox of these concrete universals,
prevents us from ever being able sensibly to generalize about a work of
art. The only generality produced is the universal agreement about each
particular case. We can no more refer to the class of *Hamlets* than we can to
the class of *particular* historical events, the class of Spanish Armadas, Great
Fires of London, Wall Street Crashes, and so on. This is not because other
Hamlets have not been written, nor because further Spanish Armadas have
not taken place, but because they are not the sort of thing that can recur.
You can't repeat an historical event, any more than you can repeat the year
in which it occurred. That unrepeatability is part of what is meant by its
being historical. It happened then. Any repetition of the event must already
be built into the event's description, and the event's typicality resolved once
and for all in that original resonance.

But Schlegel dissolves the art-work's objective boundaries in the ever-
changing generic field of its reception and, in Andrew Benjamin's phrase,
describes a 'plural event'. Historical reinterpretation allows the same event
to develop more of itself across time in art and history. Coleridge called such
repetition of sameness with a difference 'tautegory'. He contrasted it with
'allegory', in which we see a resemblance to something in an entirely different subject. Kant does not pursue this tautegorical notion of singularity
persisting across time and so becoming different, while, like a changing person, remaining the same individual. Accordingly, his aesthetic has nothing
more to say than its expressions of our sense of how we apprehend the world
and, inseparable from this, our wonder that things should be so and our
wonder at what else might be. This is to say that we pleasurably repeat, or
sublimely fail not to reiterate, our experience. In either case, nothing more
is said. Except that *that* is what the aesthetic as opposed to non-aesthetic
description does say: that there is nothing more to be said. No scientific
statement can get away with that finality or produce its pleasure.

The other option, faced with expressions of this aesthetic 'mutism' as de
Bolla felicitously calls it, is to feel challenged to evolve a new vocabulary, to
feel unlearned in the description of affect and keen to be better equipped to

describe our feelings. Perhaps existing aesthetic vocabularies are underused: the influential division of aesthetic experience between the categories of the sublime and the beautiful has for too long appeared adequate? In a once well-known article, F. N. Sibley pointed out that in practice we already use a more comprehensive and variegated vocabulary of taste and aesthetic approval. He relies, one assumes, on the Austinian premise that 'ordinary uses of words' are the philosopher's first resources, although, Austin conceded, 'it seems that we shall in the end always be compelled to straighten them out to some extent'.[7] Has the traditional sufficiency of the sublime and the beautiful possibly made acceptable our otherwise culpable lack of practice in describing wonder? Or maybe we need to be still more inventive, to look for new or undervalued words, sleepers awaiting aesthetic activation, potential but yet actual collaborators in our attempt to satisfy our need for aesthetic articulation? De Bolla cites I. A. Richards, whose interest both in 'basic English' and in 'linguistic engineering' is a byword for this kind of optimistic interventionism. We are to accept the distinctiveness of the aesthetic, but to feel provoked by it to be more discriminating. How else are we to engage in that activity inseparable from aesthetic appreciation – evaluation? It is all very well to assume a lapidary appositeness in aesthetic expression because Kant has proved that the aesthetic cannot be reduced to another discourse. But we still want to say that some art is better than other art, without falling into the nonsense of saying that they are two shots at doing the same thing. Michaelangelo's and Bernini's 'David' can be educatively compared and evaluated precisely because we do not measure them on the same scale.

This second option does appear to approach the Schlegelian exit from or development of the first option. Kant's insistence upon the particularity of aesthetic expression is opened up and given a future. Aesthetic experience, de Bolla writes, is something 'lived through', in analogy with the way that Barnett Newman literally cohabited with his 'inaugural' painting (*One-ment 1*), before he could say what he'd done. Insofar as the art-work has a material existence, it is made up of our affect in response to it over time.[8] This temporal dimension recovers the post-Kantian response to a central dilemma of Kantian aesthetics. As de Bolla points out, Kantian aesthetics is founded on a catachresis. Kantian catachresis, by which we call our aesthetic experiences objects, and refer to works of art and their qualities as if they were things, returns us once more to 'mutism' and linguistic poverty. For we do not appear to possess another way of describing the universality and necessity we wish to attribute to aesthetic experiences other than to call them objects, which they are not. The aesthetic content has no language of its own; its vicarious expression points to a native silence. When we say that the painting, the nocturne, the sky, her expression are beautiful, we solicit the same degree of agreement about our subjective feeling for these things as we more confidently expect of shared objective knowledge. The absence of any private, idiosyncratic content to the feeling of satisfaction delivered aesthetically means that aesthetic judgements are habitually expressed as if referring to objects not subjects. There is not another way of putting their claim to legitimacy. To point out that aesthetic judgements are therefore figurative, expressing subjective response in objective likeness, and so themselves produce more of what they are about, repeats the dilemma of 'mutism'.[9] They never break out of their own hermeneutical circle. In Kant's aesthetic, aesthetic expression is irreplaceably particular for the same reason that it defies analysis or expression in other terms.

At the end of his exposition of the connections beween 'mutism' and wonder, de Bolla is left with 'dignity', a very Kantian derivative. This dignity is not integrated with 'grace', as it is in Schiller's treatise. Dignity, as de Bolla puts it, responds to the utter individuality of our fate, a destiny isolated both by its loneliness and in its inability to break through its limitations into another life. For Schiller, dignity considered on its own expresses the sublime attitude by which we accept, firstly, that we can never attain completion, but, secondly, that this realization of failure is the only way our ultimate vocation can appear to us.[10] Again, the aesthetic circle is drawn. Accounts of the sublime from Longinus onwards stress its characteristic 'turn', whereby the apprehension of it replicates the same scenario of turning defeat into victory, or turning the failure to progress beyond physical constraints into the simultaneous expression of our grasp of the unconstrained.[11] Sublimity demands sublime description, a reinforcement that is also a descriptive exercise in diminishing returns. The expressionism we are dealing with here, it could be said, becomes increasingly abstracted from everything else; hence, perhaps, that attraction towards the sublime typical of the painters, Newman and Rothko, whose work de Bolla writes about so revealingly in this context.

Schiller, though, already has his exposition of 'grace'. The natural expression of a happier *schöne Seele*, grace is reserved for those times when we don't want to stand entirely upon our dignity. But it is worth remembering that Hegel's critique of the graceful life of the 'beautiful soul' raises problems akin to those belonging to the sublime attitude. Like the Stoic, the beautiful soul proposes moral self-cultivation as a solution to the intractability of the world to human purposes. The aesthetic invention where this self-perfection is made possible replaces worldly contingencies; it claims itself to be nature. But Hegel is suspicious of this aesthetic resolution of the conflict between is and ought, what we should do and what we can do. He suspects it of recasting the conflict as the effort to connect our rational with our sensuous being, producing 'merely an insincere play of alternating these two determinations [*das verstellende Spiel der Abwechslung dieser beiden Bestimmungen*]'.[12] Hegel's *verstellende* combines the senses of misplacing and playacting, depriving, that is, Schiller's fictional morality of any aesthetic excuse for having been made up. Hegel's word for this psychologism is 'abstraction [*Abstraktion*]'. When the particular aesthetic experience claims prescriptive universality it creates a self-serving nature abstracted from real nature: this is Hegel's verdict on the inescapably figural character of aesthetic objectivity; 'it is now the law that exists for the sake of the self, not the self that exists for the sake of the law'.[13] In a stand-off between virtue and 'the way of the world [*Weltlauf*]', the latter, thinks Hegel, will always prevail.[14] For him the point is to discover the necessary (Reason) within and not at an abstract remove from contingent reality. When we internalize the world as a mixture of psychological aspects, and achieve a graceful harmony between it and all the other drives of our personality, the world reduces to a purely abstract expressionism.

To put it crudely, Hegel thinks that Schiller's account of the resolution of ethical conflict, between what our reason tells us we ought to do and what the world lets us do, describes the restoration of a feel-good factor. Doing the right thing is equated with achieving psychological equilibrium. The insincerity, for Hegel, lies in pretending that such therapy exhausts the meaning of morality. On a broadly Aristotelian view, it is true, morality doesn't make sense if it is divorced from a notion of human flourishing. In this context, though, the sublime still has a part to play in emphasizing the compromises involved in the Aristotelian pursuit of human ends, or the accommodation of human desires to Greek notions of Fate. In his *Poetics* Aristotle acknowledges that the ultimate therapeutic experience, catharsis, is gained through the purging of pity and fear. These are responses to the *tragic* exposition of humanity through its heroic *failure* to be happy or fortunate. The unacceptable is not made acceptable, but art shows that we reach our boundaries in contemplating the unacceptable, and that this experience satisfies us in a peculiarly comprehensive way.

Hegel thinks Schiller's graceful aesthetic entertains a much diminished version of this dialectic. Taken outside the fatal conflict, his aesthetic harmony idealizes its competing forces, forgetting that one of those is contingent and beyond our control. Emptied of that content, the nature-drive (*Naturtrieb*) falsely internalizes a constitutionally external force. Of course, the progress of Hegel's own philosophy is to seek an evolving rational pattern in our successive definitions of what is external to us. Unlike Schelling and Coleridge, he is not interested in tracking the reverberations of an ontology continually disclosed through our repeated historical differences from it. Coleridge's *Dejection* ode does read like a Schillerian poem: 'for in our life alone does Nature live'. It just depends on how diagnostic one takes it to be. In deep depression, health may indeed appear like an impossible mastery over circumstances, an imaginative hegemony. 'Hence viper thoughts, that coil around my mind, / Reality's dark dream!' Ultimately, though, all well-being depends upon something given to us, and on our power to accept and repeat it by means of our 'shaping spirit of Imagination'; and that 'dower', the poem's religious abjection makes clear, is as much out of our power to manufacture as is the grace of God.

Finally the poem's narrator imagines the reproduction of the joy he wishes in the 'Lady', in his 'friend'. In that altruistic benediction he perhaps escapes the pathological desire for original production symptomatic of his depression. He accepts as sufficient the repetition implied when our animation of the world can be described as 'guided from above'. But there is no other access to what is 'above' other than to follow its 'guidance', or to see in our limitations a vocation, a calling, rather than a thwarting. Repetition, the recurrence of the same in different historical form, tautegory rather than allegory, fits the Jena idea that the aesthetic typically encourages its own reproduction. The art-work precipitates a plural event allowing it to be revived in different shapes no longer necessarily observing original aesthetic allegiances. This self-destroying perpetuation is a way of knowing, not an aesthetic abstraction from knowing, not the alternative to cognition it would be in Kant's and Schiller's aesthetics. Coleridge's narrator finds his well-being finally reflected back to him when re-imagined for someone *else*. Coleridge's aesthetic maintains the sense that our creative perceptions are re-enactments, repetitions in different historical situations. The result is to defamiliarize what is described rather than to describe something else. There isn't something else to describe.

Nevertheless, an aesthetic that continually historicizes itself in this way, existing in its departures from any original moment, clearly overcomes the 'mutism' inherent in Kantian aesthetics. It reworks the figurative quality, which seemed to entrap aesthetic judgement, in its own content as an openness to reformulation that abandons selfish interests. In the personal drama of *Dejection*, the care of the narrator's self is bequeathed to the other. In aesthetic terms, the selfishness abandoned is disciplinary, as the aesthetic legacy becomes a general facility to defamiliarize through the sense that our apprehensiveness is triggered when we realize that perception repeats something we cannot get at in any other terms. Equally, the apparent failure to gain immediate acquaintance with the 'infinite I AM' takes the form of a continuing discovery of the common ground shared by all our repetitions of the 'infinite I AM'. They may all be repetitions, rather than original grounding discourses, but they are all repeating the same thing. The lack of a foundational discourse, therefore, is also what powers Coleridge's striking idea of philosophy as an 'anti-Babel'. Failure to posit becomes exposition, informative in its own way. Coleridge's notebook entry where the 'anti-babel' appears describes how

Preparatory to the great anti-babel of metaphysical Science, all sorts of materials psychological & logical must be brought together / some fit, some unfit – and as even this takes ages even before the commencement of the building, the Fetchers & Carriers build Cots & Houses of them, each according to his own Fancy, with different cements – still however they are but orderly Cumuli of materials, that must surely be taken to pieces – some times 5 or 10 stones may be taken at once, unloosened – &c[15]

There is a lot going on here. Fundamentally, Coleridge describes an assemblage of materials in need of breaking down before their common philosophical or metaphysical contribution can be gauged. Surely Coleridge cannot be unaware of the paradox of raising a great building to counter the hubris of the original tower of Babel? He had made the connection between building and language before in another cryptic entry about Kubla Khan: 'Kublaikhan ordered letters to be invented for his people –' (line 1281). In Coleridge's poem, Kubla's 'miracle of rare device' is of course architectural. It repeats the original creativity of the 'fountain' from which the 'sacred river', Alph, 'momently was forced' from the 'deep Romantic chasm'. Harnessed to cultivate the city, the river's subsequent progress provides the setting for Kubla's 'pleasure dome', where the noise of its past and future can mingle, an effect somehow linked with the perfect poise of the dome. Dependency on the river's sacred passage, though, means that Kubla's achievement can only generate further repetitions, and can never call a halt to these with its own authoritative, monumental statement. The invention of language is a comparably doomed display of control since it is confirmed by everyone else's ability to use its words in their own way, in ways different from their donor. Language enfranchises rather than reduces a population; Coleridge, in Marjorie Levinson's words, 'makes his readers amass within *them* the amassing harmony'. But the alternative, as Levinson also points out, would be a *cul de sac*; the one that, I argued, Hegel criticized in Schiller's *schöne*

Seele; what Levinson calls 'the appropriation of the actual and extrinsic into psychic space'.[16] This repeats the presumption of Babel, not the originality that Babel originally presumed to emulate.

Coleridge discusses Babel at length in *The Friend*. The discussion appears in the tenth of the *Essays on the Principles of Method* that are the principal adornment of the 1818 '*rifacciamento*' of the original periodical, 'the first elements, or alphabet, of my whole system'.[17] The context is Coleridge's analysis of the intellectualism properly belonging to ideas rather than to fixed images or idols. Ideas cultivate, sensuous images civilize or lead to the architecture of civilization – cities, musical instruments, artifice generally, convenience. But this devotion to the 'agreeable' must, like Schiller's *schöne Seele*'s devotion to the 'graceful', have 'assumed' what it then 'did not, in this respect, pretend to *find*'. In other words, even an apparently single-minded devotion to accessible pleasures is predicated upon an absolute provision revealing our situatedness in the world not just as convenient and timely but as a vocation. Forgetfulness of the contingency of the dispensation we enjoy leads to the abstraction which Coleridge thinks produces polytheism. Polytheism amounts to absolute claims for the facts of experience, claims that must appear a little ridiculous, 'a whole *bee-hive* of natural Gods'. The trick here is to reverse the normal meanings of concrete and abstract. Usually we would think of the function subtending everything as an abstraction from their concrete variety. But in depicting an absolute that has temporarily contracted to be the ground of our determinations, all (determinate) concretions must seem abstract in contrast to its potential, undisclosed variety.

Coleridge marries this philosophical discussion to his interpretation of the book of Genesis. Investment of particulars of our experience with absolute authority makes each impossibly presume to exclude the other. The confusion of tongues (repeated, Coleridge seems to suggest, in the productive 'diversity' of tongues now, which, as a linguist, he enjoys) is the sign of this philosophical malfunction. Confusion, in Coleridge's interpretation, appears to preclude translation, which in his work as a philosopher he habitually practises. Diverse translation, as opposed to absolute posturing, is the continual amassing of significance that expounds more of the variety of the original it repeats. Or, as Friedrich Schlegel might say, description in one genre stimulates description in another and adds progressively to our sense of the universal precipitating both. Schlegel's way of putting this gets at Coleridge's post-Kantian rather than Kantian character. Again, the thought is led by the Jena idea of an aesthetic willing to sacrifice the exclusive autonomous realm won for it by Kant's third *Critique*.

Let us look at this distinction more closely, using a difficult but precise commentary by Werner Hamacher.[18] Like Walter Benjamin before him, Hamacher understands Schlegel to claim a dynamic advance through a critique of Kant's aesthetic isolationism as it survives in Fichte. Fichte's original insight, on Dieter Henrich's famous reading, was to see the severe limitations in the logic of reflection exposed by any explanation of self-consciousness. In Kant, the 'I think' that must accompany any experience for it to be someone's, and so *be* an experience of a subject reflecting on an object, always escapes its own jurisdiction and so remains unexplained. For our self-recognition to work we must enjoy another kind of acquaintance with ourselves that is unreflective. Hamacher, though, reverses Henrich, and claims that Fichte's call to understand self-orientation through action – or knowing something by doing it – still relies on reflection for identifying the active self. Fichte's claim to have both a reflective and a performative access to the 'I' becomes an 'irreparable inconsistency'.[19] Like Hegel, in other words, Hamacher's Fichte cannot conceive of an immediate self-consciousness that is not already mediated by some general term. Schlegel, on the other hand, takes the discussion of the grounding of experience outside the sphere of self-consciousness and relocates it in questions of genre and language. This, argues Hamacher, helps, because Schlegel's explanation turns originality into a project rather than an object. We don't witness a failure in reflection when the genre in which we currently catch our existence does not itself contain the genre describing it. Rather, this standing aside from it tropes it, like parekbasis or Chorus in a Greek play.[20] Part of the same drama of meaning, the apostrophe to or commentary on individuals and events under scrutiny, expounds more of their being. The Chorus does not presume to pronounce absolutely but is another dramatic character interacting in a continuing drama of meaning. Or, deconstructively put (and de Man was greatly attracted to Schlegel), meta-writing is another genre of writing. For Schlegel, though, such commentary, unlike a mirroring reflection, is 'progressive', because, as we have seen with Schelling, repetition is here understood not as a redundant but as an expository activity.[21] And this dynamic philosophy provides the genuine alternative to thinking of being as only to be understood if cognizable by its subject reflecting upon it.

Now Coleridge's anti-babel, to the extent that he develops the idea, shares this escape from reflection. My comments so far on the function he attributes to repetition in his main formulation of imagination and on the disseminating power by which he defines ideas have tended to show this. Common to all Coleridge's plans for an *Opus Maximum* is the idea of an encircling 'Logos' which is the 'anti-babel' unifying the different 'logoi' or disciplines constituting Coleridge's great work. In the 'Essays on the Principles of Method' in *The Friend*, Coleridge follows Plato, he claims, in defining Ideas as 'living laws', and Bacon in naming 'laws of nature, *ideas*'. This growth makes for 'the secure and ever-progressive, though never-ending, investigation of truth and reality by scientific method'. Thus he can, thinks Coleridge, 'furnished with fit and respectable credentials, proceed to the historic importance and practical application of METHOD'.[22] These credentials are Platonic and Baconian, corroborated by Hooker, but in the historical context of Coleridge's philosophy, they are post-Kantian. The sameness with his precursors' insight simultaneously measures the historical difference of his own expression of them, suiting the philosophical intervention he is using them to make. Permanence and progression harmonize in Coleridge's method not only as regards art and science, but also as regards politics. There the permanent political interest tends to hinder progressive forces, and the troping stops. But the structure of Coleridge's argument is far from end-stopped, and Coleridge's neglected general statements vaunting the enjambements of intellectual inquiry within his anti-babel are worth rehearsing.

The anti-babel can be traced through Coleridge's remarks on 'the Logos, or communicative Intelligence, Natural, Human, and Divine'.[23] This single word unifies the different words or 'logoi' of the disciplines which, if all put together, would constitute an encyclopaedia of the kind for which Coleridge contributed his *Treatise on Method*. The Christian resonance of schemes of this kind is obvious; audible also is a less doctrinaire religiosity, the kind informing most of Coleridge's speculations about life as 'the language of God himself, as uttered by Nature'.[24] These Christian and religious inflections do not add much to our understanding of Coleridge's thought; they do, as I have already said, describe a coincidence by which Coleridge could link his religious passion to his philosophical curiosity. In the terms of our argument so far, this is to say that religion is another troping or progressive repetition of our situation rather than a unique revelation that might conclude this heuristic process:

Should all words have their ground and highest source in the 'Word' that was from the beginning, it might appear that a dispute concerning words is the most important subject on which the mind of man could exert its reasoning powers.[25]

Sometimes Coleridge's religious fervour drives him to wish to repeat the Incarnation and himself become a word, a word made flesh: 'the redeemed

& sanctified become finally themselves Words of the *Word*. He concludes this Notebook fantasy: 'As he is in the Father, even so we in him'.[26] Again the repetition is evident, here Coleridge's desire to repeat Jesus' incarnation of God. Philosophically speaking, though, a Schellingian nostrum appears, in which not to accept the absolute contraction to our capabilities, so that we can progressively follow through its implications, is to undo all possibilities of coherence. Hence Schelling's explanation in the *Freiheitsschrift* of evil as an aberrant growth outside the economy of the human self's well-being, like a disease. For Coleridge, in a late (1829) Notebook entry, to imagine the 'Suspension' of the Logos is 'the synthesis of Nonsense and Blasphemy'. In 'miracles of Religion' we should 'behold the abbreviation of the Miracle of the Universe'. We presumably then set about unpacking this abbreviation and unfolding our universe rather than hope to discover an otherworldly alternative to it?[27] Its laws are diverse enough in their applications for sheer existence to resonate with the miraculous.

On the other hand, I don't think it will do to see Coleridge as a philosophical rationalist for whom religion is a provisional troping of philosophical concerns, one to be superseded by the completion of philosophy. But I want to suggest this is as unlikely as his espousal of the reverse view that philosophy occupies the rudimentary position to be consummated in religious apprehension. One *Table Talk* entry suggests Hegelian *Aufhebung* at work:

I show to each system that I fully understand and rightfully appreciate what that system means; but then I lift up that system to a higher point of view, from which I enable it to see its former position, where it was, indeed, but under another light and with different relations; – so that the fragment of truth is not only acknowledged, but explained.[28]

Coleridge's failure ever to explain this explanation must be owing at least partly to his commitment to an idea that successive disclosure rather than cyclical recapitulation was the true shape of philosophical progress. At still other times, he sounds like Kant, or a pre-Jena philosopher: 'the Noumenon, I say, is the Logos, the W O R D'.[29] To be in hock to all of these philosophical positions would be, as Wellek insisted long ago, straightforwardly confusing and muddled. On the other hand, to exonerate such contradictory allegiances by saying they all trope each other would be to make criticism impossible. Nevertheless, the philosophy of poetry and the poetry of philosophy do come closer to each other in any attempt to understand Coleridge's sense of an existence bound by its diverse repetitions of an original sameness.

Ominously for Coleridge's theology, as I have been emphasizing, this is the pattern, a philosophical pattern spoken in the language of the German philosophers, which continually recurs. Let me finish with a famous Coleridgean synopsis.

Saturday Night, April 14, 1805 – In looking at objects of Nature while I am thinking, as at yonder moon dim-glimmering thro' the dewy window-pane, I seem rather to be seeking, as it were *asking*, a symbolical language for something within me that already and forever exists, than observing any thing new. Even when that latter is the case, yet still I have always an . . . [obscure] feeling as if that new phaenomenon were the dim Awaking of a forgotten or hidden Truth of my inner Nature / It is still interesting as a Word, a Symbol! It is Λογος, the Creator! <and the Evolver!>[30]

I believe many of the themes I have been discussing are here in this entry, but strung together, unsystematically, almost paratactically. Distrust of the new, yet appreciation that the historical repetition of the same is what defines difference, are linked to Coleridge's sense that his feeling of affiliation is part of some sort of communicative logic at work in the world. Religious terminology beckons, but equally we are offered the idea that our self-consciousness is bound up with an evolving discourse that never lays claim to have abstracted from or imprisoned nature in psychic space, and to whose continuing stamina this particular philosopher must attune himself. Already Coleridge writes in an idiom that can be fruitfully glossed by the main philosophical idioms of his day, idioms that emerge from Kant and are developed by the Jena Romantics and are criticized by Hegel. Hegel's inability to see off the Schellingian alternative emerging out of Jena allows that open philosophy most congenial to Coleridge to persist. Coleridge's subsequent protestations, caught up in the embarrassments of plagiarism, obscure a deep affinity of temperament with Schelling. But nothing conclusive can be established. Coleridge's conversation with the Germans, like the one they have amongst themselves, is ongoing, perhaps infinite. We are left with a tantalizing picture of the reflective temperament, and a quintessentially intellectual attempt to use poetic and religious discourse to see round the boundaries of factual description and to feel literal reality all the more intensely through the idea that it is spoken, addressed, to us.

NOTES

1. Samuel Taylor Coleridge, *Biographia Literaria*, ed. James Engell and W. Jackson Bate (London: Routledge and Kegan Paul, and Princeton: Princeton University Press, 1983), vol. II, p. 84. This is vol. VII of the Bollingen series, *The Collected Works of Samuel Taylor Coleridge*, gen. ed. Kathleen Coburn, 16 vols. to date

(London: Routledge and Kegan Paul, and Princeton: Princeton University Press, 1957–).

2. Michael Rosen, *Hegel's Dialectic and Its Criticism* (Cambridge: Cambridge University Press, 1982), p. 109.

3. Charles Lamb, *Quarterly Review* 12 (October 1814), 100–11.

4. Jay Bernstein, *The Fate of Art: Aesthetic Alienation from Kant to Derrida and Adorno* (Cambridge: Polity Press, 1991).

5. Peter de Bolla, *Art Matters* (Cambridge, Mass.: Harvard University Press, 2001).

6. Richard Wollheim, *Art and Its Objects*, 2nd edn with supplementary essays (Cambridge: Cambridge University Press, 1980), pp. 33–4.

7. J. L. Austin, 'How to Talk', in his *Philosophical Papers*, ed. J. O. Urmson and G. J. Warnock, 2nd edn (Oxford: Clarendon Press, 1970), p. 134. F. N. Sibley, 'Aesthetic Concepts', revised version in his *Approach to Aesthetics: Collected Papers in Philosophical Aesthetics*, ed. John Benson, Betty Redfern, and Jeremy Roxbee Cox (Oxford: Clarendon Press, 2001). Sibley, like Wollheim, attributes an absolute propriety to some aesthetic expressions, 'ways of talking' he calls 'natural' (p. 17). But this is a consequence of 'taste concepts . . . [being] not, except negatively, governed by conditions at all' (p. 8), and so being, in Kantian terms, irreducibly particular. So 'natural', in this usage, is already metaphorical if we can't generalize about it, part of the aesthetic activity it describes, as Sibley partly concedes on occasion.

8. De Bolla, *Art Matters*, pp. 15, 24–5.

9. I discuss the law of diminishing returns here as it applies to Schiller's version of Kantian aesthetics in ch. 1 of my *Metaromanticism – Aesthetics, Literature, Theory* (Chicago: Chicago University Press, 2003).

10. See Friedrich Schiller, *Über Anmut und Würde*, ed. Klaus L. Berghahn (Stuttgart: Philipp Reclam, 1970), p. 113: 'So wie die Anmut der Ausdruck einer schönen Seele ist, so ist Würde der Ausdruck einer erhabenen Gesinnung. Es ist dem Menschen zwar aufgegeben, eine innige Übereinstimmung zwischen seinen beiden Naturen zu stiften, immer ein harmonierendes Ganze zu sein und mit seiner vollstimmigen ganzen Menschheit zu handeln. Aber diese Charakterschönheit, die reifste Frucht seiner Humanität, ist bloss eine Idee, welcher gemäss zu werden er mit anhaltender Wachsamkeit streben, aber die er bei aller Ansstrengung nie ganz erreichen kann.'

11. See especially Neil Hertz's classic *The End of the Line: Essays on Psychoanalysis and the Sublime* (New York: Columbia University Press, 1985).

12. G. W. F. Hegel, *Phenomenology of Spirit*, trans. A. V. Miller, with an Analysis of the text and Foreword by J. N. Findlay (Oxford: Clarendon Press, 1979), p. 384, para. 633; Hegel, *Werke*, newly edited on the basis of the *Werke* of 1832–45 by Eva Moldenhauer and Karl Markus Michel, 21 vols. (Frankfurt: Suhrkamp, 1970), vol. III, p. 466.

13. Hegel, *Phenomenology*, para. 638, p. 387; Hegel, *Werke*, 3. 469: 'es ist jetzt das Gesetz, das um des Selbst willen, nicht um dessen willen das Selbst ist'.

14. Hegel, *Phenomenology*, paras. 389–90, pp. 233–4; Hegel, *Werke*, 3. 289–90.

15. Kathleen Coburn (ed.), *The Notebooks of Samuel Taylor Coleridge*, 5 vols., each in two parts (London: Routledge and Kegan Paul, 1957–), vol. III, p. 3254.
16. Marjorie Levinson, *The Romantic Fragment Poem: A Critique of a Form* (Chapel Hill and London: University of North Carolina Press, 1986), p. 113.
17. For the discussion of Babel, see Samuel Taylor Coleridge, *The Friend*, ed. B. E. Rooke, 2 vols. (London: Routledge and Kegan Paul, and Princeton: Princeton University Press, 1969), vol. I, pp. 502–3: this is vol. IV of *The Collected Works*, ed. Coburn. For the description of the *Essays*, see a letter of November 1819, in Earl Leslie Griggs (ed.), *The Collected Letters of Samuel Taylor Coleridge*, 6 vols. (Oxford: Oxford University Press, 1956–71), vol. VI, p. 1050.
18. Werner Hamacher, 'Position Exposed: Friedrich Schlegel's Poetological Transposition of Fichte's Absolute Proposition', in his *Premises: Essays on Philosophy and Literature from Kant to Celan*, trans. Peter Fenves (Cambridge, Mass.: Harvard University Press, 1996), pp. 222–61.
19. Hamacher, *Premises*, p. 235 n. 7.
20. Ibid., p. 249: 'With parekbasis prose falls out of the role of reflection . . . Poetic parekbasis constitutes an uncontrollable, dramatical-grammatical trope whose exorbitant movement displaces the framework for every epistemological paradigm of reflective representation.'
21. In Hamacher's condensed formulation: 'By positing itself, genre poses for itself a limit and posits itself, as self-positing, beyond this limit', *Premises*, p. 230.
22. Coleridge, *The Friend*, vol. I, pp. 492–3.
23. Coleridge, *Collected Letters*, vol. III, p. 353.
24. Samuel Taylor Coleridge, *Hints towards the Formation of a More Comprehensive Theory of Life*, ed. Seth B. Watson (London, 1848), p. 17.
25. Samuel Taylor Coleridge, *Logic*, ed. J. R. de J. Jackson (London: Routledge and Kegan Paul, and Princeton: Princeton University Press, 1981), vol. II, p. 146: this is vol. XIII of *The Collected Works*, ed. Coburn.
26. Coleridge, *Notebooks*, vol. II, p. 2445.
27. Ibid., vol V, pp. 5987, 5977.
28. Samuel Taylor Coleridge, *Table Talk*, ed. K. Coburn and B. Winer (London: Routledge and Kegan Paul, and Princeton: Princeton University Press, 1990), vol. II, p. 3: this is vol. XIV of *The Collected Works*, ed. Coburn.
29. Coleridge, *Collected Letters*, vol. V, pp. 325–6.
30. Coleridge, *Notebooks*, vol. II, p. 2546.

CHAPTER 9

Elizabeth Hamilton's Translation of the Letters of a Hindoo Rajah *and Romantic orientalism*

Nigel Leask

In her pioneering 1990 essay 'Byron and the Empire in the East', Marilyn Butler demonstrated the benefit of attending to the historical contexts of British colonialism in interpreting some of the key poetic narratives of Romantic orientalism.[1] Her main example, a poetic debate between Southey and Byron about the politics of monotheistic religion under the aegis of 'orientalism' (in *The Curse of Kehama* and *The Giaour*), took on new urgency when considered in the light of contemporary arguments about the evangelization of Britain's newly won empire in India. The triumph of the evangelical party, which Southey strongly supported, resulted in the insertion of a 'pious clause' into the 1813 India Act, permitting Anglican missionaries to operate in British territory for the first time. Butler's understanding of 'Romantic orientalism' here subsumed, as it surpassed, the established scholarly understanding of the oriental topos as either a Schlegelian realm of spiritual inwardness, or else an exotic Flaubertian theatre of sexuality and cruelty in which the European ego might expatiate without limits.

Butler's approach also eschewed the traditional literary critical reading of the oriental settings of so many popular poems of the period as merely picturesque backdrops to characteristic Romantic themes of love, death, heroism, and betrayal. Neither was she entirely convinced by Edward Said's Foucauldian critique of orientalism as 'a Western style for dominating, restructuring, and having authority over the Orient',[2] although she did follow Said in reading orientalism as first and foremost a discourse of imperial power. But unlike Said (in his early work at least) she was alert to Western voices of dissent, and she was able to show Byron, in poems like *The Giaour* and *Sardanapalus*, ventriloquizing the voices of cultures in conflict, 'satirizing the new notion that the British have a God-given mission to colonise and govern other nations, or that killing people may become in the right circumstances a religious activity'.[3] I still remember my excitement on hearing Marilyn deliver this paper at the 1988 Bicentenary

Byron Conference at Trinity College, Cambridge. The new light it cast on the subject of Romantic orientalism, and the characteristic enthusiasm and encouragement with which she subsequently responded to my interest in the topic, inspired my own *British Romantic Writers and the East*, published in 1992.

In this chapter I'll return to a text discussed briefly in that work, *Translation of the Letters of a Hindoo Rajah* (1796) by the Scots-Irish novelist Elizabeth Hamilton, a novel which chronologically preceded, but also provided a context for, the debate about evangelizing British India. Marilyn Butler's passing remarks on Hamilton in her landmark study *Jane Austen and the War of Ideas* make the *Hindoo Rajah* an appropriate subject for a collection of essays in her honour, as they reveal the novel's orientalism as linked to another act of critical recovery dear to her heart. In the Austen book and elsewhere, Butler pioneered scholarly interest in Hamilton as a female novelist and moralist, in relation to her more distinguished peer group of Jane Austen, Maria Edgeworth, Mary Wollstonecraft, and Mary Shelley. This congruence of interest (as well as the pioneering work of Gary Kelly on Hamilton in *Women, Writing and Revolution*),[4] has led to an excellent critical edition from Broadview Press which now makes the novel available for study on university courses in Romanticism.

Hamilton's *Hindoo Rajah* is of course a fictional construct, the invention of a European novelist seeing her own culture through the eyes of an imagined oriental 'other'. In order to underline its fictionality, in the last section of this chapter I'll compare it with the nearly contemporaneous *Travels of Mirza Abu Taleb Khan* (1810), the historical record of the travels of its author, an Indo-Persian poet and *munshi*, in Britain and Europe between 1799 and 1803. Although Abu Taleb wrote in Persian, his book was translated and published in English in 1810 with the imprimatur of British oriental scholarship. For all the considerable differences between the novel and the travel account (I have found no evidence that Abu Taleb had read Hamilton, or vice versa, although the possibility cannot be discounted), what interests me is the fact that they share certain common concerns, as they negotiate the difficult terrain of linguistic and cultural 'translation'. As well as being, to a greater or lesser extent, instances of colonial discourse, both consider the human consequences of economic and social modernization, offer a comparison of the condition of women in Asia and Europe, and mount a moral and religious critique of upper-class British manners.

In *Jane Austen and the War of Ideas*, Butler describes Hamilton's popular first novel *Letters of a Hindoo Rajah* (which went through five editions by 1811) as 'the most amusing of the anti-jacobin [novels]', a categorization which has been upheld by a number of subsequent commentators.[5] Butler adds, however, that 'it is misleading to think of [Hamilton] as rabidly partisan: she is shrewdly moderate in tone'.[6] The view of the novel as 'anti-jacobin' is I think retrospectively influenced by the stronger ideological colouring of Hamilton's second novel, *Memoirs of Modern Philosophers* (1800), which satirizes the radical philosophy of Wollstonecraft and, particularly, Godwin with greater urgency.[7] Butler hints at this in commenting on the fact that, in the wake of the political crisis of 1798, 'the genial Mrs Hamilton becomes noticeably severer towards her miscreants', and the wayward heroine of *Modern Philosophers* is disciplined by being cast as 'a tragic female quixote'.[8]

As I hope will become evident in the course of this chapter, categorizing the *Hindoo Rajah* as an 'anti-Jacobin novel' seems a little too hasty, and as a critical generalization it's perhaps better suited to the second novel alone. After all, in her 1801 *Letters on the Elementary Principles of Education*, Hamilton proclaimed her moderate Whig politics, as well as her discomfort with Hannah More's critique of civic humanist 'virtue' and Paine's 'Rights of Man'.[9] As I'll demonstrate below, Hamilton was no admirer of Edmund Burke, and her intellectual mentors were instead the Scottish Whig philosophers of the Common Sense School, Thomas Reid and Dugald Stewart, philosophers whose analysis of the powers of the human mind informs the *Letters*, and more indirectly, the novels themselves.[10] Both these philosophers had liberal and Whig sympathies but were forced into silence on political matters by the overwrought reaction to the French Revolution engineered by Henry Dundas and his Tory followers in Scotland. Moreover, as a Scots/Irish Presbyterian Hamilton was sympathetic to the English Dissenting tradition of Priestley and Price, and, although she wrote as a Christian moralist, stood closer in ideological terms to her friend Maria Edgeworth than to the Tory evangelicalism of Hannah More.

Letters of a Hindoo Rajah is one of several early novels about India written by British or Irish women writers, and has been compared with Phoebe Gibbs's *Hartly House, Calcutta* (1789) and Lady Morgan's *The Missionary* (1811).[11] Hamilton's novel stands apart from these other works to the extent that it conforms to the 'Persian Letters' genre of pseudo-oriental reverse travel accounts. Montesquieu's interest in cultural comparison in his 1721 *Persian Letters*, and especially his interest in gender and the condition of women, may have recommended the genre to Hamilton in the first place.[12] *Hindoo Rajah*'s epistolary commentators Sheermaal and Zaarmilla (the genre is a useful vehicle for comparing and contrasting different cultural values) belong in the literary tradition of Montesquieu's Persians Usbek and

Rica, Goldsmith's Chinese Lien Chi Altangi in *Citizen of the World* (1762), or Robert Southey's Spanish Catholic Don Manuel Espriella, in *Letters from England* (1807).

As I've said, Hamilton's representations of hyperbolic oriental diction, and her imaginary 'construction' of Zaarmilla's world, are certainly 'orientalist' in the broader sense. But the novel also represents British orientalism in another, more historically specific framework. Hamilton writes with the double aim of commemorating her recently deceased brother, the orientalist scholar Charles Hamilton, who appears as the pious, benevolent, and dying Captain Percy in the early letters, and also of vindicating the moral probity of what is known as the 'orientalist' phase of Company rule in India.[13] *Letters of a Hindoo Rajah* is dedicated to Warren Hastings, patron of the scholarly programme of Sir William Jones and the Asiatic Society of Calcutta, of which body Charles Hamilton was a founding member. In addition to having translated the *Hedaya* or Islamic legal code into English, Charles Hamilton was author of a history of the Rohilla wars of 1773–4, in which he had participated as a military interpreter. In his *Historical Record*, purportedly translated from an Afghan Rohilla manuscript, Hamilton sought to exonerate the British from charges of atrocities committed during that campaign, charges which were amongst the leading articles in the impeachment of Warren Hastings conducted by Burke, Fox, and Sheridan in the years 1789–95.[14]

Hamilton's Zaarmilla is the Rajah of Almora, a Hindu kingdom recently liberated from the Rohilla yoke by the combined forces of the East India Company and Shuja-ud-daula, the Nawab of Awadh. As such he is hardly likely to be the kind of colonial subject seething with resentment against the rapid expansion of British rule in the later decades of the eighteenth century. At one point in the novel, after Zaarmilla has arrived in England, he is approached in a London coffee-house by a fashionable Whig critic of British colonial misconduct in India, who sets about apologizing to him (on his country's behalf) for the devastation of Rohilcund by the Company's army. The critic's anti-Hastings polemic is a self-conscious pastiche of Edmund Burke's speeches, drawn both from the impeachment oratory itself, and (problematically in an 'anti-jacobin' novel) from Burke's *Reflections on the Revolution in France*. 'We, Sir, are Englishmen, capable of blushing at the nefarious practices of delegated authority. Englishmen, who have not been completely embowelled of our natural entrails; our hearts, and galls, and spleens, and livers, have not been forcibly torn from our bodies, and their places supplied by shawls and lacks, and nabob-ships, and dewanes!' When Zaarmilla tries to protest that the critic has got the wrong man, that he is in fact a beneficiary rather than a victim of Hastings's policies, his interlocutor pre-empts him; 'Perceiving my intention to speak, "I know Sir, what you would say . . . You would tell me that it is we who have desolated your Empire, who have turned the fruitful and delicious garden of Rohilkund, into a waste and howling wilderness".'[15] This of course isn't what Zaarmilla would have said at all, but Hamilton's satirical point is that the Burkean impeacher shamelessly ventriloquizes the voice of the Hindu 'Other' in making his political pitch. Was Hamilton aware that this exactly mirrors her own 'construction' of Zaarmilla in *defence* of Hastings? More pertinently, the fiction of reverse travelling allows her to turn Whig criticism of British conduct from the hills of Rohilcund to the polite drawing rooms of the metropolis.

Hamilton's novel is preceded by a 'Preliminary Dissertation on the History, Religion, and Manners of the Hindoos' which draws heavily on Sir William Jones's orientalism by idealizing 'the sublime and exalted notions of the Deity, taught by the Bramins . . . only equalled in that Gospel "which brought life and immortality to light"' (p. 60). Hindu culture is praised for its tolerance, and caste (usually singled out for attack by European commentators) is commended for suppressing selfish individualism, envy, and social discontent, encouraging 'each individual [to] follow the occupation, and walk in the footsteps of his fathers' (p. 60). By contrast, the Prophet Mahomet is dismissed as 'the imposter of Mecca', and the Mogul conquest of India as 'the restless fury of Fanatic zeal' (p. 67). Vilification of Mogul India provides an opportunity to celebrate the advent of British rule in Bengal as a restoration of a Hindu golden age 'that unrelenting persecution, which was deemed a duty by the ignorant bigotry of their Musselman rulers, has, by the milder spirit of Christianity, been converted into the tenderest indulgence . . . their ancient laws have been restored to them . . . agriculture has been encouraged by . . . the security of property' and the *pax brittanica* (p. 70). Both in the 'Dissertation' and the novel itself, Hamilton quotes from her late brother's book to vindicate the Rohilla campaign as an act of liberation, rescuing oppressed Hindus from the despotic yoke of Islam, (in this particular case) Rohilla chieftains, or 'banditti of the hills' (p. 70). Hamilton's pro-Hindu and Islamophobic novel, quite apart from its spirited defence of the Hastings phase of British colonial rule, works as colonial ideology in this historically specific sense.

At one level this polemic inflects the novel's entire political framework, transforming its setting from the more-or-less imaginary orientalism of the 'Persian Letters' genre into the carefully researched context typical of the 'footnote novel'. The sort of satirical fiction associated with the serious female novel (Fanny Burney is one obvious model) is buttressed by a learned dissertation and orientalist footnotes, enabling Hamilton as a woman writer (Kelly again) 'to practice learned discourses and engage in political issues conventionally closed to [women]'.[16] Hamilton's overriding concern with promoting female education and moral agency is focused here on Charlotte Percy's conversion from self-consuming melancholy into purposeful authorship in the novel's final section. Adopting the learned 'footnote novel' is Hamilton's way of reforming a genre of female writing dismissed by Zaarmilla as 'a few letters written in the days of juvenile folly, on the subject of love', a pitifully self-indulgent genre dwarfed by the works of mighty geniuses like Kalidasa and Shakespeare (pp. 190, 192). Nonetheless, as Balchandra Rajan, Kelly, and other critics have indicated, the Hindu Zaarmilla is a feminized male protagonist in the tradition of the late-eighteenth-century novel of sensibility.[17] His liberal attitudes to women and openness to the Christian message puncture stereotypes of oriental sexual despotism and superstition: arguably many of those stereotypes are displaced onto his Hindu friend Maandaara, and Muslims in general.

Zaarmilla's gratitude to the British for his deliverance from the Rohilla yoke has been converted into strong Anglophilia by his conversations with the high-minded, fatally injured Capt. Percy, whom he has rescued from his Afghan captors after the battle of Cutterah, and who whets the Rajah's curiosity to know more about distant Britain. This, however, is where the novel's critical project warms up: Zaarmilla's starry-eyed idealization of British culture in the wake of his discussions with Percy adds to the pathos of his progressive disappointment when he embarks on his travels, as he personally encounters a very different reality on the ground. Hamilton seeks to shame her readers by refusing them the narcissistic satisfaction of self-reflection in an oriental mirror. Reflection is trumped by *com*plexion, as the reader rapidly discovers the dark-skinned Zaarmilla's moral critique darkening the bright image of British self-regard. In a revealing letter to Mrs Gregory, Hamilton dubbed *Letters of a Hindoo Rajah* 'my black baby', and, fearful that her work in progress might offend by too fiercely exposing the vices and follies of her compatriots, added that she was 'such an unnatural parent' that she would happily see it 'smothered without remorse' should her friend find fault with it.[18] The colonialist mother/child metaphor here of course qualifies the novel's bid to imagine critical autonomy and ethical agency for Zaarmilla.

Nevertheless, Hamilton's vindication of British policy in India in the 'Preliminary Dissertation' is only half the story; as it turns out the novel's interest in cultural comparison as moral critique makes it far more than merely a 'footnote novel'. Perhaps its indebtedness to the eighteenth-century 'Persian Letters' tradition conditioned its satirical imperative, as it targets upper-class British decadence, irreligion, and moral laxity, just as Montesquieu had exposed the corruption of the French interregnum in the guise of oriental despotism. Lisa Lowe, writing of *Lettres Persanes*, denies that Montesquieu's novel 'colonizes' the oriental, arguing rather that it sets out to question the act of cultural appropriation itself; 'it inverts and destabilises the very categories of observer and observed, ruler and ruled, or *persan* and *parisien*'.[19] By employing the device of contrasted oriental viewpoints in the early sections (Zaarmilla, Maandaara, Sheermaal), Hamilton exposes the difficulty both of adequately representing other cultures in general, and also of justifying Britain's legitimacy as a colonizing power in the eyes of her new Asian subjects.

Zaarmilla's distant view of Britain, as gleaned from Percy, exemplifies what Edward Said has called (in a different context) a 'textual attitude', revealed in his admission to his friend Maandaara that 'it is to the Arabic copy of those books of the Shaster, called Gospels, to which I am indebted for the accuracy of my information' (p. 87). Zaarmilla's textualist idealization of British Christian culture provides the occasion for, amongst other things, a discussion of the condition of women, as an index of progressive civilization. This provides one of the book's major themes, linking it to Hamilton's work as a Christian feminist: 'Throughout the Christian shaster, [women] are exalted to perfect equality with man. They are considered as occupying a station of equal dignity, in the intelligent creation . . . what care! What pains must we then conclude to be bestowed by Christians, on the formation of the female mind?' (p. 88). Experience will of course show that this is far from being the case, but the point is that initially Zaarmilla fails to distinguish between precept and practice.

If his early misjudgements, fully appropriate to Zaarmilla's 'feminized' and credulous character, are intended to deflate the Rajah's 'armchair occidentalism', Letters 4–6, penned by the Brahmin Sheermaal descriptive of his own travels in Britain, set out utterly to refute the Rajah's 'textual' credulity. The letters are highly critical of British colonial slavery, irreligion, and injustice, and describe conditions of class and gender inequality far exceeding those to be found in India. With the exception of parts of rural Scotland, Britain is in the grip of atheism, luxury, and vice. In contrast to the Hindu caste system with its divisions by occupation, Sheermaal finds that the British Caste system is divided into 'People of Family, People of no Family, and People of Style' (p. 122). In contrast to Zaarmilla, Sheermaal exemplifies conventional 'sexual orientalism' in his belief that women are intellectually and morally inferior to men; nevertheless his indignation is aroused by the social leeway permitted to half-educated upper-class women and 'Boarding-School Bibbys'; 'equally ignorant and equally helpless, as the females of Hindostan, their situation is far more destitute and pitiable' (p. 130). At the other end of the social scale, he compares wide-scale prostitution on the streets of London to the sacrifice of female victims on the altar of the Hindu goddess Kali. His British acquaintances seem more willing to shed tears over the Hindu custom of sati or widow-burning, than to worry about the prostitutes on their doorsteps, which he considers a far more serious social injustice.

Hamilton here aims her satire at the act of (mis)representation itself, namely the claims to naive empiricism underpinning much contemporary travel narrative and social commentary. Despite the undeniable validity of his critique, Sheermaal's view is also one-sided; he is satirically categorized as 'a systematic traveller' on the strength of his claim that 'in the bosom of experience I have found . . . expected conviction' (p. 108). Like Swift's treatment of his travelling protagonist Gulliver, Sheermaal's letters embody a double-edged satire which reflects back upon their purported author. Once again we see Hamilton's intellectual inheritance from the Scottish Enlightenment emerging in her belief in the moral value of comparing and contrasting different cultures, providing this is done with sufficient reflexivity. Sheermaal clearly fails the test; as Zaarmilla puts it, 'Can *he* be a proper judge of the peculiar customs of remote nations, who measures everything by the narrow standards of his own prejudices?' (p. 139). But this is no ethnocentric claim, following Kames or Ferguson in placing Asiatics and other 'barbarians' in the darkness of monocultural ignorance. The target here is less the benighted 'oriental' than the prejudiced and 'systematic' British observer. Hamilton's irony resounds in Zaarmilla's naive exclamation, 'Ah! What a pattern might Sheermaal have found in the travellers, and the travel-writers of Europe. How many of these does England alone, every year, pour from her maternal bosom? Happy for Sheermaal, if he had followed the laudable example of these sapient youths; how deep would then have been his observations! How important his discoveries!' (p. 139). In ironizing Indian misconceptions about England as they 'travel the other way', British readers might perceive a mirror image of their own misconceptions about India and other distant cultures.

Despite Hamilton's political support for Hastings and dependence upon her brother's orientalist scholarship throughout, her novel doesn't exempt certain aspects of British orientalism from critique. The prejudiced Brahmin Sheermaal, like some naive orientalist in reverse, over-interprets every aspect of British life as symptomatic of British religious beliefs; thus, for example, he (absurdly) accepts that the harsh enforcement of the Game Laws in England is the result of a religious veneration for partridges, a species of animal worship 'borrowed from the manners of their eastern progenitors'. (This parodies the theories of some of Charles Hamilton's fellow orientalists like Francis Wilford and Reuben Burrow that 'the Druids of Britain were Brahmins is beyond the least shadow of doubt').[20] Sheermaal also insists that the principal form of worship practised in Britain is 'the poojah of cards', a religion whose sacred pantheon is 'painted upon small slips of stiff paper' (p. 114–16). As Kate Teltscher has indicated, Sheermaal's desire to study the iconography of 'every one of these painted idols' parodies William Jones-style mythography.[21] I would add that Sheermaal's comment that 'a rich field of conjecture is already opened, to the culture of which I shall willingly devote some of the remaining years of my existence' (p. 134) clearly parodies the tone of William Jones's *Anniversary Discourses* to the Asiatic Society. Interpreting this passage I think illustrates the dangers of flattening Hamilton's lively, reflexive, and polyphonic satire into the terms of available ideologies ('anti-jacobin', 'orientalist', 'evangelical'). Dedicated to Warren Hastings, the novel nevertheless satirizes some of the intellectual tendencies of his protégé Sir William Jones, and even (by extension) of brother Charles.

Teltscher argues that Hamilton here targeted the oriental misapplication of British scholarly techniques, rather than that scholarship itself: 'Britain doesn't offer herself up to Indian scrutiny the way that the subcontinent reveals itself to the members of the Asiatic Society.'[22] But Hamilton did after all have perfectly good reasons for wishing to satirize British orientalism, her fraternal links with the Asiatic Society notwithstanding. Like the other Scottish orientalists discussed by Jane Rendall,[23] she had little time for anti-quarianism and fanciful mythographic syncretism, although the evangelical critique so prominent in writing about India after the 1813 India Act is as yet underdeveloped here. In her *Letters on the Elementary Principle of Education*, Hamilton favoured a broadly ecumenical and anti-denominationalist Christianity, taking issue with excessive emphasis on the outward forms of religion over inner faith. The same might be said of her view of Hinduism revealed in this complex instance of cultural mirroring. After all, Zaarmilla's 'natural piety' is able to flourish within the idolatrous external forms of Hindu worship, and I would suggest that Hamilton is taking British orientalism to task for concentrating to an excessive degree on the Hindu pantheon, its outward forms of worship, to the exclusion of an inner spiritual content more compatible with progressive and rational Christianity. Like Lord Teignmouth's evangelical reinterpretation of the life of

Sir William Jones, in his posthumous 1804 biography, Hamilton seeks retrospectively to infuse the intellectual deism of eighteenth-century British
orientalism with Christian piety.

The conflict between Zaarmilla's idealizing and (at least initially) 'textual'
attitude to Britain and Shermaal's prejudiced claims to 'naïve empiricism' is
tested out in the remainder of the novel. Zaarmilla's travels in British Bengal
draw heavily on William Hodges's georgic panegyric on colonial prosper-
ity in his *Travels*, published just two years before *Letters* in 1794, a debt
which Hamilton acknowledges in her footnotes. (The fact that Hodges,
like her late brother, enjoyed the patronage of Warren Hastings may have
influenced her enthusiasm for his travel account.) Zaarmilla's encounters
with Captain Percy's Anglo-Indian friends in Bengal largely bear out the
Rajah's high expectations, although he makes the usual Indian mistakes –
and Hamilton is plundering British travel accounts of cross-cultural mis-
understandings here as elsewhere – such as, in one incident, mistaking
the dancing wives of British officers for nautch-girls. Elsewhere Zaarmilla
discovers triumphantly that the custom 'which Sheermaal ignorantly pronounced a species of worship' turns out to be no more than a game of
cards, 'invented by the Europeans, as chess was by our ancestors, for the
pastime of the rich, and idle' (p. 176). He quickly rounds on Sheermaal for
criticizing card-obsessed British women – 'Base slanderer! How little does
he know of the ladies of England!' (p. 176) – without, of course, yet having
the slightest empirical foundation for his judgement.

The death of Zaarmilla's young wife having cast him into despondency,
he resolves to risk loss of caste by sailing to England to satisfy his doubts and
curiosity about 'the morals and manners of the Christians' (pp. 180–1). The
novel's second volume relates his voyage to Europe, the friendships which
he makes on shipboard, and his first impressions of England. Although
he quickly makes the acquaintance of the virtuous 'experimental philosopher' Mr Severan, Zaarmilla is horrified by the dissipation and luxury of
English fashionable life. His strictures on the Godwinian and materialist
principles favoured by upper-class dilettantes like Sir Caprice Ardent, and
his philosophical circle, Puzzledorf, Sceptic, Vapour, and Axiom, anticipate
the theme of Hamilton's *Memoirs of Modern Philosophers*. Dr Severan here
becomes a mouth-piece for Hamilton's own inductivist denunciation of
Godwinian philosophy, directly deriving from the Common Sense philosophy of Reid and Stewart; 'would [the professors of Ardent Hall] pursue
the same plan of investigation that has been so successfully adopted by
natural philosophers, that of first making themselves well acquainted with
facts, and thoroughly investigating them, before they draw conclusions,

they would perceive the necessity of allowing first principles, which are so self-evident as not to admit of any direct proof' (pp. 272–3). Zaarmilla's Hindu candour and spiritual 'common sense' intuitively align themselves with Severan's Christian metaphysics against 'French' atheism, materialism, and scepticism, which is denounced in orientalized language: 'The poojah of Philosophers is performed to certain Idols, called Systems . . . Never did the most bigoted derveish of the Mussulmans, betray more abhorrence at the sight of the Idols of the Pagoda, than is evinced by the worshipper of system towards a Christian priest!' (p. 257). (In *Letters on . . . Education*, Hamilton glossed this criticism by insisting: 'Of systems I have none, save the system of Christianity'.)[24]

Zaarmilla's attitude to the Wollstonecraftian feminist Miss Ardent seems rather more sympathetic than has been claimed by critics who want to read the *Letters* as straightforward 'anti-jacobinism'. At one point Miss Ardent's practical objection to the difficulties for women of accommodating themselves to Vapour's hare-brained utopianism leads the latter into a misogynistic outburst; '"Women!" repeated Mr Vapour, with a contemptuous smile; "we shall not then be troubled with – women. In the age of reason, the world shall contain only a race of men!!"' (p. 261). Zaarmilla's experience of the corruption of British women in general leads him to recant his earlier views on Christian feminism. 'Send for the pious Bramin Sheermaal', he requests Maandaara at the end of Letter 13, 'tell him, that my heart reproaches me, for the injustice I was guilty of towards him; I implore his pardon, for the incredulity with which I regarded his account of the conduct of Christians' (p. 243), and, especially, Christian women. Aroused by his first-hand experience of the moral corruption and irreligion of Georgian Britain, Zaarmilla is willing to eat humble pie.

Yet all is not lost for British self-esteem in this fall from grace in the eyes of her new Hindu subjects. In the final section of the novel, Zaarmilla once again falls in with Percy's friend Mr Denbeigh, who introduces him to the idyllic and virtuous society of Violet-Dale, a pointed contrast to the moral confusion of Ardent Hall. The world of Ardent Hall dissolves into slapstick comedy and melodrama, as Sir Caprice unsuccessfully attempts to transform unproductive swallows into honey bees, and ends up by embracing Methodism. On a graver note, Dr Sceptic's nephew commits suicide, illustrating the fatal consequences of false philosophy. But Zaarmilla's high ideal of British female piety is restored by Lady Grey, who criticizes fashionable sensibility as 'too often a name for selfishness', in its place advocating active virtue. Although here sounding almost Wollstonecraftian, Hamilton parodies Axiom and Puzzledorf's desire to attribute Lady Grey's doctrines to Hume or any other modern philosopher; 'I have taken [my principles]', says her Ladyship, 'from the doctrines and examples of Jesus Christ and the Apostles' (p. 278). Lady Grey eventually marries Dr Severan, while Emma Denbeigh weds the benevolent Darnley, and Charlotte Percy, Elizabeth Hamilton's self-portrait, is rescued from despondency by embracing authorship at the behest of Mr Denbeigh, an 'employment of [her] leisure hours which is both innocent and rational' (p. 303). In conclusion Zaarmilla is able to report that 'notwithstanding the progress of philosophy, and the report of Sheermaal . . . Christianity is *not yet entirely* extinct; but, like Virtue and Wisdom, it has still some adherents, in the retired scenes of life' (p. 307). Despite the Rasselassian mood of its final passages, the *Hindoo Rajah* ends on a note of optimism: 'though vice and folly have the appearance of being every where predominant . . . it is only the superficial observer, who will from thence infer the non-existence of Wisdom and Virtue' (p. 306).

One lesson of the novel – a variant of the common eighteenth-century Quixote theme that *both* education and worldly experience are needed to temper judgement – is the danger of making blanket generalizations about other cultures. Hamilton suggests that whilst certain societies are unquestionably more morally and intellectually progressive than others, particularly those blessed with Christian revelation, progress brings its own dangers, and social development is always likely to be uneven. Just as static, non-progressive Hindu India can produce a Zaarmilla as well as a Sheermaal, so a nominally progressive Britain can produce the corrupt Sir Caprice Ardent, as well as a Captain Percy or a Lady Grey. The mirror of Zaarmilla's 'primitive' Hindu piety exposes the corruption and luxury of British manners, just as the Christian morality and civic virtue embodied in the better sort of Britons indicates to Hindus the path of true social progress.

Hamilton's employment of the 'Persian Letters' vehicle for the purposes of moral satire was generally praised by contemporary reviewers. The radical *Analytical Review*, in its October 1796 issue, regretted Hamilton's support for Warren Hastings and her espousal of Scottish Common Sense philosophy, but nevertheless approved Hamilton's views on education, and her rational feminism in general.[25] Even conservative reviewers didn't seem to take offence at her ideal of Hindu virtue in the persona of Zaarmilla, any more than at the positive representation of Brahmins in novels like *Hartly House, Calcutta*, or *The Missionary*. This is perhaps less surprising when we consider the extent to which (despite contemporary evangelical attacks on Brahmins by Charles Grant and Robert Southey, as discussed by Marilyn Butler)[26] British 'orientalism' promoted Hindu elites at the same time as it criticized the Islamic religion of the displaced Mogul rulers of India. C. A. Bayly writes that, in consequence of this orientalist policy, 'hierarchy and the Brahmin interpretation of Hindu society which was theoretical rather than actual over much of India as late as 1750 was firmly ensconced a century later'.[27] One note of criticism was struck by the *Monthly Review* for October 1796, when it opined that 'Miss H. is less happy in her descriptions of Hindoo manners than in her delineations of scenes at home', thereby warning women writers off the orientalist 'footnote novel' genre.[28] It was advice that Hamilton heeded in choosing domestic settings for both her subsequent novels, *Memoirs of Modern Philosophers* (1800) and *Cottagers of Glenburnie* (1808).

In the final section of this chapter, I turn to Abu Taleb Khan's travel account, which has been described as 'one of the most comprehensive accounts of the West by an Indian Muslim . . . a successful translation of one cultural system into another'.[29] Abu Taleb's book is I think beholden to the fictional European 'Persian Letters' genre (by the end of his European sojourn, he was well read in English and French literature) as well as to the rich Indo-Persian tradition of travel writing. It is therefore appropriate that he was popularly known, during his residence in London, as 'The Persian Prince', his protests notwithstanding. Although of course marking a different cultural and religious space from 'Hindoo Rajah', the designation of 'Persian Prince' located Abu Taleb in a culture of popular orientalism somewhere between Montesquieu's Usbek and a fashionable masquerade at Vauxhall.

Although Abu Taleb's English translator consequently feared that the travel account would be 'read like a novel', the historical facts of its author's life were on record. Abu Taleb ibn Muhammed Isfahani was a Shiite Indo-Persian *munshi* (cleric) born in Lucknow in 1752, a former revenue officer for the Nawab of Awadh who had married into the Bengali nobility. He had unsuccessfully solicited British patronage in Calcutta for a decade before embarking upon a three-year voyage to Britain and Europe in 1799, depressed by the rapid collapse of his familiar Mogul world. Despite the similarities here with the experience of his fictional Hindu counterpart Zaarmilla, like many of the high functionaries of the Company regime in this period he was an extremely literate representative of the Indo-Muslim court culture excoriated by Hamilton and other British orientalists. Abu Taleb's *Travels* began life as a Persian-language manuscript entitled the *Masir-I Talibi* composed in 1803–4 upon his return to Calcutta. A copy was taken to Britain, and translated into English by Charles Stewart, Professor of Persian at the Company College at Haileybury, and published by Longman in 1810 under the title of *Travels of Mirza Abu Taleb Khan, in Asia, Africa, and Europe*. A second English edition was published in 1814, and a Persian-language abridgement was published in Calcutta in 1812, edited by Abu Taleb's sons, and reissued in 1827 and 1836.[30]

Abu Taleb's social class and Company connections gave him, like Zaarmilla, an entrée into British high society; as he himself put it, 'I may perhaps be accused of personal vanity by saying, that my society was courted, and that my wit and repartee, with some impromptu application of Oriental poetry, were the subject of conversation in the politest circles'.[31] His portrait was painted six times, and he was presented to the King and Prince of Wales, as well as to members of high society, including Lord Cornwallis, Warren Hastings, Horatio Nelson, and the Prime Minister William Pitt. Abu Taleb's flattering comments on individuals in British high society hardly mask the generally critical nature of his account of English manners, offering another strange similarity with Hamilton's novel. Although as a member of the Shiite Indo-Persian nobility Abu Taleb's religious views were latitudinarian, and his world view was far more secular than that of many contemporary Muslim commentators, he did note the irreligion characteristic of late-Georgian Britain. By chance Hamilton's critique of 'modern philosophers' is endorsed in Abu Taleb's employment of the Persian words 'khariji u failasuf' ('dissenters and philosophers') to describe the dominant intellectual influences on English religious life.[32] Abu Taleb's most sustained criticism, again chiming with a common theme in the writings of Hamilton and other Whig moralists, was that British civilization was threatened by excessive luxury, urging that Britons study the history of the early Arabs and Tartars, whose empire was founded upon 'the paucity of their wants' (II, 37).

In the second volume of his *Travels* Abu Taleb turned from personal narrative to systematic description of England, and in Chapter 17 he listed the twelve principal vices of the English: irreligion, pride, obsession with making money, indolence, irascibility, propensity to waste time in eating, sleeping, and dressing, excessive luxury which threatened the continuing strength of their empire, intellectual arrogance masking ignorance (particularly of foreign and oriental languages), selfishness (notably in their governance of Bengal), sexual promiscuity, prodigality, and contempt for the customs of other nations. Although he admired the balance of the British constitution, Abu Taleb made devastating criticisms of the English Common Law, and of the exercise of British law in Calcutta. But balancing his devastating critique of English manners, he offered in Chapter 20 a list of the 'virtues' of the English, which he named as honour, meritocracy, propriety, social conscience, conformity to fashion, sincerity, good sense, sound judgement, and hospitality. Nonetheless, twenty-nine pages on the vices of the English (*razai'l-I Ingilish*) are hardly balanced by five on their virtues (*fazai'l-I Ingilish*), and my reading is based on Stewart's English translation, which I suspect moderates the critical spirit wherever possible.

Stewart's translation emphasizes the trope of defamiliarization (for the English reader) reminiscent of Sheermaal and Zaarmilla's fictional 'mis-readings' of European culture. Oriental hyperbole and florid metaphor abound: for example, Abu Taleb describes how whales observed on the voyage are like 'large elephants' with 'immense nostrils' which 'threw up water to the height of 15 yards' (1, 44). The House of Commons is described in a high-coloured orientalist metaphor, Whigs and Tories likened to 'two flocks of Indian paroquets, sitting upon opposite mango trees, scolding at each other; the most noisy of whom were Mr Pitt and Mr Fox' (1, 282). Abu Taleb's comments on the British upper-class fashion for classical sculpture call to mind Sheermaal's account of the 'poojah of cards', infused with an Islamic dislike of anthropomorphic representation and idolatry; 'over the chimney pieces they place some of the heathen deities of Greece . . . It is really astounding that people possessing so much knowledge and good sense, and who reproach the nobility of Hindostan with wearing gold and silver ornaments like women, should be thus tempted by Satan to throw away their money upon useless blocks' (1, 120).

Abu Taleb's obsessive interest in the condition of women offers both a continuity and a contrast with the Christian feminist concerns of Hamilton's *Letters of a Hindoo Rajah*. If Hamilton's Zaarmilla manifests a sentimental sympathy for women proper to a 'feminized' Hindu, Kate Teltscher is surely right to suggest that Abu Taleb sports with a correspond-ing masculinist stereotype of the lascivious Muslim.[33] He openly confesses that 'I am by nature amorous and easily affected at the sight of [female] beauty' (II, 139) and, as his interpolated Hafiz-style 'Ode to London' makes clear, his experiences in Britain are troped as an erotic encounter with 'the British Fair'. A keen observer of women, Abu Taleb is fascinated by female promiscuity amongst the Dutch at the Cape, Asian-Irish mixed marriage at Cork, High Society women in London and Paris, *cicisbeism* in Italy, and unveiled Ottoman wives in Istanbul.

Throughout the narrative, Abu Taleb represents himself as an accom-plished gallant and flirt. Visiting Captain Baker's house near Cork, he flat-ters one of his host's daughters who has inquired whether his tea is sweet enough 'I replied, that, having been made with such hands, it could not but be sweet. On hearing this, all the company laughed, and my fair one blushed like a rose of Damascus' (I, 102). In London, he 'gave himself up to love and gaiety', at one point curtailing his trip around the English shires because 'Cupid had planted one of his arrows in my bosom, [and] I found it impossible to resist the desire of returning to the presence of my fair one' (I, 175). Presumably this refers to Miss Julia Burrell, the addressee of one of his Hafiz-style odes in parallel English-Persian text, published separately in 1802.[34] Even Abu Taleb's devastating catalogue of the vices of the English is excused as an act of gallantry to the command of Lady Spenser, wife of the First Lord of the Admiralty: 'Her Ladyship particularly requested, nay commanded me, to write an account of my Travels, and to state my opinions, candidly, of all the customs and manners of the English; and without fear or flattery, freely to censure whatever I thought reprehensible amongst them' (I, 285). Abu Taleb's moral strictures on English manners are thus legitimized by the figure of Lady Spenser as female moralist, a legitimacy which at once domesticates his cultural alterity, and brings his remarks closer to the conventions of self-criticism familiar to European readers from the 'Persian Letters' genre, particularly salient in Hamilton's *Hindoo Rajah*.

Perhaps aware of contemporary interest in comparing oriental and occidental sexual manners, Stewart published Abu Taleb's essay on the 'Vindication of the Liberties of Asian Women', which had first appeared in the *Asiatic Annual Register* in 1801, as an appendix to the *Travels*. (Did the title consciously allude to Wollstonecraft's famous treatise on the condition of European women, with its numerous orientalist allusions?) The *Vindication* takes the form of a dialogue between Abu Taleb and an unnamed English lady who had 'censured [oriental] men for their unkindness, and the women, also, for submitting to be so undervalued' (II, 401). Abu Taleb sets out to criticize the sexual orientalism so prevalent in early-nineteenth-century Europe, reversing the stereotype of progressive Europe where the triumph of chivalry has permitted women considerable social freedom, compared to their confinement and suppression in oriental cultures. He concludes, possibly drawing on his own experience as a frustrated lover of English women, by finding the latter actually more oppressed than their Asian sisters, despite their much vaunted social freedom. Asian women were permitted, he insisted, to own private property, control the domestic environment of the *zenana*, have easier access to divorce, and expect to maintain custody of their children in the event of separation from their husbands. Whereas Zaarmilla's critique of the condition of English women lay in the discrepancy between the 'theoretical' ethical respect for women allegedly enjoined in the Bible and the social reality, Abu Taleb's diagnoses

Western gender relations as systematically flawed, and attacks the hypocrisy of European sexual orientalism. It's difficult to imagine Hamilton's (or, for that matter, Wollstonecraft's) reaction to Abu Taleb's *Vindication*, but it's likely they would have been put off by the note of libertinism barely concealed beneath the surface. It would presumably have been easier for British feminists to credit the work if the author had been an Asian *woman* rather than a self-confessed Bengali Don Juan. Too much was at stake, in Europe's self-promoting narrative of the links between social progress and the emancipation of women, to have admitted the validity of Abu Taleb's case, or to have accepted his *Vindication* as anything but the work of a frustrated oriental voluptuary.

In his long review of Abu Taleb's *Travels* published in the *Quarterly Review* in 1810, Reginald Heber accepted the book's authenticity, claiming it (inaccurately as it turns out) as 'the first description of European manners and characters, which has, as far as we know, appeared in an Oriental language'.[35] He openly linked it to the 'Persian Letters' genre, speculating that because 'no real oriental traveller had yet appeared' in Britain until Abu Taleb's arrival, 'his place and character were eagerly assumed by European writers, who under the names of Turkish Spies, Ambassadors of Bantam, and Chinese and Persian Tourists, endeavoured to instruct, as impartial spectators of European feuds and follies; or to amuse, by ridiculous oppositions of our own manners and characters with their own'.[36] Yet, Heber confesses, there was now something tawdry about the fake orientalism of the genre, especially in a culture rapidly becoming expert in the languages and ethnography of its oriental colonies. 'Amusing as they were, these Turks and Persians wanted the charm of reality. They were "Bigg's French beads and Bristol Stones", in comparison with the glorious treasures of Golconda: and the difference in interest was almost the same as between a view of the Great Mogul himself, and the well-bred Sultan of a French tragedy or an English masquerade'. Hence his pleasure in announcing that in the persona of Abu Taleb 'the reality . . . has at last made his appearance'.[37] Heber's announcement seems to signal a general transformation in European representations of the orient in the Romantic period. As Michael Harbsmeier has indicated, the eighteenth-century genre of 'Persian Letters' more or less died out, following in the wake of the defunct genre of the epistolary novel: 'a few Orientalists sometimes did their best to authenticate fictitious accounts . . . but more often they tried all they could to find the genuine texts of this sort and to make them accessible for the European reading public through translation'.[38] As the nineteenth century drew on, European orientalism seemed increasingly split between what Said has designated a 'dream-like Orient', and an exercise in philological world-building wedded to imperial expansion, as 'the [colonial] reality made its appearance'.

Given what we have seen of Abu Taleb's critical strictures on British society and manners, it hardly seems fair to follow Juan Cole in accusing him (and other members of the Indo-Persian service elite) of merely collaborating with the British colonial authorities, although he was keen to solicit employment from the new masters of Bengal.[39] Nonetheless, it is a fact that the printed form and textual dissemination of Abu Taleb's *Travels* (in English, Persian, and Urdu) depended on a contemporary perception, by Heber and others, of its value as propaganda for British power in South Asia. For all that, unable to appeal to the idealized Brahminical virtue of the sort we saw informing the orientalism of Hamilton's *Hindoo Rajah*, Abu Taleb sought to analyse and judge British culture according to the standards of his own Indo-Persian and Mogul world view, resisting the reformist agenda of European colonizers. As Tabish Khair has indicated, this has led to a double forgetting of Abu Taleb's text; 'if British officers [increasingly] found India's Persian heritage a threat to their power and hegemony . . . Hindu nationalists – as well as the Westernised bourgeoisie – have continued to skip the five hundred years of Persian influence in India'.[40] Abu Taleb's account of Britain conforms neither to the agenda of Hamilton's *Hindoo Rajah*, which appropriates a Hindu (definitively *not* an Indo-Muslim) perspective in order to moralize British readers, nor with the newly familiar colonial axiom that 'West was best'. Even when filtered through an 'orientalist' English translation, Abu Taleb's *Travels* demand that we reconsider our sense of colonial interaction as a one-way street between those articulate Europeans who possessed the power of representation, and their colonial subjects who were silent or ventriloquized objects of that power.

NOTES

1. Marilyn Butler, 'Byron and the Empire in the East', in Andrew Rutherford (ed.), *Byron: Augustan and Romantic* (Basingstoke: Macmillan, 1990), pp. 63–81. An earlier version of this essay appeared as 'The Orientalism of Byron's *Giaour*', in Bernard Beatty and Vincent Newey (eds.), *Byron and the Limits of Fiction* (Liverpool: Liverpool University Press, 1988), pp. 78–96.
2. Edward Said, *Orientalism* (London: Penguin, 1985), p. 3.
3. Butler, 'Byron and the Empire in the East', p. 76.
4. Gary Kelly, *Women, Writing and Revolution 1790–1827* (Oxford: Clarendon Press, 1993).

5. Marilyn Butler, *Jane Austen and the War of Ideas* (Oxford: Clarendon Press, 1975: with new introduction, 1987), p. 108. The designation is accepted, with some qualifications, by Pamela Perkins and Shannon Russell in the introduction to their excellent recent edition of the *Translation of the Letters of a Hindoo Rajah* (Peterborough, Ontario: Broadview Press, 1999), p. 14.

6. Butler, *Jane Austen and the War of Ideas*, p. 108.

7. Although according to Elizabeth Benger, in *Memoirs of the Late Mrs Elizabeth Hamilton*, 2 vols. (London, 1818), in *Modern Philosophers* 'the alliance of morals and politics was carefully disclaimed, and consequently Aristocrats and Democrats agreed to laugh at what was ridiculous' (vol. i, p. 132).

8. Butler, *Jane Austen and the War of Ideas*, p. 111.

9. Elizabeth Hamilton, *Letters on the Elementary Principles of Education*, 2 vols., 2nd edn (Bath, 1801), vol. i, p. 224: 'these rights [of man], which are derided by prejudice, despised by luxury, and trampled on by pride, must ever be held sacred by justice and humanity'. For her defence of virtue, see vol. i, p. 335.

10. See Jane Rendall, 'Writing History for British Women: Elizabeth Hamilton and the *Memoirs of Agrippina*', in Clarissa Campbell-Orr (ed.), *Wollstonecraft's Daughters: Womanhood in England and France, 1780–1920* (Manchester: Manchester University Press, 1996), pp. 79–93, and Harriet Guest, *Small Change: Women, Learning, Patriotism, 1750–1810* (Chicago: Chicago University Press, 2000), pp. 328–34.

11. See Kate Teltscher, *India Inscribed: European and British Writing on India, 1600–1800* (Oxford: Oxford University Press, 1995), pp. 134–42; Balchandra Rajan, 'Feminizing the Feminine: Early Women Writers on India', in Alan Richardson and Sonia Hofkosh (eds.), *Romanticism, Race, and Imperial Culture* (Bloomington and Indianapolis: Indiana University Press, 1996), pp. 149–72.

12. Like her intellectual mentors Kames, Ferguson, and Stewart, Hamilton's *Letters on . . . Education* attempts to illustrate the influence of early associations on the mind by drawing upon travellers' records of foreign cultures, most notably those of the East and West Indies.

13. See my *British Romantic Writers and the East: Anxieties of Empire* (Cambridge: Cambridge University Press, 1992), pp. 91–103 for further clarification.

14. Charles Hamilton, *An Historical Relation of the Origin, Progress, and Final Dissolution of the Government of the Rohilla Afghans, in the Northern Province of Hindostan, Compiled from a Persian Manuscript* (London, 1787).

15. Elizabeth Hamilton, *Letters of a Hindoo Rajah*, ed. Pamela Perkins and Shannon Russell, pp. 244–5. All subsequent references to this edition are given in brackets in the text.

16. Kelly, *Women, Writing and Revolution*, p. 133.

17. Rajan, 'Feminizing the Feminine', p. 156; Kelly, *Women, Writing, and Revolution*, pp. 128–38.

18. Elizabeth Benger, *Memoirs of the Late Mrs Elizabeth Hamilton*, vol. i, p. 126.

19. Lisa Lowe, *Critical Terrains: French and British Orientalisms* (Ithaca, N.Y.: Cornell University Press, 1991), p. 58.

20. Quoted in my *British Romantic Writers and the East*, p. 107; see also my essay 'Francis Wilford and the Colonial Construction of Hindu Geography', in Amanda Gilroy (ed.), *Romantic Geographies* (Manchester: Manchester University Press, 2000), pp. 204–22.

21. Teltscher, *India Inscribed*, p. 140.

22. Ibid., p. 141.

23. Jane Rendall, 'Scottish Orientalism: From Robertson to James Mill', *Historical Journal* 25.1 (1982), 43–69.

24. Hamilton, *Letters on . . . Education*, vol. 1, p. 18.

25. Anthologized in Hamilton, *Letters of a Hindoo Rajah*, ed. Perkins and Russell, p. 318.

26. Butler, 'Byron and the Empire in the East', pp. 70–4.

27. C. A. Bayly, *Indian Society and the Making of the British Empire* (Cambridge: Cambridge University Press, 1988), p. 158.

28. Anthologized in Broadview edition, ed. Perkins and Russell, p. 315. See note 25.

29. Gulfishan Khan, *Indian Muslim Perceptions of the West during the 18th Century* (Karachi: Oxford University Press, 1998), pp. 100, 178.

30. It should be noted that numerous manuscript versions also circulated in Indian and British libraries, and are described by a contemporary Persian scholar as being 'similar in content' (Khan, *Indian Muslim Perceptions of the West*, p. 116).

31. Abu Taleb Khan, *The Travels of Mirza Abu Taleb Khan, in Asia, Africa, and Europe, during the Years 1799–1803*, trans. Charles Stewart, 2 vols. (London: Longman, 1810), vol. 1, p. 162. Subsequent references are given parenthetically in the text, in the form (1, 162). Reginald Heber's ill-spirited comment on this passage was 'Poor Abu failed to understand that he was only entertaining from the Caftan outwards'. Review of Abu Taleb Khan's *Travels*, *Quarterly Review* 8 (August 1810), 88.

32. Gulfishan Khan, *Indian Muslim Perceptions of the West*, p. 219.

33. Kate Teltscher, 'The Shampooing Surgeon and the Persian Prince: Two Indians in Early 19th Century Britain', *Postcolonial Interventions* 2.3 (2000), 421.

34. Ibid., p. 420. Teltscher suggests that the poem is unusual in naming its female object, alluding to the absence of *purdah* in England.

35. Reginald Heber, Review of *Travels*, *Quarterly Review* 8 (August 1810), 80–93, 92.

36. Ibid., p. 81.

37. Ibid.

38. Michael Harbsmeier, 'Early Travels to Europe: Some Remarks on the Magic of Writing', in Francis Barker et al. (eds.), *Europe and Its Others*, 2 vols. (Colchester: Essex University, 1985), p. 79.

39. Juan Cole, 'Invisible Occidentalism: 18th Century Indo-Persian Constructions of the West', *Iranian Studies* 25.3–4 (1992), 1–16.

40. Tabish Khair, 'Remembering to Forget Abu Taleb', *Wasafiri* 34 (Autumn 2001), 34–8, 38.

CHAPTER 10

Jane Austen and the professional wife

Janet Todd

The early cultural image of Jane Austen was crafted in large part by her nephew J. E. Austen-Leigh in his *A Memoir of Jane Austen* (1870).[1] He composed his work when he was in his seventies and far removed both from his 'dear Aunt Jane' – she had died over half a century before – and from her historical time. While her letters depicted a woman embedded in her era; acutely aware of intellectual and cultural trends; visitor to Bath, London, Southampton, and Godmersham; and patron of circulating libraries and art galleries, Austen-Leigh's Jane Austen was a retiring Victorian lady rooted in a quiet and picturesque country village. She lived in 'entire seclusion from the literary world' and was 'always very careful not to meddle with matters which she did not thoroughly understand . . . She never touched upon politics, law, or medicine', he wrote.[2]

In *Jane Austen and the War of Ideas* (1975) Marilyn Butler taught us how absurd this statement was in relation to politics and helped inaugurate a period of intense interest in Austen as social commentator, concerned with the presumed masculine spheres of state politics and the professions. In the present chapter I want to follow this route using contemporary writing about the professions to shed light on Austen's texts. At the same time I recognize that the emphasis is itself a response to the Austen-Leigh tradition of depoliticizing Austen and can be a source of only one of the numerous approaches to the novels. Although she draws on the same contemporary world as her more definite and didactic contemporaries, Austen is not an historian, teacher, or recorder; she investigates rather than portrays social transformations and explores rather than pronounces on ethics.

THE PROFESSIONS

The professions in the early nineteenth century have been described by Harold Perkin as forming a class or culture with its own ideology of intelligent and moral service, already politically inflected when Jane Austen depicted it. The class, according to Perkin, existed outside the aristocratic, entrepreneurial, and working-class groups and was not simply the ruling classes' 'thinkers' and 'active conceptualizing ideologists', as Karl Marx defined its members. Rather it was a protean class, assuming the guise of other classes at will. Like merchants and traders, men of the professions – the law, medicine, the church, and the military – were not immune from market forces but were also valued according to a notion of service. True, the clergy had their living, a guaranteed but not hereditary income provided by the laity, lawyers and medical men accepted fees, while military men had their pay and prizes; yet all were regarded as somehow serving a community or the nation and all acted on trust and drew status from this trust – although only the highest levels actually received much respect and reward. 'Being by nature hierarchical interests dependent on patronage . . . the professions fitted snugly into the old dependency society.'[3]

Enriching Perkin's analysis, Brian Southam noted that, during the second half of the eighteenth century, the traditional 'learned professions' – the church, the law, and medicine – assumed a social character as 'liberal professions', that is occupations which, along with the profession of arms, were suited to a gentleman – and indeed useful to his character. By the turn of the nineteenth century, the provision of a profession was not just monetary but moral and disciplinary. As General Tilney remarks in *Northanger Abbey*, it is 'expedient to give every young man some employment'.[4]

The entry of gentlemen into the professional class boosted status, but the corollary within the church was that clerical duties atrophied and a few sermons taken from books and the odd baptism or funeral could comprehend the functions of a hunting, dining vicar, with other pastoral activities left to a poorly paid curate. This situation changed around the beginning of the nineteenth century, a time of urbanization and higher living standards, when, according to Perkin, professional men grew less dependent on a few rich patrons and more on their own groups as clients. They became institutionalized and more 'respectable', to use an increasingly significant term. To enhance their prestige lawyers formed local societies culminating in the Law Society in 1825, while apothecaries and surgeons, general practitioners of the time, gained status through the Royal College of Surgeons in 1800 and the Apothecaries' Act of 1815. Prompted by the Evangelical Movement the Anglican clergy took up their sacred and social duties with more vigour, emphasizing in dress and demeanour their difference and freedom from the laity.[5]

With such developments the professions could be seen as the repository of social and moral values like probity, honesty, prudence, and sobriety, spreading outwards into the wider community. The conduct-book writer Jane West believed that the virtues of professional men should mark all gentlemen: 'punctuality and regularity in money transactions' were no longer simply 'counting-house requisites', she wrote in *Letters to a Young Lady* (1806). Entering the national debate about the education of a modern gentleman even of the highest rank, she declared that arithmetic 'has been of more real service to the world, than all other remains of classical learning or science'.[6]

Along with emphasis on professional work and the national significance of professional values came stress on the qualities demanded of wives of professional men, rising in status along with their husbands. Gary Kelly remarks that the 'professions are central to Austen's novels, and the Austen sisters were educated to be such men's wives – itself considered a profession by many'. The domestic woman became 'a female version of the professional man' requiring 'the same kind of self-discipline and method ("virtue" and "reason")', albeit not the 'same intellectual training'.[7] So, for instance, in *Strictures on the Modern System of Female Education* (1799) Hannah More declared that, as men are trained for professions, so women must be trained to be 'daughters, wives, mothers, and mistresses of families'. Anticipating Mr Knightley she asserted, 'when a man of sense comes to marry, it is a companion whom he wants'.[8] Jane West defined wifehood as a 'scene of enlarged usefulness, activity, and responsibility',[9] while James Fordyce in *Sermons to Young Women* (1766) insisted on the importance of a wife being 'an oeconomist', whatever the husband's income, and he pitied men deceived into marrying expensive women – though deception was hardly possible since everyone knew how little economy was taught in girls' boarding schools. Pupils learned how to make an elegant table but never to connect elegance with frugality. A wife must understand economics, know how to budget and manage an income.[10] So frequent is this economic injunction in contemporary conduct-book discourse that the usual charge that Jane Austen's novels were too concerned with 'brass' seems merely ignorance of a cultural obsession.[11] Of course it helped if the woman brought money as well as frugal habits into a union; even Hannah More creating a good evangelical clergyman's wife in *Coelebs in Search of a Wife* (1809) gave her a fortune to bestow on her spouse.[12]

Hester Chapone's *Letters on the Improvement of the Mind* (1773) made a special plea for financial transparency: it is 'a very ill sign, for one or both of the parties, where there is such a want of openness, in what equally concerns them'. A duty especially falling to women was the organization of charity. In 1797 Thomas Gisborne advised wives to urge benevolence on their successful professional self-made husbands, while clergymen's ladies in particular should make community charity their business, despite a temptation to stint in favour of their own children – the church made no provision for clergy widows, as Mrs Bates of *Emma* reveals.[13]

Gisborne is more open than Chapone about the difficulties of marriage to a professional man who, unlike the gentleman of leisure, is much about his business and may mix with undesirable people, often leaving his wife solitary and exposed to temptation. The wife should respond by making her home attractive and her mild and tender self a contrast 'to the violence, the artifice, the unfeeling selfishness' her husband meets in the outside world. Wives of military or naval officers are especially tried. In long separations when they manage families alone they must guard against extravagance and levity, while avoiding awakening 'the censorious tongue of malice'. If they lead unsettled wandering lives with their husbands, they find themselves mixing too much with men, failing to develop domestic habits, and learning to love 'roving', 'amusement', card-playing, and the 'mischievous trash' of circulating libraries. They must counter so evil a fate 'with unremitting vigilance'.[14] As usual it is left to Jane West to provide the darkest picture of a professional marriage unrestrained by excellent wifely qualities. Men might become rich by 'successful adventure, professional skill, patient diligence, or laborious industry', but imprudent wives can reduce all to 'bankruptcies, suicides, helpless widows and destitute orphans'. For West good wifeliness is a duty to England: 'the wife cannot show her patriotism better than by relieving her partner from the weight of domestic incumbrance, and acting as a faithful steward and intelligent agent in every affair which can be submitted to her management'.[15]

The professions feature in all of Austen's novels but in those conceived early in her life there is less criticism of leisure and idleness than in the later three. Edward Copeland has argued that in the 1790s people on fixed income faced difficulties and that these 'early novels share a common economic vision – the danger of losing it all, the chance of hitting it rich, huge losses, huge gains, everything riding on luck and the main chance'.[16] The later novels however, exploring the social and economic changes of the war and immediate post-war years, fit with Perkin's history of the professions and look at a more intimate connection between work, money, morality, and men; the getting of money comes to exist in a moral framework. In this it is possible to see a reflection of Austen's own experience as described in her letters on publication, copyright, and money, for, despite Austen-Leigh's insistence that his aunt of 'humble mind' wrote only 'for her own amusement', in Chawton she clearly participated in the most significant development in this social change: 'the general rise in the status of the professional intellectual' seen best in the profession of letters.[17] As Marilyn Butler observed, even though Austen 'never became consciously or through real-life communications a *woman* novelist', she did come to consider herself a spokesperson for the new professionals, a group emerging from, 'but intellectually impatient with, the gentry'.[18]

THE PROFESSIONS IN *EMMA*, *MANSFIELD PARK*, AND *PERSUASION*

The novels conceived at Chawton, *Emma*, *Mansfield Park*, and *Persuasion*, display marriages between professional working men, whose work is central to their characters, and women who are suited through experience and temperament to be their wives – and part managers. Through the preparation for such marriage the resplendent individualism of the thinking heroine, delivered with all the techniques of internal monologue, free indirect speech, and shifting narrative voice, is tempered by an awareness of necessary negotiation between that individualism and familial and communal social need.

Mansfield Park urges the importance of being professional, whether in ministering, acting, or soldiering. The clerical Edmund Bertram and the sailor William Price stand against the extravagant Tom Bertram and the philandering Henry Crawford, who idly thinks he might like to try both their professions but who soon realizes the pleasure of pursuing pleasure – in much the same way as he later tires of thinking he wants the modest Fanny for his wife. With her experience of Dr Grant, his sister sees the church as a place of sloth and indulgence, in status far below the military and the law, while idle landowning excels any work. Rushworth's property allows him to 'escape a profession' (*MP*, p. 161) in her view, despite the fact that the notion of profession gives Edmund part of his character and value. Mary's worldly attitude provokes her would-be lover into expressing his sense of his clerical calling – and the discussion trickles through the second half of the book.

Mansfield Park is set firmly in the Napoleonic War years and Austen's contemporary reading connects the text with this context. In January 1813 she wrote to Cassandra that she was reading 'an essay on the Military Polic[y] and Institutions of the British Empire, by Capt. Pasley of the Engineers' and finding it 'delightfully written & highly entertaining'. She was, she declared, 'much in love with the Author'.[19] Pasley was a paternalistic imperialist but his main purpose in writing was not to encourage empire but to rally the despondent British at a particularly depressing moment in their struggle against France, or 'thraldom' as he called possible defeat and invasion. He felt his countrymen had lost their will to struggle and win:

The justice of going to war, for a necessary object, has never for a moment been disputed in any age or country, except by a few fanatics. War should not be lightly entered into, nor should any warlike enterprise be rashly undertaken: but when once undertaken, those who have drawn the sword should never give way to despair, on account of difficulties or dangers, foreseen or not foreseen. The art of war is the art of surmounting difficulties, and of setting danger at defiance.[20]

Essential to the war effort was moral purpose in the home and the nation, the 'active principle' (*MP*, p. 463) that Sir Thomas Bertram finds lacking in most of the inhabitants of Mansfield Park. Pasley reiterated the point that England needed professional military leadership if it was to defeat France. The novels Austen conceived in the 1790s featured well-dressed, leisured militiamen and absentee, half-hearted or ridiculous clergymen; in *Mansfield Park,* however, she presents the military and the church as the two serious professions that potentially support the country in a difficult and sapping war, the one defending it abroad, the other establishing at home those principles for which men were fighting.[21]

The implied praise of the navy in the presentation of the young, frank, and aspiring William Price draws on the earlier national enthusiasm for Admiral Nelson, rather waning when Austen was writing the novel since further naval victories had not been forthcoming. At the same time the book is not wholeheartedly enthusiastic about the navy, as John Peck has argued – witness William's lament about his lack of promotion, which is brought about in the end only because his sister has caught the eye of an influential man, while Mary Crawford's admiration for the service is based on its fashion rather than use.[22] The main profession displayed in the book is of course the church. The heroines of two out of three of the 1790s novels marry clergymen but only in *Mansfield Park* do the implications of the choice emerge.

Shortly after reporting her enjoyment of Pasley, Austen addressed her sister, 'Now I will try to write of something else; – it shall be a complete change of subject – Ordination.'[23] Recent critical consensus is that this was written after *Mansfield Park* had been started and refers to queries about the process of clerical training, not the subject of the novel. Yet one can argue that 'ordination' is a possible key to an aspect of *Mansfield Park*, which discusses the value of the clergyman and of religion within the nation,[24] not only in time of war but also in an era when, as Edmund noted, the clergy were improving and congregations with them: 'there is more general observation and taste, a more critical knowledge diffused, than formerly; in every congregation, there is a larger proportion who know a little of the matter, and who can judge and criticize' (*MP*, p. 340).

Religion, the faith of the Church of England, forms part of the structure and cement of community and ultimately the nation, and Edmund sees the clergyman as being at the centre of both. The country rector could support the local landowner as Southam and Perkin have argued, but he also had civic functions in his own right such as acting as magistrate, administering poor relief, and 'reporting on the manpower available for wartime service in the volunteers'.[25] In his insistence on political centrality, Edmund directly opposes the obsequious Mr Collins's ideas in *Pride and Prejudice*. Collins subordinates clerical influence to social, so allowing Lady Catherine de Burgh to usurp not only his clerical function but also the masculine power of magistrate and commissioner of the peace. His lack of understanding of the clerical role influences his notion of a wife, whose main purpose, as he sees it, is to gain the approval of his patroness. Women are interchangeable as long as they are reasonably well-born and well-bred – and he is happy to have whichever Bennet girl is on offer and, when rejected, he takes the next woman he meets. It is in keeping with that 'light, bright and sparkling' book that, in Elizabeth's words, he happens to meet with 'one of the very few sensible women who would have accepted him' (*P&P*, p. 178), a woman suited by expectation and family training to her social and economic wifely role.

Edmund Bertram has a higher notion of the clergyman:

[he] has the charge of all that is of the first importance to mankind, individually or collectively considered, temporally and eternally – [he] has the guardianship of religion and morals, and consequently of the manners which result from their influence. No one here can call the *office* nothing. If the man who holds it is so, it is by the neglect of his duty, by foregoing its just importance, and stepping out of his place to appear what he ought not to appear. (*MP*, p. 92)

The Mansfield family, however, has had no positive image of a clergyman: the parsonage has been inhabited by two trivial men, Mr Norris and Dr Grant, both concerned to shield their home from the churchyard. When Maria Bertram visits the house at Sotherton, she is relieved to see it separated from the church, so it avoids the 'annoyance of the bells' (*MP*, p. 82). In similar vein Henry Crawford wants to turn Edmund's 'mere Parsonage House' into a gentleman's 'residence' (*MP*, p. 243) with no sense of its situation within a clerical community.

The choice before Edmund is of the church as vocation or mere source of income, dramatized in his choice of wife between the sprightly, metropolitan Mary Crawford and the retiring, rural Fanny Price. Even when most attracted to Edmund Mary can imagine spending no more than half the year in the country and then only with the best society; indeed a single wet afternoon in the Grants' parsonage appals her. Sir Thomas had once proposed that Edmund have both the good livings of Thornton Lacey and Mansfield, an outcome prevented by his eldest son's extravagance,[26] but on his return from his dangerous expedition he speaks eloquently of the duties of a resident clergyman. (Although the telescoped ending includes Edmund gaining the richer Mansfield living, it is unclear whether this makes him a pluralist – like Austen's father and brother.) Agreeing with Sir Thomas, Edmund intends to be 'constantly resident' in his parish, believing with him that 'human nature needs more lessons than a weekly sermon can convey' (*MP*, pp. 247–8). He will be a country parson and proud of his post. London is not the nation, certainly not its moral centre: 'We do not look in great cities for our best morality', he asserts (*MP*, p. 93). In London fine preaching is admired like a branch of acting, as Henry later suggests when, with his thespian skills, he imagines giving a good sermon and receiving 'capital gratification' (*MP*, p. 341). Edmund's rural clergyman will be a model of behaviour as well as a preacher, an arbiter not of manners but of conduct. Interestingly, this fits with a distinction Richard Lovell Edgeworth made in his *Essays on Professional Education* (1809), where he discusses the education of men destined for the church:

Well-dressed crowds weep while they listen to a fashionable orator in the pulpit, the next moment they relapse into habits of dissipation . . . It should . . . be established in the minds of young clergymen, as an article of morality, as well as a principle of criticism, that the excellence of sermons, especially for country congregations, depends more on simplicity, and clearness of expression, than upon ornament, or what is commonly called fine writing.[27]

Edmund knows that the good clergyman begets the good local community: 'as the clergy are, or are not what they ought to be, so are the rest of the nation' (*MP*, p. 93). Following this serious social sentiment, it is fitting that an angry Mary mocks him as a Methodist, that most socially despised form of Anglican evangelicalism.

Like Fanny, Mary is deracinated, depending on relatives for a home; but where the stationary Fanny chose as prop and defence a firm morality, the peripatetic Mary has armoured herself with wit and liveliness. Given her developed personality she would not be a useful wife for a resident clergyman, who cannot follow her in seeing it as a 'point of honour' to promote people's enjoyment at the expense of puffing their 'vanity and pride' (*MP*, pp. 82–3). Had Edmund continued in his love he would have faced the dilemma described by a clergyman contemporary with Austen, who confided to his diary his misgivings about loving an unsuitable woman: 'She seems to be an utter stranger to God; and yet I fondly think I could be happy with her. But how can two travel together, except they be agreed? Were I (as I now think happy enough) to marry her, what distress might it not occasion . . . When I consider matters soberly, I must needs be ensured of enjoying more true happiness in marriage with a pious woman . . . than with a graceless, gay, dissipated lady.'[28] A wife with money was useful but she might negate her usefulness by trying to make her husband live beyond his income, as Austen noted in the example of her brother James's genteel first wife. Mrs Norris's remark is pertinent: 'A fine lady in a country parsonage was quite out of place' (*MP*, p. 31).

Against her self-interest Mary does come to love Edmund but, like her brother, she fantasizes about dominating a 'good' character: as Henry Crawford anticipates the 'felicity of forcing' (*MP*, p. 326) Fanny to care for him, Mary imagines Edmund's 'sturdy spirit' bending towards her, seeing the conquest as 'sweet beyond expression' (*MP*, p. 358). Towards the end of the novel Mary's manners and wit falter under the promptings of unwelcome desire: when she contemplates a married clerical fate she becomes rude and snobbish, close here to the disdainful, over-familiar aristocrats Sir Thomas deplores (while not aristocrats, the Crawfords are associated with their metropolitan libertine lifestyle).[29] She rattles on about conquests to a hostile Fanny and sends her a crass letter speculating on Tom's death and Edmund's elevation – like Isabella Thorpe with Catherine Morland she also imagines arch and inappropriate responses in the other. Such acts seem out of her social character but have been prepared for by her growing need both to have Edmund and to have him in the worldly mould she wants. So the letter appears here to exhibit in part what Edmund had called the 'right of a lively mind' (*MP*, p. 64) precisely not to think of her correspondent, in part the corruption he later laments. All Austen novels display men whose characters have been diminished or at least not improved by injudicious marriages – Mr Elton in *Emma*, potentially a serviceable clergyman, is lessened in value for the community by marriage to a vulgar, presuming wife. Such men have mostly followed beauty, but there may be equal error for a clergyman in marrying primarily for liveliness and charm.

Fanny Price, Mary's rival, is the least liked of Austen heroines, arriving in print immediately after the most approved, Elizabeth Bennet. But she gains purpose when read in conjunction with Edmund's choice of profession. Fanny is not destined for Pemberley, nor indeed for Mansfield Park – perhaps that should be left to the more spirited Susan Price – but for a life in a rural parsonage. Where Mary lacks any sense of the rhythms of agriculture, Fanny, although not mentioned directly in terms of farming, is aware of changing seasons and their needs.[30] On the road to Sotherton she notes a harvest, cottages, cattle, and children where the others remain absorbed in sexual feelings. She spends much of the novel helping her selfish aunts and when at home in Portsmouth uses the little money she has to aid family peace and improve her sister's manners and mind. Like the eclectic church she will serve, Fanny is open to ideas and thoughts – hence the novel's stress on her reading – and she is religious without being pious or evangelical, seeing morality as process not as an adherence to a code, a struggle rather than a single conquest or conversion. She is certainly not all goodness. She is quickly ashamed of her natural home and, in the talk with her uncle, lies about her main reason for rejecting Henry. She spends much of the book consumed by jealousy and is censorious about Mary, who, on little evidence, is pronounced 'cruel' and 'ungrateful' (*MP*, pp. 63 and 456), the latter so loaded a word in Fanny's lexicon that her judgement appears warped by her own experience. She is frequently, though silently, angry and despite their similar situations there is no sympathy between her and her female cousins, except in Fanny's mind: she cloisters her virtue. None the less she aspires to social goodness: she examines herself and struggles against wayward impulses and poor health, the latter simply a given rather than a virtue or vice. She has known neglect but Edmund's responsive kindness has made 'tears delightful' (*MP*, p. 152), so that she learns to assimilate pain into her personality. With her seriousness, her active sense of duty, her moral fastidiousness, and keen sense of the power of self-restraint and self-denial, she would make a good clergyman's wife: with her, Edmund's profession would follow 'moral ordination' and become a common pursuit.[31]

Writing of the clergyman's wife, Gisborne stressed that she needed the womanly virtues more than other women: 'the apostle well knew that the want of any of them would prove, in the way of example, far more prejudicial in the wife of a clergyman than in another person . . . if religion have its genuine effect on her manners and disposition, if it render her humble and mild, benevolent and candid, sedate, modest and devout; if it withdraw her inclinations from fashionable foibles and fashionable expences; if it lead her to activity in searching out and alleviating the wants of the neighbouring poor' then she becomes a 'fellow-labourer' with her husband.[32] Unlike the parson's wife of the Victorian era she was not expected to pursue an independent ministry and the emphasis here and in Austen's novel is on a social, moral, and economic rather than spiritual role.[33]

The distinction between Henry Crawford on the one hand and William Price and Edmund Bertram on the other continues in *Emma* in the contrast of George Knightley and Frank Churchill, made openly patriotic by their Christian names – Frank underlining the point when he declares, 'I am sick of England – and would leave it to-morrow, if I could' (*E*, p. 365). But this is a less war-engrossed and more unstable society than that in *Mansfield Park* – one reason for Emma's many social mistakes – so the larger social picture of the professions emerges, the way in which the law, and medicine, less gentlemanly pursuits than the church and military, are also rising in status. The point is made through two ubiquitous but silent characters, Mr Cox the attorney and Mr Perry the apothecary.

Emma has a complex, rather intense relationship with her barrister brother-in-law, and happily her sister's marriage could not 'raise a blush' (*E*, p. 358). Yet she is uneasy at the idea of the law in general and she considers the family of Highbury's Mr Cox 'very vulgar' (*E*, p. 232). She dismisses Mrs Elton's efforts to achieve gentility through implying that her father was 'in the law line' by demoting him into a 'drudge of some attorney, and too stupid to rise' (*E*, p. 183). The difference of rank between barrister and attorney was real but the gap was closing, as Richard Cronin has pointed out in his introduction to *Emma*, owing to the fact that by 1800 attorneys came to stand between client and barrister, so forcing the higher-status barristers into financial dependence on the attorneys who commissioned them.[34] The great difference Emma observes between the ranks derives in part from the wives – the genteel Isabella versus the vulgar Mrs Cox.

Medicine comes below law in status. In *Mansfield Park*, when the well-born Edmund named the gentlemanly professions, he listed the church, arms, and the law, claiming that as younger son he must have been intended for one of these. Medicine was not of high enough status to appear in this list, not even at the level of the university-educated physician who overtopped the more lowly surgeon and apothecary. Jane Austen was well aware of medical status. In a letter to her niece Anna Austen, an aspiring novelist, she wrote, 'I have also scratched out the Introduction between Lord P. & his Brother, & Mr. Griffin. A Country Surgeon (dont tell Mr C. Lyford) would not be introduced to Men of their rank.'[35] Below the surgeon and apothecary was the druggist who sold medicines and was not supposed to give consultations, although he very frequently did so. In a village or small town he could indeed become the main medical man as Perry is within Highbury.[36] Isabella and her father argue about the merits of their favourite medical men, the London apothecary Mr Wingfield, and Highbury's Mr Perry. John Knightley evidently believes that Perry is little better than a druggist, who makes his tidy income from selling his drugs as well as from advising and prescribing for a fee.[37] But in Highbury he is respected as both a medical man and a therapist, understanding the hypochondria of Mr Woodhouse and the depression of Jane Fairfax. He is constantly present, glimpsed by Emma walking or riding, keeping an eye on community health, circulating gossip, and ministering to the prejudices of the village's richest inhabitant, Mr Woodhouse.

Perry is very aware of his betwixt-and-between status and is worried about setting up a carriage although he has the funds. As friend to many of the gentry and patron of the poor he thinks he might have the social position; yet he also fears he could be thought presumptuous by the born gentlemen, and indeed Mr Weston, who has himself risen through his own entrepreneurial efforts, does think the carriage a little premature. Happily Mr Perry has chosen a suitable wife, for it is she who makes the action acceptable. In a community so much concerned with health, Mr Perry's own can be alleged as reason for this otherwise lavish move. Highbury soon learns that the setting up of the carriage was owing to his wife's 'persuasion', as she thought his being out in bad weather did him 'a great deal of harm' (*E*, pp. 344–5). Ill health has an equalizing tendency and in a book which, as John Wiltshire has observed, is 'littered' with 'para-medical paraphernalia', the luxury rank-inflected consumer item can be disguised as a health aid.[38]

Austen heroines do not marry lawyers and doctors, and for *Emma* one must go outside the usual professional categories to consider a role touched upon in several of the novels and subsumed by Edgeworth into the professional class, that of gentleman farmer. Although in *Principles of Political Economy and Taxation* (1817) the economist David Ricardo opposed the landlord living on unearned rents to the professional man and the capitalist serving and managing industry, it is possible to see the landowning farmer of the late eighteenth century as serving the community by filling many of the social and patriotic functions of professional men, as well as displaying similar specialized knowledge, quite unlike the idle rentier and absent landowner.[39] Edgeworth demanded that 'To be a good landlord, and a good magistrate', a man must 'have a desire to serve his tenants, and to do justice to all who appeal to him' and he should encourage his tenants to improve themselves and their farms. His actions ought to be based on good economic and agricultural theory. Such gentlemen farmers are 'agriculturalists' experimenting 'for the benefit of their estates, and of their country'.[40] The noted agriculturist Arthur Young made a similar point when, describing recent changes in agriculture, from rotations of crops to enclosure of land, he observed in *Rural Oeconomy* that gentlemen who had in earlier times left matters to their stewards now managed their farms and studied 'husbandry' and 'rural oeconomics'.[41]

Austen often pits sensible professional men against silly landowners, but she does not follow Mary Wollstonecraft into praising the entrepreneurial unlanded class at the expense of the gentry with inherited land and wealth. Rather, she seems to desire social and economic virtues in both groups: each must function in a new capitalist world but each must fulfil old responsibilities and retain a duty of care to those below them. Reputedly Austen's favourite landowning character, Mr Knightley is an attractively anachronistic figure, but he has some modern qualities, as Emma at first fails to understand. He inhabits a low unmodernized old English manor house with an estate untouched by fashionable landscaping; yet he is also an up-to-date farmer who reads 'Agricultural Reports' and talks of drainage with his brother. He is 'improving' in agricultural mode, perhaps enclosing his fields, but he is taking into account community susceptibilities. No feudal landlord, he considers the villagers of Donwell before changing a path across his land (*E*, p. 106). He recognizes as near equals the rising professional men of Highbury, as well as his own land steward and tenant farmer Robert Martin, who dines with his brother in London and whose potential wife, Harriet, he tries to instruct in 'modes of agriculture' (*E*, p. 361).

But Knightley has his weak spots. He may know about agriculture but he lacks culture. There is no evidence that he reads the kind of books that Emma, despite her lack of serious application, has read, the novels and romances of the day, and he has little of what Edgeworth also requires in the country gentleman, 'those principles of taste, which will enable him to lay out his own grounds, or to judge of the advice of the professional improver'.[42] He has no sense of improvement for pleasure and the grounds of Donwell Abbey fall far short of the aesthetic standards of Pemberley. Like his brother he has a low opinion of women. John Knightley had chosen to marry an adoring but silly wife and, although George later declares he always loved the cleverer sister and states *à propos* of Mr Collins that a man wants a companion in a wife, he also expresses deeply patriarchal notions of marriage. He lauds Mrs Weston's wifely compliance and describes her readiness to submit her 'own will' as a 'very material matrimonial point' (*E*, p. 38), the kind of statement reminiscent of the conduct books both Austen and Mary Wollstonecraft abhorred. He learns his mistake before he decides to take on Emma and, as proof of his development, makes the sacrifice of moving from his masculine domain of Donwell into Hartfield, where the woman must always be preeminent. Though kindly, both Knightleys are ill at ease in company. John, in consequence of his marriage, indulges himself in either staying at home or being rude when forced abroad and George does not always dance or make small talk when he should. Both brothers fulfil the French caricature of the English as taciturn and bluntly sincere, dispensing with conversational politeness as well as gallantry towards women.[43]

At first sight Emma, an idle man's snobbish daughter, seems an unsuitable candidate for the wife of a magistrate and responsible landowner – except in the useful fact that she is rich and will bring her large dowry to a husband short of ready money. She will also bring her intellectual feminine capital of taste and aesthetic sensibility. She has presumably had much to do with the 'pretty' grounds of Hartfield which contrast so decidedly with the workaday estate of Donwell. But she, like Mr Knightley, has to shift in some attitudes; she is helped in this by the fact that she has to pay a heavy price for each slight social error she makes. She was out of date when she dismissed Robert Martin as a member of the 'yeomanry' (*E*, p. 29) and no gentleman, where Mr Knightley refers to him as a 'gentleman farmer' (*E*, p. 62), and she learns that no one in the community, even Miss Bates, can be slighted by a woman of her status. She comes to accept social change and bind not fracture the community. She never quite recognizes the integrity of other people's lives but she does begin to notice the restrictedness of her own. John Knightley tells her: 'Your neighbourhood is increasing, and you mix more with it' (*E*, pp. 311–12). Some reserve will still be necessary to her married role however, which demands '[g]eneral benevolence, but not general friendship' (*E*, p. 320), a phrase she uses in criticizing the likeable parvenu Mr Weston. In short she will in the end fill the role Jane West prescribed in *Letters to a Young Lady*:

To you my dear young friend who are by birth appointed to that most enviable of situations a country gentlewoman, I can with peculiar applicability point out the beneficial consequence of prudence, gentleness, decent respect to your own rank, kind attention to the wants and comforts of others, and regard to religious duties, as reflected in the appearance of a village which looks up to you as its standard of rights.[44]

'[K]ind attention to the wants and comforts of others' is exactly Emma's forte. Within the walls of Hartfield she oils society, keeping the various ranks and types happy and contented, ministering unostentatiously and with immense patience both to her selfish father and to his long-suffering guests, avoiding transgressing their food fads and idiosyncrasies. Unlike the disruptive Frank Churchill with his 'cheerful lack of consideration in matters of health'[45] she accepts people's unease as disease, without mocking or trivializing it. She is tireless in keeping the domestic atmosphere harmonious, shielding her father from his son-in-law's irritation and soothing the latter with her careful talk. Only outside Hartfield does she seem insensitive: in her attitude to the Bateses, the attorney, and the merchant turned country gentleman, as well as to the unfortunate Jane Fairfax. With marriage and increased status the discernment and compassion practised indoors must move out. 'Must' here hides a slight uneasiness left at the end of the novel, which does not quite display this improvement. The equal friendship with Jane is cut off in *Emma* and the equal marriage unobserved.

Robert Miles called *Persuasion* the Jane Austen novel 'most touched by history';[46] like no other it refers directly to military and political events. The patriotism of 'English verdure' in *Emma* (p. 360), of understated English values against superficially attractive French principles, no longer suffices for a victorious nation which has to look within and see its own social and economic fissures. *Persuasion* subtly chronicles social change and, in terms of its implied politics, seems Austen's most radical completed work. The line of great houses stretching from *Sense and Sensibility*'s Norland through Pemberley to Mansfield Park and Donwell Abbey ends in Kellynch-Hall, up for rent because it lacked the economic 'method, moderation, and economy' (*P*, p. 9) of its proprietor's dead wife and as a result 'they were gone who deserved not to stay, and . . . Kellynch-hall had passed into better hands than its owners' (*P*, p. 125). Yet the fate of Kellynch does not argue a complete replacement of the social model of *Emma*. The estate is rented out because its owner is foolish and extravagant and has not, like Mr Knightley, seen his landowning as part duty, part business. Nina Auerbach, whose lively article 'O Brave New World'[47] did so much to open up criticism of the novel, goes too far in seeing the Elliots as entirely dispossessed, the old guard routed by the proponents of new feeling. In fact the future promises no landed renewal: Kellynch will revert to its owner if his lawyer manages things honestly – after all he may now have his daughter's interests to consider since she has gone off with the heir. Despite Auerbach's conclusion that the meritocratic 'navy *is* Jane Austen's vision of a brave new world', it is hard to see anything entirely revolutionary in a service whose policing according to Charles J. Rzepka included 'the Bourbon restoration, the Quadruple Alliance, the Indian Raj, and the Peterloo Massacre'.[48]

With all the caveats, however, the novel does give the impression that the moral significance vested in the clergy in *Mansfield Park* and in the 'untainted' landowner in *Emma* settles here in the naval world – but only when that world includes naval wives. As *Mansfield Park* had staged a debate about the role both of the cleric and of his wife, so *Persuasion* analyses women's role not only in the traditional world of families and hereditary houses but also in the new shifting world of self-made men.

Mrs Clay associates the navy with other professions since it too demanded 'toil and a labour' (*P*, p. 20) and opposed the leisured life. Less tentatively than the law and medicine, seen hesitantly advancing in *Emma*, the profession of arms allowed men not born into the gentry to enter its ranks; as Sir Walter remarks, it brings 'persons of obscure birth into undue distinction' (*P*, p. 19). The navy added to the usual professional mixture of potential achieved wealth and public trust, an overt national significance, as Anne gently urges in her first intervention in the novel. In some ways it was closer than the army to the learned professions, for success required more specific training and skill. In *Britannia Rules: The Classic Age of Naval History* (1977) C. Northcote Parkinson argued that, at the start of the Revolutionary and Napoleonic Wars, the British navy was far more amateur than the French but that, under the reforms of Lord Saint Vincent – perhaps referred to in *Persuasion* in the wizened Lord St Ives – which aimed to put the service on a proper financial and regulatory footing, it became professionalized. At the same time it retained its dashing quality. As Richard Lovell Edgeworth remarked concerning the sailor's education: 'it must be the object to excite enthusiasm, not to subject him to the nice calculations of prudence, or the more accurate judgements of reason'. The taking of a prize, a kind of sanctioned piracy on the high seas, required courage or obstinate self-belief, which young Wentworth found so lacking in Anne Elliot: 'He should ascend the hill to seize his prize, without listening to the abusive voices, that perpetually dissuade him from his enterprise', Edgeworth wrote.[49] Where a boy being educated for the church 'should never be applauded for pleading his cause well, for supporting his own opinion', the boy destined for the navy should be ready to hold 'sturdily' to his main principles. He should 'pursue his own course steadily, regardless of the clamours of the great or little mob'.[50]

According to these precepts Wentworth becomes something like Edgeworth's ideal sailor. But the very qualities that make for success at sea may render a man unfit for life on land. Like Mr Knightley, Captain Wentworth has a limited notion of female roles. He may have a point against his sister when he argues that the naval way of life at sea has no place for women, but on shore he knows little of the sex. After his long absence he only looks at Anne physically, then carelessly attends to the pleasing but trivial

Musgrove girls as if they were another species from himself, as interchangeable as Charles Musgrove must once have found the Elliot sisters – with such dreary and disturbing results. Had Louisa not toppled from the Cobb he might have found himself tied in marriage to the wrong woman.

In many qualities Anne contrasts with Wentworth, who himself asserts complementary gender roles in a crude but not entirely mistaken way. Throughout the novel she seems in training for the helpmate sort of wife a sailor will need and the conduct-book writers approve by the very habits of service that have in part rendered her depressed through the first chapters of the book and which, unlike Fanny Price's qualities in a kinder fable, have made no dent in the habits of her immediate family. Monica Cohen has argued that '*Persuasion* wants us to see structural affinities between the nineteenth century's incipient professionalism and a domesticity aimed at expanding the woman's sphere by defining it as social and ethical expertise'.[51] Anne is indeed almost professional in her social piano-playing – her fingers are 'mechanically at work' (*P*, p. 72) – and she habitually acts as companion and nurse to her peevish sister and her children. Faced with the recumbent Louisa Musgrove at Lyme, the active Captain Wentworth is less than competent, where Anne, reprising the scene where Wentworth knows what to do when she is overwhelmed by her sister's child, makes decisions and takes charge.

Conduct books stress nursing as women's business,[52] as Charles Musgrove does when he excuses himself and his wife as they leave for a dinner party. Anne agrees: 'Nursing does not belong to a man . . . A sick child is always the mother's property' (*P*, p. 56). Wentworth shows his first real 'glow' and 'gentleness' (*P*, p. 114) towards her when he sees her as nurse. However, she is never close to being a professional nurse, a role left to the lower-class Nurse Rooke, whom Anne pointedly fails even to notice. When Anne makes the role of nurse into a cross between a lady and an angel – 'What instances must pass before them of ardent, disinterested, self-denying attachment, of heroism, fortitude, patience, resignation' (*P*, p. 156) – Mrs Smith, informed by Nurse Rooke, responds that a nurse is much more likely to face weakness, selfishness, and impatience. In other words, Anne knows little of the *profession* of nursing – her nursing, like that of Mrs Harville, exists in the sphere of the family.

Outside these service roles Anne, unlike her robust lover, struggles against physical weakness and she sees no shame in suffering. Although much has been made of the feminism of the sea-going Mrs Croft, who is indeed admired within the book and who excels in prudence and financial acumen, the final paragraph of the novel, as Rzepka notes, suggests not that Anne will follow this liberated childless sister-in-law to sea but that she will be a landlocked, anxious wife within a family – though it should be noted that the only sign of her new status as chosen woman is the possession of a mode of transport, a smart landaulette. Mrs Croft declares herself unfit for the traditionally female role of watcher and waiter, which Anne claims for herself: like Mary Musgrove she gets 'imaginary complaints' (*P*, p. 71) when left alone to face the kind of life so many women endured. Indeed, when she tries to act in a healthcare role she ends up with a blister as large as a 3s piece. Anne will be too 'tender' (*P*, p. 233), as her friends know, but there is no evidence from her past that she will fancy herself unwell. With her mothering skills she emerges as a maternal figure, not, as Sandra Gilbert and Susan Gubar argued in *The Madwoman in the Attic*, a woman heading for life 'on the water' unconfined 'to a female community of childbearing and childrearing'.[53]

Like Emma, Anne will also bring to wifehood her feminine capital of accomplishments and literary knowledge. Wentworth does not quote from literature and in this again he reveals the education Edgeworth planned for a boy destined for the army or navy: 'Early progress in literature is not essential', for the naval boy requires enthusiasm rather than the 'judgements of reason'. The literary Captain Benwick has not been as successful as Wentworth – although he at least chose to read the properly inspirational Walter Scott, 'calculated' in Edgeworth's view 'to inspire a martial taste'.[54]

I should end where I began – with a caveat. In *Persuasion*, perhaps even more than in *Mansfield Park* and *Emma*, external texts only illuminate the edges of the novel and I think it unwise to argue, with some of the critics I have found most helpful in this chapter, that Austen's use of certain political and social positions suggests that she and her novels endorse them. For instance, although I have found Charles Rzepka's article most useful, I cannot quite accept his conclusion that marriage in *Persuasion* is a statement of conservative and evangelical ideals of domestic economy and feminine nurturing, and that Anne's famous reflections on women's exclusion from public activities 'appears less a critique of the status quo than a resignation to her own emotionally exposed position at the end of the book, a position that, to judge from Austen's use of the harsh word "fate", seems almost biologically ordained'.[55] For all the conservative, gendered complementarity of the central marriage, the romantic close moves outside any discussion of professional men or appropriate wives that has intermittently taken place over the novel – as the silence of Captain Harville after Anne's great speech of love and constancy testifies. In this pivotal conversation in the White Hart inn, both sailor and stationary woman imply the insufficiency of much of the gendered and specific activity they are lauding. Harville uses images from the sea and Anne from the land, yet both have suffered from the spheres they appeal to: Harville has been left wounded and relatively poor, excluded from the maritime world that informs his speech, while Anne is making a sacrificial ideal of precisely those aspects of her life that have blighted her youth and would continue to blight her life if this second chance at love had not intervened. In the final rewritten denouement, then, we are not in the realm of ethics, politics, or indeed any historical representation but of fiction, fantasy, excess, and romance. Anne Elliot does not choose a husband for his moral and military qualities – rather she puts on this handsome raconteur the weight of a total desire unforeseen in conduct books: on him depended 'all which this world could do for her' (*P*, p. 237).

NOTES

1. J. E. Austen-Leigh, *A Memoir of Jane Austen* (London: Richard Bentley, 1870).
2. Austen-Leigh, *Memoir*, p. 25.
3. Karl Marx, *German Ideology*, in Marx, *Selected Writings in Sociology and Social Philosophy*, ed. T. B. Bottomore and Maximilien Rubel (Harmondsworth: Penguin Books, 1963), p. 79; Harold Perkin, *The Origins of Modern English Society*, 2nd edn (London: Routledge, 2002), p. 254.
4. B. C. Southam, 'Professions', in Janet Todd (ed.), *Jane Austen in Context* (Cambridge: Cambridge University Press, 2005), pp. 366–76. See also Lawrence Stone and J. C. Fawtier, *An Open Elite: England 1540–1800* (Oxford: Clarendon Press, 1984), p. 228. David Spring terms some men of the rank Perkin has located as the professional classes – the clergymen, lawyers, and military officers – the 'pseudo-gentry', 'primarily because they sought strenuously to be taken for gentry'. See his 'Interpreters of Jane Austen's Social World: Literary Critics and Historians', in Janet Todd (ed.), *Jane Austen: New Perspectives, Women and Literature* (New York and London: Holmes and Meier, 1983), pp. 53–72. Jane Austen, *Northanger Abbey*, in *The Novels of Jane Austen: The Text Based on Collation of the Early Editions by R. W. Chapman* (London: Oxford University Press, 1969), p. 176. All subsequent quotations from Austen's novels refer to R. W. Chapman (ed.), *The Novels of Jane Austen*, 3rd edn (Oxford: Oxford University Press, 1988) and are included parenthetically in the text.
5. See Perkin, *Modern English Society*, pp. 254–5.
6. Jane West, *Letters to a Young Lady*, 4th edn, 3 vols. (London, 1811), vol. 1, pp. 303–4.

7. Gary Kelly, 'Education', in Todd (ed.), *Jane Austen in Context*, pp. 252–61; Kelly, *Revolutionary Feminism: The Mind and Career of Mary Wollstonecraft* (London: Macmillan, 1992), p. 16.

8. Hannah More, *Strictures on the Modern System of Female Education*, 2 vols. (London, 1799), vol. I, pp. 97–8.

9. West, *Letters to a Young Lady*, vol. II, p. 451.

10. James Fordyce, *Sermons to Young Women*, 14th edn, 2 vols. (London, 1814), vol. I, pp. 175–7.

11. Hannah More, in *Coelebs in Search of a Wife*, 6th edn, 2 vols. (London, 1809), also noted the improper education of girls left ignorant of domestic economy: 'when I hear learning contended for on one hand, and modish accomplishments on the other, I always contend for the intermediate, the valuable, the neglected quality, so little insisted on, so rarely found, and so indispensably necessary' (vol. II, pp. 181–2). See W. H. Auden's expression of unease in 'Letter to Lord Byron', in his *Collected Longer Poems* (New York: Random House, 1969), p. 41, at seeing 'An English spinster of the middle class / Describe the amorous effects of "brass"'.

12. Irene Collins, in her *Jane Austen and the Clergy* (London: Hambledon Press, 1993), p. 130, discusses the qualities and requisites of the model clergyman's wife.

13. Hester Chapone, *Letters on the Improvement of the Mind, Addressed to a Young Lady* (1773; London, 1810), pp. 75–6; Thomas Gisborne, *An Enquiry into the Duties of the Female Sex*, 11th edn (London, 1816), chapter 12: 'On the Duties of Matrimonial Life'.

14. Gisborne, *Duties of the Female Sex*, pp. 347, 366–9.

15. West, *Letters to a Young Lady*, vol. I, pp. 141–4, 303–4.

16. Edward Copeland, 'Money' in Todd (ed.), *Jane Austen in Context*, pp. 317–26.

17. Perkin, *Modern English Society*, p. 255. The male members of Austen's own family were much involved in the 'old' professions: her father's family included medical men and lawyers and her mother's clergymen. Two of her brothers entered the church; two more brothers served in the navy throughout the French wars.

18. Marilyn Butler, *Jane Austen and the War of Ideas*, 2nd edn, with new introduction (Oxford: Clarendon Press, 1987), p. xliv.

19. Deirdre Le Faye (ed.), *Jane Austen's Letters*, 3rd edn (Oxford: Oxford University Press, 1997), 24 January 1813, p. 198.

20. C. W. Pasley, *Essay on the Military Policy and Institutions of the British Empire*, 3rd edn (London, 1811), p. 231.

21. The writing of *Mansfield Park* also coincides with the period when the British government attempted to curb abuses in the administration of the Church of England: in 1812–13 a bill was passed giving better pay to curates and there was much agitation against pluralism.

22. John Peck, *Maritime Fiction: Sailors and the Sea in British and American Novels, 1719–1917* (Basingstoke: Palgrave, 2001), 'Jane Austen's Sailors', pp. 30–49.

23. Le Faye (ed.), *Jane Austen's Letters*, 29 January 1813, p. 202.

24. The Prince Regent's librarian, James Stanier Clarke, amused Austen by recommending that she 'delineate in some future Work the Habits of Life and Character and enthusiasm of a Clergyman' (Le Faye (ed.), *Jane Austen's Letters*, 16 November 1815, p. 296); *Mansfield Park* went some way towards this although Austen avoided the evangelical tone which the emphasis on 'enthusiasm' suggests.

25. Southam, 'Professions', p. 368.

26. Southam stresses that these prosperous livings were a feature primarily of the richer south of England. He writes: 'At one end of the scale (according to a parliamentary enquiry in 1802) about 1000 church livings were worth less than £100 per annum, with another 3000 between £100–150, barely enough to live on. But it was another story for country parishes in the prosperous south. Ownership of the glebe (the church agricultural land), together with the tithes, produced an income that rose in step with the rising value of both the land and its produce, a boom that lasted until 1814. In the 1770s, Mr Austen's two Hampshire parishes were worth about £200. Thirty years later, their value had gone up more than four-fold: the tithes were producing £600 and the glebe £300. This change in the economics of farming and land ownership had much to do with the attraction that the church increasingly held for the sons of the gentry . . . beyond the fortunate clerics remained a body of clergymen, calculated in 1805 to number up to 45% of those ordained, who never found a church living and were forced into dead-end employment as penurious curates hired for as little as £50 a year, or who turned to teaching or some other occupation outside the church' (ibid., pp. 368–71).

27. Richard Lovell Edgeworth, *Essays on Professional Education* (London, 1809), p. 101.

28. William Jones, *The Diary of the Reverend William Jones 1771–1821*, ed. O. F. Christie (London, 1929), cited in Collins, *Jane Austen and the Clergy*, p. 132.

29. Although in *The Country and the City* (Frogmore: Paladin, 1975) Raymond Williams has warned us how difficult it is to oppose the Bertrams and the Crawfords socially, Avrom Fleishman has persuasively argued for cultural links between the Crawfords and the aristocracy. For a discussion of the social context of *Mansfield Park*, see Fleishman's *A Reading of 'Mansfield Park': An Essay in Critical Synthesis* (Minneapolis: University of Minnesota Press, 1967), pp. 40–1. The hostility between gentry and aristocracy is investigated by R. W. Chapman in *Jane Austen: Facts and Problems* (London: Oxford University Press, 1949), pp. 197–9.

30. The good wives of clergymen in the earlier novels are all connected to farming: Elinor is concerned with pasturage for cows and Charlotte Lucas for cows and poultry. Irene Collins wonders whether in creating Fanny, Austen was trying to break away from the farming image to present a better type of parson's wife, since it is difficult to imagine her engaged with poultry and apple picking (*Jane Austen and the Clergy*, p. 139). I would argue that there are enough hints about Fanny and rural life to suggest her suitability as wife for a farming vicar.

31. From Thomas Chalmers, *On the Power, Wisdom and Goodness of God*, quoted in Boyd Hilton, *The Age of Atonement: The Influence of Evangelicalism on Social and Economic Thought, 1795–1865* (Oxford: Clarendon Press, 1988), p. 84.

32. Gisborne, *Duties of the Female Sex*, p. 361.

33. See also Collins, *Jane Austen and the Clergy*, p. 131.

34. Richard Cronin, introduction to *Emma* (Cambridge: Cambridge University Press, 2005), pp. xxi–lxxiv.

35. Le Faye (ed.), *Jane Austen's Letters*, 10–18 August 1814, p. 268.

36. See John Wiltshire, 'Medicine', in Todd (ed.), *Jane Austen in Context*, pp. 306–16.

37. See J. R. Watson, 'Mr Perry's Patients: A View of *Emma*', *Essays in Criticism* 20 (1970), 334–43, and Fiona Stafford, introduction to *Emma* (London: Penguin Classics, 2003), p. 458n.

38. John Wiltshire, *Jane Austen and the Body: 'The Picture of Health'* (Cambridge: Cambridge University Press, 1992), p. 112.

39. Elsewhere T. R. Malthus in his *Principles of Political Economy* (1820) saw the landowner's unproductive consumption as initiating activity in the other professional classes.

40. Edgeworth, *Professional Education*, pp. 256, 268–9.

41. In his *Rural Oeconomy: Or, Essays on the Practical Parts of Husbandry* (London, 1770) Arthur Young also made the point that many professionals including 'Physicians, lawyers, clergymen, soldiers, sailors, merchants' had turned farmers (pp. 174 and 177).

42. Edgeworth, *Professional Education*, p. 274.

43. See Michèle Cohen, 'Manliness, Effeminacy and the French: Gender and the Construction of National Character in Eighteenth-Century England', in Tim Hitchcock and Michèle Cohen (eds.), *English Masculinities 1660–1800* (London: Longman, 1999), pp. 44–61.

44. West, *Letters to a Young Lady*, vol. III, pp. 347–8.

45. Watson, 'Mr Perry's Patients', p. 337.

46. Robert Miles, *Jane Austen* (Tavistock: Northcote House, 2002), p. 57.

47. Nina Auerbach, 'O Brave New World: Evolution and Revolution in *Persuasion*', *ELH* 39 (1972), 112–28.

48. Charles Rzepka, 'Making It in a Brave New World: Marriage, Profession, and Anti-Romantic *Ekstasis* in Austen's *Persuasion*', *Studies in the Novel* 26.2 (Summer 1994), 99.

49. Jane Austen appreciated the drawbacks and rewards of the navy when she remarked to her naval brother that the 'Profession has its' douceurs to recompense for some of its' Privations'. Le Faye (ed.), *Jane Austen's Letters*, 3–6 July 1813, p. 214.

50. Edgeworth, *Professional Education*, pp. 88, 110, 113, 123, 143. Edgeworth even educates naval men for their time on land: 'At seasons of the year when exercises in the open air are not convenient, the pupil may amuse himself within doors with carpenter's, smith's and turner's tools' (p. 116). Captain Harville seems to

have had this training, for in his house he carpenters and glues, making toys, needles, and nets.

51. See Monica Cohen, 'Persuading the Navy Home: Austen and Married Women's Professional Property', *Novel: A Forum on Fiction* 29.3 (1996), 346–66.
52. See, for example, Gisborne, *Duties of the Female Sex*, pp. 11–12.
53. Sandra M. Gilbert and Susan Gubar, *The Madwoman in the Attic: The Woman Writer and the Nineteenth-Century Literary Imagination* (New Haven: Yale University Press, 1984), p. 181. Women did sometimes go to sea with their husbands, though perhaps not as often as is depicted here. Mrs Croft is making a feminist case for a greater female role at sea, but it is only one among many possible roles for women.
54. Edgeworth, *Professional Education*, p. 126.
55. Rzepka, 'Making It in a Brave New World', 106.

High instincts and real presences: two Romantic responses to the death of Beauty

Jerome McGann

> Beauty is momentary in the mind –
> The fitful tracing of a portal;
> But in the flesh it is immortal.
>> (Wallace Stevens,
>> 'Peter Quince at the Clavier')

Few passages in twentieth-century poetry are better known than this. It reformulates the idea and ideal of Beauty in mortal rather than ideal terms. In this view, as Stevens also famously wrote, 'Death is the mother of beauty' because from death is born 'the heavenly fellowship / Of men that perish and of summer morn' ('Sunday Morning').

But are we confident of our confidence in these poetical formulations? Or let me ask the question another way: does Stevens's mortalist perspective on *to kalon* involve anything more than a stylistic flourish? Is Beauty immortal in the flesh? Do we agree with that, do we agree that Stevens actually means us to assent to that statement? To the *idea* being pronounced, presumably, *by* the statement? I ask these questions in order to clarify the full depth of the paradox involved here. For we would have to cognize in some fashion the truth of the statement that Beauty is immortal in the flesh. In that event our mortal, enfleshed minds would have not an immersion in some immortal Being of Beauty but only Beauty's fitful and momentary trace. For that is how our mortal minds work, according to this presentation on the matter.

THE PROBLEM OF BEAUTY

The standard approach to these issues and problems in Stevens is through a certain way of reading Wordsworth, as the normative commentaries by Harold Bloom and Helen Vendler show. In this line of interpretation, whose primary source is Coleridge, the mind's fitful view of Beauty is taken as an emblem of what it means to be a perishing person. Beauty is what

Yeats called 'the land of the heart's desire' precisely because and as it escapes our ceaseless efforts to possess it. Beauty is immortal, then, not from its transcendental reality *as such* but from our mortal experience of its perpetual flight.

We know that way of thinking about Beauty is as foundational as Pythagoras, Plato, and Plotinus. We also know what new depths and difficulties Beauty gained with the coming of Enlightenment. Scholars have traced 'the decay of beauty as an ideal and as a technical enterprise in the last two centuries' to the historical moment when Beauty passed between the Scylla of empirical and sensationalist philosophy and the Charybdis of the aesthetics of sensibility.[1] Those reciprocating powers placed the ancient ideal of Beauty in – quite literally – mortal peril.

The problem is fully articulated in Kant and the subsequent tradition of idealistic philosophy, which struggles to preserve a transcendental ground for human judgements in the face of the radical process of secularization set in motion by Locke. In this tradition, Beauty and Sublimity are both conceived as *a priori* categories. Our human affective responses to 'the Sublime and the Beautiful' signal their reality through the persistence of the erotic dialectic of distance and desire. Most important here is the emergence of Sublimity as the determining category of both morality and aesthetics, displacing *to kalon*. That shift licensed art and poetry to experiment with novel, and distinctly disharmonic, forms of order – a signal feature of all Romantic practices. Mountain glory is a function of mountain gloom, as Wordsworth makes abundantly clear in those key books of *The Prelude*, VI and XIV.

The problem of Beauty during the past two centuries followed upon that initial Kantian displacement. So far as art and poetry are concerned, the move would relegate comedy and satire to a secondary order of practice until the cultural emergence of sensibilities we now associate with postmodernity. A famous passage in Kant's *Critique of Judgement* forecasts this cultural trajectory. Distinguishing between the Beautiful and the Sublime, Kant says that the former 'represents freedom rather as in *play* than as exercising a law-ordained *function*'. Sublimity, by contrast, is for Kant a figure for that function, 'which is the genuine characteristic of human morality, where reason has to impose its dominion upon sensibility'.[2] When freedom appears better imagined as play rather than as ordained law, the dark spell cast upon Beauty will begin to be lifted.

Of course Beauty does not disappear from the practice of art in 'the last two centuries'. Indeed, we can see from our current perspective that the exile of Venus would eventually supply her with the privilege of historical backwardness. That fact becomes clear, I think, through an examination of certain crucial moments in our Anglophone culture when the crisis of the ideal of Beauty was most saliently engaged. My aim here is to indicate how certain roads were taken and others refused, and what differences followed from those choices. Ultimately I shall also be arguing that we might usefully retrace this history – rethink it – in order to see why the malaise of Beauty was but a nightmare 'owing to [our angelic] metaphysics', as Blake's devil told his benighted angel.

Recall when the two plunged into 'eternity' together in Plates 17–20 of *The Marriage of Heaven and Hell* (1790). An 'immense' Gothic city unfolds itself though angel eyes, an 'infinite Abyss' of 'fiery tracks', 'terrific shapes', and 'monstrous' forms 'advanc[ing] . . . with all the fury of a spiritual existence'. When the angel flees from his own scary vision, the devil 'remain'd alone, & then this appearance was no more, but I found myself sitting on a pleasant bank beside a river by moon light hearing a harper who sung to the harp'. This famous poetical event has rarely (if ever) been seen for what, in at least one important sense, it clearly is: a conflict between an imagination of reality as Sublime and an imagination of it as Beautiful. Blake is of course knowingly 'of the devil's party' in this conflict – that is to say, on the side of Beauty rather than Sublimity.

Because so much of Blake's work is bent upon exposing the evil of a world consumed by what he called 'the torments of love and jealousy', we forget – commentators forget – that he is a poet committed to Beauty, and that his Sublime is a nightmare function. He puts his position with great simplicity in the incomparable 'Auguries of Innocence' sequence:

> God appears and God is light
> To those poor souls who dwell in Night,
> But does a human form display,
> To those who dwell in realms of day.
> (lines 129–32)

Insofar as we see a 'decay of beauty . . . in the past two centuries', it appears to have progressed under the auspices of a God of light and in neglect of the human form so beloved of Blake. At least that is the story I shall try to sketch now.

WORDSWORTHIAN BEAUTY

We begin with Wordsworth and the 'Preface' to *Lyrical Ballads*, which has dominated English-language aesthetic discourse since it appeared in

1800. This is a remarkable fact given the essay's notorious lack of intellectual rigour. Early traditionalists like Jeffrey had an easy time ridiculing Wordsworth's theory and practice of 'poetic diction', as it has come to be called. Coleridge, Shelley, and Byron – unhappily in the first instance, gleefully in the latter two – followed and elaborated Jeffrey's line of attack. Coleridge's is an especially interesting case. *Biographia Literaria* is – explicitly if also reluctantly – a long set of glosses on Wordsworth's brief polemic.

The *Biographia* is the first in a line of idealist responses to Wordsworth's novel explanation of poetry. René Wellek's contempt for the 'Preface' (in his *History of Modern Criticism* (1955–92)) is barely disguised. For him, pronouncements on aesthetic matters must at any rate *aspire* to a philosophical – if not a Kantian – coherence, the way *Biographia Literaria* aspires (a work Wellek can respect, despite its fractures and incompletions, as he cannot respect Wordsworth's 'Preface'). The quest for a coherent *philosophy* of Beauty dogs the subject to this day, as James Kirwan's very interesting book has shown yet again.[3] Wordsworth, however, like Byron (!), is clearly indifferent to these kinds of systematic attitudes or aspirations. When in his 'Ode: Intimations of Immortality' he speaks of 'the philosophic mind' he is thinking in aesthetic not in systematic terms. The whole of the 'Preface' is framed as a contractual problem between poet and audience. It is an explanation of a new type of sympathetic cultural exchange. For all its personal rhetoric, *Biographia* is, by sharp contrast, a brief for ideas about the essential principles of poetry.

Let's examine Wordsworth's two key, and closely related, ideas – an idea about language and an idea about feeling. He proposes the language of 'low and rustic life' as a measure for poetical discourse because he wants to make sincerity of feeling the central aesthetic issue. The focus of traditional rhetoric is on rules of decorum, not the language of the heart. This vantage gives it no ready means to study or anatomize its forms of expression. Consequently, these will be – as Gertrude Stein might say – always stanzas in performance, never stanzas in meditation. The show must go on.

Crucial to realize is the way Wordsworth's 'Preface' is installing a version of Schiller's myth of naive and sentimental poetry. Wordsworth proposes to make an aesthetic measure of 'low and rustic' language as a means to rethink the grounds of art from an experiential rather than a synthetic or rational position. Whether such a language or such a culture actually *exists* is only heuristically important. Wordsworth means to imagine its existence – ultimately, to persuade us to suspend willingly our disbelief in its existence – in order to gain a fresh way of thinking about art, poetry, and culture. 'The Idiot Boy' – which seems to me both the most ambitious as well as the greatest poem in the 1798 *Lyrical Ballads* – could not be more explicit in its demonstrative argument. In its world, things, animals, and people are all 'bound each to each' in the natural piety of their immediate sympathetic relations, and their alliances comprise an exponent for Wordsworth's new poetical contract. Sensations, feelings, emotions: these organize the world and the character of Wordsworth's poetry, which sets its face against the more customary signs of artistic action: wit, intelligence, Beauty. The poetry is replete with all three of those traditional signs of art, but they arise to our awareness – if they arise at all – only in forms of ruin, of which the idiot boy's ruined – that is to say, innocent – mind is the signifying monkey.

Lyrical Ballads and its 'Preface' thus originate a new rhetoric for poetry, one that is founded in – indeed, that culminates – the eighteenth-century traditions of sentiment and sensibility. So complete is Wordsworth's adherence to this recent moral and philosophical tradition that we will look in vain in the 'Preface' for any sign that Beauty is a function of poetical or artistic practice. When Wordsworth speaks of poetry he gravitates to words like 'sensation', 'feeling', 'pleasure', 'emotion', and their cognates, *never* to any form of the word 'beauty'. The latter enters the 'Preface' only three times, in fact, and on each occasion it references a transcendental category of the natural world ('the beautiful and permanent forms of nature', for example, or 'the beauty of the universe').

Those forms, however, have grown difficult of access. They are especially elusive to the eye of the picturesque tourist, who is Wordsworth's emblem of aesthetic decadence. One begins a passage to those 'beautiful forms' – actually, to their precincts, not to the forms themselves – only through a felt confrontation with their desolated apparitions. Wordsworth himself says that the procedure is 'indirect' ('Preface') – that is to say, it is symbolic. 'The Ruined Cottage' and 'Michael' were both written to make just that point. They are 'the simple Wordsworth's'[4] simplest statements of one of the momentous arguments of Romanticism: that when Beauty comes to us now, it comes disguised, veiled, or disfigured.

In Burke's more spectacular and political terms, the passage (back) to the Beautiful will have to be via its terrorized remains, the world of the Sublime. As James Chandler has shown, Wordsworth follows Burke's lead in a lower – a sublimated – register. Think of *The Prelude*, that great discourse on the subject of the recovery of Beauty. Wordworth's poem tells us how to regain his – our – Derwent origins, the world of primal Beauty, through a series of 'self destroyings', 'visionary dreariness', and a regular discipline of fear. We come into the world 'trailing clouds of Glory' and pass from thence to darker circumstances. All this is the fallen world of Mountain Gloom and

Mountain Glory, where we work out our salvation in fear and trembling. The world of Derwentwater, the world of Beauty, lies somewhere else – beyond, in some magical place where we are cradled in our nurse's or our mother's arms, as we are at the outset of *The Prelude*, or play children's games at the edge of the sea, as we do at the end of the 'Intimations' Ode.

This influential Romantic myth has many regenerated forms. All rest in the primary assumption – literally, the working assumption – that 'Energy is the only life and is from the Body, and Reason is the bound or outward circumference of Energy'.[5] Human life begins not in a primal generative idea but in a primal sympathetic exchange – in a contract, as the 'Preface' assumes. This is why feeling and emotion ground every Romantic art: because the Romantic model for these processes of exchange is human and sentimental. They are incarnational and experiential processes, not inherited and transcendental.

Coleridge shared the general Wordsworthian view that poetry, properly executed, would lead one to 'see into the life of things'. 'Imagination' was Coleridge's name for that revelatory function, and he declared that in point of imagination Wordsworth 'stands nearest of all modern writers to Shakespeare and Milton'.[6] He also agreed that 'pleasure' was the immediate object of poetry and that the attainment of this object came through 'a union of deep and subtle thought with sensibility; a sympathy with man as man'.

But Coleridge also argued that Wordsworth's poetry had certain 'characteristic defects' which reflected an ill-considered theoretical position. The sign of this deficiency was what Coleridge called Wordsworth's '*matter-of-factness*'. The *Biographia* is a polemical effort to establish a correct view of poetry at a moment when its very (Wordsworthian) successes threatened to corrupt a clear understanding of its essential character. Wordsworth's idealization of the language of 'low and rustic life' is, for Coleridge, what would later be called 'the fallacy of imitative form'.[7] It leads Wordsworth into 'a laborious minuteness and fidelity to the representation of objects' and 'the insertion of accidental circumstances'. The only justification for such irrelevant details, Coleridge thinks, is to provide factive grounds for Wordsworth's poetical representations.[8] For in Coleridge's view poetry is what Aristotle laid down: a discourse of imitative probabilities. Wordsworth's poems thus 'contrav[ene] the essence of poetry', which 'is essentially ideal [and which] avoids and excludes all accident' and circumstantiality.

Coleridge's attack on Wordsworth's facticities follows from his primary concern, which is to fence poetry from any theory or practice that would secularize its condition. Thus Wordsworth's idea of a 'primal sympathy'

seems to Coleridge far too mortalized: Hartleian rather than Aristotelian;
even, at times, pantheistic:

> And 'tis my faith that every flower
> Enjoys the air it breathes.
> (Wordsworth, 'Lines
> written in Early Spring')

This way of thinking and writing tends to establish poetry on the secular ground of material embodiment. Wordsworthian sympathy emerges
through what he famously called 'a wise passiveness' before the 'living forms'
of other beings, both natural and human. But Coleridgean sympathy functions at a different – at what he regarded as a higher and more spiritual –
level. It is the sympathy emblemized by the theoretical relation between
the Primary and the Secondary Imagination, and thus between the eternal
act of God's creation and its repetition in the finite mind. The Coleridgean
imagination 'struggles to idealize and to unify' its often 'opposite and dis-
cordant' materials[9] and create works that reflect the operation of its ideal
origin, the way the natural world reflects the agency of its divine Creator.
In Wordsworth, however, creation is an exchange function.

One final, crucial point must be observed. In praising the sympathetic
structure of Wordsworth's poetry Coleridge says that this is 'the sympathy . . . of a contemplator, rather than a fellow-sufferer or co-mate (*spectator, haud particeps*)'. Because Wordsworth's pathos develops at a 'meditative'
remove from his subjects, the poetry exhibits 'the gift of imagination in the
highest and strictest sense of the word'[10] – that is to say, of the imagination
as Coleridge imagines it in the *Biographia*. Wordsworth stands to his poetry
the way God stands to the world he is supposed to have created. Whether
or not we agree with that deific view of Wordsworth's poetic practice, cultural history from Arnold and Bradley to Abrams, Bloom, and Hartman
has followed that line.

BYRONIC BEAUTY

However that may be, Romanticism developed another major type of sympathetic structure. D. G. Rossetti gave it a name in 1848: he called it the
'poetry of the inner standing-point'.[11] Its greatest exemplar was also its most
famous, Lord Byron.

Byron's difference springs from the sympathy he kept with inherited
forms – cultural as well as political – whose limitations and even decadences
he was well aware of. In *Manfred* he calls this transcendental order 'the dead

but sceptred sovereigns who still rule / Our spirits from their urns' (3.4.42–3). His transactions with that order, unlike Wordsworth's, took an agonistic form, as we see in the undertaking of *Childe Harold's Pilgrimage*. At the thematic level the poem reveals the ruination of the order of Beauty. The first two cantos come to argue that this ruin is a condition half perceived and half created. The poem's first instalment tracks those ruins from England through the decadence of the French Revolution on the Peninsula to Greece, the *fons et origo* of the Western myth of the 'matchless' 'Beauty' that Byron explicitly invokes at the beginning of the initial cantos ('To Ianthe'). Cantos 3–4 then resume the tale in a post-Napoleonic context in order to engage with various forms of Sublimity, which for a Romantic is what remains when access to the order of Beauty has become troubled.

Byron's handling of the Spenserian stanza is perhaps the most striking index of how his verse cooperates in replacing the order of Beauty with an order of Sublimity. From Ariosto through Spenser and on to Thomson and Beattie, this stanza became a kind of emblem of a metrical form that could hold in balanced equipoise a great variety of poetical materials. Byron chooses the stanza and then forces it to perform unnatural imaginative acts. It is an astonishing virtuoso display. In Byron's hands the Spenserian stanza becomes not a thing of Beauty or a refuge of order but either a shirt of Nessus he must wear, or a weapon he can wield. Indeed, neither this nor that, but both at once.

Wordsworth's project is slightly but significantly different. He writes his famous 'Preface' to install a new form of the Sublime – a psychomachia – in place of the model developed through the extravagant terrors and horrors of the Gothic. In the event Beauty fades from view, absented by the onset of 'the picture of the mind' and its intense Glory. This is Wordsworth's way of turning the problem of Beauty – its disappearance and loss – into a *felix culpa*. In that redemptive transformation Beauty ceases to be a problem needing address. What occupies the poet is the need to investigate, map, and ultimately get possessed by the sensational dynamic he has discovered ('I recognize thy glory'). This is the fruit of the dialectic of pleasure, which may be intense and even alienating or, reciprocally, sympathetic and healing.

We do not, in Wordsworth's Romantic scheme, actually make contact with *to kalon*. Instead, we generate or contact a *feeling for* it. The feeling then stands as the emblem and sign of its alienated presence. For this Beauty, in such a Romantic imagination, is always 'moving about in worlds not realized'. This Beauty is a transcendental category, something known only to the impeccable taste of God. Feeling, on the other hand, is quotidian, and Wordsworth will work to convince us that if we cultivate feeling and sympathy, rather than taste, we will position ourselves in as close a relation to the 'beauteous forms of nature' as we might need or imagine in this world.

Now let's look again at Byron. Whereas Wordsworth does not struggle against the ideal of an alienated Beauty, Byron does.

> Of its own beauty is the mind diseased,
> And fevers into false creation: – where,
> Where are the forms the sculptor's soul hath seized?
> In him alone. Can Nature show so fair?
> Where are the charms and virtues which we dare
> Conceive in boyhood and pursue as men,
> The unreached Paradise of our despair,
> Which o'er-informs the pencil and the pen,
> And overpowers the page where it would bloom again?
>
> Who loves, raves – 'tis youth's frenzy – but the cure
> Is bitterer still, as charm by charm unwinds
> Which robed our idols, and we see too sure
> Nor Worth nor Beauty dwells from out the mind's
> Ideal shape of such; yet still it binds
> The fatal spell, and still it draws us on,
> Reaping the whirlwind from the oft-sown winds;
> The stubborn heart, its alchemy begun,
> Seems ever near the prize – wealthiest when most undone.
>   (*Childe Harold*, canto 4, stanzas 122–3)

For Byron, the feeling for *to kalon* reaches perfection in a perfection of suffering and unpleasure. Like Laokoon toiling with his serpents, Byron wrestles and tears at the Spenserian form he has both inherited and chosen. As a result, Byron stages his use of the stanza as an emblem of what he elsewhere called, echoing Milton, the last infirmity of noble minds. *To kalon* is a 'nympholepsy of some fond despair', 'a faith whose martyrs are the broken heart' (*Childe Harold*, canto 4, stanzas 115, 121). It defines this state of crucifixion because Beauty has emerged as a disease of human desire and imagination. But note that Beauty is not absconded, as it is in Wordsworth. On the contrary, Beauty in Byron is always being revealed, but revealed divested of its illusions.

Think of how differently Byron and Wordsworth conduct us on their touristic journeys. In 'The Ruined Cottage' Wordsworth puts us in the hands of a guide who will instruct us in a forgotten piece of local history. 'I see around me here / Things which you cannot see.' In a first vision these things appear ruined, terrors and desperations to the feeling mind. But in a further view they emerge through those nightmares as signs of something else we can scarcely see or believe: natural harmony and 'tranquil restoration'.

That is one moral of the story. The other is that only a privileged Romantic eye has the visionary skill required to perceive this invisible salvation history. This eye has cultivated habits of sympathetic attention. Seeing through it we come to feel 'the deep power of harmony' – Beauty's absent presence – in unimagined localities.

By sharp contrast, *Childe Harold's Pilgrimage* escorts us through a series of celebrated European places: nature reserves on one hand, museums on the other. Nor is Byron a *spectator ab extra* tracking after or along 'untrodden ways'. So the poem assumes the fame of these famous places as emblems and touchstones of *to kalon* – that 'ideal beauty' which possesses 'all unquiet things' and moves them to 'fever into false creation'. Beauty is not an absent presence in Byron, it is fully apparent, known to all. As he moves through its famed localities, the forms of Beauty make an exhibition of their defeatures and illusions. This is the Byronic Sublime: the agony of Beauty in presence and in the present. The *agon* of Byron's Spenserian pilgrimage replicates that story from an inner standing-point.

BEAUTY AS REAL PRESENCE

Byron's *Don Juan* style 'turns what was once romantic' – the tormented narratives and pilgrimages – 'to burlesque' – the comic manner initiated in the gossipy tale of *Beppo*.[12] The change exposes certain undiscovered resources awaiting a Romanticism that works from an inner standing-point. In the comic procedures of the late poetry – their sources are, significantly, Sternean and Quixotic, not Spenserian and Miltonic – Byron becomes one of his own primary objects of amusement. 'The moral of all human tales'[13] is that every tale – *this* tale of *Don Juan* – is one of those tales, and they are all tales of defeat. They are also the teller's tale and, if the reader will agree not to stand aside, reading and paring his fingernails like a god or *spectator ab extra*, they are the audience's as well.

> I have spent my life, both interest and principal,
> And deem not, what I deemed, my soul invincible.
> (*Don Juan*, canto 1, stanza 213)

That view of the matter will set the figure of Beauty on an important new footing. Byron's soul is vincible and, as a result, so will be the soul of his soul, his epipsyche, his art and its emblematic forms: those fragile creatures Julia, Haidée, Aurora Raby. These are the *figurae* of Beauty who preside over Byron's world, 'the literary lower empire' which his poem exposes, satirizes, and participates in.[14] The revelation of these splendid minor deities requires submission to the empire of the *Musa Pedestris*. Sublimity is abandoned in order to possess Truth and Beauty in a human register.

Here is one of Byron's restored incarnations of Beauty, a vision of spring in the winter of his Romanticism. He is setting the scene for the climactic feast on Lambro's island with a description of Haidée.

> Of all the dresses I select Haidée's:
>   She wore two jelicks – one was of pale yellow;
> Of azure, pink, and white was her chemise –
>   Neath which her breast heaved like a little billow;
> With buttons form'd of pearls as large as peas,
>   All gold and crimson shone her jelick's fellow,
> And the striped white gauze baracan that bound her,
> Like fleecy clouds about the moon, flow'd round her.
>
> One large gold bracelet clasp'd each lovely arm,
>   Lockless – so pliable from the pure gold
> That the hand stretch'd and shut it without harm,
>   The limb which it adorn'd its only mould;
> So beautiful – its very shape would charm,
>   And clinging as if loth to lose its hold,
> The purest ore inclosed the whitest skin
> That e'er by precious metal was held in.
>
> Around, as princess of her father's land,
>   A like gold bar above her instep rolled
> Announced her rank; twelve rings were on her hand;
>   Her hair was starr'd with gems; her veil's fine fold
> Below her breast was fasten'd with a band
>   Of lavish pearls, whose worth could scarce be told;
> Her orange silk full Turkish trowsers furl'd
> About the prettiest ankle in the world.
>
>   (*Don Juan*, canto 3, stanzas 70–2)

Such Beauty, neither an absent presence nor a disease of the mind, has cast out the spirits of symbolism. We are not asked to 'see into the life of things', as if these exquisite surfaces were insufficient, nor are we led along by the fever of an 'unquenched soul'. But neither is the attitude anything like Wordsworth's famous 'wise passiveness'. The latter is a discipline of self-absorption, a method for regaining contact with blocked springs of feeling. Here, however, nothing seems blocked or concealed: the invitation is to discreet, meticulous attention. And so the actual action of the verse, fleet and delicate as Haidee, incarnates its ostensible, its ostensive, subject.

Of course in each case – Wordsworth's, Byron's – the style of address never ceases to be Romantic – that is to say, personal. *Don Juan*, like *Childe Harold*, fixes our attention on Byron and his acts of linguistic expression. But what we watch in *Don Juan* is Byron giving up his faith in unseen seraphs and pledging his allegiance to their mortal models. These are still what *Childe Harold* names 'false creations', that is to say, beings fashioned from the mind's idealized and idealizing desires. The difference in *Don Juan* is that their irreality has become the measure of their Beauty rather than the sign of their absence or Sublimity. The wonder of these wonderful stanzas rests in their exquisite simplicity and concern for small detail and pure appearance. 'The mind's ideal shape[s]'[15] emerge in the pace of the verse and its clear concern that every smallest feature of the language be rendered at something like full value. Every rhyme must be weighed out, every last lingual seen and sounded:

> With v*iands and* sherbets in ice – *and* wine.

Syllables assume an absolute condition, even if it means that metrical rules might have to be bent or broken. The syllabic correctness of the line 'The tables, most of ebony inlaid' prepares the lovely outbreak of the next line, where the three syllables of 'I-vo-ry' insist upon full presence.[16]

Or is it Byron who insists, as if answering the call for attention from these small worldly divinities? Reading the verse Romantically we should say it is indeed Byron who is charming us. But then we will also notice how the charm seems to slip into the language as such, as if Byron were wearing his words the way Haidee wears her clothing and jewellery.

This is verse with designs upon the reader and the reader's responses. The 'feeling' in this poetry is no longer in the poem or the poet; it has been licensed to the reader. Is it Haidee's doing that she makes such a striking appearance? Well, presumably she *has* chosen her accoutrements. But that choice having been made – as we may willingly suspend our disbelief to believe – Haidee becomes an apparition, absolute, like an incarnate god. Which is why Byron, observing such a creature stepping – *mirabile dictu* – through his own text, remarks that 'it would not be idolatry to kneel' before her.[17]

Underlying this passage is the familiar dynamics of sensibility. But in this passage the dynamic has been arrested so that all its features may be examined. Byron's feelings do not measure this poetic action, as Wordsworth's feelings always do. That is why the poet speaks of 'idolatry' in relation to Haidée. As a result, sympathetic exchange here turns to admiration and wonder, and the subjectivity of the Romantic ego is reciprocally objectified.

Haidée as mortal goddess thus comes to index the medium of which she has been made. The 'conversational facility' of Byron's poem establishes and maintains its fundamentally Romantic style, which – like all Romantic styles – rides on what Wordsworth famously called 'the feeling of my loss'.[18] In passages like this, however, we observe Byron using that style to (as it were) execute itself. When 'feeling comes in aid of feeling' in Wordsworth,[19] an exchange of human sympathy revivifies a faith in an absent god. *Don Juan's* verse, by contrast, has discovered an exchange of wonderment as the obverse of *Childe Harold's* exchanges of despair. A famous passage in *Beppo* describes Byron's discovery that 'Truth and Beauty at their best' are actual human beings, what he calls 'Love in Life!':

> Love in full life and length, not love ideal,
>   No, nor ideal beauty, that fine name,
> But something better still, so very real,
>   That the sweet Model must have been the same;
> A thing that you would purchase, beg, or steal,
>   Wer't not impossible, besides a shame:
> The face recalls some face, as 'twere with pain,
> You once have seen, but ne'er will see again;
>
> One of those forms which flit by us, when we
>   Are young, and fix our eyes on every face;
> And, oh! the Loveliness at times we see
>   In momentary gliding, the soft grace,
> The Youth, the Bloom, the Beauty which agree,
>   In many a nameless being we retrace,
> Whose course and home we knew not, nor shall know,
> Like the lost Pleiad seen no more below.
>
> (*Beppo*, stanzas 13–14)

That this Beauty takes the form of a 'Love in full life and length' is a tellingly mortalized view. Temporality rules, and it is transpsychic. The forms seizing Byron are not, as he thought in *Childe Harold*, 'in him alone'. They are 'very real,' and if he calls them 'nameless being[s]' it is partly because he actually saw them in Florence – 'leaning' from balconies, imaged in paintings by Giorgione – and partly to make the witty point that they are more substantial and wondrous than 'ideal beauty, that' merely 'fine name' for insubstantial things.

Byron's erotic reaction to these charming creatures becomes an emblem for his poetic method. Figured as a flirtation with the reader, this poetry develops a natural (non-divine) creation by sympathy of sexual liaison and attraction – a condition Byron repeatedly develops in the insistent and frank eroticism of his work. In the order of art this kind of creation is a reciprocating material semiosis where author and reader are engaged with each other at the inner standing-point of the poetry they have together undertaken.

While Romantic melancholy recurs through *Don Juan*, then, the poem celebrates creation's escape from its creator. The famous and much lamented nineteenth-century disappearance of god – the god of nature, the god of art – becomes here the locus of a neo-pagan order of Beauty, whose Real Presence leaves one at a loss very different from the loss felt in the absence of Beauty. The translation of Haidée into Beauty's figural form measures the textual effacement of the Romantic Lord Byron, who becomes, like Swinburne's Sappho, 'now no more a singer but a song'.[20] This effect – the translation of the Romantic ego into what Charles Bernstein wittily calls a 'textual experience'[21] – is the aesthetic gift of choosing to write at an inner standing-point.

The event, once again, contrasts sharply with equivalent Wordsworthian experiences, those spots of time that in a 'flash [reveal] the invisible world'. The very intensity of such moments effaces what the poet desires to perceive. Byron's Haidéean beauties linger awhile, if not for ever, as if meeting an obligation laid upon them by their remarkable mortality. For Beauty here insists that its particular material virtues be attentively marked. Responding to such Beauty, Byron's verse turns from pyrotechnics to precisions. The verse is more important than the versifier, the creature than the creator.

BEAUTIFUL MINDS

Blake warned his monotheist world against 'choosing forms of worship from poetic tales'.[22] He was thinking about the way social institutions – thrones, principalities, powers, and dominions, as they are called in the New Testament – turn art into ideology. Byron's idolatry, however, is the reverse of that. In plain terms – and his poetry, like Thomas Paine's prose, cultivates plain speaking –

I wish men to be free,
As much from mobs as kings – from you as me.
                                        (*Don Juan*, canto 9, stanza 25)

That view of freedom is 'a vision never before communicated to man', as Shelley called another of Byron's great discourses on freedom, *Cain*.[23] The passage describing Haidee exhibits the Beauty of that vision's Truth – as does her story, as do all the stories Byron tells in *Don Juan*.

These remain to this day countercultural stories. 'To what serves mortal beauty', Hopkins famously asked, and his answer – that it serves to celebrate the grandeur of God – sees poetry as a form of worship rather than a poetic tale. Read that way, it is used – as Wordsworth is used, as Wordsworth *wanted* to be used – to reify an idealist regimen and, more problematic still, an abstract and moralizing approach to art and poetry.

Byron's answer to Hopkins's question would have been what Laura Riding's answer *was*: 'Nothing'.[24] Mortal Beauty is not in service. It is – for good and ill alike – absolutely free. It is an egg laid by a free-ranging chicken.

This intellectual stance, like Byron's tomb, is located far from the centre of official culture. Indeed, its cultural displacement has been arranged through a kind of pre-emptive strike against some of its key practitioners: Byron, Poe, and Swinburne in the nineteenth century, for instance; Stein, Laura Riding, and John Cowper Powys in the twentieth. The intellectual claims of Byron's work are regularly discounted, even by his admirers. He is represented as a great force of nature – Key West rather than the idea of Order thereat. So, 'When he thinks he is a child':[25] this is what cultural mandarins like Goethe and Arnold, impressive creatures in their own way of course, tell us about Byron.

They have worse things to say about Poe. Artists from Baudelaire to Balthus and Borges understood the importance of Poe's art and ideas, just as they recognized Poe's immediate Byronic source. Only when we take our view from the Anglophone academic centre does that history fade out of the light of common day. Its disappearance might be more lamented than the disappearance of god, so lamentable to the high priests of the imperium. The fate of Beauty I've been tracing here – *its* crisis and apparent 'decay' – is precisely an *historical* phenomenon, and – more precisely still – the legacy of a culture committed to choosing forms of worship over poetic tales. Worse still, turning poetic tales into forms of worship.

'The death of a beautiful woman', Poe notoriously observed, is 'the most poetical subject in the world'. This thought is strictly a poetic tale. A line of feminist thinking, turned ideological and debased, has followed our early modern moralists in reading that sentence through a set of realist conventions. The move drags the sentence away from its wicked, brilliant, and (in several senses) *original* context. There it forms a crucial moment in Poe's deliberately anti-Wordsworthian manifesto 'The Philosophy of Composition' (1846), where a new type of 'philosophic mind' is advanced for the artist. It is actually a mind that reaches very far back. The mind once insisted on the Beauty of the crucifixion of Jesus and of the suffering of St Sebastian, and it demonstrated, despite all evidence, that nature is a heracleitean fire and the comfort of the resurrection. Those remarkable poetic tales have remarkable nineteenth-century counterparts. Poe was right. The death of a beautiful woman *is* (*was*) the most poetical subject in that world. For better and for worse is this true.

How Poe's haunting mind fashioned such a poetic tale remains to this day an expurgated story. The tale haunts the margin that separates high culture from popular culture because that is where Beauty's tomb was built, at the public place celebrating her living defeat and death. The place is preoccupied with monuments – small ones like Rossetti's famous sonnet:

> A sonnet is a moment's monument,
> Memorial from the soul's eternity
> To one dead deathless hour
> > (Dante Gabriel Rossetti,
> > 'The Sonnet')

and great ones like Delacroix's amazing picture of *Freedom Expiring on the Ruins of Missolonghi*. Poe's mind proposed to raise up (and succeeded in raising up) a body of Beauty from the 'wormy circumstance' – that comic and crepuscular phrase is Keats's[26] – where Beauty found herself in the nineteenth century. Under the auspices of that mind, Beauty emerges like Venus from the brackish sea of nineteenth-century gift books and periodicals.

I close, then, by giving a few of the characteristic features of this beautiful mind – a 'beautiful mind', let me add, about as far removed as one could imagine from a recent preposterous movie named of the same name.

The mind is fundamentally comic and self-aware. It works by a willing suspension of beliefs, not a willing suspension of disbeliefs. It is reverent of irreverence. It is responsible for the invention of the celebrated 'religion of beauty' that flourished in the late nineteenth century. Also for the similar religion of beauty that flourishes today, the religion attended to in Johanna Drucker's superb study *Sweet Dreams*.[27] When it thinks it *is* a child – but not in the sense that Goethe meant; rather, in Blake's sense. Like the god it displaces, this mind imagines itself master of a universe which, however, it knows to be fantastic. All its relationships are, as Wordsworth and Coleridge thought, basically sexual and, as Byron saw, as promiscuous as its lovers.

Finally, it cannot live without Beauty. It proves this by signing a contract to live, with others, in impossible worlds, the only truly possible ones, and to procreate there. As Keats knew, 'A thing of beauty is a joy for ever'. So its children cannot die.

NOTES

1. Frederick Turner, *Beauty: The Value of Values* (Charlottesville and London: University Press of Virginia, 1991), p. 17.
2. Immanuel Kant, *The Critique of Judgement*, trans. James Creed Meredith (Oxford: Clarendon Press, 1952), 1.120.
3. James Kirwan, *Beauty* (Manchester and New York: Manchester University Press, 1999).
4. John Danby, *The Simple Wordsworth: Studies in the Poems 1798–1807* (London: Routledge and Kegan Paul, 1960).
5. Blake, *Marriage of Heaven and Hell*, Plate 4.
6. Samuel Taylor Coleridge, *Biographia Literaria*, ed. Walter Jackson Bate and James Engell, 2 vols. (Princeton: Princeton University Press, 1983), ch. 22.
7. Yvor Winters, 'Poetic Convention', in his *Primitivism and Decadence* (New York: Arrow, 1937).
8. Coleridge, *Biographia Literaria*, ch. 22.
9. Coleridge, *Biographia Literaria*, ch. 13.
10. Coleridge, *Biographia Literaria*, ch. 13.
11. See J. J. McGann, *Dante Gabriel Rossetti and the Game that Must be Lost* (New Haven and London: Yale University Press, 2000), p. 159 n.11: 'He used this phrase twice, once in a prose note to the poem "Ave" and again in his rejoinder to Buchanan, the essay "The Stealthy School of Criticism"'.
12. Byron, *Don Juan*, canto 4, stanza 3.
13. Byron, *Childe Harold's Pilgrimage*, canto 4, stanza 108.
14. Byron, *Don Juan*, canto 11, stanza 62.
15. Byron, *Childe Harold*, canto 4, stanza 123.
16. Byron, *Don Juan*, canto 3, stanza 69.
17. Byron, *Don Juan*, canto 3, stanza 74.
18. Byron, *Don Juan*, canto 15, stanza 20; Wordsworth, 'Elegiac Stanzas', line 39.
19. Wordsworth, *The Prelude* (1805), book 11, lines 325–6.
20. Swinburne, *Thalassius*, line 474.
21. Charles Bernstein, 'Community and the Individual Talent', *Diacritics* 26 (1996).
22. Blake, *Marriage of Heaven and Hell*, Plate 11.

23. Shelley's letter to John Gisborne, 26 January 1822.

24. Laura Riding, *Anarchism is Not Enough* (London: Jonathan Cape, 1928).

25. J. P. Eckermann, *Conversations with Goethe*, trans. S. M. Fuller (Boston: Hilliard Gray, 1839), 18 January 1825.

26. Keats, 'Isabella, Or The Pot of Basil', stanza 49.

27. Johanna Drucker, *Sweet Dreams: Contemporary Art and Complicity* (Chicago: Chicago University Press, 2005).

Marilyn Butler: a bibliography

Heather Glen

BOOKS

Maria Edgeworth: A Literary Biography, Oxford: Clarendon Press, 1972.

Jane Austen and the War of Ideas, Oxford: Clarendon Press, 1975; repr., with new introduction, 1987.

Peacock Displayed: A Satirist in His Context, London: Routledge, 1979.

Romantics, Rebels, and Reactionaries: English Literature and Its Background, 1760– 1830, Oxford: Oxford University Press, 1981; repr. 1989, 1996.

Ed., *Burke, Paine, Godwin and the Revolution Controversy*, Cambridge: Cambridge University Press, 1984.

Ed. with Janet Todd, *The Works of Mary Wollstonecraft*, 7 vols., London: Pickering and Chatto, 1989.

Ed., Maria Edgeworth, *'Castle Rackrent' and 'Ennui'*, Harmondsworth: Penguin, 1992.

Ed., Mary Shelley, *Frankenstein or, the modern Prometheus: The 1818 Text*, London: Pickering and Chatto Women's Classics, 1993. Reissued by Oxford University Press, World's Classics, 1994.

Ed., Jane Austen, *Northanger Abbey*, Harmondsworth: Penguin, 1995.

Gen. Ed., *The Works of Maria Edgeworth*, 12 vols., London: Pickering and Chatto, 1999–2003.

ARTICLES, CONTRIBUTIONS TO BOOKS, PUBLISHED LECTURES

With C. E. Colvin, entry on Maria Edgeworth, *Cambridge Bibliography of English Literature*, vol. III, 1969, pp. 665–70.

'The Uniqueness of Cynthia Kirkpatrick: Elizabeth Gaskell's *Wives and Daughters* and Maria Edgeworth's *Helen*', *Review of English Studies* 23, 1972, 278–90.

'The Woman at the Window: Radcliffe, Wollstonecraft, Austen', *Women & Literature*, n. s. 1, 1980, 128–48.

'Disregarded Designs: Austen's Sense of the Volume', in David Monaghan (ed.), *Jane Austen in a Social Context*, London: Macmillan, 1981, pp. 49–65.

'Myth and Mythmaking in the Shelley Circle', *English Literary History* 49, 1982, 50–72; repr. in Kelvin Everest (ed.), *Shelley Revalued: Essays from the Gregynog Conference*, Totowa, N.J.: Barnes and Noble, 1983, pp. 1–19.

'Godwin, Burke and *Caleb Williams*', *Essays in Criticism* 22, 1982, 237–57.

'Satire and the Images of Self in the Romantic Period: The Long Tradition of Hazlitt's *Liber Amoris*', *Yearbook of English Studies*, 1983, 209–25; repr. in Claude Rawson (ed.), *English Satire and the Satiric Tradition*, Oxford: Blackwell, 1984, pp. 209–25; repr. in G. A. Rosso and Daniel P. Watkins (eds.), *Spirits of Fire: English Romantic Writers and Comparative Historical Methods*, Rutherford, N.J.: Fairleigh Dickinson University Press, 1990, pp. 153–69.

'Learning and the Learned Journals: Literature', *Times Literary Supplement*, 16 December 1983, 1397–8.

Introduction to Jane Austen, *Selected Letters*, Oxford: World's Classics, 1985 (repr. of R. W. Chapman's 1955 edition).

'Nymphs and Nympholepsy: The Visionary Woman and the Romantic Poet', in Rolf Breuer, Werner Huber, and Rainer Schöwerling (eds.), *English Romanticism: The Paderborn Symposium*, Essen: Blaue Eule, 1985, pp. 11–31.

'Peacock, Ceres and the Twice-Born Bacchus', *Keats-Shelley Memorial Bulletin* 36, 1985, 57–76.

'History, Politics and Religion', in J. D. Grey, A. W. Litz, and B. C. Southam (eds.), *Jane Austen Handbook*, London: Athlone Press, 1986, pp. 190–209.

'The Case for an Antithetical Historical Criticism', in J. J. McGann (ed.), *Historical Studies and Literary Interpretation*, Madison: University of Wisconsin Press, 1986, pp. 25–47.

'Literature as a Heritage: Or Reading Other Ways'. Inaugural lecture delivered at the University of Cambridge, 10 November 1987. Cambridge: Cambridge University Press, 1988.

'Revising the Canon', *Times Literary Supplement*, 4–10 December 1987, 1349, 1359–60.

'Romanticism in England', in Roy Porter and Mikulás Tiech (eds.), *Romanticism in National Context*, Cambridge: Cambridge University Press, 1988, pp. 37–67.

'The Orientalism of Byron's *Giaour*', in Bernard Beatty and Vincent Newey (eds.), *Byron and the Limits of Fiction*, Liverpool: Liverpool University Press, 1988, pp. 78–96.

'Oxford's Eighteenth-Century Versions', *Eighteenth-Century Life* 12, 1988, 128–36.

'Repossessing the Past: The Case for an Open Literary History', in Marjorie Levinson et al., *Rethinking Historicism*, Oxford: Basil Blackwell, 1989, pp. 64–84.

'Romantic Manichaeism: Shelley's "On the Devil" and Byron's Mythological Dramas', in J. B. Bullen (ed.), *The Sun is God: Painting, Literature and Mythology in the Nineteenth Century*, Oxford: Clarendon Press, 1989, pp. 13–37.

'Byron and the Empire in the East', in Andrew Rutherford (ed.), *Byron: Augustan and Romantic*, Basingstoke: Macmillan, 1990, pp. 63–81.

'Telling it like a Story: The French Revolution as Narrative', *Studies in Romanticism* 28 (Fall 1989), 345–64. Another version, 'Revolving in Deep Time: The French

Revolution as Narrative', in Keith Hanley and Ramon Selden (eds.), *Revolution and English Romanticism*, Hemel Hempstead: Harvester Wheatsheaf, 1990, pp. 1–22.

'Plotting the Revolution: The Political Narratives of Romantic Poetry and Criticism', in Kenneth Johnston, Gilbert Chaitin, Karen Hansen, and Herbert Marks (eds.), *Romantic Revolutions: Criticism and Theory*, Bloomington: Indiana University Press, 1990, pp. 133–57.

Introduction, *Mansfield Park*, Oxford: World's Classics, 1990.

Introduction, *Emma*, London: Everyman's Library Classics, 1991.

Part-author with Mark Philp of General Introduction, 'Godwin's Novels', to Philp (gen. ed.), *Collected Novels and Memoirs of William Godwin*, 8 vols., London: Pickering and Chatto, 1992, vol. 1, pp. 22–47.

'Literary London', in Celina Fox (ed.), *London: World City 1800–1840*, New York and London: Yale University Press, 1992, pp. 187–98.

'John Bull's Other Kingdom: Byron's Intellectual Comedy', *Studies in Romanticism* 31, 1992, 281–94.

'The First *Frankenstein* and Radical Science: How the Original Version of Mary Shelley's Novel Drew Inspiration from the Early Evolutionists', *Times Literary Supplement*, 9 Apr. 1993, 12–14.

'Culture's Medium: The Role of the Review', in Stuart Curran (ed.), *Cambridge Companion to British Romanticism*, Cambridge: Cambridge University Press, 1993, pp. 120–47.

'Gray Suits and Black Leather Jackets, Or, Is There an Anglo-American Feminist Criticism?', *Tulsa Studies in Women's Literature* 12, 1993, 209–22.

'Ambush: The Politics of National Curriculum English', *Critical Quarterly* 35, 1993, 8–12.

'Orientalism', in David B. Pirie (ed.), *The Penguin History of English Literature: The Romantic Period*, 1994, pp. 395–447, 488–92.

'Doubting Visionaries: Thomson, Barry and the Future of the Arts', in Brian T. Allen (ed.), *Towards a Modern Art World*, Studies in British Art 1, New Haven and London: Yale University Press, 1995, pp. 67–78.

'Editing Women', *Studies in the Novel* 27, 1995, 273–83.

'E. P. Thompson and the Uses of History', *History Workshop Journal* 39, 1995, 71–8.

'Edgeworth's Stern Father: Escaping Thomas Day, 1795–1801', in Alvaro Ribeiro and James G. Basker (eds.), *Tradition in Transition: Women Writers, Marginal Texts, and the Eighteenth-Century Canon*, Oxford: Oxford University Press, 1996, pp. 75–93.

'Romanticism and Nationalism: Talking to the Dead', *Questione Romantica: Rivista Interdisciplinare di Studi Romantici* 2, 1996, 41–52.

'Shelley and the Empire in the East', in Betty T. Bennett and Stuart Curran (eds.), *Shelley: Poet and Legislator of the World*, Baltimore: Johns Hopkins University Press, 1996, pp. 158–68.

'Burns and Politics', in Robert Crawford (ed.), *Robert Burns and Cultural Authority*, Iowa City: University of Iowa Press, 1997, pp. 86–112.

'"The Purple Turban and the Flowering Aloe Tree": Signs of Distinction in the Early Nineteenth-Century Novel', *Modern Language Quarterly* 58, 1997, 475–95.

'Antiquarianism (Popular)', in Iain McCalman (ed.), *An Oxford Companion to the Romantic Age: British Culture 1776–1832*, Oxford: Oxford University Press, 1999, pp. 328–38.

'Blake in His Time', in Robin Hamlyn and Michael Phillips (eds.), *William Blake*, London: Tate Gallery, 2000.

'Irish Culture and Scottish Enlightenment: Maria Edgeworth's Histories of the Future', in Stefan Collini, Richard Whatmore, and Brian Young (eds.), *Economy, Polity, and Society: British Intellectual History 1750–1950*, Cambridge: Cambridge University Press, 2000, pp. 158–80.

'Edgeworth's Ireland: History, Popular Culture, and Secret Codes', *Novel* 34, 2001, 267–92.

'Edgeworth, the United Irishmen, and "More Intelligent Treason"', in Heidi Kaufman and Chris Fauske (eds.), *An Uncomfortable Authority: Maria Edgeworth and Her Contexts*, Newark: Delaware University Press, 2004, pp. 33–61.

REVIEWS

Review of B. C. Southam, *Jane Austen's Literary Manuscripts*, *Essays in Criticism* 15, 1965, 337–41.

Review of C. J. Rawson, *Henry Fielding and the Augustan Ideal under Stress: 'Nature's Dance of Death' and Other Studies*, *Essays in Criticism* 24, 1974, 298–300.

'Fielding, Whose Contemporary?', *Essays in Criticism* 25, 1975, 272–6, 478–9. [An exchange with C. J. Rawson arising from review above.]

Review of R. F. Brissenden, *Virtue in Distress: Studies in the Novel of Sentiment from Richardson to Sade*, *Notes and Queries* 23, 1976, 373–4.

Review of Juliet McMaster (ed.), *Jane Austen's Achievement: Papers Delivered at the Jane Austen Bicentennial Conference at the University of Alberta*, *Notes and Queries* 25, 1978, 562–3.

Review of Jerome McGann, '"Don Juan" in Context', *Essays in Criticism* 28, 1978, 52–60.

Review of Timothy Webb, *Shelley: A Voice Not Understood*, *English* (Leicester) 28, 1979, 78–83.

Review of John Kinnaird, *William Hazlitt: Critic of Power*, *English* (Leicester) 29, 1980, 50–6.

Review of Herschel Moreland Sikes (ed.), *The Letters of William Hazlitt*, *English* (Leicester) 29, 1980, 50–6.

Review of Ioan Williams, *The Idea of the Novel in Europe, 1600–1800*, *Notes and Queries* 27, 1980, 373–4.

Review of J. R. de J. Jackson, *Poetry of the Romantic Period*, *English* (Leicester) 29, 1980, 239–45.

Review of Janet Todd, *Women's Friendship in Literature*, *Essays in Criticism* 31, 1981, 246–9.

Review of Nancy K. Miller, *The Heroine's Text: Readings in the French and English Novel 1722–1782*, Essays in Criticism 31, 1981, 246–9.

Review of Terry Eagleton, *The Rape of Clarissa: Writing, Sexuality and Class Struggle in Samuel Richardson*, Times Literary Supplement, 12 Nov. 1982, 1241–2.

Review of Jerry C. Beasley, *Novels of the 1740s*, Times Literary Supplement, 12 Nov. 1982, 1242.

Review of Warren Roberts, *Jane Austen and the French Revolution*, English Historical Review 97, 1982, 204–5.

Review of Dimiter Daphinoff (ed.), *An Alternative Ending to Richardson's 'Clarissa'*, Times Literary Supplement, 12 Nov. 1982, 1241.

Review of David Pirie, *William Wordsworth: The Poetry of Grandeur and of Tenderness*, and of Jonathan Wordsworth, *William Wordsworth: The Borders of Vision*, London Review of Books, 5 Dec. 1983, 18–19.

Review of T. A. J. Burnett, *The Rise and Fall of a Regency Dandy: The Life and Times of Scrope Berdmore Davies*, Keats-Shelley Memorial Bulletin 34, 1983, 80–5.

Review of Michael Stapleton, *The Cambridge Guide to English Literature*, London Review of Books 5.15, 1983, 14–16.

Review of Leslie Mitchell, *Holland House*, Keats-Shelley Memorial Bulletin 34, 1983, 80–5.

Review of Janet Coleman, *English Literature in History, 1350–1400: Medieval Readers and Writers*, John Barrell, *English Literature in History 1730–80: An Equal, Wide Survey*, and Roger Sales, *English Literature in History 1780–1830: Pastoral and Politics*, London Review of Books 5.15, 1983, 14–16.

Review of Paul F. Betz (ed.), *Benjamin the Wagoner*, London Review of Books 5.12, 1983, 18–19.

Review of Percy G. Adams, *Travel Literature and the Evolution of the Novel*, Times Literary Supplement, 22 June 1984, 689.

Review of Helen Vendler, *The Odes of John Keats*, Hudson Review 37, 1984, 143–50.

Review of George Deacon, *John Clare and the Folk Tradition*, Eric Robinson (ed.), *John Clare's Autobiographical Writings*, Margaret Grainger (ed.), *The Natural History Prose Writings of John Clare*, and Anne Tibble (ed.), *The Journal, Essays, the Journey from Essex*, London Review of Books 6.22/23, 1984, 3–5.

Review of Olivia Smith, *The Politics of Language, 1791–1819*, and Jerome J. McGann, *The Beauty of Inflections: Literary Investigations in Historical Method and Theory*, London Review of Books 7.22, 1985, 11–13.

Review of John Halperin, *The Life of Jane Austen*, New York Times Book Review, 24 Feb. 1985, 25.

Review of Thomas C. Faulkner (ed.), *Selected Letters and Journals of George Crabbe*, Times Literary Supplement, 3 Jan. 1986, 3–4.

Review of J. F. Burrows, *Computation into Criticism: A Study of Jane Austen's Novels and an Experiment in Method*, London Review of Books 9.12, 1987, 11–13.

Review of Chris Baldick, *In Frankenstein's Shadow: Myth, Monstrosity and Nineteenth-Century Writing*, London Review of Books 10.9, 1988, 12–13.

Review of Gayatri Spivak, *In Other Worlds*, Times Literary Supplement, 11–17, March 1988, 283–4.

Review of Michael Mason (ed.), *Lyrical Ballads*, Susan Eilenberg, *Strange Power of Speech: Wordsworth, Coleridge and Literary Possession*, and Nicholas Roe, *The Politics of Nature: Wordsworth and Some Contemporaries*, London Review of Books 14.15, 1992, 12–13.

Review of Jerome J. McGann (ed.), *The New Oxford Book of Romantic Period Verse*, London Review of Books 16.20, 1994, 33–4.

Review of John Sutherland, *The Life of Walter Scott*, London Review of Books 17.17, 1995, 10–11.

Review of Christopher Ricks, *Essays in Appreciation*, London Review of Books 18.15, 1996, 15–16.

Review of Ian McIntyre, *Dirt and Deity: A Life of Robert Burns*, London Review of Books 18.3, 1996, 9–10.

Review of David Nokes, *Jane Austen: A Life*, and Claire Tomalin, *Jane Austen: A Life*, London Review of Books 20.5, 1998, 3–6.

Index

Abu Taleb Khan, Mirza 14–15, 195–6
  reviewed by Heber 199
  Travels of Mirza Abu Taleb Khan 184, 195,
    196–8, 200
  'Vindication of the Liberties of Asian
    Women' 198–9
Aikin, Arthur 81, 82
Aikin, Rev. John (father of Anna Barbauld) 80,
  81, 83
Aikin, John (brother of Anna Barbauld) 25,
  81–2, 87, 88
  career 91–3
  Evenings at Home 91, 92
  Poems (1791) 91
  politics 88–9
  relationship with Anna Barbauld 93
Aikin, Lucy 9, 23, 31, 81, 91
  and Mary Godwin Shelley 86
  as memoirist 89, 90–2, 94
  Epistles on Women 89–90
  on Barbauld's poetry 85
  on Godwin 86
  politics 93–4
  reviews of 90
Anderson, Perry 66–7
Auerbach, Nina 217
Austen, Jane 15
  Emma 207, 211, 213–14, 215–17, 218
  Mansfield Park 207–12, 213, 217, 218
  Persuasion 207, 217–21
  Pride and Prejudice 209
  Sense and Sensibility 217
Austen-Leigh, J. E. 203, 206
Austin, J. L. 171

Baker, Herschel 40
Balázs, Bela 130–1
Balibar, Etienne 125–6
Balzac, Honoré de 121
Barbauld, Anna Laetitia 6, 22–3, 28–33
  and Dissent 26, 35

and family 80–1, 93
and Mary Wollstonecraft 86–7
Eighteen Hundred and Eleven 85, 90
Evenings at Home 91, 92
Poems (1773) 84, 85
on education 30
political interventions 87
'Thoughts on the Devotional Taste' 22, 25
Barbauld, Rochemont 81
Barrell, John 17, 57
Barruel, Abbé 154
Beddoes, Thomas 145
Benedict, Ruth 111
Benjamin, Walter 169, 177
Bentham, Jeremy 8
Bergson, Henri 129
Blake, William 21, 22, 149, 228, 239
  Auguries of Innocence 228
  Marriage of Heaven and Hell 228
Bloom, Harold 16, 226
bluestockings 22, 23–6, 27–9, 32, 34
Bonaparte, Napoleon 51
Bromwich, David 41, 60
Buffon, Georges 148–9
Burke, Edmund 11, 12, 26, 45, 48, 55, 142–3
  on France 143–4, 151
  on the Sublime and the Beautiful 230
  pastiche of 186–7
Burrow, Reuben 191
Butler, Marilyn 1–4, 6, 11, 16, 17, 35, 120–1
  as editor 98–9
  Jane Austen and the War of Ideas 184–5, 203
  on Maria Edgeworth 119, 123, 124–5, 155
  on Hazlitt 40
  on Marlow 64
  on Romantic orientalism 183–4
  on Shelley 65
  Romantics, Rebels, and Reactionaries 163–6
Byron, George Gordon, Lord 14, 16, 64
  Beppo 235, 237, 238–9
  Cain 240

Childe Harold's Pilgrimage 74, 233, 234, 235, 237
Don Juan 235–8, 239
Godwin on 106–7
Manfred 232–3
on Wordsworth 229
Sardanapalus 183
The Giaour 183

Carter, Elizabeth 22, 24, 25, 28, 34
Chandler, James 230
Chapone, Hester 205
Clairmont, Claire 64
Clarendon, Earl of 70
Clarke, J. C. D. 4
Cobbett, William 43, 44, 55
Cohen, Monica 219
Cole, Juan 200
Coleridge, Samuel Taylor 13–14, 43, 56, 145, 226
    and German philosophy 165–6, 180
    as European intellectual 163–4
    Biographia Literaria 80, 165, 168, 229, 231–2
    Christabel 165, 168
    Dejection 174
    Kubla Khan 165, 166, 167, 175
    The Friend 176, 178
    on Anna Barbauld 85
    on Babel and 'anti-babel' 175–6
    on the Edgeworth children 142
    on Wordsworth 231–2
Colley, Linda 3, 5
Connolly, Claire 124, 138
conversation 21–2, 27–8, 30–1
    bluestocking 24–5
    and Dissent 6–7, 33, 34, 35, 100
    Hannah More on 24–5
    in education 146–7
    polite 33–4
Cooper, James Fenimore 121
Cooper, Thomas Abthorpe 103
Copeland, Edward 206
Cromwell, Oliver 65, 70
Cronin, Richard 213
Crook, Nora 71, 72

Dart, Greg 47, 48, 49
Darwin, Erasmus 149
Deane, Seamus 40
de Bolla, Peter 169, 170, 171–2
de Dominis, Antonio 149
de Genlis, Stéphanie 153
Deleuze, Gilles 12, 126–30, 131, 132
Descartes 148–9
de Staël, Madame 111
Dissent 3–4, 9, 17, 22

and free discussion 6–7, 23, 100
and education 3–4, 9, 12, 81, 82, 83–5
gentrification of 9, 22, 23
politics of 3, 22–3, 32, 83, 88–9, 93–4
Dreier, Carl 131
Drucker, Johanna 241
Dyson, George 103

Edgeworth, Honora Sneyd 141, 155
Edgeworth, Lovell 140–1, 152, 155
Edgeworth, Maria 11–12, 17, 34
    influence on Scott 119–20, 122–3, 125
    Memoirs of Richard Lovell Edgeworth 146
    Patronage 124–5, 134, 135–7
    Practical Education 140, 142, 143, 144, 146, 148–52, 153, 154, 155
    stories for children 155, 156, 156–7
    Tales of Fashionable Life 124
    The Absentee 123–4, 134
Edgeworth, Richard Lovell 11, 141, 155–6, 210
    on professional education 214, 218, 220
Edgeworth, Sneyd 148–9, 157, 158
Eisenstein, Sergei Mikhailovich 131–2
Enfield, William 26, 83
Everest, Kelvin 100

Ferris, Ina 120, 123
Fichte, Johann Gottlieb 165, 168, 177
Fordyce, James 205
Fox, Charles James 91
Fuseli, John Henry 87
Frye, Northrop 52

Gadamer, Hans-Georg 169
Gilbert, Sandra 220
Gisborne, Thomas 205–6, 212
Godwin, Mary Jane 105–6, 108, 109
Godwin, William 7, 8, 10, 23, 33, 69, 86, 145, 185
    and Elizabeth Inchbald 109–11
    and his children 104–5
    and his mother 105–6
    and letter-writing 101–2
    and rational Dissent 68, 100
    as professional author 107–9
    as promoter of women writers 109–11
    at Marlow 64, 65
    editions of works 99–100
    Essay on Sepulchres 65
    Fleetwood 101
    History of England, for the use of schools and young persons 78
    History of the Commonwealth of England 65, 70, 73, 108
    Life of Chaucer 108
    Lives of Edward and John Phillips 65

Godwin, William (*cont.*)
  literary opinions 106–7
  Mandeville 65
  on Mary Wollstonecraft 82, 102, 104
  on the English revolution 70
  Political Justice 102, 103, 104, 109
  political views 106
Goldsmith, Oliver
  Citizen of the World 186
Guattari, Felix 12, 126–30, 131
Gubar, Susan 220
Guest, Harriet 27
Guillory, John 84
grand narratives 3, 4–5

Habermas, Jürgen 21
Hamacher, Werner 177
Hamilton, Charles 186, 187, 191
Hamilton, Elizabeth 14, 15
  Cottagers of Glenburnie 195
  on Godwin 104
  pastiche of Burke 186–7
  Letters on the Elementary Principles of
    Education 185, 191, 193
  Memoirs of Modern Philosophers 185, 192, 195
  politics 185
  reviews of 194–5
  Translation of the Letters of a Hindoo
    Rajah 184–94, 200
Hampden, John 65, 66, 67, 68–9, 70
  as portrayed in *Charles I* 70
Harbsmeier, Michael 199
Harling, Philip 42
Hartman, Geoffrey 16
Hastings, Warren 5, 186, 187, 191
Hays, Mary 31, 33, 34–5, 109
Hazlitt, William 7–8
  and Dissent 7, 42
  and Hobbes 50–1
  critical reputation 40–1
  Notes of a Journey through France and
    Italy 51–2
  on Coleridge 56
  'On the Jealousy and Spleen of Party' 52
  on London 45, 46, 47–51, 53, 54
  on Malthus 46
  'On the Literary Character' 46
  on Wordsworth 45, 46–7, 51
  radical journalist 42–4
  'What is the People?' 53–7
Heber, Reginald 199
Hegel, Georg Wilhelm Friedrich 165, 166,
  168
Hobbes, Thomas 50–1
Hodges, William 192

Hogg, Thomas Jefferson 64, 67
Hooke, Robert 146–7
Holcroft, Thomas 103, 111, 145
Hölderlin, Friedrich
  on interruption 165, 166
Hopkins, Gerard Manley 240
Hume, David
  History of England 71–3
Hunt, Leigh 64, 65
  The Examiner 68, 69–70, 73–4

Imlay, Fanny 105
Inchbald, Elizabeth 109–11
Israel, Jonathan 3, 4

Jameson, Fredric 52
Jeffrey, Francis 67–8
Johnson, Joseph 7–8, 23, 24, 31, 32, 87
  and Aikin family 82
  publisher of Barbauld 87
  publisher of Godwin 108
  trial 88
Johnson, Samuel 137
Jones, Sir William 187, 191

Kant, Immanuel 165, 166, 169, 170, 171–2, 177,
  227
  Critique of Judgment 227
Kelly, Gary 184, 205
Kierkegaard, Søren 165–8
Kirwan, James 229

Lamb, Charles 169
Langford, Paul 6
Leibniz, Gottfried Wilhelm 165, 166
Levinson, Marjorie 3, 175–6
Locke, John 227
Lowe, Lisa 189
Lukács, Georg 120, 121–2, 123

Macaulay, Catharine 67, 70
McCormack, W. J. 124
Mackenzie, Henry 134
Malthus, Thomas 46, 85
Marshal, James 104, 105–6
Martineau, Harriet 111
Midon, Francis 69
Miles, Robert 217
Milton, John 22, 34, 65, 68
  Godwin on 107
Montagu, Elizabeth 6, 22, 23, 25, 28–9, 30–1, 32,
  34, 86–7
Montesquieu, Charles-Louis de Secondat, Baron
  de
  Persian Letters 185, 189, 195

More, Hannah 22, 32–3, 34, 185
  Coelebs in Search of a Wife 205
  *Strictures on the Modern System of Female
    Education* 205
  The Bas Bleu 24, 33–4
  'Thoughts on Conversation' 24–5, 28
Morgan, Lady 134
Morton, Timothy 64

Nicholson, William 111
Nora, Pierre 66

O'Brien, Karen 72
Opie, Amelia 109
orientalism 14, 183, 186, 191–2, 194–5, 199–200

Parkinson, C. Northcote 218
Pasley, C. W. 207–8
Peck, John 208
Perkin, Harold 203–4, 206–7
Pine, Thomas 44, 55
Peacock, Thomas Love 63–4, 65, 69
Plato 227
Plotinus 227
Pocock, J. G. A. 67
Poe, Edgar Allan 240–1
Porter, Roy 3, 5–6
Price, Richard 22, 100, 142, 143
Priestley, Joseph 58, 81, 87
  and Barbauld 22–3, 26–7
  on education 83, 143
Pythagoras 227

Ricardo, David 214
Richards, I. A. 165, 167, 171
Richardson, Alan 140, 154, 158
Robinson, Mary 80, 81, 109
Robison, John 154
Rodgers, Betsy 81
Rogers, Samuel 38
Rosen, Michael 165, 166, 167
Rossetti, Dante Gabriel 232, 241
Rousseau, Jean-Jacques 12, 55, 145, 153
Rowe, Elizabeth 26
Rzepka, Charles J. 217, 220

Said, Edward 183, 200
Samuel, Richard
  'Nine Living Muses of Great Britain' 24
Schelling, Friedrich Wilhelm Joseph von 13,
    169
Schiller, Friedrich 15, 16, 172, 173, 229
Schlegel, Friedrich von 170, 176, 177
Scott, Mary
  The Female Advocate 24

Scott, Sir Walter 12, 220
  and Maria Edgeworth 12, 122–3, 125
  and ethnographic realism 121–2
  and sentimentalism 133–4
  on chivalry and romance 128
  Ivanhoe 132
  The Bride of Lammermoor 121–2, 132
  Waverley 122, 133, 137
sentimentalism 5–6, 10, 12, 89, 133–4
Shelley, Mary 86
  as a child 105
  at Marlow 64, 68
  Falkner 101
  Frankenstein 65, 66
  on *Charles the First* 73
  on Percy Bysshe Shelley 74
Shelley, Percy Bysshe 8–9, 51
  at Marlow 63–5
  Charles the First 67, 68, 70–3
  Godwin on 107
  'On Christianity' 74
  on Byron's *Cain* 240
  on Wordsworth 229
  republicanism 67–8
Sibley, F. N. 171
Simpson, David 45
Smith, Adam 134
Smith, Charlotte 33
Smith, Nigel 64
Southam, Brian 204
Southey, Robert 14, 43, 53, 55, 73
  'For a Column at Newbury' 66, 73
  Letters from England 186
  The Curse of Kehana 183
Sterne, Laurence 133
Stevens, Wallace 226
Stewart, Charles 195–6, 197, 198

Teltscher, Kate 191, 197
Thompson, E. P. 43
Tooke, Horne 145
Trimmer, Sarah 152–3, 154
Trumpener, Katie 123

Vendler, Helen 226
Vesey, Elizabeth 22, 23, 24, 31

Wakefield, Gilbert 81, 85, 87, 88
Walpole, Horace 31
Warrington Academy 3, 9, 81, 82, 83–5
Watts, Isaac 23
Wedgwood, Thomas 145–6
Wellek, René 229
West, Jane 205, 206, 216
Whale, John 57

Wilford, Francis 191
Williams, Helen Maria 31, 38
Wollstonecraft, Mary 31, 33, 111, 185, 215
    death 104
    in the Johnson circle 34–5
    marriage to Godwin 102
    on education 143
    Vindication of the Rights of Woman 147, 198
Worden, Blair 68
Wordsworth, William 5, 7, 16, 68, 145
    'Ode on the Intimations of Immortality' 231

Preface to *Lyrical Ballads* 228–30,
    233–4
'spots of time' 66, 106
The Excursion 5, 45, 46, 48, 169
'The Idiot Boy' 229–30
The Prelude 227, 230–1
'The Ruined Cottage' 234–5
Wright, Frances 111

Yeats, William Butler 227
Young, Arthur 214–15